Hebert

D1515418

IN GOOD TASTE

IN GOOD TASTE

A CONTEMPORARY APPROACH TO COOKING

VICTOR GIELISSE, CMC, MBA

MARY E. KIMBROUGH, R.D., L.D.

KATHRYN G. GIELISSE

PRENTICE HALL

UPPER SADDLE RIVER, NJ 07458

Library of Congress Cataloging-in-Publication Data

Gielisse, Victor.
    In good taste: a contemporary approach to cooking/Victor
  Gielisse, Mary Kimbrough, Kathryn G. Gielisse.
      p.   cm.
    Includes index.
    ISBN 0-13-591595-3
    1. Cookery.   2. Nutrition.   I. Gielisse, Kathryn G.
  II. Kimbrough, Mary (Mary E.)   III. Title.
  TX714.G54   1999
  641.5—dc21   98–27195
                                                              CIP

Director of Production and Manufacturing: Bruce Johnson
Managing Editor: Mary Carnis
Editorial/production supervision: WordCrafters Editorial Services, Inc.
Interior design: Laura Ierardi
Cover design: Ruta K. Fiorino
Manufacturing buyer: Ed O'Dougherty
Acquisition editor: Neil Marquardt
Editorial Assistant: Jean Auman
Marketing manager: Frank Mortimer, Jr.
Cover photo: Dave Gresham
Art Director: Marianne Frasco

 © 1999 by Prentice-Hall, Inc.
Simon & Schuster/A Viacom Company
Upper Saddle River, New Jersey 07458

Printed in the United States of America

10   9   8   7   6   5   4   3   2   1

ISBN 0-13-591595-3

Prentice-Hall International (UK) Limited, *London*
Prentice-Hall of Australia Pty. Limited, *Sydney*
Prentice-Hall Canada Inc., *Toronto*
Prentice-Hall Hispanoamericana, S.A., *Mexico*
Prentice-Hall of India Private Limited, *New Delhi*
Prentice-Hall of Japan, Inc., *Tokyo*
Simon & Schuster Asia Pte. Ltd., *Singapore*
Editora Prentice-Hall do Brasil, Ltda., *Rio de Janeiro*

EXAMPLE IS NOT THE MAIN THING IN INFLUENCING OTHERS,

IT IS THE ONLY THING.

Albert Schweitzer

THIS BOOK IS DEDICATED TO ALL THE YOUNG, AS WELL AS THE YOUNG

AT HEART, FOOD SERVICE PROFESSIONALS. TO THOSE OF US WHO HAVE A

PASSION FOR FOOD, OUR TRADE, AND RESPECT FOOD'S OVERALL

INTEGRITY AND CULTURAL IMPACT.

Victor Gielisse, CMC, MBA

CHOOSE A JOB YOU LOVE AND YOU WILL NEVER HAVE TO WORK

A DAY IN YOUR LIFE.

Confucius

MY INSPIRATION FOR BEING A PART OF THIS BOOK CAME FROM

THE MAN I MOST ADMIRE AND WHO TRULY LIVES BY THESE WORDS.

I DO NOT KNOW ANYONE WHO IS MORE IN LOVE WITH HIS PROFESSION

THAN MY HUSBAND!

Kathryn Gielisse

FOR MY MENTORS AND THOSE WHO ALLOW ME TO MENTOR THEM. MOST

OF ALL MY PARENTS WHO ARE THE GREATEST MENTORS OF ALL:

WILLIAM R. KIMBROUGH AND VIRGINIA HUGHES KIMBROUGH.

Mary E. Kimbrough, R.D., L.D.

CONTENTS

@

@

FOREWORD

@

Brillat Savarin, the first historian of gastronomy, once made the statement, "Tell me what you eat and I will tell you who you are." Throughout history, food was always associated with culture, status, and economic well-being. Having been guided by Brillat Savarin's statement, The Culinary Institute of America began in the early 1980s to seriously evaluate its mission as a leading culinary institution to teach and provide nutritious food without compromising our culinary principles, which demand that food must taste good and be well presented and properly served.

The then-relatively raw and unpolished concept of nutritious food has grown and matured into a more sophisticated yet realistic approach that is presented in *In Good Taste: A Contemporary Approach to Cooking.* Victor and Kathryn Gielisse and Mary Kimbrough have built upon the Institute's nutrition principles, which allow for the creativity needed to provide healthful and pleasurable dining experiences without the obvious punishment often associated with nutritious and dietetic food.

Besides the recipes, the book also discusses the health benefits of wine, as well as providing a comprehensive dictionary of herbs and spices. In addition, an entire chapter is devoted to the pros and cons of biotechnology and its relationship to a healthier living standard.

I recommend *In Good Taste* as a valuable resource for food service professionals, particularly those involved in the healthcare field.

Ferdinand E. Metz, CMC
President, The Culinary Institute of America

PREFACE

Our vision for contemporary cooking has evolved through years of collaboration with other food service professionals and through our own experiences. Contemporary cooking is the integration of culinary tradition and nutrition science. The abundance of food in the marketplace allows the potential for unlimited culinary delights. By selecting flavorful ingredients and using healthful cooking techniques, we can enhance our quality of life. Our goal is to erase any perception that healthful food must be tasteless and uninspiring. Food *can* taste good while still being healthful.

We want to share our respect and passion for the art of cooking. Sharing the pleasures of the table can establish and nourish friendships, build cultural understanding, and create synergy within families. Food nourishes both the body and the soul.

The principles of contemporary cooking are built upon the solid foundation of traditional cooking. Culinarians can shift to a contemporary style of cooking simply by following these principles of ingredient selection, preparation, and cooking methods, while utilizing flavoring and seasoning techniques.

Nutrition is a science that is meant to be applied. A basic understanding of nutrition will allow a culinarian to choose techniques, ingredients, and portion sizes that have positive health benefits.

The recipe section is organized by menu course (appetizer, salad, etc.) to help the culinarian create a complete healthful meal. We have strived for authenticity in traditional recipes while employing contemporary cooking principles. We hope that our style of contemporary cooking will become a natural way to cook.

We believe in sharing professional knowledge and cultural experience with the next generation of culinarians, nutrition and food service professionals, and consumers. We challenge you to build upon the recipes and ideas you find in this text and savor the adventure of doing so. In the words of Auguste Georges Escoffier, one of the most brilliant chefs of all time, *"Faites semples,"* or make it simple!

Victor, Mary, and Kathryn

ACKNOWLEDGMENTS

@

We wish to thank all the staff at Prentice Hall/Simon & Schuster Education Group for their trust and faith in the project, and for allowing us to share our experience with our readers. A special thank-you and our most sincere gratitude go to our editor, Neil W. Marquardt. Our sincere appreciation also goes to Rose Mary Florio, Jean Auman, Mark Cohen, and Robin Baliszewski for their guidance, encouragement, and professionalism.

Our special appreciation goes to Allyn L. Giacomazzi, Michelle Landry, R.D., L.D., Rana Rittgers-Simonds, M.S., R.D., L.D., Alicia Taylor, and the Administration and Nutrition Service staff of Zale Lipshy University Hospital, for their ever-present encouragement and generous support. We would also like to thank Vickie Vaclavik, PhD, R.D., for her knowledge, experience, and technical support throughout the project.

We wish to thank Ferdinand E. Metz, CMC, President of The Culinary Institute of America, for his years of friendship, encouragement, and inspiration, and for his insightful perspective on our work.

Thanks also to Thomas L. Wright, Vice President of Culinary Education of Johnson & Wales University, for his professional support and friendship; and to Thomas L. Wright, Robert Nograd, CMC, and Linda Beaulieau, of Johnson & Wales University, for their collective thoughts, dedication, and thorough review of our work.

The following people were also instrumental in the development of the book:

Jeffrey Akens

Nancy D. Berkoff, R.D., EdD, C.C.E.

Donna Burg

Lori Stickley

Ron De Santis, C.M.C.

Mark V. Erickson, C.M.C.

Klaus Friedenreich, C.M.C.

Ken Gladysz, C.W.C.

Leopoldo Gonzalez

David Greshan

Anthony Griffin

Pat R. Haverfield

Roland Henin, C.M.C.

David Holben

David P. Kellaway, C.M.C.

Eric Kopelow, C.E.C.

David Meginis, C.M.C.

Chris Northmore, C.M.P.C.

Robin Plotkin, R.D., L.D.

Tracy Pursell, R.D., L.D.

Michael Robbins, C.M.C.

Leopold Schaeli, C.M.C.

John M. Shoop, C.M.C.

Rudolph Speckamp, C.M.C.

Dan Stewart, C.E.C.

Jennifer Thomas

Ken Udoomzak

Marti Vinson, M.S., R.D., L.D.

Cynthia Weber, PhD, R.D., L.D.

DR. GRUNDY'S GUIDELINES

❡

Nutrition scientists and physicians know how important it is to eat a balanced, nourishing diet. They also know that many people think following a healthy diet can sometimes be boring and tedious. Authors Victor and Kathryn Gielisse and Mary Kimbrough set out to change that perception, and they've done it! You will discover that for yourself in the following pages. They emphasize food that is fresh, well prepared, and pleasing to the eye. They show how intermingling flavors and textures enhances the appeal of a menu. The result is a low-fat, healthy, delicious way to eat. The authors have mastered these elements by marrying the art of food preparation with the science of nutrition. The information they present will give you valuable resources to help you develop menus of your own.

The National Institutes of Health, the American Heart Association, and the American Cancer Society agree on general guidelines for a healthful diet. Foremost, dietary intake of saturated fats should be limited. Sources of saturated fat include milk and cream, butter, cheese, ice cream, visible fat on meat as well as fatty cuts of meat. These foods should be replaced by low-fat varieties when possible. Fat intake should emphasize monounsaturated fats, which can be more beneficial because they do not elevate blood cholesterol levels. Sources of monounsaturated fat include olive oil and canola oil. A healthful diet should contain an abundant supply of whole grains, fresh fruits, and vegetables. Fruits and vegetables are rich in antioxidants and fiber, which may protect against heart disease and certain types of cancer.

It is important to pay attention not only to what you eat, but also to how much you eat. The meals in this book may assist with weight management. A healthful diet does not require calculating each gram of fat, carbohydrate, and protein. Rather, a balanced approach can be taken to maximize the pleasure of eating. If you overindulge one day, then cut back the next. Monitor portion sizes. Allow yourself an occasional "treat." Moderation, balance, and variety are the best ways to follow a healthful diet. *Stick to it for a lifetime!*

Scott M. Grundy, M.D., Ph.D.
Professor, Internal Medicine
Director, Center for Human Nutrition
The University of Texas Southwestern
Medical Center at Dallas

ABOUT THE AUTHORS

Victor Gielisse, CMC, MBA, is the Dean of Culinary Arts, Baking & Pastry Studies at The Culinary Institute of America in Hyde Park, New York. He is one of fifty-five culinary experts in the United States who can claim the prestigious title of Certified Master Chef. Chef Gielisse was formerly the president of CFT/Culinary Fast-Trac and Associates, Inc., a professional organization dedicated to solving problems unique to the food service industry.

Chef Gielisse is an Ambassador to The Culinary Institute of America and was named Chef of the Year by that organization in 1991. He also holds an honorary Doctor of Culinary Arts degree from Johnson & Wales University. His former restaurant, Actuelle, garnered numerous national awards and was applauded in such publications as *Food & Wine* and *Bon Appetit*, and was named one of *Conde Nast Traveler* Magazine's 50 Best U.S. Restaurants Worth the Journey. He is featured in the series "Great Chefs of Great Cities," which airs on the Discovery Channel as well as on the Public Broadcasting Service network. His literary contributions include authoring his first book, *Cuisine Actuelle;* co-authoring the video and cookbook *In Good Taste;* and receiving national and international recognition in several high-profile literary projects such as *Dining at Home with the Great Chefs of The World, Superchefs, Taste of Texas, Becoming a Chef,* and *Great Chef, Great Cities,* to mention just a few. He also served as a contributing editor to The American Culinary Federation's *The National Culinary Review* magazine.

A native of the Netherlands and certainly one of this country's most multifaceted chefs, he was highlighted in 1992 on a Fox network's "Hometown Heroes" segment for receiving the Jefferson Award for his efforts to feed the hungry and homeless in Dallas. For all his acclaim, he remains a chef with an interest in the consumer rather in the food critic. His approach emphasizes freshness, health, and elegant simplicity.

Mary E. Kimbrough, R.D., L.D., is director of Nutrition Services at Zale Lipshy University Hospital at Southwestern Medical Center. A registered dietitian with a Bachelor of Science in nutrition from The University of Texas at Austin, she has more than 16 years of food experience in the health care industry.

Kathryn and Victor Gielisse and Mary Kimbrough

Her literary contributions include co-authoring the cookbook and video *In Good Taste: A Contemporary Approach to Nutritional Cooking,* in collaboration with Dr. Scott Grundy of the Center for Human Nutrition at UT Southwestern Medical Center and Chef Gielisse, Development Chef at Zale Lipshy University Hospital.

Active in professional organizations, Mary has served as president of the Dallas Dietetic Association. She serves on the executive board of the National Society on Healthcare Foodservice Management and the American Dietetic Association's Food & Culinary Professionals Practice Group. Mary has been a guest speaker with Chef Gielisse at professional organizations such as the Greater New York, Texas, and Dallas Dietetic Associations, spreading the message that "Nutritious Can Be Delicious."

In February 1998, Mary was awarded the Silver Plate Award by IFMA (International Foodservice Manufacturers Association) in recognition of her dedication and excellence in the healthcare food service industry. This excellence earned the Nutrition Services Department an IVY award in 1998 from *Restaurant and Institution* magazine. The IVY is the nation's foremost accolade for excellence in food service.

Armed with the philosophy that hospital food can be both healthful and tasty, Mary and her staff created the Culinary Enhancement program when the hospital opened in 1989. Her innovative approach brought Cafe 5151, a dining establishment and catering service operating within the hospital, into existence in the summer of 1994. Quality, attention to detail, specialized training, and excellence in presentation are hallmarks of the cuisine, as well as all the services, offered at Zale Lipshy University Hospital.

Kathryn G. Gielisse is President of CFT/Culinary Fast-Trac and Associates, Inc., a professional organization dedicated to solving problems unique to the food service industry. Born in Houston, she is a third generation Texan. She was also an operating partner in *Actuelle,* a Dallas five-star restaurant that garnered numerous national awards and was applauded in such publications as *Food & Wine, Conde Nast Traveler,* and *Bon Appetit.* Her first literary accomplishment was co-editor of the cookbook *Cuisine Actuelle.*

After attending The University of Texas, Kathryn began a career in sales and marketing, joining Westin Hotels for a twelve-year career in the hotel industry. She was National Sales Manager, Catering Director, and a member of the Hotel Opening Task Force. She was a member of the management team of the Westin Oaks Hotel in Houston and the Westin Galleria Hotel in Dallas.

She finds time to volunteer and has served on several boards, including Vice President of the Women's Auxiliary of the March of Dimes Birth Defects Foundation and Publicity Chairman of the Parents Board of The Parish Day School in Dallas, where she participated on numerous committees.

While balancing her family and business, Kathryn is currently enrolled in a university degree program to complete her MBA. But her most important and cherished role is being a mother to her compassionate, intelligent, and beautiful daughter, Marykathryn. Kathryn resides in Hyde Park, New York, with her husband Victor and their daughter Marykathryn.

GETTING BACK TO BASICS IS CRUCIAL IN PUTTING OUT DISHES
THAT REPRESENT A REGION. SOMETIMES FOOD TASTES BEST
IN ITS SIMPLEST FORM.

Chef Victor Gielisse, CMC

THE SECRET OF WINNING IN LIFE IS THAT FIRST YOU MUST BELIEVE
YOU ARE.

Chef John M. Shoop, CMC

IF ONE HAS A GOOD SOUL, A LOVE FOR CREATING SOMETHING THAT DID
NOT EXIST BEFORE, THE REST WILL COME.

Chef Roland G. Henin, CMC

PART ONE

OUR PHILOSOPHY ON FOOD AND WINE AND THE EFFECT ON LIFESTYLE

@

CHAPTER 1
GASTRONOMY, THE ESSENTIAL ART, AND THE ALLIANCE OF TASTE AND HEALTH

CHAPTER 2
WINE WITH FOOD CAN BE PART OF A HEALTHFUL LIFESTYLE

@

Consumed by today's hectic lifestyle and work styles, Americans are overwhelmed by a continuous flow of information on how we should eat and what foods are better for us. We hear, "Less salt, less fat, less meat, less sugar, less alcohol." With all the attention-getting and "politically correct" cue cards, it may appear to the consumer that in fact nothing is good for you. Americans say that conflicting and confusing health and nutrition information is their biggest obstacle to eating right. From the consumer's point of view, the food service industry may not be doing enough to answer their concerns, which include the following issues:

- Misleading nutritional claims in food advertising and on products
- Distrust of food service manufacturers and operators regarding food safety
- Misunderstanding of the new concepts of processes such as biotechnology

CHAPTER 1

GASTRONOMY, THE ESSENTIAL ART, AND THE ALLIANCE OF TASTE AND HEALTH

@

Today's consumers are actively involved with their physical well-being and conscious of their health, therefore they demand information regarding what goes into their bodies.

Do we have to choose between healthy eating habits and great tasting food, or can we use flexibility in finding the proper balance to combine the two? By fusing these two aspects of eating, we can improve our attitude toward creating a better quality lifestyle. In order for the consumer to make intelligent and well-informed purchasing choices, the food service industry has to provide, on a timely basis, information that is honest and accurate. Today's consumers are not opposed to such information; in fact, they would like to see products in the market with correct information available that can advise them of exactly where the product originated, how it was grown, how it was processed, and how it arrived at the store.

Times are changing and so are technologies. The next decade will see a possible 30 percent increase in food service facilities nationwide, without an increase in the population. So, to stay competitive, food service professionals will have to find the proper balance and accommodate the needs, perceptions, and regimen of their clientele.

We believe this balance can be achieved through simplifying and utilizing sound cooking techniques, by placing an emphasis on quality, purchasing top-quality products at an affordable cost, and using a contemporary approach to cooking. Food service professionals can provide today's consumer with food that not only looks good but, first and foremost, tastes good and has the added bonus of being good for you.

The challenge for culinarians is to prepare traditional, classical foods and integrate them with new and modern ideas. We have to preserve the traditional specialties, combine them with what is valuable in modern cooking techniques, and serve flavorful, yet very distinctive food. The result for each of us as culinarians must be an ever-pressing effort to refresh one's repertoire and skill.

Begin by refining the cooking techniques that bring out flavors and textures. Experiment with such dishes as Spiced Braised Brisket with Wild Mushroom Risotto or Country Style Brown Shrimp Etouffee or Southwest Lentil Ragout. Take a new look at the vegetarian options available today.

Provide healthy alternatives to meat and seafood with different grains such as quinoa, bulgur wheat, kasha, couscous, barley, and certain varieties of rice. Do not overcook fruits and vegetables, and strive to rediscover the multiple applications of pungents and roots such as garlic, shallots, leeks, parsnips, yams, and celeriac.

Revisit your sauce production, creating more natural jus. Incorporate the use of vegetables and pulps in addition to infusions. Experiment with different coatings on food. Instead of only bread crumbs, utilize varieties of nuts, bran flakes, potatoes, rice paper, whole wheat filo dough, and herb crepes. Focus on creating desserts such as steeped, marinated seasonal fruits with sorbets or ices or sautéed peppered pineapple with fruit sauce.

Instead of being sautéed, fish can be steamed on a bamboo or wire rack over citrus juices, ginger, and fennel. The vapors infuse the fish with a delicate aroma and flavor. Fruit sauces can be prepared as a salsa by pureeing the fruit with the other ingredients.

The taste of the food is determined primarily by the quality of the main ingredients, the preparation and cooking method applied, and the addition of the appropriate seasonings, flavorings, and herbs. Proper serving temperature and visual presentation also influence perception of taste.

There are plenty of additional techniques to bring out the taste in food. For example, put an emphasis on simple, tasty grilled foods. Foods may be prepared in aluminum foil as well as in the microwave. An eating establishment can do a lot to avoid the stigma of being labeled a "nutritional restaurant," through consciously and actively taking into consideration the heightened level of expectation held by the consumer of today.

Today, a restaurant that captures the fast-growing health and nutrition conscious market segment may have the competitive edge over other establishments. Studies have shown that consumers with the greatest concern for restricting their intake of foods high in fat, sodium, and cholesterol are also those with the greatest propensity to frequent fine restaurants and dining establishments.

It is an excellent idea for a food service operator to form an alliance with a local health practitioner. Working together in partnership, the chef and the dietitian can combine the art of cooking with the science of nutrition and transform each favorite food item into a lighter version, without losing its finesse.

Although restaurants have not traditionally been venues for the promotion of good nutrition, it is becoming increasingly important for chefs and restaurants to recognize the necessity of good nutrition. As chefs, we should do the research and apply our culinary skills to create a product that is not only creative and tasty, but nutritious as well. We should then educate our sales staff to promote these attributes. With the increasing number of meals being eaten away from home, chefs can have a decisive impact on the health of the nation as a whole. The consumer today will seek out food service establishments that provide the best in quality, taste, service, health, and excitement.

Obviously, healthy can be tasty, and today there is plenty of help in this area. We need only to look at the varieties of inventive recipes that focus on this topic in the abundance of cookbooks and magazines on the market. There are approximately 250 cookbooks published annually on the subject of a healthier approach to cooking.

Yet, with the ready availability of nutrition information, adopting a healthful eating behavior pattern still depends on the different ways that people interpret the meaning of healthy eating habits, balance, moderation, and nutrition. In order to further captivate the attention of the consumer, we must instill a feeling of rediscovery of the intense and sensual qualities of food and the pleasure one derives from flavorful and exciting foods. Food appeals to all our senses, a factor often overlooked in many discussions, and appropriately reflects a basic need for the beauty of sight, sound, taste, feeling, and emotion.

We can achieve this by preparing foods that are simple, light and contemporary in style, yet provocative in flavor, through sensible execution and with a focus on quality and healthful ingredients. This will offer consumers a greater diversity in taste, address their need for convenience and quality, and provide the best in nutritional value.

Of all the arts, gastronomy is perhaps the most indispensable, elemental, understandable, and comforting. Gastronomy has evolved into a "whole table culture," which encompasses factors beyond surroundings. It now extends to psychological factors, including inducing the perfect mental disposition for the dining experience. Fine gastronomy can involve the simplest of meals, prepared to perfection, with all the components in harmony. The fundamentals of gastronomy have barely changed through the years.

However, changing lifestyles and demographics with an increasing public awareness of the importance of nutrition to overall health have shifted the consumer's interest from the long-drawn-out meals of old to today's meals with reduced portion sizes, less caloric intake, yet better nutritional value. To nourish oneself according to dietary guidelines presents challenges, not only for the person who eats but also for the person preparing the meals. Despite these challenges, the following basics still apply: The food must be appealing, look good, taste good, and have a variety of textures. The food must also contain all the necessary nutrient values in the required amounts and provide substantial variety.

CHAPTER 2

WINE WITH FOOD CAN BE PART OF A HEALTHFUL LIFESTYLE

@

We feel it is important to share our views on wine with the reader since the role of wine in the diet has changed dramatically. Today research confirms the positive role that moderate wine consumption can play in our lives (see Chapter 3, Mediterranean Diet Pyramid and Guidelines for Sensible Wine Drinking).

Wine consumption in true moderation, although heavily debated, has a long history. The more important issue, however, is for consumers to have adequate and factual information. Given accurate information, one can make educated and informed choices regarding alcoholic beverage consumption and the effect responsible wine consumption can have on an individual lifestyle. This book does not attempt to provide this level of information, which is easily attainable. Our recommendations and opinions on wine and health are based on our experience in the hospitality and food service industry. However, they are not meant to be construed as components or requirements of a healthful lifestyle.

Over the centuries, the rules and recommendations on storage, service, and drinking of wine have grown out of the experiences of many knowledgable wine experts. They discovered how we could treat wines to best service us.

In simple terms, wine is the naturally fermented juice of ripe grapes. It may be a staple item in most kitchens. To enjoy wine is to drink the wine you prefer, albeit in moderation, and it is always a matter of personal taste.

WINE TASTING

As with food, over time one learns about wines by tasting and identifying the refined characteristics, as well as appreciating the flavor and bouquet. The best time to taste wine is usually before a meal, never after a hearty meal because your sense of taste is still influenced by the meal.

Light is very important, because it will affect how you perceive the wine's clarity and brilliance. The temperature in the tasting room should preferably be around 68 to 70 degrees Fahrenheit (21°C). (Storage temperatures for red wines should ideally be 55 to 60 degrees Fahrenheit [16°C] and for white wines, 46 to 54 degrees Fahrenheit [12°C].)

A great deal can be learned from the actual sight test. Visual examination reveals, to some extent, the alcoholic content of the wine (high-alcohol-content wines tend to stick to the glass and run off more slowly). The sight test also allows one to judge the wine's clarity and detect unfiltered and murky wines. Tiny gas bubbles in wine could be the result of a second fermentation. On the other hand, there are some naturally sparkling wines whose mild effervescence does not affect the clarity.

With red wines, the depth of the color (depending on the variety of grapes and the length of time the grapes were left to ferment) decreases with time. As a general rule, a good bright red, tending toward cherry red, usually denotes good quality. In the case of red wines, the visual test is a good indicator of whether the wine is mature or on the decline.

The nose and smell test will allow you to recognize the aroma closely linked to the grape variety, referred to as the primary aroma. A secondary aroma develops after fermentation and can be somewhat fruity and even flowery. During the further maturation process, both primary and secondary aromas will merge into a final aroma, referred to as the wine bouquet. This can be a somewhat floral combination, yet it releases a whole new range of aroma.

The actual taste test is the last, perhaps most crucial step in analyzing the wine. After you have examined the wine and explored its aroma, gently sip the wine and roll it around in your mouth. The first sip will not always be the truest indicator of the wine's qualities, since your taste buds adjust to the tasting process. The second and third sips will bring forth additional taste sensations and enable one to make a more complete assessment. The tongue plays the lead role in tasting and distinguishes the five basic tastes. It can identify bitterness, saltiness, acidity, sweetness, and umami (savoriness) at the tip and sides of the tongue.

You should drink wine from a glass that has a large bowl and a stem, as this will further allow you to admire the color as well as the clarity. With experience and practice you will be able to determine the alcoholic strength of the wine and define the sugar and acidity.

Although there are specific relationships between wine and food, from a taste perspective, it should always be our goal not to let one overshadow the other but instead complement one another in their own unique way. Above all, remember, personal taste and choice are always the first consideration.

We have referred to the enjoyment of food being influenced by all of our senses; this is also very true for wine enjoyment. Focus on your emotional frame of mind when enjoying wine, as this will influence your preferences.

GUIDELINES FOR SELECTING AND SERVING WINES

In selecting wines to enjoy with food and in menu planning, consider some very general guidelines. Don't become caught up in the right and wrong of wine selection, but consider the blending of the individual flavors from a sensual perspective and have fun with the complexity of the possible pairings. Some simple guides to consider are:

- Dry wines are served before sweet wines.
- White wines are served before red wines, the exception being (sweet) white dessert wines that are served after the meal.
- Young red wines are served prior to the more intense and complex older red wines.
- Red Bordeaux are generally served before red Burgundies.
- White Burgundies are generally served before white Bordeaux.
- In Germany, Moselle wines are generally served before the Rhine wines.

Today, exceptions to the rules may be dictated by the individual tastes of those making the menu selections.

As discussed with food, our recommendation for enjoying good quality wines is variety. Today the market offers us a wide variety of options—Chardonnay, Sauvignon Blanc, Pinot Blanc, and Pinot Gris as well as a very fine, high quality selection of Cabernet Sauvignon and Merlots. Some of these match many of the great Pomerols of France, as well as the great *premier cru* Burgundies. Additional choices are endless with the Pinot Noirs and Syrahs.

During the last two decades, our profession has seen tremendous progress in how we perceive, purchase, prepare, cook, serve, and consume food products. A very similar development has occurred in the wine industry. Today at least 70 percent of the wine purchased in the United States originates from California; thus the wine production clearly speaks for itself. Between 1970 and 1990, U.S. vineyards grew in area by 300 percent. Today the United States is the sixth largest producer of wine in the world.

The following are our suggestions for pairing wines with fine cuisine.

As an Aperitif. Champagne has all the stimulating attributes of an aperitif. Champagnes come in several styles and are truly versatile; they can be served with a variety of foods.

Champagne is dry and fruity, with a clean, rich flavor. The more mature Champagnes are buttery and classic, with a distinct nutty profile. Champagnes with soul such as the mature Special Cuvées and rare vintages blend beautifully with fresh gingerbread!

Rosés go well with bold foods such as game and pâtés.

A Zinfandel is full of deep berry flavor, but will not overpower or compete with delicate food.

A light, dry sherry served as an aperitif should be slightly chilled, never icy cold, in order to fully enjoy the beautiful bouquet. Avoid serving spicy olives or salted peanuts with an aperitif, as the salt will negatively affect the flavor of the wine.

Shellfish Appetizers and Hors d'Oeuvres. Preferably serve these with light, dry white wines, also Brut Champagne, white Burgundy or Rhône wines, Chablis, dry Moselle, Rhine wines, dry white Bordeaux, and Sauvignon Blancs. These are known for their balanced yet crisp flavor.

Savory Hors d'Oeuvres, Vegetarian and Provençal Vegetable Dishes. These go very well with a simple, light red, such as a Pinot Noir or rosé, as well as the fleshy reds like a Pomerol, the California Merlots, or an Australian Shiraz.

Poached Seafood. It is preferable to serve this with a dry wine, not to be confused with only white wines, as a light red is also delightful with a flavorful fish dish. Sole, depending on the ingredients in the preparation, usually goes well with a somewhat sharper, dry white wine, particularly if the preparation includes tomatoes. If a cream-based sauce is used, select a wine with more depth, such as white Burgundy.

Sautéed and Roasted Fish. A good choice is a simple, light red wine, such as a young Cabernet or Pinot Noir. Salmon, for example, will pair well with a young Pinot or even a fine light Burgundy. Tuna is complemented by wines with a fruity character, such as Sauvignon Blanc. New Zealand is producing some very fine Sauvignon Blancs and Chardonnays.

White Meats and Chicken. Light red Bordeaux, Cabernet Sauvignon, and Burgundy wines, as well as dry white wines, are excellent with white meats and chicken. Chicken is perhaps the most versatile of all dishes as far as wine selection is concerned, so base the wine selection for a poultry dish on its preparation and additional ingredients.

Pasta Dishes. Italian foods call for Italian wines, or a similar selection. Chianti is the obvious choice with pasta, pizza, and Italian food, particularly when a heavy meat sauce is used. Pesto, basil and cilantro sauces go best with a Sauvignon Blanc. An Italian Chardonnay or an equivalent will complement pasta dishes with a cream sauce.

Red Meats, Roasts, Rotisserie Items. These items work well with the fuller, more developed Bordeaux, Merlot, Cabernet, or Burgundy wines, as well as dry white wines of a higher niveau.

Wild Game and Game Birds. Game goes well with fully developed, high-caliber red Bordeaux, Cabernet, and Burgundy, also high-end, dry Rhine wines. Venison is particularly complemented by the grand vintage Bordeaux, as well as a high-quality, rich white Alsace, Tokay, or Pinot Gris.

Ethnic Dishes. Cajun food goes well with Pinot Noir or a dry Gewurztraminer.

Cold Meat Platters, Pâtés, Galantines. These go exceptionally well with young, fruity, red wines, dry Champagnes, Beaujolais, and selected dry white wines.

Sweet Desserts and Ice Cream Desserts. Desserts go with sweet or semi-sweet white wines or *demi-sec* Champagne. One could also skip dessert altogether if a wonderful dessert wine or Champagne is offered.

Cheese and Hot or Cold Cheese Dishes. These are normally served prior to a sweet dessert and work well with a high-caliber Bordeaux, Cabernet, Burgundy, or Rhône wine, but of course a high-quality vintage Port is also appropriate. Remember, strong cheeses will mask the flavor of wine, therefore serve mild, top-quality cheeses with fine wines.

Other points to consider:

- A high-quality dry Champagne is appropriate to be served throughout the meal period.
- A dry sherry is also appropriate with a variety of fish dishes, although one should consider the alcohol content.

COOKING WITH WINE

The natural flavor of wine makes it ideal for cooking. The alcohol partially evaporates in the deglazing and reducing process, depending on the cooking method, as well as the length of cooking time. Wine "burns off" more easily than hard liquor. The longer it is kept over (or in) a flame, the more alcohol tends to evaporate and less is left in the food. However, people with alcohol intolerance or those taking medications that do not mix with alcohol should always be cautious.

Any wine used in cooking should be a good wine to maximize the flavor contribution. This does not mean it must be an expensive vintage bottle; good cooking wines can be found at reasonable prices.

In the kitchen we use many fortified and dessert wines, such as Madeira, Marsala, Port wine, vermouths, and sherry, all to enhance simple dishes and add excitement to food preparation. Sherry is commonly used in trifles, dessert applications, and soup applications. Madeira and Marsala are both used in dessert preparations, warm gratin, and the preparation of zabaglione. Madeira is also utilized in a variety of cooking applications, such as in soup preparations like a real turtle soup or oxtail soup.

Progress is great, but the traditional classics still have a lot to offer. Madeira must always be of high quality and dry. We believe that when cooking with wines in the kitchen the chef should utilize a good-quality wine and that price should not be the main consideration in its purchase.

When cooking with wine, it is the flavor of the wine that ultimately enhances the dish. Practice restraint and do not drown the dish in wine. When cooking chicken, veal, fish, and sweetbreads, use a delicate, medium-dry white wine. Red meats such as lamb, beef, and game are traditionally prepared with red wines. In the classical cuisine we find certain traditional dishes prepared with red rather than white wine, such as coq au vin, civet de homard, or filet de sole matelote.

Apart from being an obvious flavor enhancer, wine is also used to increase moisture and tenderness. Fish marinated in white wine or meats steeped in red wine are enhanced in both texture and taste. Fish need not be marinated for more than an hour, but meats such as rabbit, hare, wild duck, venison, or beef may be left up to four days, depending on the brine and the intended use. Marinades can consist of one part high-quality olive oil to three parts dry red or white wine, depending on use, and include herbs, bouquet garni, garlic, onions, and peppercorns. (See Chapter 5, Flavor Enhancers and Marinades.)

Spicy foods may tend to overpower wine, but one can try a good Gewurztraminer with spicy cuisine. We found that the pungent aroma and sweet taste works well with spicy dishes. Thai cuisine particularly goes well with an Alsace Pinot Blanc for crisp refreshment. However, in the case of curries from India and the Middle East, perhaps the best choice is a glass of well-chilled beer!

COOKING WITHOUT WINE
Although there is truly no substitute for the flavor of wine, if you wish to replace the wine with another liquid, use high-quality beef, chicken, veal, vegetable, or fish stock to complement the food. Citrus juices or apple cider or juice will be a fine substitute for wines called for in dessert recipes.

Overall, national consumption of alcoholic beverages may be down, in part due to consumers who are increasingly selective and discerning in their consumption.

In a commercial food service setting where menu compatibility and flexibility are important, a varied, yet exclusive selection of fine-quality wines should be offered. This attention to variety, quality, and selection will complement and enhance the overall food and beverage service program. Today the worldwide market encompasses educated consumers, with unique cultural, religious, ethnic, and dietary backgrounds, which makes food and wine pairings even more specific and demanding.

At the fine restaurants of The Culinary Institute of America, The American Bounty, The Escoffier Room, and St. Andrews Cafe, customers are offered a wine list that features, in addition to wine by the bottle, a choice of 3-, 4-, or 5-ounce-glass servings. This enables the guest to be selective and expand his or her tasting enjoyment and overall wine experience.

The Chef Instructors of St. Andrews Cafe agree that wine and food should complement one another and encourage guests to experiment with different combinations of food and wine, tasting wines outside their normal selections.

An interesting and unusual combination is found when tasting a Cabernet Sauvignon with a fine chocolate dessert. Unique is the experience of the harmony in such an unlikely match.

In that St. Andrews is a health-conscious restaurant, non-alcoholic wines are also offered to their guests. These can be fresh and fruity and a fine accompaniment to a delicious, nutritious, and well-prepared meal. Today the consumer can find many varieties of non-alcoholic beverages readily available, including beers, wines, and sparkling wines.

Experience and education are the keys to wine appreciation and enjoyment. However, we sometimes overlook the real pleasures from the experience of enjoying a wonderful wine with a delicious meal. Those experiences, and the pleasure they produce, are longer lasting than the material possession of the same monetary value. What we sometimes forget is that in comparison, the material things we can measure are the most meaningless possessions and that it is really the pleasurable experiences, shared with those we love, that have true value.

As America matures as a nation, developing a sincere appreciation of the most basic but most pleasure-filled things in life, its enjoyment of the pleasures of fine wine with well-prepared food will grow as well!

To learn more about the health effects of moderate wine consumption, you can send for the federal government's Dietary Guidelines or consult with your health-care practitioner (see pages 26–32).

DEVELOPING YOUNG CULINARIANS CONTINUES TO BE A PRIORITY FOR THE FOOD SERVICE INDUSTRY . . . IF WE ARE TO HAVE DEVELOPED, WELL TRAINED AND MOTIVATED STAFF.

Chef Leopold K. Schaeli, CMC

PLAIN COOKING CANNOT BE ENTRUSTED TO PLAIN COOKS.

Countess Morphy

IF ALL YOU'VE GOT IS WHERE YOU ARE FROM, YOU SHOULD BE GETTING OUT MORE.

Billy Connolly

OUR RECIPE FOR A HEALTHFUL CUISINE

❦

❦

With the increased emphasis on health and fitness, the American diet today may focus on extremes. Examples of these extremes include practices such as eliminating all fat from the diet, and consuming excessive amounts of those vitamins that have been shown to have a positive effect on health. The fallacies and confusions regarding the nutritional aspects of a healthful diet are abundant. Focusing on any single nutrient can give the false impression of following a healthful diet. The focus instead should be on the cumulative effect of the consumption of foods within a meal, a day, a week, or a lifetime. A healthful diet should include a wide variety of foods. Incorporating variety in food selection, including colors, textures, and flavors, will ensure a diet full of the essential nutritional components. This diet can be appealing, tasty, and healthful.

According to a study conducted by the American Dietetic Association, the most common perceived hurdles to eating well include the fear of giving up foods (40 percent), confusion or frustration over nutrition studies and reports (23 percent), and the belief that a healthful eating style takes too much time (21 percent). The conquest for a healthy diet does not require the elimination of favorite foods. Just as good cooking begins with good ingredients, a healthful diet begins with the essential nutritional components.

CHAPTER 3

BUILDING THE RECIPE WITH THE ESSENTIAL INGREDIENTS, FROM A NUTRIENT PERSPECTIVE

@

Just as in cooking we select the best ingredients in order to create a wonderful recipe, in nutrition we have to include all of the required nutrients (carbohydrates, protein, fat, vitamins, minerals, water) to build a healthful diet. A basic understanding of nutrients is essential for effective and healthful contemporary cooking. *Nutrients* are those substances that are essential to life and which the body cannot manufacture. The body acquires these substances from food.

CALORIES

A calorie is simply a measurement, or unit, of energy. It is not a nutrient per se, but rather a reflection of the amount of energy food provides.

Calories = Energy

The body requires energy to function. Simply said, when the amount of energy consumed balances the energy expended, body weight is stable. The average caloric intake for healthy adults is about 2,000, but calorie requirements are extremely individualized and are based on many factors including age, weight, height, and activity level. Figure 3.1 provides a simple formula by which adults can determine their approximate calorie requirements. For those who desire weight change, the calorie intake and/or energy expenditure must be altered appropriately. It is important to recognize that while some foods are more calorically dense, or high in calories, the nutritional value of food is not based solely on the calorie content but on the nutrients it contains. Energy consumed but not utilized by the body is eventually stored as fat, regardless of its original source.

The calorie-containing nutrients include carbohydrates, protein, and fat. Alcohol, although not a nutrient, also provides energy.

The number of calories in a single gram of these substances is as follows:

Carbohydrates   4
Protein   4
Fat   9
Alcohol   7

To determine your baseline daily calorie needs, multiply your current weight in pounds by the number of calories per pound shown below. For example, for a 35-year-old weighing 130 pounds: 130 pounds × 12 calories per pound = 1560 calories per day. Note: Variations in metabolism and physical activity affect each individual's calorie needs.

Ages 20–30	weight × 13–15
Ages 30–40	weight × 12
Ages 40–50	weight × 11
Ages 50+	weight × 10

FIGURE 3.1   Simple Formula for Figuring Calorie Needs

NUTRIENTS

CARBOHYDRATES

Carbohydrates are food starches, sugars, and fibers. Established guidelines recommend that 55 to 60 percent of total calories come from carbohydrates. There are three categories of carbohydrates: simple, complex, and fiber.

Simple: Single or double sugars

Complex: Long chains of sugars (starches)

Dietary fiber: The indigestible portion of complex carbohydrates

Simple and complex carbohydrates break down to glucose (the form of sugar used by the body). They are an important source of energy for the body.

Fiber, although not a nutrient, performs a role in the digestive process including the prevention and treatment of constipation. A diet high in fiber also reduces the risk of certain cancers and high blood cholesterol levels. Fiber is divided into two groups: water-soluble and water-insoluble. Table 3.1 gives further information on these two types.

PROTEIN

Protein is the major structural component of muscle, bone, skin, tissues and organs, and body fluids. One-fifth of the total body weight is protein, sec-

TABLE 3.1   Soluble and Insoluble Fiber

	Type of Fiber	*Sources*	*Functions*
Soluble	Gums, mucilages, pectin	Oat bran, jams and jellies, fruit	Bind fatty substances; decrease blood cholesterol; regulate the body's use of sugar.
Insoluble	Cellulose, hemicellulose, lignin	Raw fruits and vegetables, whole grains, legumes	Promote bowel regularity; lower risk of certain cancers.

ond only to water weight. Established guidelines recommend that 10 to 15 percent of calories in a healthful diet come from protein. Proteins are composed of amino acids strung together in different configurations. Approximately 22 different amino acids have been identified, nine of which are essential. *Essential* means the body cannot manufacture them, so they must be provided by the diet. A *complete protein* is one that contains all of the nine essential amino acids. An *incomplete protein* lacks, or has limited amounts, of one or more essential amino acids. Animal protein is more complete than plant protein. Most protein in animal products provides essential amino acids in ratios needed by the human body. However, some animal protein, such as gelatin, is inadequate in essential amino acids. Complete proteins are considered high quality; incomplete proteins are considered low quality.

Protein from vegetables and grains is usually incomplete. It is possible to combine incomplete proteins to make a complete protein. Incomplete proteins which, when grouped, form complete proteins are called *complementary* proteins.

FAT AND CHOLESTEROL

Fat in food is self-evident in many animal products but is also found in dairy foods (butter fat), plant oils, and processed foods that have had fat incorporated into them. Americans may spend a lot of time and energy focusing on ways to decrease or eliminate fat from the diet. In humans, fat is a fundamental part of the body structure and has many essential functions. For example, it aids in the transport of fat-soluble vitamins, and it provides an efficient way for the body to store energy. Established guidelines recommend that for a healthful diet, less than 30 percent of total calories come from fat.

There are several different types of fat, each with properties that affect both health and food preparation. Although some fats are more healthful, all fats have the same high caloric content, and therefore the total amount of fat should be considered in meal planning. Fats are categorized as saturated, monounsaturated, and polyunsaturated. Fat in food may contain all three types, though one type usually predominates.

1. Saturated Fat. Saturated fats originate mainly in animal products and are solid at room temperature. Examples of saturated fats include most fats from meat, fish, poultry, lard, butter, milk, and milk products. High dietary intake of saturated fat can lead to elevated blood cholesterol, a risk factor for cardiovascular (heart) disease. (See Chapter 4, Cardiovascular (Heart Healthy) Diet, page 45.)

2. Monounsaturated Fat. Monounsaturated fats are mostly of plant origin. Avocados, olives, olive oil, peanuts, peanut oil, and canola oil are all high in monounsaturated fat. These fats are usually liquid or semi-solid at room temperature. Of all the fats, monounsaturated fat has the most beneficial effect on blood cholesterol levels.

3. Polyunsaturated Fat. Polyunsaturated fats are also from plants. Sunflower, cottonseed, corn, safflower, and some fish oils are all polyunsaturated fats. These fats are usually liquid at room temperature. When used in place of saturated fats, they can lower the level of cholesterol in the blood.

Monounsaturated fat and polyunsaturated fat can be made saturated for stability and extended shelf life through a process called hydrogenation. *Hydrogenation* causes fats to be solid at room temperature; for example, when vegetable oil is hydrogenated, it becomes vegetable shortening. Other examples include stick margarine and many snack foods (i.e. cookies, crackers). Hydrogenated fats act similar to saturated fats in the body and therefore should be limited.

The recommendations suggest that dietary intake for each category of fat should be no greater than 10 percent of total calories or one-third of fat calories.

4. Cholesterol. Dietary cholesterol is a type of fat found in small amounts in foods of animal origin including meat, poultry, fish, shellfish, egg yolk, milk, and lard. Cholesterol is also manufactured by the body; it is necessary for the body and is found in every cell. Some foods which are cholesterol-free may not be fat-free.

VITAMINS AND MINERALS

Vitamins and minerals are calorie-free nutrients and are needed in small quantities, thus are called micronutrients. They are essential because the human body cannot manufacture them in adequate quantities. Vitamins are divided into two categories: fat-soluble and water-soluble. *Fat-soluble* vitamins are stored in the liver and in fatty tissue. *Water-soluble* vitamins are not stored, but rather are excreted in the urine when consumed in excess of body requirements. It is more common to have deficiencies of water-soluble vitamins than fat-soluble vitamins, although a vitamin deficiency of any kind is increasingly rare in the United States (see Table 3.2).

Minerals are categorized as either *macrominerals* or *trace minerals*, depending upon the amount needed by the body. Macrominerals are needed in higher volumes than trace minerals (see Table 3.3).

ESTABLISHED GUIDELINES FOR NUTRIENTS

Recommended Dietary Allowances (RDAs) are standards set for the daily intake of various nutrients. They are considered to be adequate quantities for practically all healthy people. The RDAs are based upon the recommendations of the Food and Nutrition Board of the National Academy of Science National Research Council. The tenth and most recent edition of the RDAs was published in 1989.

TABLE 3.2   Quick Reference to Vitamins

Vitamin	Good Food Sources	Adult RDA or Estimated Safe and Adequate Intake[1]	Functions
Fat-Soluble:			
Vitamin A	Liver, fish, egg yolks, fortified milk, butter, fortified margarine, cream, cheese, dark green, deep orange, and yellow vegetables	1000 RE (male 11+ years) 800 RE (female 11+ years)	Normal bone development and tooth formation. Vision. Growth. Maintenance of mucus-forming cells. Immune function.
Vitamin E	Vegetable oils, nuts, seeds, beef liver, milk, eggs, butter, fortified cereals, wheat germ, leafy green vegetables	10 mg (male 11+ yrs) 8 mg (female 11+ yrs)	Antioxidant (protects vitamin A and unsaturated fatty acids from oxidation). Protects red blood cells from damage.
Vitamin D	Eggs, liver, butter, fortified margarine, fortified milk, fatty fish, sardines, salmon, exposure to sunlight	5 mcg (1–50 yrs) 10 mcg (51–70 yrs) 15 mcg (71+ yrs)	Formation of bone and teeth. Promotes absorption of calcium and phosphorus.
Vitamin K	Vegetable oils, green leafy vegetables, liver	80 mcg (male 25+ yrs) 65 mcg (female 25+ yrs)	Required for production of blood clotting factors.
Water-Soluble:			
Vitamin C (Ascorbic Acid)	Citrus fruits, berries, melons, potatoes, tomatoes, peppers, greens, raw cabbage, papayas, mangos	60 mg	Collagen synthesis. Antioxidant. Wound healing and immune function. Enhances iron absorption.
Thiamin (Vitamin B$_1$)	Pork, liver and other organ meats, wheat germ, whole-grain and enriched breads and cereals, legumes	1.5 mg (male 15–50 yrs) 1.2 mg (male 51+ yrs) 1.1 mg (female 15–50 yrs) 1.0 mg (female 51+ yrs)	Energy metabolism. Normal appetite. Growth. Digestion. Nerve function.

(continued)

TABLE 3.2   Quick Reference to Vitamins (continued)

Vitamin	*Good Food Sources*	*Adult RDA or Estimated Safe and Adequate Intake*[1]	*Functions*
Water-Soluble (continued):			
Riboflavin (Vitamin B$_2$)	Milk and milk products, eggs, organ meats, green leafy vegetables, whole-grain and enriched breads and cereals	1.7 mg (male up to 50 yrs) 1.4 mg (male 51+ yrs) 1.3 mg (female up to 50 yrs) 1.2 mg (female 51+ yrs)	Energy metabolism. Growth.
Niacin	Lean meats, poultry, fish, peanuts, organ meats, brewer's yeast, whole-grain and enriched bread and cereals	19 mg (male 19–50 yrs) 15 mg (male 51+ yrs) 15 mg (female 19–50 yrs) 13 mg (female 51+ yrs)	Energy metabolism.
Pyridoxine (Vitamin B$_6$)	Yeast, wheat germ, pork, liver, legumes, potatoes, bananas, whole-grain cereals	2.0 mg (male) 1.6 mg (female)	Red blood cell production. Synthesis and breakdown of protein. Synthesis of unsaturated fatty acids. Growth.
Folic Acid (Folacin, Folate)	Organ meats (liver), green leafy vegetables, legumes, asparagus, broccoli, whole-grain cereal, nuts	200 mcg (male) 180 mcg (female)	Helps produce DNA and RNA. Essential for normal maturation of red blood cells.
Cobalamin (Vitamin B$_{12}$)	Liver, kidney, meat, eggs, cheese, fish	2.0 mcg	Red blood cell formation. Coenzyme in protein synthesis.
Panthothenic Acid	Fresh vegetables, kidney, liver, egg yolks, yeast, wheat bran	4–7 mg	Energy metabolism. Biosynthesis of fatty acids.
Biotin	Milk, egg yolks, yeast, kidney, liver, mushrooms, bananas, strawberries, watermelon	30–100 mcg	Energy metabolism.

[1] mg = milligram

mcg = microgram

RE = Retinol equivalents

IU = International Units

The RDA values vary according to age and sex, and for pregnant and breastfeeding women. They are intended only to be guidelines for meeting the nutritional needs of most healthy people.

A more comprehensive set of guidelines are the Dietary Reference Intakes (DRIs), which were established as a response to increased public awareness about health and nutrition. DRI values include EARs (Estimated Average Requirements), AIs (Adequate Intakes), and UIs (Tolerable Upper Intake Levels), as well as RDAs. These new values indicate a safe and optimal range of nutrient consumption. DRIs for calcium, fluoride, magnesium, vitamin D, and phosphorus were published in the first volume. Other nutrients will be published as they are evaluated. The various DRI values are defined as follows:

TABLE 3.3 Quick Reference to Minerals

Mineral	Good Food Sources	RDA or Estimated Safe and Adequate Intake[1]	Functions
Macro:			
Calcium	Milk and milk products, salmon and sardines with bones, dark green leafy vegetables, tofu, dried beans and peas, products fortified with calcium	1000 mg (19–50 yrs) 1200 mg (51+ yrs)	Formation and maintenance of teeth and bones. Muscle contraction and relaxation. Nerve transmission. Necessary in clotting of blood.
Phosphorus	Milk and milk products, egg yolks, meat, poultry, nuts, fish, beans, whole-grain cereals, chocolate	700 mg	Formation and maintenance of teeth and bones. Energy production. Protein synthesis and fat transport. Component of DNA and RNA.
Magnesium	Whole grains (wheat bran), green leafy vegetables, nuts, meat, milk, dried beans and peas, chocolate, tofu	400 mg (male 19–30 yrs) 420 mg (male 31+ yrs) 310 mg (female 19–30 yrs) 320 mg (female 31+ yrs)	Part of over 300 enzymes in the body. Cardiac function and nerve function. Bone growth. Energy production.
Potassium	Meat, milk, whole grains, fruits, vegetables, dried beans and peas	2000–3500 mg	Fluid and acid–base balance. Muscle contraction. Blood pressure regulation. Nerve impulse transmission.

(continued)

TABLE 3.3 Quick Reference to Minerals (continued)

Mineral	Good Food Sources	RDA or Estimated Safe and Adequate Intake[1]	Functions
Macro (continued):			
Sodium	Table salt, processed foods	500–2400 mg	Fluid and acid–base balance. Muscle contraction. Nerve impulse transmission.
Chloride	Table salt, processed foods	750 mg (minimum)	Fluid and acid–base balance. Component of hydrochloric acid in stomach.
Sulfur	Dried beans and peas, nuts, eggs, milk, cheese, meat, fish, poultry	No RDA established	Acid–base balance. Component of the amino acids cysteine and methionine and the vitamins thiamin and biotin essential in the detoxification process.
Trace:			
Iron	Liver, red meats, poultry, fish, legumes, dried fruits, whole-grain and fortified breads and cereals, green leafy vegetables, egg yolks	10 mg (male) 15 mg (female)	Part of hemoglobin (carries oxygen in blood). Part of myoglobin (stores oxygen in muscles). Immune function.
Iodine	Iodized salt, seafood, dairy products, white bread	150 mcg	Part of thyroxin (thyroid hormone) which helps regulate metabolic rate, growth, and development.
Selenium	Shellfish, organ meats, egg yolks, milk, grains and vegetables grown in selenium-rich soil	70 mcg (male) 55 mcg (female)	Part of an enzyme that works with vitamin E as an antioxidant (prevents cell damage).
Fluoride	Fluoridated water, tea, seafood	3.8 mg (male) 3.1 mg (female)	Present in teeth and bones. May reduce bone loss. Helps prevent tooth decay.
Copper	Organ meats, shellfish, nuts, dried beans and peas, whole grains, chocolate, raisins	1.5–3.0 mg	Part of many enzymes. Helps make hemoglobin (to carry oxygen in red blood cells). Aids in formation of protective covering of nerves.

(continued)

TABLE 3.3   Quick Reference to Minerals (continued)

Mineral	Good Food Sources	RDA or Estimated Safe and Adequate Intake[1]	Functions
Trace (continued): Chromium	Whole-grain breads and cereals, brewer's yeast, meats, vegetables, oils, egg yolks	50–200 mcg	Energy release from glucose. May enhance the action of of insulin.
Manganese	Tea, dried beans and peas, whole grains (bran), nuts, fruits, beet greens	2.0–5.0 mg	Normal tendon and bone structure. Energy production. Blood formation.
Molybdenum	Dried beans and peas, dark green leafy vegetables, organ meats, whole-grain breads and cereals	75–250 mcg	Energy metabolism. Iron storage.
Cobalt	Liver, kidney, oysters, clams, milk, meat, poultry	No RDA established	Part of vitamin B_{12}. Healthy nerves and red blood cells.
Zinc	Poultry, eggs, beef, liver, oysters, fish, whole-grain breads and cereals, nuts, wheat germ, milk, beans	15 mg (male) 12 mg (female)	Wound healing and immunity. Taste and smell acuity. Growth. Sexual development and reproduction.

[1]mg = milligram

mcg = microgram

EAR (Estimated Average Requirement): The intake that meets the estimated nutrient need of 50% of the individuals in a group specified by age and sex, plus pregnant and breastfeeding women.

RDA (Recommended Dietary Allowance): The intake that meets the nutrient need of almost all (97–98%) individuals in a group specified by age and sex, plus pregnant and breastfeeding women.

AI (Adequate Intake): The average observed or experimentally derived intake by a defined population or subgroup that appears to sustain a defined nutritional state, such as normal circulating nutrient values, growth, or other functional indicators of health.

UI (Tolerable Upper Intake Level): The maximum intake by an individual that is unlikely to pose risks of adverse health effects in almost all (97–98%) individuals.

SODIUM

Sodium is a mineral that the body needs in very small amounts. It merits special attention because it is so abundant in the food supply that many people consume greater amounts than is healthy. Sodium combined with chloride becomes *sodium chloride*, or *table salt*. Salt is a common flavor enhancer used in cooking and can also contribute to the texture in processed foods. Table salt is not the only form of sodium that we consume. Monosodium glutamate (MSG), sodium bicarbonate (baking soda), and sodium caseinate are common food additives. Sodium content will be indicated by the words "sodium," "salt," or "Na" (the chemical symbol for sodium). Sodium is prevalent in processed foods; the Nutrition Fact Label indicates sodium levels in a food product.

One teaspoon of salt contains approximately 2,400 mg of sodium. Most healthy people need approximately 500 mg (about 1/4 teaspoon of salt) daily to maintain normal body functions. The RDA for sodium is 2,400 mg or less per day; however, the average American consumes between 4,000 and 6,000 mg of sodium daily. Excess sodium is normally excreted by the body.

Sodium regulates the fluid balance of the body and can affect blood pressure. Some individuals are more sensitive to the effects of excessive sodium intake. Excessive sodium in the diet is linked to high blood pressure, which contributes to heart and kidney disease. A healthy diet should be limited in high-sodium processed foods and beverages; smoked, salted, and cured meats; canned or pickled foods, and luncheon meats and cheeses. "Fast foods" are generally high in sodium and should be limited. Additional information can be found in Chapter 4, Sodium-Restricted Diet.

Salt substitutes are available for individuals who are sensitive to sodium. Many of the salt substitutes replace sodium with potassium; therefore, there may be risks related to overconsumption of potassium for some individuals.

WATER

Water is essential to life, yet it is sometimes overlooked as a nutrient. The human body is composed of approximately 55 to 75 percent water by weight. It is vital to maintain an adequate level of water in the body. Water supports the transport of nutrients and waste throughout the body and regulates body temperature. Sources of water for the human body include foods and beverages (milk, juices, flavored drinks, and water itself). Although virtually all foods contain some water, many foods have a high water content, especially fresh fruits and vegetables including tomatoes, oranges, watermelon, celery, and iceberg lettuce. Water is needed in large quantities in comparison to all other nutrients. Calorie-free, low-sodium, caffeine-free, and fat-free, water is the optimal beverage choice to satisfy thirst! In addition, many communities fluoridate their water supplies; fluoride promotes healthy bones and teeth.

Selecting the right ingredients when cooking is only half the process involved in creating a recipe. The choice of cooking techniques to use and the tools to execute these techniques must also be considered. They influence the visual appeal of the meal and can also enhance the flavor. Using the tools available can help prepare a healthful diet. The Dietary Guidelines, the Food Guide Pyramid, and the nutrition information available on food labels may all be useful tools in recipe development and food preparation.

DIETARY GUIDELINES

The Dietary Guidelines offer principles of food selection to meet nutrient needs (RDAs). These guidelines provide suggestions for minimizing the risk for developing certain diseases while maintaining or improving overall health. They are developed by the Dietary Guidelines Advisory Committee of the U.S. Department of Agriculture (USDA) and the U.S. Department of Health and Human Services and are designed for healthy people age two years and older. The guidelines were first developed in 1980; the third and most recent version was completed in 1995. Guidelines have evolved from simple dietary restrictions to practical suggestions for positive lifestyle changes.

1. **Eat a variety of foods.** An interesting and healthful diet requires a variety of foods. There is not one "super food" or "super nutrient" which is more important than any other. Healthful eating requires the selection of foods based not only on the nutrient content but also on taste and sense of satisfaction. A healthy diet can incorporate preferences and need not exclude certain foods or food groups. Variety adds contrasting tastes and colors and is a natural way to meet nutrient needs. When planning meals for others, selections should be made based on food groups while considering diversity, ethnicity, enjoyment, and lifestyle. Also utilize various cooking techniques, especially those which preserve nutrient value. Moderate the use of convenience foods and incorporate more fresh foods.

2. **Balance energy consumption and energy expenditure.** Some people focus excessively on the energy nutrients, especially fat, to avoid or combat obesity. A healthier approach is to focus on portion control, healthful food choices, and expending the energy consumed. To maintain a healthy weight, energy consumed (carbohydrate, protein, fat) must be balanced with energy expended by physical activity. For the obese individual to achieve a healthy weight, energy expended must be greater than energy consumed.

3. **Choose a diet with plenty of grain products, vegetables, and fruits.** A diet rich in grains, vegetables, and fruits is naturally healthful. These food

groups are nutrient dense; in other words, per calorie, they are high in carbohydrates, vitamins, minerals, and fiber. They are naturally low in fat. They contribute to satiety, the feeling of satisfaction after eating a meal. The fiber present in grains, vegetables, and fruits has also been shown to help fight cancer and heart disease.

For optimal health, choose a diet with grains, vegetables, and fruits as the largest component, with less emphasis on meat. Consider meat as a side dish instead of the center of the plate.

4. Choose a diet low in fat, saturated fat, and cholesterol. Fat contributes to the satiety, flavor, and enjoyment of a meal. When including fats in your diet, choose more monounsaturated or polyunsaturated fats and less saturated fats and cholesterol (see p. 31). A diet high in fat, particularly saturated fat, can result in elevated levels of blood cholesterol, and can lead to heart disease, cancer, and obesity. A natural way to reduce fat intake is to choose leaner cuts of meats, smaller portions, and low-fat dairy products, while utilizing healthful cooking techniques that do not add fat.

5. Choose a diet moderate in sugar. Sugar in the diet comes from natural sources (fruit sugars and milk sugars) or from foods to which sugar has been added (processed foods). An overindulgence in high-sugar foods means consumption of "empty" calories (calories with few nutrients) and promotes tooth decay. Instead, choose foods with naturally occurring sugars and fiber, vitamins, and minerals—fresh fruit or a baked sweet potato, for example.

6. Choose a diet moderate in salt and sodium. Salt has long been used as an enhancer of food flavor, but an overconsumption can contribute to high blood pressure and heart disease. A diet high in fresh, unprocessed foods will be lower in sodium. Processed and convenience foods are generally high in sodium content; therefore, it is important to moderate their use in the diet. And of course, table salt should be used with moderation, since a single teaspoon of salt meets the guideline for an entire day's intake.

7. If you drink alcoholic beverages, do so in moderation. In addition to enhancing the pleasure of a meal, moderate consumption of wine may lower the risk of heart disease. However, alcohol is high in calories with very few nutrients and therefore, from a nutritional standpoint, not the best choice of calories.

For some people, consumption of alcohol can lead to addiction. It can also contribute to health problems including heart disease, cancer, and liver disease.

FOOD GUIDE PYRAMID

In 1992, the USDA developed the Food Guide Pyramid to replace the Basic Four Food Groups. The Food Guide Pyramid (see Figs. 3.2 and 3.3) is a graphic depiction of the Dietary Guidelines, and was designed to translate the

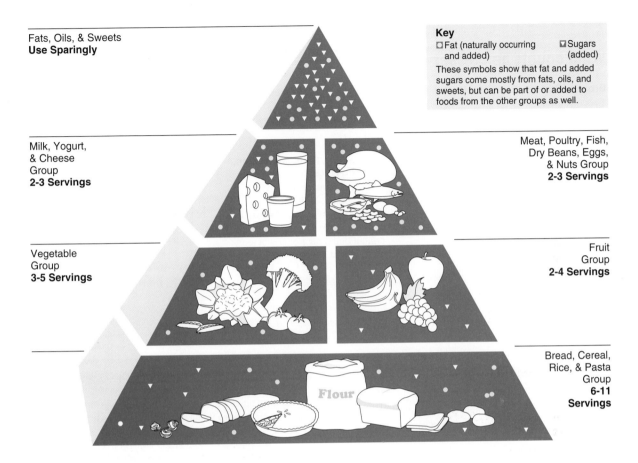

Fats, Oils, & Sweets
Use Sparingly

Key
☐ Fat (naturally occurring and added)   ☑ Sugars (added)
These symbols show that fat and added sugars come mostly from fats, oils, and sweets, but can be part of or added to foods from the other groups as well.

Milk, Yogurt, & Cheese Group
2-3 Servings

Meat, Poultry, Fish, Dry Beans, Eggs, & Nuts Group
2-3 Servings

Vegetable Group
3-5 Servings

Fruit Group
2-4 Servings

Bread, Cereal, Rice, & Pasta Group
6-11 Servings

Flour

Use the Food Guide Pyramid to help you eat better every day. . .the Dietary Guidelines way. Start with plenty of Breads, Cereals, Rice, and Pasta; Vegetables; and Fruits. Add two to three servings from the Milk group and two to three servings from the Meat group.

Each of these food groups provides some, but not all, of the nutrients you need. No one food group is more important than another — for good health you need them all. Go easy on the fats, oils, and sweets, the foods in the small tip of the Pyramid.

FIGURE 3.2   The USDA Food Guide Pyramid. U.S. Department of Agriculture, Human Nutrition Information Service, August 1992, Leaflet No. 572. To order a copy of "The Food Guide Pyramid" booklet, send a $1.00 check or money order made out to the Superintendent of Documents to: Consumer Information Center, Department 159-Y, Pueblo, Colorado 81009

RDAs into practical advice. Eating "by the Pyramid" ensures the consumption of nutrients the body needs for energy, growth, and health. The pyramid shape emphasizes the key concepts of variety, moderation, and proportionality. The pyramid shape also helps to emphasize that no single food or food category can meet all the nutrient requirements. Fats, oils, and sweets are positioned at the tip of the pyramid illustrating that they should be used sparingly, but need not be eliminated entirely from the diet. The broad bottom of the pyramid conveys that cereals and grains are the foundation of a healthy diet. The pyramid illus-

What counts as one serving?

Breads, Cereals, Rice, and Pasta
1 slice of bread
1/2 cup of cooked rice or pasta
1/2 cup of cooked cereal
1 ounce of ready-to-eat cereal

Vegetables
1/2 cup of chopped raw or
    cooked vegetables
1 cup of leafy raw vegetables

Fruits
1 piece of fruit or melon wedge
3/4 cup of juice
1/2 cup of canned fruit
1/4 cup of dried fruit

Milk, Yogurt, and Cheese
1 cup of milk or yogurt
1-1/2 to 2 ounces of cheese

**Meat, Poultry, Fish, Dry Beans,
Eggs, and Nuts**
2-1/2 to 3 ounces of cooked lean
    meat, poultry, or fish
Count 1/2 cup of cooked beans,
    or 1 egg, or 2 tablespoons of
    peanut butter as 1 ounce of lean
    meat (about 1/3 serving)

Fats, Oils, and Sweets
LIMIT CALORIES FROM THESE
especially if you need to lose weight

> The amount you eat may be
> more than one serving. For
> example, a dinner portion of
> spaghetti would count as two
> or three servings of pasta.

How many servings do you need each day?

	Women & some older adults	Children, teen girls, active women, most men	Teen boys & active men
Calorie level*	about 1,600	about 2,200	about 2,800
Bread group	6	9	11
Vegetable group	3	4	5
Fruit group	2	3	4
Milk group	**2-3	**2-3	**2-3
Meat group	2, for a total of 5 ounces	2, for a total of 6 ounces	3, for a total of 7 ounces

*These are the calorie levels if you choose lowfat, lean
foods from the 5 major food groups and use foods from
the fats, oils, and sweets group sparingly.

**Women who are pregnant or breastfeeding, teen-
agers, and young adults to age 24 need 3 servings.

A Closer Look at Fat and Added Sugars

The small tip of the Pyramid shows fats, oils, and
sweets. These are foods such as salad dressings,
cream, butter, margarine, sugars, soft drinks, candies,
and sweet desserts. Alcoholic

beverages are also part of this
group. These foods provide
calories but few vitamins and
minerals. Most people should go
easy on foods from this group.

Some fat or sugar symbols are
shown in the other food groups.
That's to remind you that some
foods in these groups can also be
high in fat and added sugars, such
as cheese or ice cream from the milk group, or french
fries from the vegetable group. When choosing foods
for a healthful diet, consider the fat and added sugars
in your choices from all the food groups, not just fats,
oils, and sweets from the Pyramid tip.

FIGURE 3.3   Using the USDA Food Guide Pyramid

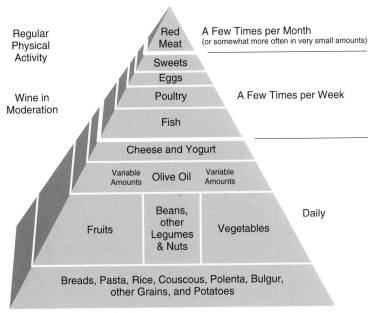

Regular Physical Activity

Wine in Moderation

Red Meat — A Few Times per Month (or somewhat more often in very small amounts)

Sweets

Eggs

Poultry — A Few Times per Week

Fish

Cheese and Yogurt

Variable Amounts — Olive Oil — Variable Amounts

Fruits

Beans, other Legumes & Nuts

Vegetables — Daily

Breads, Pasta, Rice, Couscous, Polenta, Bulgur, other Grains, and Potatoes

FIGURE 3.4 The Mediterranean Diet Pyramid. ©1996 by Oldways Preservation & Exchange Trust. Reprinted by permission.

trates that all food types are allowed and can be enjoyed as part of the healthy diet.

MEDITERRANEAN DIET PYRAMID

In 1993, a panel of international experts on diet, nutrition, and health reviewed and researched the composition and health implications of diets consumed over the last 50 years in the Mediterranean region. They focused on diets of adults from Crete, much of the remainder of Greece, and Southern Italy. Their research shows that individuals who consume a diet based on the Mediterranean Diet, as it has come to be called, have low rates of coronary heart disease and of many types of cancers. In addition, these people have long life expectancy.

The Mediterranean Diet Pyramid (see Fig. 3.4) is characterized by the predominance of fruits, vegetables, breads, cereals, potatoes, legumes, nuts, and other complex carbohydrates such as polenta, couscous, and bulgur. Olive oil is the primary source of fat and represents an entire section of the pyramid. The main sources of protein in this pyramid are dairy products, primarily yogurt and cheese. Fish and poultry are consumed in low to moderate amounts. High-fat sources of protein including red meat and eggs are consumed in low amounts; therefore the diet is low in saturated fat. The total fat intake ranges from about 25 to 35 percent of energy intake throughout the region.

GUIDELINES FOR SENSIBLE WINE DRINKING

When consumed moderately, preferably with food and as part of family and social gatherings, wine can be part of a well-balanced lifestyle, adding pleasure to everyday living for healthy adults.

STATEMENT OF PRINCIPLES

BECAUSE throughout human history, wine drinking has been an important part of religious rituals, social relationships, family gatherings, and celebrations of the pleasure of living, and

BECAUSE moderate, sensible wine consumption can contribute to a healthy diet and lifestyle, and

BECAUSE integration of sensible wine drinking into the lifestyle of many cultures helps to prevent alcohol abuse, and

BECAUSE society has a responsibility to teach all people, especially young people, about sensible drinking, and

BECAUSE of intense international interest in the benefits of wine,

The following guidelines define sensible drinking and should be widely circulated.

KEY ELEMENTS

AWARENESS of the world-wide scientific consensus that moderate alcohol consumption contributes to good health.

ACKNOWLEDGEMENT of the current scientific evidence associating moderate wine consumption with healthy diets and lifestyle benefits.

APPRECIATION of wine's role in traditional rituals, celebratory festivities and as an accompaniment to meals.

ACCEPTANCE of responsible wine consumption along with disapproval of excessive consumption.

AGREEMENT upon the freedom of choice to either drink or abstain.

10 GUIDELINES FOR SENSIBLE WINE DRINKING

1. Wine should be consumed by healthy adults only in moderation.

2. Wine should be consumed as part of social, family, celebratory or other occasions, but not as their central focus.

3. Wine is best consumed with food or around mealtimes.

4. Society as a whole and families should accept the responsibility for teaching all people, including the young, about sensible wine drinking, because education helps prevent alcohol abuse.

5. Moderate, non-disruptive drinking is socially acceptable, while excessive drinking and any resulting behavior that violates legal or social standards are unacceptable.

6. Parents who drink should drink sensibly, presenting themselves as examples of moderation.

7. Wine drinking should follow clear, consistent and sensible customs that emphasize moderation and discourage binge drinking.

8. The choice of abstinence for any religious, health or personal reasons must be respected.

9. Wine drinkers should know the difference between moderate use and abuse, and drinking must be avoided in situations where it puts the individual or others at risk.

10. Wine should be consumed slowly to enhance the taste of food and to add to the enjoyment of everyday living.

The Guidelines acknowledge that consumption is not for everyone, and that the legal purchase and public possession age in the U.S. is 21. At the same time , the Guidelines urge society and parents to take a more active role in teaching young people about responsible drinking customs so they are prepared to make informed choices.

Moderate drinking is defined by the Dietary Guidelines for Americans as two 5-ounce glasses a day for men and one glass for women. Somewhat higher levels of consumption are reflected in the U.K. Sensible Drinking Guidelines and are associated with health advantages in many scientific research studies. Factors such as weight, height, drinking pattern and time of consumption level must be considered for each individual.

Drinking is not recommended for people who are at risk for alcohol abuse, for people who take certain medications, for pregnant women, or for people whose consumption of wine may put themselves or others at risk.

These guidelines were developed by Oldways Preservation & Exchange Trust and R. Curtis Ellison, M.D., Boston University School of Medicine; Dwight Heath, Ph. D., Brown University; Stanton Peele, Ph. D.,Independent social science researcher; David Pittman, Ph. D., Washington University, St. Louis; Archie Brodsky, Massachusetts Mental Health Center at Harvard Medical School; Meir Stampfer, M.D., Dr. P.H., Harvard School of Public Health.
© 1996 Oldways Preservation & Exchange Trust. Reprinted with permission.

FIGURE 3.5 Guidelines for Sensible Wine Drinking. © Oldways Preservation & Exchange Trust. Reprinted with permission.

One notable difference in the Mediterranean Diet Pyramid from the Food guide Pyramid is the addition of wine consumed in low to moderate amounts (one glass per woman, two glasses per man daily). The Mediterranean Diet Pyramid also focuses on weekly and monthly recommendations and addresses individual foods more than does the Food Guide Pyramid.

Regularly scheduled physical activity also contributes to very low rates of obesity. The Mediterranean Diet Pyramid includes the provision of exercise.

The Mediterranean Diet Pyramid is designed to complement rather than replace the Food Guide Pyramid. In addition to the dietary guidelines, it addresses the benefits of exercise and moderate consumption of wine. Since this alternative style of eating reflects taste preferences, flavor, palatability, and the pleasure of the dining experience, some culinarians find the Mediterranean Diet Pyramid more appealing than the Food Guide Pyramid. (See Appendix E for multicultural food guide pyramids.)

SENSIBLE WINE DRINKING GUIDE

Consumption of wine with a meal is traditional in many Mediterranean regions. Wine consumption in moderation adds pleasure to the meal. The pleasure of drinking wine should be balanced with responsible nutrition.

The accompaniment of wine with a meal in the Mediterranean Diet is based on the premises of tradition and moderation. Research indicates that moderate consumption of wine may have a positive effect on lowering the incidence of heart disease and certain types of cancer. Wine consumption, however, is not appropriate for all individuals. The guidelines shown in Figure 3.5 introduce Americans to the concept of enjoying wine with a meal.

NUTRITION LABELING

Nutrition Product Label. Nutrition labeling is a useful tool for making informed decisions concerning a healthful diet (see Fig. 3.6). Consumers use these labels to determine if they are following the recommended Dietary Guidelines. Food labeling regulations introduced in 1994 require 595,000 food products to meet guidelines set by the U.S. Food and Drug Administration (FDA) and the USDA. These regulations standardize labeling to make product comparison easier; the FDA determined 139 reference serving sizes for practical comparison. Some products, such as cuts of meat, raw fish, and 20 of the most commonly eaten fruits and vegetables, do not require an individual food label, but nutritional values may appear on posters, flyers, or packages.

Product Claim Requirements. If a manufacturer makes a health claim and prints it on a food label, it must follow established criteria from the FDA Product Claim Requirements. Claims such as "low fat," "low cholesterol," "low sodium" fall under this guideline. (See Fig. 3.7 and Table 3.4).

Labeling for Restaurants and Food Service. The label is especially important to food service professionals who are nutrition conscious and want to actively

The New Food Label at a Glance

The new food label will carry an up-to-date, easier-to-use nutrition information guide, to be required on almost all packaged foods (compared to about 60 percent of products up till now). The guide will serve as a key to help in planning a healthy diet*

Serving sizes are now more consistent across product lines, are stated in both household and metric measures, and reflect the amounts people actually eat.

The **list of nutrients** covers those most important to the health of today's consumers, most of whom need to worry about getting too much of certain nutrients (fat, for example), rather than too few vitamins or minerals, as in the past.

The label of larger packages may now tell the number of calories per gram of fat, carbohydrate, and protein.

New title signals that the label contains the newly required information.

Calories from fat are now shown on the label to help consumers meet dietary guidelines that recommend people get no more than 30 percent of the calories in their overall diet from fat.

% Daily Value shows how a food fits into the overall daily diet.

Daily Values are also something new. Some are maximums, as with fat (65 grams or less); others are minimums, as with carbohydrate (300 grams or more). The daily values for a 2,000-and 2,500-calorie diet must be listed on the label of larger packages.

Nutrition Facts

Serving Size 1 cup (228g)
Servings Per Container 2

Amount Per Serving

Calories 260   Calories from Fat 120

% Daily Value*

Total Fat 13g	**20%**
Saturated Fat 5g	**25%**
Cholesterol 30mg	**10%**
Sodium 660mg	**28%**
Total Carbohydrate 31g	**10%**
Dietary Fiber 0g	**0%**
Sugars 5g	
Protein 5g	

Vitamin A 4%	•	Vitamin C 2%	
Calcium 15%	•	Iron 4%	

* Percent Daily Values are based on a 2,000 calorie diet. Your daily values may be higher or lower depending on your calorie needs:

	Calories	2,000	2,500
Total Fat	Less than	65g	80g
Sat Fat	Less than	20g	25g
Cholesterol	Less than	300mg	300mg
Sodium	Less than	2,400mg	2,400mg
Total Cartbohydrate		300mg	375mg
Dietary Fiber		25g	30g

Calories per gram:
Fat 9 · Carbohydrate 4 · Protein 4

* This label is only a sample. Exact specifications are in the final rules.

FIGURE 3.6 Product Label Requirements. *Source:* U.S. Food and Drug Administration, 1994

The New Food Label at a Glance

Health Claims: For the first time, food labels will be allowed to carry information about the link between certain nutrients and specific diseases. For such a "health claim" to be made on a package, FDA must first determine that the diet-disease link is supported by scientific evidence.

Health claim message referred to on the front panel shown here

FROZEN MIXED VEGETABLES
— IN SAUCE —

NET WT. 8.9 oz. (252 g)

- Low Fat
- Cholesterol Free
- Good Source of Fiber

See back panel for nutrition information

Ingredients: Broccoli, carrots, green beans, water chestnuts, soybean oil, milk solids, modified starch, salt, spices.

"While many factors affect heart disease, diets low in saturated fat and cholesterol may reduce the risk of this disease."

Claims: While descriptive terms like "low," "good source," and "free" have long been used on food labels, their meaning — and their usefulness in helping consumers plan a healthy diet — have been murky. Now FDA has set specific definitions for these terms, assuring shoppers that they can believe what they read on the package.

Ingredients still will be listed in descending order by weight, and now the list will be required on almost all foods, even standardized ones like mayonnaise and bread.

FIGURE 3.7 Product Claim Requirements. *Source:* U.S. Food and Drug Administration, 1994

TABLE 3.4 Label Claims

Free	The food must contain no or only "physiological inconsequential" amounts of fat, saturated fat, cholesterol, sodium, sugars or calories.
Low, Little, Few, and Low Source of	The food can be eaten frequently without exceeding dietary guidelines for fat, saturated fat, cholesterol, sodium or calories.
Fat-Free	The food has less than .5 grams of fat per serving.
Low Fat	The food has 3 grams of fat or less per serving.
Low saturted fat	The food has 1 gram or less of saturated fat per serving; not more than 15% of a serving's calories are from saturated fat.
Low sodium	The food has 140 mg or less of salt per serving.
Very low sodium	The food has 35 mg or less of salt per serving.
Low cholesterol	The food has 20 mg or less of cholesterol per serving.
Low calories	The food has 40 calories or fewer per serving.
Reduced, less and fewer	The nutritionally-altered product must contain at least 25% fewer calories than the regular or reference food product
Light or Lite	The nutritionally altered product must contain at least one third or 50% less fat than the reference product. Light in sodium means that the nutritionally-altered product contains 50% or less sodium in a low-calorie or low-fat food, than the regular or reference product. Light may still be used to describe color, as in "light brown sugar."
High	The food must contain 20% or more of the daily value for a desirable nutrient per serving.
More	The food must contain at least 10% or more of the daily value for protein, vitamins, minerals, dietary fiber, or potassium that the reference product.
Good Source	The food contains 10 to 19% of the daily value per serving for the specific nutrient such as calcium or dietary fiber.
Lean	The meat, poultry, game, fish or shellfish item contains less than 10 grams of fat, less than 4 grams of saturated fat and less than 95 mg of cholesterol per serving and per 100 grams.
Extra Lean	The meat, poultry, game, fish or shellfish item contains less than 5 grams of fat, less than 2 grams of saturated fat, and less than 95 mg of cholesterol per serving and per 100 grams.

promote good nutrition to their customers. All health claims or claims of nutrient content on menus, or claims orally presented to the customer, must be substantiated. This information must be provided either verbally or in written form to those who request it. Health claims must meet established FDA criteria. Key phrases such as "low fat," "low cholesterol," "low sodium" and symbols which appear in menus are also regulated. Nutritional claims must be supported with credible references, such as a reliable cookbook or computer software program. A registered dietitian can also provide nutritional expertise.

SUGAR SUBSTITUTES

Sugar, both natural and refined, is abundant in the American diet. It functions to provide flavor (sweetness), color, bulk, tenderness, and texture, and it can act as a preservative. Sugar occurs naturally in fruits, vegetables, and milk. The Dietary Guidelines and the Food Guide Pyramid both recommend that sugar be used sparingly for a healthful diet. With increased public awareness of these recommendations, there is a demand for low-sugar, low-calorie products. Sugar substitutes make the development of these products possible. Two types of sugar substitutes are available: sugar alcohols and artificial sweeteners.

Sugar Alcohols. These do not contain ethanol (the alcohol in alcoholic beverages), as the name might suggest. A sugar alcohol molecule is actually a chemically altered sugar molecule. Sugar alcohols also occur naturally in many fruits and vegetables. The most common sugar alcohols are mannitol, sorbitol, and xylitol. Although sugar alcohols provide 4 calories per gram, they do not require insulin to be metabolized and they are absorbed slowly and incompletely. They do not cause dental caries because they are not metabolized by cavity-causing bacteria. As an additive to food, they add sweetness, retain moisture, and provide texture in the place of sugar. Sugar alcohols are commonly found in sugarless gum, candies, jams, and jellies.

Diabetics can utilize sugar alcohols in moderation. However, some people are sensitive to sugar alcohols, which, especially if consumed in high amounts, can have a laxative effect.

Artificial Sweeteners. Artificial sweeteners have gained popularity with the demand for sugar-free and low-calorie foods. Thirty to 800 times sweeter than sucrose (table sugar) and noncaloric, they add intense sweetness without adding calories. Artificially sweetened products are available in many forms, from pudding and yogurt to cookies and ice cream. There are FDA-approved artificial sweeteners available to consumers: acesulfame-K, aspartame, saccharine, and sucralose. Two others, cyclamate and alitame, are under investigation by the FDA for approval.

Artificial sweeteners can be used by almost all people. They are especially useful for diabetics and individuals interested in weight control. People with PKU (phenylketonuria), an uncommon metabolic disorder, need to restrict the use of aspartame. Artificial sweeteners are not recommended for infants and

TABLE 3.5 FDA Approved Sweeteners

Name	Benefits/Uses	Limitations	Brand Names
Acesulfame-K	Heat stable for baking and cooking, no bitter aftertaste	Does not add bulk.	Sunette Sweet One Swiss Sweet Nutrataste
Aspartame	Tabletop sweetener, can be encapsulated with hydrogenated oil for baking	Contains phenylalanine and cannot be consumed by individuals with PKU.	NutraSweet Equal
Saccharine	Tabletop sweetener	Carcinogenic in laboratory animals.	Sweet 'n Low Sugar Twin Necta Sweet SweetTen
Sucralose	No unpleasant aftertaste; keeps its sweet taste over time when exposed to high temperatures; no calories; does not promote tooth decay.	*Not identified.	Splenda

*Newly approved by the FDA.

children, not because they are unsafe but because children require adequate calories for growth.

The ingredient list on a food label indicates the type of sugar substitute in the product. Table 3.5 lists some of the uses and current brand names of acesulfame-K, aspartame, saccharine, and sucralose.

FAT REPLACERS

Like sugar substitutes, fat replacers have become commonplace in the American diet. With increased awareness of heart disease and a concern for body weight, people are aware of the need to limit daily fat intake.

Fat serves many functions: texture, flavor, mouth feel, moisture retention, structure in baked goods, heat transmission, and stability. Thus, it is hard to replace. Fat replacers fall into three categories: carbohydrate based, protein based, and fat based. Manufacturers combine different fat replacers in order to achieve a product that most closely resembles the full-fat product.

Carbohydrate-based Fat Replacers. These are derived from cereal grains and plants and act as a thickening agent. They are the most commonly used fat replacers and have been in use for years. Oatrim® is a treated flour, providing 1 calorie per gram as a fat replacer. It is used to replace fat in products such as ice cream, frozen desserts, salad dressings, and baked goods.

Protein-based Fat Replacers. These are made from milk, egg, or plant sources. They can simulate the creaminess and mouth feel traditionally found in high-fat foods such as cheese and frozen desserts. Simplesse® is an FDA-approved fat replacer developed by the NutraSweet Corporation containing 1.2 calories per gram. Products containing Simplesse® include ice creams and yogurts. Both carbohydrate-based and protein-based fat replacers reduce calories in the fat component of the food by over half.

Fat-based Fat Replacers. These are chemically altered fats or synthetic fats. The body cannot absorb these replacers, so they pass through the body without adding calories. Their flavor is similar to fat and they can model fat's cooking properties. They are utilized in cooking oils and shortenings for deep-frying foods such as chips and snack foods. Olestra is a fat-based replacer with FDA approval.

CHAPTER 4

SPECIAL REQUESTS

SPA, VEGETARIAN,
AND MODIFIED DIETS

Enlightened culinarians can create a healthful diet using tools such as the Food Guide Pyramid and healthy cooking techniques as guidelines. There are times, however, when people want to follow special guidelines for weight management, for religious or social requirements, or for the prevention or treatment of certain diseases. It is challenging for culinarians to develop appealing food items that satisfy these special requirements. This chapter provides an overview of the most frequent special requests and the basic tools to produce these diets.

SPA CUISINE

With an increasing public interest in health, spas have emerged combining pleasure and healthfulness. There are over 100 spas currently in the United States, with many hotels and resorts adding spa amenities to their existing operations. In general, spas are enjoyed by those in good health as a preventive health measure combining healthful eating, fitness activities, and relaxation. Some people utilize spa resources to improve health by reducing weight or blood cholesterol.

Spa food is typically low in calories and fat without sacrificing flavor. Meals planned in accordance with the Dietary Guidelines are acceptable for the average spa guest. Many spas offer menus designed for weight loss or maintenance with set calorie levels and reduced fat, cholesterol, and sodium content (see Modified Diets for Disease Management). Many guests select a spa based on upon the reputation of the food, which is a function of the creativity of the chef and the expertise of a registered dietitian. The recipes presented in this book follow the general guidelines for spa cuisine and would prove to be excellent choices for most spa guests.

VEGETARIAN DIETS

With the abundance of fresh fruits and vegetables, grains, and legumes available today, more and more people find following some form of vegetarian diet a feasible way to eat. Vegetarians focus their diet on plant-based products including grains, legumes, nuts, vegetables, and fruits rather than animal-based products such as meat, eggs, and milk products.

Some vegetarian diets exclude all forms of animal products, while others simply exclude red meat. Following is a brief description of the various types of vegetarian diets.

Vegan: A strict vegetarian, or vegan, excludes *all* animal products such as meat, poultry, fish/seafood, eggs, milk, cheese, and other milk products from the diet. Foods with small amounts of animal product, such as casein and whey, may be avoided as well as foods that involve animal products in processing. Honey may also be avoided.

Lactovegetarian: Excludes meat, poultry, fish/seafood, and eggs from the diet, but includes milk and milk products.

Lacto-Ovo-Vegetarian: Excludes meat, poultry, and fish/seafood from the diet, but includes eggs, milk, and milk products.

Pescovegetarian: Excludes meat and poultry from the diet, but includes fish/seafood, eggs, milk, and milk products.

Semivegetarian: Excludes meat from the diet, but includes poultry, fish/seafood, eggs, milk, and milk products.

Fruitarian: Excludes meat, poultry, fish/seafood, eggs, milk and milk products, grains, legumes, and most vegetables from the diet. Diet includes fruits and vegetables that are botanical fruits (tomatoes, eggplant, avocado, and zucchini), as well as nuts and seeds.

NUTRIENT GUIDELINES FOR VEGETARIAN DIETS

Carefully planned vegetarian diets can easily provide the nutrients necessary to sustain life. The key is to consume enough calories, choose a wide variety of foods, and pay attention to certain nutrients.

Protein. Most vegetarians do not have difficulty consuming adequate amounts of protein in their diet. While animal products are the most expedient sources of high-quality protein, the body will make its own complete proteins if adequate calories and varied plant foods are consumed.

Calcium. Many people do not realize that calcium is abundant in vegetables. Vegans can obtain sufficient calcium from plant sources alone, and tofu, dried figs, seeds, and calcium-fortified cereals and juices are excellent sources of calcium. Vegetarians who consume milk and milk products easily meet calcium requirements.

Iron. Plant sources are loaded with iron; for example, dried beans, dark leafy vegetables, dried fruits, and iron-fortified breads and cereals are excellent sources. Simultaneously consuming foods high in vitamin C can enhance iron absorption.

Vitamin B$_{12}$. Vegans must supplement vitamin B$_{12}$ in their diet because this vitamin is naturally present only in animal foods. However, many foods are fortified with vitamin B$_{12}$, including fortified cereals. It is therefore not a common deficiency in most vegetarian diets.

Vitamin D. A vitamin D supplement may be indicated for vegetarians who do not consume milk or milk products. Vitamin D status can be improved in vegetarians through exposure to sunlight. Sunlight converts a vitamin D precursor (a substance normally manufactured by the human body) into vitamin D.

Riboflavin. Riboflavin is found in milk and milk products as well as leafy green vegetables, whole grains, and legumes.

Zinc. Zinc is found in legumes, whole grains, milk, and milk products; however, phytic acid and oxalates found in whole grains reduce zinc absorption.

The vegetarian is not immune from concerns about fat and calories. Oils, nuts, butter, milk fat, seeds, and seed spreads are high in fat. Cheese is a food common in the vegetarian diet that is high in protein and calcium; however, cheese is also high in fat and cholesterol. Some vegetarians consume too many calories by eating large amounts of these high-fat, high-calorie foods. Many products are available in reduced-fat, reduced-sodium, or reduced-calorie form. The recommended Dietary Guidelines for fat, cholesterol, sodium, and fiber for vegetarians are consistent with those for all healthy adults.

With increased interest in vegetarian diets, culinarians are challenged to provide tasty, flavorful, and healthful vegetarian options. Vegetarian menus are easy for creative and knowledgable culinarians to plan. The Vegetarian Food Guide (Fig. 4.1) is a good place to start in planning a vegetarian meal or diet. Resources for vegetarians can also be found in vegetarian cookbooks and magazines and on the Internet. A registered dietitian is also an excellent resource.

MEAT ANALOGS

Processed vegetable protein products can substitute for meat and meat products. These products are widely accepted by vegetarians. Soy is a popular and versatile ingredient. The soybean is high in protein and calcium and can be incorporated into the vegetarian diet in many different forms: soy milk, miso, tempeh, textured soy protein (TSP), tofu, fermented products (soy cheese, soy yogurt), soy flour, soy concentrate, soy isolate, and the soy bean in its whole form. Meat extenders and analogs can be used to mimic meat in recipes. Legumes can also add substance to a meatless entree. Virtually any recipe can be adapted to a vegetarian diet, even for strict vegans, but substitutions may alter the taste, quantity, and presentation of vegetarian dishes, particularly baked goods.

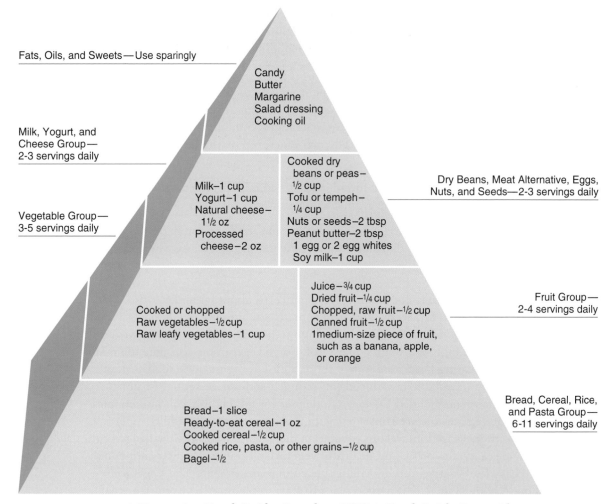

Fats, Oils, and Sweets—Use sparingly

Candy
Butter
Margarine
Salad dressing
Cooking oil

Milk, Yogurt, and
Cheese Group—
2-3 servings daily

Dry Beans, Meat Alternative, Eggs,
Nuts, and Seeds—2-3 servings daily

Vegetable Group—
3-5 servings daily

Milk–1 cup
Yogurt–1 cup
Natural cheese–
1½ oz
Processed
cheese–2 oz

Cooked dry
beans or peas–
½ cup
Tofu or tempeh–
¼ cup
Nuts or seeds–2 tbsp
Peanut butter–2 tbsp
1 egg or 2 egg whites
Soy milk–1 cup

Juice–¾ cup
Dried fruit–¼ cup
Chopped, raw fruit–½ cup
Canned fruit–½ cup
1 medium-size piece of fruit,
such as a banana, apple,
or orange

Fruit Group—
2-4 servings daily

Cooked or chopped
Raw vegetables–½ cup
Raw leafy vegetables–1 cup

Bread, Cereal, Rice,
and Pasta Group—
6-11 servings daily

Bread–1 slice
Ready-to-eat cereal–1 oz
Cooked cereal–½ cup
Cooked rice, pasta, or other grains–½ cup
Bagel–½

FIGURE 4.1   A Vegetarian Food Guide. Based on USDA Food Guide Pyramid.

MODIFIED DIETS FOR DISEASE MANAGEMENT

Diet and nutrition play an important role in the management of many diseases. Some people voluntarily restrict their intake of foods they believe are detrimental to their health. Others are encouraged by physicians to follow dietary modifications as a means of managing specific disease states. As a culinarian, it is important to understand what these modifications are as well as the rationale supporting them. More importantly, it is the chef's challenge to create foods that comply with dietary restrictions while remaining appetizing and tasty. This task is made easier by using healthful cooking techniques and healthful ingredients.

There are many modified diets for disease management; this book will provide an overview of the most common. To obtain more information about these and other diets, contact a registered dietitian. To find one in your area, call the American Dietetic Association's referral hotline at 1-800-366-1655. To speak to a registered dietitian, call the American Dietetic Association's consumer hotline at 1-900-225-5267.

CARDIOVASCULAR (HEART HEALTHY) DIET

Cardiovascular diets focus on controlling dietary intake of total fat, saturated fat, cholesterol, and sodium. With the prevalence of cardiovascular disease in the United States, these guidelines are recommended for *all* healthy Americans two years of age and older, since they are also preventative.

The following dietary factors are linked to cardiovascular disease:

- High intake of saturated fat
- High intake of dietary cholesterol
- High intake of sodium
- Imbalance between calorie intake and energy expenditure, leading to obesity

Management of this disease includes dietary modification, weight management, and increased physical activity. Dietary management includes the following elements:

- Limiting the intake of total fat, saturated fat, cholesterol, and total calories
- Using monounsaturated fat as opposed to saturated fat
- Increasing the intake of dietary fiber through whole-grain breads and cereals and fresh fruits and vegetables
- Limiting the intake of dietary sodium

The American Heart Association guidelines for a healthy diet recommend the following:

Total fat intake	≤ 30% of total calories
Saturated fat intake	8–10% of total calories
Polyunsaturated fat intake	up to 10% of total calories
Monounsaturated fat intake	10–15% of total calories
Cholesterol intake	< 300 mg per day
Sodium intake	≤ 2,400 mg per day

SODIUM-RESTRICTED DIET

Sodium is an essential mineral responsible for maintaining blood volume and blood pressure. It is also involved in transmitting nerve impulses. In cooking, sodium compounds are used as flavor enhancers, food additives, and preservatives. Sodium occurs naturally in very low concentrations in most plant foods and in moderate concentrations in animal products.

In certain individuals, sodium intake is directly related to elevated blood pressure. A diet restricted in sodium is indicated for the management of diseases including hypertension (high blood pressure), liver disease, cardiovascular disease, and renal (kidney) disease.

Most health groups recommend an average daily intake between 2,400 mg and 4,000 mg or less of sodium for healthy adults. Therapeutic (i.e., for treatment of disease) sodium-restricted diets range from 500 mg to 4,000 mg ("no added salt") per day. A "no added salt" diet utilizes foods naturally low in sodium. Natural flavor enhancers are used instead of adding salt.

A low-sodium diet may be bland; the use of other flavor enhancers is encouraged, and a creative chef can do a great deal to improve palatability.

SOFT DIET

The soft diet is a transition diet from liquids to solids following surgery. It may also be indicated when one is too weak or does not have sufficient teeth to chew the foods on a regular diet. It is designed to prevent or minimize gastrointestinal problems related to digesting high-fiber and gas-forming foods. Most raw fruits and vegetables are omitted. Tough meats with gristle are excluded. Gas-forming vegetables, dried beans and peas, whole-kernel corn, coarse breads, cereals, and crackers, and highly seasoned or fried foods are excluded from the soft diet.

MECHANICAL SOFT DIET

A mechanical soft diet includes foods that require minimal chewing and are easy to swallow. It is indicated for people who have difficulty chewing and/or swallowing, including people with few or no teeth, poorly fitting dentures, or mouth sores. It is indicated following surgical procedures in the head, neck, and mouth which compromise the ability to chew. This diet may also be indicated for people who have temporarily or permanently impaired motor function (i.e., chewing, swallowing).

Foods included on a mechanical soft diet should be soft and moist or altered through grinding, chopping, or mashing so that they can be easily chewed and swallowed. Most raw fruits and vegetables are excluded except those easy to chew (bananas, peeled ripe peaches or pears). Vegetables should be cooked until tender. Seeds, nuts, and skins should be avoided. Tough meats with gristle should be avoided; other meats should be ground and moistened with soup or gravy. Soft breads and cereals are generally well tolerated.

PUREED DIET

A pureed diet requires no chewing and is easy to swallow. Pureed foods are completely blenderized, while mechanical soft foods are ground or chopped into small pieces. The indications for a pureed diet are similar to those for a mechanical soft diet.

A pureed diet includes liquids, strained soups, and pureed meats, fruits, and vegetables. Soups or gravies may be added to foods in the pureeing process to add smoothness to facilitate swallowing and enhance the nutritional value. Solid foods may be included based on individual tolerance.

Commercial thickening agents are available to add cohesiveness to liquids and pureed foods. Thickened liquids promote a safer swallowing process in people with impaired motor function.

CALORIE-CONTROLLED OR WEIGHT-LOSS DIET

The Census Bureau estimates that in 1990 approximately 58 million adults suffered from obesity. Obesity is the excessive accumulation of fat in the body, technically defined as a body weight greater than 125 percent of desirable weight. Obesity results when the energy consumed through eating exceeds the energy expended through metabolism, normal activities of daily living, and exercise. Health risks associated with obesity include high blood pressure, stroke, diabetes, degenerative joint disease, and functional impairment.

The goal of weight management is to achieve a healthy weight through gradual, safe loss of body fat. A moderate weight loss of even 10 percent may reduce some health risks. Successful weight management should include a good eating plan, behavior modification, and an exercise regime.

Total calories consumed should be reduced by no more than 20 to 40 percent of the usual dietary intake. The distribution of carbohydrate, protein, and fat in the diet should adhere to the Dietary Guidelines (55 to 60 percent carbohydrate, 10 to 15 percent protein, less than 30 percent fat), with a reduction in total calories. The diet should be well balanced to provide the Recommended Daily Allowances.

Fat is the most calorically dense nutrient. It has more than twice as many calories per gram as both carbohydrate and protein. Small amounts of high-fat foods, therefore, add excessive calories to the diet. Limiting high-fat food items such as sauces, gravies, butter or margarine, salad dressings, and sour cream can result in a substantial reduction in total calories. Consumption of concentrated sweets such as pies, cakes, cookies, candy, and ice cream should also be limited. These food items contain a lot of calories and do not contribute proportional nutrients.

For long-term adherence, a weight-reduction diet should promote a feeling of satiety or satisfaction. Weight-reduction diets provide fewer total calories and less fat, so the perception of feeling hungry or unsatisfied is common. The addition of fiber-rich foods and roughage can add bulk to the diet and produce a feeling of satiety or satisfaction. Using the contemporary style of cooking — healthful cooking techniques, elimination of unnecessary fat and calories, healthful, flavorful, and appetizing meals — can help people stay with a weight-reduction diet and actually achieve results.

DIABETIC DIET

Diabetes Mellitus is a chronic disorder in which the body cannot properly use carbohydrate in the foods consumed. The body may also have difficulty using fats and proteins properly. Diet therapy plays an integral role in the management of Diabetes Mellitus. For many diabetics, effective dietary management may delay or even eliminate the need for daily injections of insulin or oral medication.

Although diets must be customized for each individual, there are some common goals for the dietary management of diabetes:

- ◉ Maintain normal blood sugar levels (prevent high or low blood sugar levels.)
- ◉ Limit the intake of total fat, saturated fat, and cholesterol.
- ◉ Achieve and maintain a healthy weight.
- ◉ Promote overall good health through optimal nutrition.

Historically, diabetic diets have been very restrictive, but this resulted in poor compliance. The American Diabetes Association developed new guidelines in 1995 which empower individuals to take an active role in meal planning and the overall management of the disease. The emphasis is on balancing total carbohydrate consumption, including both simple and complex carbohydrates, throughout the day. The diabetic must eat regular meals to maintain normal blood sugar.

As a culinarian, it is important to recognize that many people follow diets modified or restricted in specific nutrients. This may be necessary for disease management or may be a personal preference. You should have a basic understanding of the rationale and general guidelines for the most common diets. See Appendix D for specific diet guidelines.

@

There is an ancient Roman proverb, "De gustibus non est disputandum" or "You cannot argue about taste," which is mankind's fundamental wisdom, argued every day and night, by fools.

Chef Charles Boley, CMC

A good dinner sharpens the wit, while it softens the heart.

John Doran

Active listening leads to instant success.

Chef Ronald De Santis, CMC

Foods that fit, nutritional, yes! But let's look at the specifics. Delicious, flavorful, well-prepared food. Creative, innovative, attractive and well presented providing a realistic experience for your customer.

Chef Roland G. Henin, CMC

@

PART THREE

NUTRITIONAL COOKING

@

CHAPTER 5

INGREDIENTS, FLAVOR ENHANCERS, AND MARINADES

CHAPTER 6

CONTEMPORARY COOKING METHODS

@

Food service professionals can benefit by establishing alliances with food producers, growers, and suppliers who are committed to bringing consistently high-quality food products to the marketplace.

Successful cooking begins with the selection and purchase of the best quality, freshest, and most wholesome ingredients available. The recipes in this book are based on the premise of using the freshest product available, in addition to some minimally processed foods, in the ingredient selection.

CHAPTER 5

INGREDIENTS, FLAVOR ENHANCERS, AND MARINADES

@

INGREDIENTS

Always strive to utilize seasonal ingredients at the peak of freshness, when they are full of flavor. The best ingredients are those in which the natural flavor and integrity of the product has not been compromised. At times this can be a challenge, since convenient processed foods are widely available in quantity, as well as variety. However, reliance on processed foods that contain excessive artificial ingredients, such as food colorings, food flavors, preservatives, or unnecessary additives, should be avoided.

FLAVOR ENHANCERS

In gastronomy there are five fundamental taste perceptions: salty, sour, sweet, bitter, and umami (savory.) All other taste sensations are the result of a combination of these qualities. Taste is a subjective and much-debated issue. Perhaps it is justifiable to conclude that our other senses have a tremendous influence over how we appreciate and understand taste, particularly that of smell. Of all the senses, smell is the most evocative and sensual. The merest hint of an aroma—a precious perfume or the scent of fresh fruit and herbs—can instantly conjure up a past experience in a way in which sight, sound, and touch cannot.

Through the centuries, the value of herbs and spices in both the medical and culinary fields has been evident. Herbs and spices can actually increase the appetite and promote proper digestion. It is also interesting to note that herbs and spices, albeit in small quantities, contain vitamins, minerals, and oils, and some act as natural preservatives to deter the spoilage of food. In cooking with the appropriate addition of herbs and spices we can actually enhance our health.

Despite the increased awareness of healthful cuisine which limits the use of salt, salt is still a very important seasoning agent. There are very few dishes in the culinary repertoire that do not require the addition of some salt; however, moderation is the key factor from both a medical and a culinary perspective.

Fresh herbs play a particularly important role in seasoning for low-sodium or low-fat diets.

A well-known Swiss, Paracelsus, who lived from 1493 to 1541, said, "Nothing is poison, and everything is poison, it all depends on the quantity."

During the years of the East Indisch Company, many of today's known spices and herbs were first introduced to Europe. However, it was the French and English traders and settlers, in an attempt to break the monopoly of the East Indisch Company, who brought many herb plants and roots to the United States.

Pepper played an important role in history. So important was the role of pepper that it became one of the motives in the many discovery travels of Columbus and even Vasco da Gama as they searched for this valuable and mysterious spice. During the Middle Ages, pepper was an indicator of status and well-being and was frequently used as a legal method of exchange. In the year 410 AD, Alarik I with his army of West Gothen conquered Rome and demanded the price of three thousand pounds of pepper.

One of the most cosmopolitan of spices is the red pepper, and it is likely to appear in some form throughout the continents. It is interesting that the word *pep*, which indicates spirit and energy, originated from the word *pepper*. Oregano originated in Italy, whereas sage came from Yugoslavia and bay leaf from Turkey. The much beloved herbs tarragon and marjoram came from France.

Mustard seed originated in northern Europe and Britain and was ultimately brought to the United States, which is now a major producer of this product. Ginger was brought to the United States by the Spanish during the sixteenth century. Although Jamaica produces some of the best ginger worldwide, Africa and India also produce and export vast amounts of ginger. Paprika, primarily from Spain, is produced in Central Europe, Hungary, and California.

The use of fresh herbs is still widely underutilized in today's kitchens. Aromatics and pungents such as shallots, garlic, spring onions, ginger, horse-radish, onions, lemon grass, and leeks have an important part to play in the kitchen with regard to seasoning. Other seasoning agents such as sugars, honeys, fruit syrups, vinegars, and citrus fruits play an equally important role in cooking.

Fresh herbs should be used whenever possible, to capture the full benefit of the natural juices and aromas. Certain herbs are best when added at the last moment, ensuring optimum flavor. Some of these more delicate herbs are chives, parsley, dill, chervil, lemon grass, and tarragon. Herbs that can tolerate more lengthy cooking processes include oregano, thyme, leaf coriander, fennel, and peppermint.

Herbs and spices are available in a wide variety of styles and packaged quantities. The preservation of fresh herbs uses three basic methods: puree with oil, freeze or preserve in vinegars, or dry upside down and store in air-tight containers.

To develop a feel for the use of herbs and spices, it helps to divide them into groups according to similar traits. Basil, chervil, chives, and parsley are

CHAPTER 6

CONTEMPORARY COOKING METHODS

@

Healthful food does not have to be boring or tasteless. Eating a balanced diet is more interesting if you vary the way in which you prepare your food. Different cooking techniques may not only cut down on fat and calories, but also add new textures and flavor to favorite dishes.

Many of the cooking techniques that are used today can be adapted to healthful cooking with just a few minor alterations. The exception to this is pan-frying or deep-frying. The key element in adapting a cooking technique into a nutritional cooking application is to make sure that the use of fat is kept to a minimum.

Start with ingredients of high quality, that are naturally flavorful. This is of utmost importance when creating great-tasting foods. Focus on capturing flavor wherever possible. Taste is affected by the freshness, the level of seasoning, and the use of quality ingredients.

Presentation and eye appeal involve proper portion size, basic cooking fundamentals, and the arrangement of the food on a platter or plate. Although presentation and eye appeal are important, they are secondary to taste.

DRY-HEAT COOKING METHODS

ROASTING

Roasting is a cooking method suitable for large cuts of meats, poultry, and some seafood products, but in general it involves cuts that provide multiple servings. Ideally the cut of protein to be roasted should be tender and naturally marbled for best results. Marinades and spice rubs are frequently used to assist in the flavoring, tenderizing, and preservation of the food (e.g., Marinated Roast Pork Loin with Savoy Cabbage and Lentils).

In most situations, roasting requires a low-sided, open roasting pan with a roasting rack to adequately hold the meat above the bottom of the roasting pan, allowing fat to drip away from the meat. The type of roasting pan will vary depending on the size of the meat or poultry to be roasted.

CHEF'S NOTES

6 *Flavor the food to be roasted with either a marinade or a spice/herb rub.*

6 *Use the proper oven temperature for roasting according to the guideline of the recipe. A temperature setting that is too high will cause shrinkage and excessive drying.*

- Roast the product, until the desired internal temperature is reached.

- Do not cover the roast during the cooking process, or it will steam the meat and result in a less tender, less juicy roast.

- Baste the roast frequently.

- Remove excess fats, leaving just enough for proper caramelization during the roasting process, as this will enhance the flavor.

- Test roast for doneness with an oven thermometer, and consult local health department ordinances for specific temperature requirements.

- Do not pierce the roast with a fork when turning or removing from the oven, as this causes a loss of natural juices and less perceived tenderness.

- If making a pan sauce or pan gravy, add a variety of root vegetables to the roasting pan during the final 45 minutes of roasting.

- Allow for carry-over cooking, as the roasted meat will continue to cook after it is removed from the oven.

- Be sure the roast rests prior to carving for maximum fiber tenderization.

- Carve roasts across the grain, to shorten meat fibers and promote the perception of tenderness.

- Serve roasts with vegetable coulis, jus, or vinaigrettes.

GRILLING AND BROILING

Grilling and broiling are other dry-heat cooking methods using direct heat with the addition of a minimal amount of oils or fats (e.g., Grilled Flank Steak with Balsamic Glaze and Herbed Brown Rice). The grill is a heat source that radiates and conducts heat from below, using a heat source such as charcoal or hard woods. When broiling, the heat source radiates and conducts from above, with limited conduction from the grids of the broiler. The types of broilers are convection gas or electric and conventional gas or electric. The grilling method also works well with vegetables. Both the grilling and broiling techniques are very popular since the food can be cooked very quickly with no holding times, which may diminish quality.

CHEF'S NOTES

- Flavor the food to be grilled or broiled with either a marinade or a spice/herb rub. If the meat has been marinated, pat it dry with clean paper towels to remove excess marinade.

- For best results, and to avoid sticking, use a thoroughly cleaned, seasoned, and properly pre-heated grill. The grill and broiler must be cleaned frequently to prevent fat buildup and excessive smoking during the cooking process.

- Allow meat to lose its chill before grilling, while staying within health department temperature guidelines for safety of foods.

⑥ Foods receive additional flavor from the caramelization process.

⑥ Use a small stainless steel spatula or tongs to turn the food product. Do not pierce or press the foods with a fork because juices will be lost and the meat will dry out.

⑥ Allow the grill or broiler to sufficiently cook the food on one side before turning.

⑥ Experiment with a variety of different wood chips.

⑥ If using wooden skewers, soak them in cold water ahead of time to prevent them from drying out from the heat.

DRY SAUTÉING

Dry sauté is a quick cooking method using a well-seasoned, nonstick pan with the addition of a minimal amount of oils or fats (e.g., Salmon Fillet with Arugula and Fennel). In general, a vegetable spray or oil is used in a heated pan. It is best to use a nonstick pan to avoid sticking. Once the desired pan temperature is reached, wipe the excess oil from the pan and add the food item. Turn the food only when the desired caramelization is achieved.

Once the food item is cooked, remove it from the pan and keep it warm. The pan can be deglazed with stock or sauce depending on the item being prepared. If excessive fat is evident, it should be removed. When using a dry sauté, it is important to keep sauces light and simple and use warm vinaigrettes, coulis, and/or relishes. Serve sautéed items with grain pilafs, polenta, leguminous stews, pastas, or risottos.

The dry sauté technique is very popular since the food can be cooked very quickly with no holding times, which may diminish quality.

CHEF'S NOTES

⑥ Reserve well-seasoned and nonstick pans which you will use only for the dry sauté method. This will give you the best results when using this cooking method. A well-seasoned, nonstick pan is an essential element for success with this procedure.

⑥ Season foods with aromatics and spices for added flavor. For variety, experiment with different herbs and spices.

⑥ Foods receive additional flavor from the caramelization process.

STIR-FRYING

Stir-frying is a quick cooking method similar to the dry sauté method in that foods are cooked quickly over a high heat source without the addition of fat. This cooking method is normally used with a wok. However, one can use a well-seasoned, deep, nonstick pan. It is important to keep the food moving in the stir-fry method; it should constantly be lifted and turned to allow all food surfaces to be exposed to the hot pan.

Use a seasoned, preheated wok or nonstick pan. Apply vegetable spray and remove any excess. Add the ingredient with the longest cooking time first, generally the main ingredient, and stir-fry. It is important to remember that ingredients must be added in the proper sequence due to cooking times. The food item with the shortest cooking time is always added last. While moving the foods freely, add the additional products, including the herbs, spices, and stock as desired.

CHEF'S NOTES

ⓖ *It is best to use vegetables with high moisture retention.*

ⓖ *Shellfish work great with the stir-fry method because they cook quickly.*

ⓖ *Use small pieces of chicken, beef, pork, or lamb when stir-frying.*

ⓖ *When using a liquid to deglaze, use high-quality yet low-fat stocks.*

ⓖ *Stir-fried foods must be served immediately after cooking for best appearance, flavor, and texture.*

PAN-SMOKING

Pan-smoking is a wonderful and simple technique using indirect heat, that exponentially enhances flavor without additional fats. This technique works well with fish, scallops, and prawns, also poultry, pork, beef, and game (e.g., Pan-Smoked Salmon with Italian White Beans and Saffron Broth).

The objective of smoking is to caramelize the exterior of the protein and cook the interior just enough to impede bacterial growth.

Use dry wood chips for a fast, hot smoke at the start, or use chips that have been soaked in water and drained. Moist chips give a slower, more sustainable smoke than dry chips.

To prepare a smoking pan, place wood chips on the bottom of the pan. Place roasting rack on top of the chips. Place smoking pan over a direct heat source, until smoke aroma becomes apparent. Place product to be roasted on rack, close lid, and allow flavor to develop.

Always use caution when opening a smoking pan, due to heat and smoke fumes.

For larger cuts of meat one can still use the smoking technique; however, this is best accomplished in an enclosed charcoal grill over indirect heat and is best done outdoors using high-quality charcoal briquettes and wood chips for additional flavor.

CHEF'S NOTES

ⓖ *Use fine mesquite wood chips to give the product a distinctive flavor.*

ⓖ *Season foods with aromatics and spices for added flavor. For variety, experiment with different herbs and spices.*

ⓖ *Experiment with a variety of wood chips such as alder, cherry, hickory, walnut, mesquite, and apple.*

ⓖ *Soak wood chips in water for at least 20 to 40 minutes, and drain thoroughly prior to use. This will cause the wood to smolder rather than burn.*

STEAMING

Steaming is a beneficial cooking technique that cooks food by the hot surrounding vapors. Foods are placed in an enclosed cooking unit but do not come in contact with the liquid medium such as water, stock, court-bouillon, or broth. The liquid can be enhanced with aromatics, vegetables, and citrus fruits. This method, when applied correctly, will result in virtually no flavor loss and excellent moisture retention. Steaming techniques are very popular since the food can be cooked very quickly with no holding times. Additional information on this technique can be found in Chapter 10.

CHEF'S NOTES

⊚ *Steaming works well for lean and tender pieces of protein, particularly small individual portions.*

⊚ *Steaming is recommended for cooking vegetables, since it retains flavor, moisture, and nutrient value.*

⊚ *To retain all flavor, moisture, and nutritional value, wrap seafood items in blanched cabbage, leek, or lettuce leaves.*

POACHING

Poaching is a cooking technique in which the food is completely submerged in a hot stock or liquid and cooked at a constant temperature of approximately 180 to 185 degrees Fahrenheit (82–85°C). The cooking liquid is enhanced by aromatic ingredients such as herbs, vegetables, citrus fruits, or spices. The poaching technique works especially well with tender food products. This technique differs from simmering in that simmering foods are cooked at a slightly higher temperature of 185 to 200 degrees Fahrenheit (85–95°C). In the poaching procedure, the cooking liquid is brought to the appropriate temperature, the aromatics or seasoning agents are added, then the food product to be poached is submerged. The food product is cooked over direct heat, then removed, and kept moist and warm until serving.

CHEF'S NOTES

⊚ *Use an aromatic broth.*

⊚ *To prevent food from drying out, it is best not to poach items before they are needed.*

⊚ *Cook items for the shortest possible holding time.*

⊚ *Do not allow liquid to come to a boil.*

⊚ *Poached items are best served with flavorful sauces or relishes to boost the overall flavor profile.*

SHALLOW POACHING

Shallow poaching is a cooking technique using a combination of seasoned stock and hot steam vapors. The particular cooking liquid selected is of critical importance to the overall success of the dish (e.g., Chicken Breast in Herb Broth with Root Vegetables and Roasted Garlic). To enhance the flavor profile, add pungents, spices, and aromatics to the stock. Additionally, one can add wine, citrus fruits, or mushrooms. The flavor profile will depend on the recipe and individual taste preference.

Place aromatics in the bottom of a casserole, add the item to be poached and the liquid cooking medium, bring to a simmer, not a boil, and cover with parchment paper. Finish the cooking process in the oven or over a direct heat source. Never bring cooking liquid to a boil when using this method. Remove the cooked product, keeping it warm and moist until serving. The remainder of the cooking liquid is commonly referred to as the "cuisson." This can be used for the preparation of a light sauce or dressing.

Additional information on this technique can be found in Chapter 10.

CHEF'S NOTES

⑥ *Shallow poaching is superb for small individual portions, such as seafood.*

BRAISING

Braising is a cooking method that involves both dry and moist heat. This technique is used for larger pieces of meat yielding multiple servings (e.g., Spiced Braised Beef Brisket with Wild Mushroom Risotto). In general, prior to braising, the meat is marinated for a specific period of time, since less tender and more muscular cuts of protein are used in this cooking method. The meat is quickly seared (dry heat) prior to being added to the cooking liquid that has been enhanced with roasted vegetables and aromatics. In general, a large casserole or braising pan is used. It is important to make sure the lid fits tightly on the pan to hold in the steam. The moist cooking promotes tenderization of less tender meat fibers. Place seared protein item in a casserole on a bed of roasted vegetable mirepoix. Add the cooking liquid and quickly bring to a simmer over direct heat. Add aromatics, spices, and herbs. Cover and finish cooking in the oven, according to the timing requirements of the recipe.

CHEF'S NOTES

⑥ *Marinate proteins with aromatics and spices for added flavor. For variety, experiment with different herbs and spices.*

⑥ *For added flavor, sear the meat prior to braising.*

⑥ *To prepare a sauce for serving with the protein, reduce the cooking liquid and puree the roasted vegetables to naturally bind the sauce, without the addition of flour.*

⑥ *For approximately two pounds of protein, use five ounces of roasted vegetable mirepoix and 32 ounces of cooking liquids. Always use high-quality stocks or broth.*

STEWING

Stewing, although similar to the braising technique, does have a few differences (e.g., Country-Style Beef Stew). In general, the protein is cut into bite-size pieces. The amount of cooking liquid may vary from the recipe being prepared. As in the braising technique, a less tender and more muscular piece of protein is used, and it is marinated for added flavor enhancement. Pan-sear or blanch the main protein. Remove from sauté pan and place in casserole, add roasted vegetables and cooking liquid. Add spices and herbs, bring to a simmer, cover, and cook until tender.

CHEF'S NOTES

⊚ *Pan-searing adds additional flavor and caramelization.*

⊚ *Marinate foods with aromatics and spices for added flavor. For variety, experiment with different herbs and spices.*

⊚ *Do not allow stew to boil excessively during the cooking process; this will cause the protein to shrink and toughen.*

⊚ *Always use high-quality, well-flavored stock, sauce, or broth.*

❦

SAVE THE FLAVOR!!! IT IS REALLY IMPORTANT TO RETAIN AS MUCH OF THE NATURAL JUICES OF THE FOOD AS POSSIBLE, THAT'S WHERE THE FLAVOR IS. THE MORE NATURAL JUICES YOU SAVE, THE LESS YOU HAVE TO CREATE OR TAINT THE DISH WITH SURROGATE FLAVORS.

Chef Mark V. Erickson, CMC

DINNERTIME IS THE MOST WONDERFUL PERIOD OF THE DAY, AND PERHAPS ITS GOAL—THE BLOSSOMING OF THE DAY. BREAKFAST IS THE BUD.

Novalis

A SKILLED RÔTISSEUR IS AN ARTIST.

Brillat-Savarin

COOKERY IS NOT CHEMISTRY, IT IS AN ART. IT REQUIRES INSTINCT AND TASTE RATHER THAN EXACT MEASUREMENTS.

X. Marcel Boulestin

❦

PART FOUR

THE RECIPES

CHAPTER 7
ABOUT OUR RECIPES

CHAPTER 8
APPETIZERS, SALADS, AND SALAD DRESSINGS

CHAPTER 9
STOCKS, SOUPS, SAUCES, RELISHES, AND SPREADS

CHAPTER 10
MAIN COURSE SELECTIONS

CHAPTER 11
VEGETABLES, POTATOES, GRAINS, AND LEGUMES

CHAPTER 12
DESSERTS, BREADS, AND QUICK BREADS

In an era when time and convenience have taken precedence over the joy of real foods, we believe now is the time to step back and think about the importance of actually enjoying your food, and perhaps to rediscover the kitchen. We make time for so many things, but rarely do we spend enough time in preparing our own foods. Have we forgotten how to cook, or is it that we simply do not make time for this traditional and cultural experience?

As Americans have become more concerned with health, while focusing primarily on the reduction of fats in our diet, the number of overweight Americans has risen to an all-time high. Research suggests that as a nation, we rely too much on fast foods, food substitutes, and especially processed, prepared, and packaged meals.

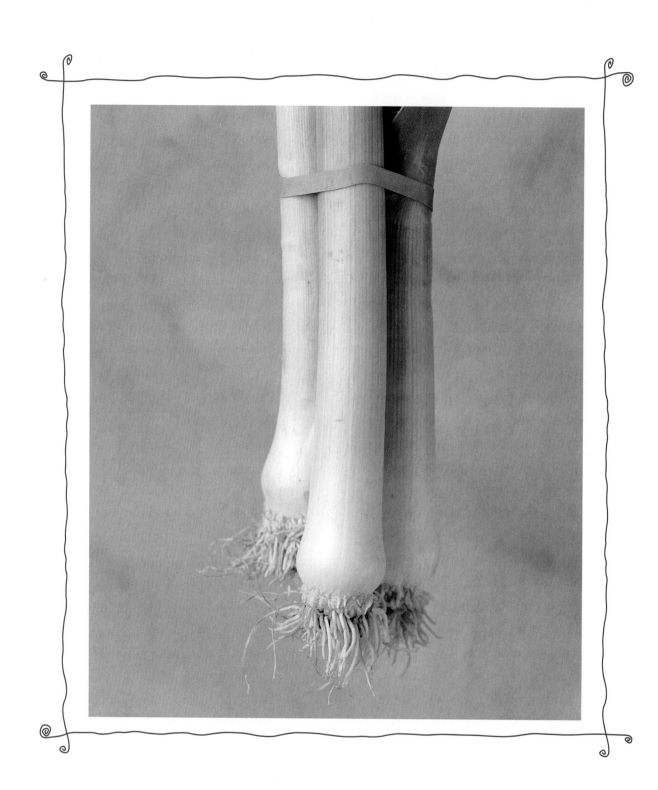

CHAPTER 7

ABOUT OUR RECIPES

Good cooking need not be expensive. This is probably one of the biggest misconceptions today. While we agree that many specialty foods cost more, excellence in cooking is not equated with extra expense.

In developing a healthful cooking repertoire, roasting, grilling, broiling, baking, pan-smoking, steaming, and poaching are among the best contemporary cooking methods used to prepare foods (see Chapter 6).

The most essential component in all cooking is taste. In healthful cooking, taste is of particular importance since it will be a major factor in reinforcing one's desire to select and prepare more healthful foods. The opportunities to achieve taste in cooking are endless and are influenced by the food products, cooking techniques, natural flavorings, pairings of products and flavors, and accompanying beverages.

Flavor enhancers such as fresh herbs and spices of every variety have no appreciable calories and no appreciable fat, therefore particularly in nutritional cooking they can be used as taste dictates and will exponentially enhance the flavor profile of food. Experiment with the use of high-quality herbs and spices in lieu of additional salt. Rather than adding salt, awaken your taste buds with a swirl of fresh lemon or lime juice or cracked white, black, or pink pepper. It is important that herbs and spices are properly stored and handled to retain the freshness and maximum flavor profile. Think about pureeing tomatoes and bell peppers with fresh basil and oregano for a pasta sauce.

In healthful cooking, stocks carry many of the flavors in the dish. When cooking and sautéing vegetables, use a high-quality stock rather than oil or butter. We use our own stocks from the recipes found in the introduction to Chapter 9, or a high-quality commercial product. Stocks, herbs, spices, vinegars, and fruit juices have minimal effect on the overall nutritional value of the recipe and can be used in a creative manner.

Sugar may be used for sweetening, but fruit juice concentrates, blended fresh or frozen fruit, and dried fruit all add sweetness, along with some vitamins and minerals as an added dividend. In baking, the use of fruit juice concentrates and fruit purees naturally reduces the amount of fat calories. Pureed berries with a dash of orange liqueur will enhance the flavor profile for an angel food cake. Also, nonfat yogurt or applesauce can be used as fat replacers in baking.

Food tastes best, and is best for us, in its simplest forms. Honest food preparation should be within the grasp of anyone. Good cooking begins with quality ingredients. Therefore, only rely on quality flavor enhancers and be selective in the purchase of all your ingredients, including vinegars, oils, condiments, herbs, spices, and citrus fruits. Always insist on the best-quality ingredients available.

The nutritional analysis appearing with each recipe was based on the recipe as written. It is our premise that cooking is an art and not an exact science; however, when cooking in this healthful style certain guidelines will apply. We may not always choose to measure, but in the case of fats and oils it is imperative to follow the recipe to ensure the nutritional integrity of the dish.

The same rule applies to the use of salt and high-sodium ingredients. In some recipes we have specified the amount of salt to be added to a dish. We consider ⅛ teaspoon of salt per serving to be adequate in dishes in which we say "salt to taste" or "adjust seasoning with salt." Our nutritional data is based on no additional salt added to the recipe. In some recipes, we use products high in flavor that may be high in sodium, such as olives, capers, and condiments, or prepared mustard, Worcestershire sauce, soy sauce, and some vinegars (see Table 7.1). Seasoning adjusted "to taste" is according to your individual taste. This leaves the addition of salt to the discretion of the culinarian based on taste and nutritional requirements. However, salt should always be used with restraint. Remember, 1 teaspoon (6 grams) of salt equals 2400 mg of sodium.

CHEF'S NOTES

⦿ *Reduce the use of processed foods. When using processed or prepared foods, incorporate fresh ingredients whenever possible.*

⦿ *Develop skill and techniques in relying on the natural flavors of the food.*

⦿ *When appropriate, use egg substitute rather than whole eggs, to reduce the amount of fat and cholesterol.*

⦿ *Use oils sparingly, and select high-quality olive oil or a monounsaturated oil.*

⦿ *Experiment with stocks to be used as natural flavor enhancers. Use only high-quality stocks.*

TABLE 7.1 Sodium Content of Condiments

Condiment	Amount	Sodium Content (mg)
Ripe olives	1 large	38
Capers*	1 tsp.	100
Soy sauce	1 tsp.	256
Teriyaki sauce	1 tsp.	209
Worcestershire sauce	1 tsp.	78
Mustard, prepared	1 tsp.	63

Source: Joan A. T. Pennington, *Bowes and Church's Food Values of Portions Commonly Used.* Philadelphia: J. B. Lippincott, 1994.

*Product label: Sysco Imperial Capers Nonpareilles

⑥ Cooking in this style can be more economically viable in that one becomes more disciplined in working with the ingredients.

⑥ Using modified cooking techniques will aid in eliminating the use of excessive fats and oils.

⑥ The nutritional analysis of the recipes in this book was completed by the Nutrition Services staff of Zale Lipshy University Hospital, Southwestern Medical Center, Dallas, Texas, using the computer software program Computrition, copyright 1991–1994.

BENCHMARKS OF HEALTHY COOKING

BENCHMARK ONE: SELECT QUALITY INGREDIENTS (WITH THE END RESULT IN MIND)

⑥ Maintain an awareness of the utilization of seasonal products.

⑥ Use produce at the height of ripeness to enjoy the perfect flavor.

⑥ Always emphasize the use of top-quality ingredients.

⑥ Utilize fresh products whenever possible.

⑥ Choose products with little or no processing. Nutrients are lost from foods at each step of processing. In addition, processed foods may contain manufacturing byproducts, such as additives and colorings.

⑥ Create as much variety in ingredients as possible.

BENCHMARK TWO: CHOOSE METHODS OF PREPARATION TO PRESERVE FLAVOR, TEXTURE, APPEARANCE, AND NUTRITIONAL VALUE

⑥ The key to better low-fat cooking is to derive maximum flavor from each ingredient that is used in the preparation and cooking procedure.

⑥ Use the proper cooking technique for the food product to ensure retention of natural quality.

⑥ Snip fresh herbs and add to foods last.

⑥ Oven-roast whole spices and seeds, then crush them in a mortar and pestle prior to use; apply the same technique with nuts such as walnuts, pecans, and filberts.

BENCHMARK THREE: MONITOR THE TOTAL USE OF FATS

⑥ Adjust the intake of dietary fat gradually to allow the body time to appreciate the changed pattern in eating behavior, and to develop and value the different flavors, textures, and tastes that accompany a healthier approach to food preparation.

- Always select the appropriate oil for a specific cooking method.
- Use lean animal products and trim any excess fat and skin.
- Reduce the use of animal fats and fat-laden foods such as eggs, cream, and butter.

BENCHMARK FOUR: INCORPORATE PLANT-BASED ITEMS WHENEVER POSSIBLE

- Offer additional varieties of plant foods, increasing the intake of fruits and vegetables, particularly raw or steamed, such as carrots, broccoli, spinach, and squashes.
- Redistribute the percentage of protein from animal and plant sources, using more plant offerings in conjunction with—or without—animal proteins.
- Focus on appreciating whole grains such as brown rice, whole wheat, and oats. When purchasing whole-wheat bread, be sure the first ingredient listed on the label is whole-wheat flour; if not, the product was made with a refined flour.

BENCHMARK FIVE: INCREASE THE USE OF SEASONINGS AND FLAVOR ENHANCERS AS OPPOSED TO SALT

- Develop the natural flavor in individual foods.
- Enhance flavors with natural sauces, reductions, juices, etc.

BENCHMARK SIX
Consider the moderate addition of wine as part of a healthy lifestyle.

BALANCING THE PLATE

In healthful cooking you should build your menu on a foundation of vegetables, starches, and/or grains. Basically, the menu can start with these foods, with an added complementary protein portion or the recommended 3 to 4 oz. serving of meat. The meat portion can appear to be a much heartier portion when served on a vegetable/starch base.

In developing menus, it might be helpful to use the following guideline as a tool to structure balanced menus. Use this as a general rule, but not your ruler!

A five-course meal based on the nutritional guidelines could take the following shape: carbohydrates at 55 to 60 percent, proteins at 10 to 15 percent, and fats at less than 30 percent. The important point to remember in any sort of menu planning is to focus on total daily (or meal) calorie intake and not on the composition of any one food product. All these guides are flexible but can be helpful in menu planning.

There are two basic styles of "building" the plate, both of which are based on the idea that combining the protein with the starch can create a visually larger portion of protein. One style involves constructing the plate with the starch or vegetables as the base. The meat portion then tops the base, thus adding height to the plate. The second style incorporates the protein into a recipe, as in main course recipe White Bean Cassoulet (page 214).

The following are some additional serving suggestions for lean meat:

⊚ Instead of serving one 3 to 4 oz. chop, use two 1.5 to 2 oz portions to create better plate coverage.

⊚ Slice roasted meats thin or precut into scallopinies and fan over the plate or on top of a starch/vegetable medley.

⊚ Shave meat when preparing fillings for sandwiches. Meat can be stacked to give the illusion of a larger portion. Adding a vegetable slaw to a sandwich further reinforces the illusion of quantity.

⊚ To give additional plate coverage and eye appeal, include healthful sauces, such as vegetable coulis, stock reductions, and fruit or vegetable relishes.

SAFE FOOD HANDLING AND STORAGE

The basic concept of food safety is to take as many precautions as possible, no matter how minor they seem, to prevent, eliminate, or minimize any kind of unacceptable contamination. Such a program is called the HACCP system (hazard analysis critical control point), which identifies critical control points (CCPs). CCPs are practices, procedures, and preparation steps (e.g., frequently checking food storage temperatures) taken as a preventive measure to eliminate, prevent, or minimize the potential for contamination.

This system requires not only standard operating procedures but also, for a dining establishment, documentation. Documentation will provide the operator with written proof that safe food handling practices are operational. Health departments can review this information from products received log sheets, market lists, shift opening and closing checklists, food preparation product log sheets, and so on.

All those actively involved in the preparation and service of food have an obligation to ensure the cleanliness of the kitchen and related work areas. Food safety is an important concern, and its assurance is a responsibility that falls on everyone in the production chain. There is no excuse for inadequate sanitation and food handling practices.

Implementing a successful HACCP system can provide numerous benefits for the food service operation, including consistent product quality, less profit loss from product quality complaints, less profit loss from from food-borne illness complaints, less profit loss due to product waste, an accurate documented track record of products prepared, and increased consumer trust due to safe food handling practices.

⊚

Receiving, storage, and preparation are all key elements to a safe food handling program and each have proper product flow procedures. The following are important criteria in the product receiving:

- Never assume that all the food you receive is good enough to eat.
- Purchase government-inspected food. This is especially important in all categories of dairy products, meat, poultry, fish, and shellfish.
- Purchase from reputable purveyors. Visit their facilities to make sure high sanitation standards are maintained.
- The receiving dock and related areas should be well lit and kept very clean.
- Schedule deliveries to allow adequate time for the proper inspection and receiving of all the food products.
- Have the appropriate equipment available for the receiving clerk (e.g., clean hard-plastic storage containers in different colors for different perishable foods, thermometers, scales, plastic gloves, etc.).
- Always verify truck delivery temperatures.
- Record the delivery temperatures of all perishables at time of receipt. Be sure that all product received is within the shelf life, and reject any expired products.
- All refrigerated food should be received at 33 to 38 degrees Fahrenheit (0.6–3°C).
- All frozen product should be received at 0 degrees Fahrenheit (−18°C) or below, and not above 10 degrees Fahrenheit (−12°C).
- Reject produce and fruits that show unacceptable signs of mold, off-color, odor, or pest infestation, or are crushed and limp in appearance.
- All food packages should be intact and in good condition to protect the integrity of the content.

- Store all food products so as to maximize proper air circulation and prevent any microbial growth or cross-contamination.
- Check and maintain all food storage refrigeration unit temperatures.
- Dry storage room should be kept at 60 to 80 degrees Fahrenheit (16–27°C).
- Do not store any food products on floors.
- All products must be stored at least 6 inches away from walls and floors.
- Check all canned, potentially hazardous products for leaks, missing labels, rust spots, dents, torn packaging, and any other signs of contamination.

- Never use foods from swollen, leaking, or dented containers. Put them on a damaged goods shelf. Do not taste any food which may be of questionable safety.

- Walk-in refrigeration units should be kept at 33 to 38 degrees Fahrenheit (0.6–3°C). Check temperatures often and keep records. Observe the "cold chain": Keep it cool, keep it dry, keep it moving.

- Walk-in freezer units should be kept at 0 degrees Fahrenheit (−18°C) or below. Since food can deteriorate in the freezer, wrap foods so as to be moisture-proof and to avoid freezer burn, odor absorption, and dehydration.

- Date-stamp all perishable food product upon receipt. Rotate all product with the FIFO system (first in, first out).

- Store non-food items, cleaning supplies, and all toxic chemicals in designated areas only, away from food and kitchen equipment.

- Keep all storage areas clean and sanitary.

PRODUCT FLOW PROCEDURES: FOOD PREPARATION

Potentially hazardous foods are foods that are capable of supporting rapid growth of harmful microorganisms. Examples include: most meats, seafood, poultry, pasta, cooked vegetables, eggs, most cheeses, milk, and most dairy products. Potentially hazardous foods must be stored at below a maximum of 41 degrees Fahrenheit (5°C) at all times, except during the necessary steps of the preparation phase.

Many food products are not classified as potentially hazardous because they do not support rapid growth of harmful bacteria. However, proper temperature control is still critical since the quality of most product begins to deteriorate rapidly when subjected to temperature fluctuations. It is therefore essential that all foods be handled properly and temperatures controlled to ensure that foods are of the highest and safest quality possible.

When preparing food products, it is important to follow some basic, yet critical, food handling procedures. Below is a list of some of the most important points in safe food handling:

- Always work in a clean, well-lit area.
- Make sure all your equipment, including pots, pans, and utensils, are clean.
- Only use clean, sanitized utensils to handle food.
- Disposable gloves may be used when it is not practical to use a utensil.
- Wash hands prior to, and after, handling any food products or utensils, after coughing or sneezing, and always prior to returning to your work station, particularly after using the toilet.
- Wash hands frequently during the preparation and cooking process.

- Cover bandages during food preparation to avoid cross-contamination, since bandages have holes where bacteria can escape.
- Use paper towels to dry hands and wipe up spills.
- Wash and sanitize cutting boards before and after food preparation.
- Use each cutting board for only one food group, such as protein, vegetables, dairy, and cooked foods. Do not cross-utilize cutting boards.
- Clean and wash all fruits and vegetables prior to use.
- Avoid handling food when you are sick.
- The best way to defrost food is in the refrigerator. Do not defrost food on the counter! In emergencies, thaw wrapped foods under cool running water.
- Any leftover cooked food should be stored in clean, shallow containers with a food depth not to exceed two inches or five centimeters, and refrigerated within 1.5 to 2 hours.
- The best way to cool cooked foods is to place the open container in an ice bath and rapidly cool before storing.
- Store all foods on shelves at least six inches off the floor. Never store raw food or unwashed produce above foods not requiring further cooking or washing.
- Never place cooked food back onto the same plate or platter which held the raw product, unless it has been completely sanitized.

During hot food preparation, observe the cooking temperature guidelines. The guidelines, as listed below, are the recommended temperatures to which specific proteins must be cooked before service (also given are the harmful organisms that otherwise may result). In addition, it is advised to consult your local health authorities for additional specific area requirements. Keep meat, poultry, fish, and all other potentially hazardous food at safe temperatures, below 41 degrees Fahrenheit (5°C) or above 140 degrees Fahrenheit (60°C).

Poultry and stuffed meats*	165°F (74°C)	Salmonella
Ground beef and pork	155°F (68°C)	E. coli
Pork, ham, sausage, and bacon	150–155°F (68°C)	Trichinella spiralis
Rare roast beef	140°F (60°C)	
Fish and fish products	140–145°F (60–63°C)	

*Note: It is preferable to cook the filling prior to stuffing the meat. However, the safest method is to cook and serve the stuffing separately.

Through implementation, constant monitoring, and training, a safe food handling program will provide your customers with a safe and reliable source of food. Safe food handling will assist in limiting potential complaints from food-borne illness and poor product quality, and will minimize waste of food products.

CHAPTER 8

APPETIZERS, SALADS, AND SALAD DRESSINGS

To get the best results begin with the best ingredients possible. Treat everything with respect, use common sense, apply fundamentals in cooking, and you will end up with a great end product.

Chef Rudy Speckamp, CMC

Learn the fundamentals of cooking, do them well and do them consistently.

Chef Edward Janos, CMC

Do not confuse efforts with results; after all the fads have passed, traditionally well-prepared foods will survive the test of time.

Chef Milos Cihelka, CMC

Eating and drinking hold body and soul together.

Alsatian proverb

APPETIZERS

SALADS

An asterisk following a recipe title indicates that the recipe also appears in another chapter.

Innumerable ingredients and virtually every cooking method can be enlisted to make dishes that will delight and whet the appetite for the courses to follow.

Practically every world cuisine offers some type of appetizer, many having their own unique word for *appetizers,* such as Italian antipasto, French hors d'oeuvres, Greek mezes, Japanese sushi or sashimi, Spanish tapas, Chinese dim sum, and the Scandinavian smorgasbord.

However, appetizers are said to have originated in Imperial Russia, and were called *zakuski.* They were adopted by the French as appetite stimulants called *hors d'oeuvres.*

Hors d'oeuvre literally translated means "aside of the work." During impressive dinners you will often find a lavish selection of hors d'oeuvres preceding the dinner. These are generally served during a reception gathering. Hors d'oeuvres should be kept small, in selection and size, as large portions will diminish, rather than stimulate, the appetite.

In selecting appetizers, choose high-quality ingredients that will not be duplicated in the entrée selection of the dinner. It is also advised to serve cold appetizers prior to the soup, and warm appetizers after the soup.

Today salads are virtually a must with every meal, not only to aid in the digestive process but also as an appetite stimulant. One need not always think of salads as simple salad greens. There are many compositions of salads that utilize a variety of preparation methods, as well as ingredients. In this category, taste, creativity, and endless possibilities offer the passionate culinarian a broad palate with which to experiment.

SALADS

Salads are an important staple of the healthful diet. A mixture of colorful salad greens and raw vegetables, or grains tossed with chopped vegetables or fruit, add to the pleasure and satiety of the meal.

Salads can help to increase the number of high-fiber, low-fat food items in the diet. The deeper the green of the vegetable, the higher it is in vitamin A, vitamin E, calcium, and iron. Dark orange vegetables may be high in beta-carotene. Salads can assist in giving textural pleasure and bulk to a meal with little or no added calories. Salads may be served at any time in a meal; the recipes in this section highlight their versatility. They can serve to stimulate or suppress the appetite at the beginning of a meal.

SALAD DRESSINGS

Salad dressing can greatly alter the healthful aspect of a meal. Often, too much emphasis is placed on its role as flavoring the salad instead of as a complementary condiment to the salad, enhancing the taste of the dish. Salad dressings are traditionally the biggest contributors to fat and calories found in salad recipes (see Table 8.1).

Traditionally, vinaigrettes are made with oil and vinegar or other acid in a 3:1 ratio. Balance the flavor with other ingredients such as citrus fruits and fresh herbs.

- ⑥ Use a 1:1:2 ratio of oil to acid to lied stock. For lied stock, combine 1 tablespoon of cornstarch in 3 tablespoons of cold water, creating a "slurry." Add the slurry to one cup of hot stock. Chill the lied stock prior to use.
- ⑥ Increase the proportion of acid and/or replace some of the fat with fruit jams, stock, or water, to a ratio of 0.5:2:1 oil/acid/other liquid.

Creamy or emulsified salad dressings are generally prepared with oil, vinegar, and egg yolks. Creamy dressings can be created healthfully by adding lower-fat ingredients such as fat-free ricotta cheese, low-fat yogurt, or fat-free sour cream or buttermilk to a vinaigrette to reduce the need for oil and replace the egg yolks.

Today, there are fat-free and reduced-fat versions of "mayonnaise" that can replace traditional mayonnaise in many recipes. Remember, these "mayonnaise" versions may not always be the best choice, considering not only the flavor aspect but the fact that these products still have significant calorie and sodium content (see Table 8.2).

Today's commercial mayonnaise is much lower in cholesterol due to the reduction in the number of egg yolks used in its preparation.

When creating a healthful version of salad dressings, it is important to remember that oils should be chosen carefully. Select an oil that will provide the greatest depth in flavor and integrity. Choose monounsaturated and polyunsaturated oils such as canola oil, olive oil, or safflower oil for their flavor profile and their healthful benefits.

Complement these oils with select vinegars such as rice vinegar and champagne vinegar.

TABLE 8.1   Vinaigrettes

Type	Amount	Calories	Fat (gm)	Cholesterol (mg)
Traditional homemade vinegar and oil[1]	1 oz. or 2 Tbsp.	144	16	0
Commercial vinaigrette[1]	1 oz. or 2 Tbsp.	114	11	0
In Good Taste Simple Vinaigrette[2]	1 oz. or 2 Tbsp.	43	4	0

[1]From Joan A. T. Pennington, *Bowes and Church's Food Values of Portins Commonly Used*. Philadelphia: J. B. Lippincott, 1994.

[2]See recipe, this chapter.

TABLE 8.2   Mayonnaise-Type Salad Dressings

Type	Amount	Calories	Fat (gm)	Cholesterol (mg)
Commercial mayonnaise[1]	1 oz. or 2 Tbsp.	200	22	12
Fat-free mayonnaise[2]	1 oz. or 2 Tbsp.	20	0	0
In Good Taste Creamy Basil Mayonnaise[3]	1 oz. or 2 Tbsp.	37	2	0

[1]From Joan A. T. Pennington, *Bowes and Church's Food Values of Portins Commonly Used.* Philadelphia: J. B. Lippincott, 1994.

[2]Nutrition Product Label: Kraft Free Nonfat Mayonnaise Dressing

[3]See recipe, this chapter.

Some vinegars are high in sodium. When preparing a healthful salad dressing, it is important to taste the dressing before adding any additional salt. To add salt to a dressing, it is best to first dissolve the salt in the vinegar before incorporating it into the oil.

Less expensive vinegars like wine vinegar can be used to create flavored vinegars by adding fruit purees, chopped herbs, and aromatics.

Condiments such as capers, prepared mustard, anchovies, and bacon, even though they are used in small quantities in vinaigrettes and salad dressings for flavor, can be high in sodium and will increase the overall sodium content of the dressing. They will wilt salad greens if dressing or vinaigrettes are added to greens too far in advance of serving, due to the osmotic effect of salt.

When purchasing condiments, make it a habit to review the label to identify those that are higher in sodium, and consider selecting the reduced-sodium versions, such as low-sodium soy and teriyaki sauce.

BASIL SHRIMP POCKETS

SERVES 8

INGREDIENTS	AMOUNT/U.S.	METRIC
For the Pockets:		
Shrimp, peeled, deveined, cold	14 oz.	392 gm
Ricotta cheese, nonfat	3 oz.	84 gm
Basil, snipped	1 Tbsp.	5 gm
Lemon juice	½ tsp.	5 ml
Kosher salt	to taste	to taste
Fresh, cracked white pepper	to taste	to taste
Wonton wrappers (quality)	24	24
Egg whites, slightly beaten	2	2
For the Sauce:		
Red onion, minced	2 Tbsp.	42 gm
Ginger root, fresh, grated	1 Tbsp.	5 gm
Lime, juice of	3	3
White wine, dry	4 fl. oz.	120 ml
Evaporated skim milk	4 fl. oz.	120 ml
Garnish:		
Cilantro leaves	½ oz.	15 gm
Fish Sauce (p. 88)	16 fl. oz.	480 ml

CHEF'S NOTES

Substitute lobster, scallops, or a firm fish for the shrimp.

PREPARATION OF THE POCKETS

1. Puree shrimp in food processor. Add ricotta and pulse machine on and off a few times until the ricotta is just incorporated.
2. Place shrimp mixture in bowl and stir in basil, lemon juice, and salt and pepper to taste. The mixture can be stored in the refrigerator for a couple of days if necessary.
3. If needed, cut wonton wrappers into quarters. Lay on a clean surface and place ½ tablespoon of filling onto each wonton. Brush the edges with egg white and fold over into a triangle and twist to form. Refrigerate or freeze prior to use.

PREPARATION OF THE SAUCE

1. Combine red onion, ginger root, lime juice, and wine. Reduce by half. Add Fish Sauce and evaporated skim milk. Simmer until the flavor and consistency are properly developed, about 10 minutes.
2. Cook wontons in simmering salted water for 3–4 minutes.
3. Drain wontons using a colander and toss with prepared sauce.

PRESENTATION

Serve in soup plates and garnish with cilantro leaves.

NUTRITION PER SERVING

Calories 454, protein 25 gm, fat 8 gm, carbohydrates 67 gm, cholesterol 98 mg, sodium 674 mg

FISH SAUCE *

SERVES 8

INGREDIENTS	AMOUNT/U.S.	METRIC
Fish stock, high-quality	16 fl. oz.	480 ml
Cornstarch	1 Tbsp.	15 gm
Evaporated skim milk	4 fl. oz.	120 ml
Kosher salt	to taste	to taste
Fresh, cracked white pepper	to taste	to taste

PREPARATION

1. Bring stock to a boil; reduce to simmer.
2. Moisten cornstarch with a little cold evaporated skim milk, stir into simmering stock.
3. Slowly stir rest of evaporated skim milk into simmering stock, a little at a time. The stock should not be too thick, but it should coat the spoon.
4. Adjust to taste with salt and pepper.

NUTRITION PER 2 OZ./60 ML SERVING
Calories 22, protein 2 gm, fat 0.5 gm, carbohydrates 4 gm, cholesterol 0.5 mg, sodium 20 mg

FILO TRIANGLES WITH FETA CHEESE AND PICKLED MUSHROOMS

YIELD: 16 TRIANGLE PASTRIES

INGREDIENTS	AMOUNT/U.S.	METRIC
Feta cheese	8 oz.	224 gm
Red peppers, cleaned, roasted, peeled, seeded, chopped	2	2
Basil, fresh snipped	2 Tbsp.	10 gm
Flat parsley, chopped	2 Tbsp.	10 gm
Fresh, cracked white pepper	to taste	to taste
Filo pastry	10 sheets	10 sheets
Vegetable spray	as needed	
Clarified butter	2 Tbsp.	30 ml
Pickled Mushrooms (p. 90)		

PREPARATION

1. In large mixing bowl, crumble feta cheese. Add chopped, roasted pepper flesh. Add basil, parsley, and adjust seasoning with pepper. Mix thoroughly. Adjust herb level as desired.
2. Preheat oven to 350°F (175°C).
3. Place filo pastry on clean surface. Cut each sheet into three even strips; spray with vegetable spray. Use single strip for each pastry.
4. Place ½ oz. filling at near bottom of strip. Fold into triangle from the bottom up. Continue folds along entire strip.
5. Place triangle on cookie sheet, brush with clarified butter, and bake in oven until golden brown for approximately 15 minutes. Serve hot with Pickled Mushrooms.

NUTRITION PER TRIANGLE

Calories 91, protein 3 gm, fat 5 gm, carbohydrates 8 gm, cholesterol 16 mg, sodium 214 mg

CHEF'S NOTES

One of the crowning culinary achievements of Middle Eastern kitchens is the filo (or phyllo) pastry made of a simple unleavened dough of flour, water, cornstarch, oil, and salt. This pastry, in tissue-paper-thin layers, is fragile and delicate, and it comes ready to use for a wide assortment of savory and sweet pastries. In Greece, the flaky layers are used in a crisp appetizer of spinach and feta cheese known as spanakopita. *In Turkey, where cheese and lamb are used, it is called* beaurele. *In Morocco, spicy chicken and almond concoctions are called* bastillo. *The pastry is best known for its use in Greek baklava, which is a cinnamon-filled, multi-layered pastry.*

Today, frozen filo is readily available and widely used in many applications. The dough may be stored in the freezer for two to three months; however, handle the package with care and use as soon as possible after purchase, as the sheets are delicate and break easily. It is best to have all other ingredients completely ready prior to working with filo dough, since it may dry out rapidly.

PICKLED MUSHROOMS

SERVES 8

CHEF'S NOTES

*Serve with Filo Triangles
(p. 89) or as a condiment.*

INGREDIENTS	AMOUNT/U.S.	METRIC
Mushrooms, fresh	12 oz.	336 gm
Garlic, minced	3 cloves	3 cloves
Olive oil	1 Tbsp.	15 ml
Chicken stock	2½ fl. oz.	75 ml
Rosemary needles, cracked	½ Tbsp.	2.5 gm
Chives, short-cut	1 Tbsp.	5 gm
Parsley, fresh, chopped	½ Tbsp.	2.5 gm
Lime, juice of	1	1
White balsamic vinegar	1 Tbsp.	15 ml
Kosher salt	to taste	to taste
Fresh, cracked white pepper	to taste	to taste

PREPARATION

1. Clean and quarter mushrooms. Heat oil with garlic, add quartered mushrooms, and sauté for 3 minutes.
2. Add stock, reduce by one-third.
3. Add herbs and vinegar and lime juice. Adjust seasoning with salt and cracked white pepper.

NUTRITION PER 2 TBSP. SERVING

Calories 30, protein 2 gm, fat 2 gm, carbohydrates 4 gm, cholesterol 0 mg, sodium 2 mg

FILO TRIANGLES WITH FETA CHEESE AND SPINACH

YIELD: 25 TRIANGLE PASTRIES

INGREDIENTS	AMOUNT/U.S.	METRIC
Red onion, finely chopped	5 oz.	140 gm
Garlic, minced	5 cloves	5 cloves
Olive oil	1 Tbsp.	15 ml
Spinach leaves, fresh, blanched, chopped	8 oz.	224 gm
Kosher salt	to taste	to taste
Fresh, cracked white pepper	to taste	to taste
Feta cheese	8 oz.	224 gm
Cottage cheese, low-fat	4 oz.	112 gm
Basil, fresh snipped	1 Tbsp.	7 gm
Oregano leaves, snipped	1 tsp.	3 gm
Egg substitute	4 oz.	120 gm
Filo pastry	12 sheets	12 sheets
Vegetable spray	as needed	
Clarified butter, unsalted	2 Tbsp.	30 ml

CHEF'S NOTES

Make sure clean bowls are always used, and use plastic gloves or utensils to mix food.

PREPARATION

1. In medium saucepan, sweat the finely diced onions and garlic in olive oil. Add the drained, chopped spinach leaves and heat thoroughly. Adjust seasoning with a little salt and pepper. Place in clean stainless steel bowl and cool mixture.

2. In large mixing bowl, crumble feta cheese. Add cottage cheese, basil, oregano, and adjust seasoning with pepper. Mix thoroughly. Set aside.

3. Preheat oven to 350°F (175°C).

4. In stainless steel bowl, beat egg substitute, combine with cheese mixture, and fold mixture into spinach mixture.

5. To assemble, place filo pastry on clean surface. Cut each sheet into three even strips; spray with vegetable spray. Use single strip for each pastry.

6. Place approximately 1 oz. filling at bottom of sheet. Fold into triangle from the bottom up.

7. Place on cookie sheet, brush with clarified butter, and bake in oven until golden brown for approximately 15 minutes. Serve hot.

NUTRITION PER TRIANGLE
Calories 77, protein 3 gm, fat 4 gm, carbohydrates 6 gm, cholesterol 11 mg, sodium 160 mg

SPICY PEPPERED SHRIMP

YIELD: 30 PIECES

Serve shrimp with a tomato relish or with herb vinaigrette.

Pickling liquid can be reused, provided clean equipment and utensils are used throughout.

INGREDIENTS	AMOUNT/U.S.	METRIC
Shrimp, 16/20 count fresh or frozen cleaned, cooked, peeled, deveined, refrigerated	30 pc.	30 pc.
Rice vinegar	8 fl. oz.	240 ml
Water	12 fl. oz.	360 ml
Kosher salt	½ Tbsp.	8 gm
Garlic, sliced	2 cloves	2 cloves
Mustard seed	1 Tbsp.	5 gm
Celery seed	½ Tbsp.	2.5 gm
Cumin seeds	2 tsp.	4 gm
Juniper berries	8	8
Bay leaves	3	3
Cloves	4	4
Brown sugar	2 Tbsp.	30 gm
Jalapeno pepper, sliced	1	1

PREPARATION

1. In stainless steel sauté pan, place all ingredients except shrimp; bring to a rapid boil for 1 minute. Cool thoroughly.
2. Combine cold pickling liquid with cold shrimp. Marinate overnight.

NUTRITION PER PIECE

Calories 36, protein 4 gm, fat 1 gm, carbohydrates 3 gm, cholesterol 28 mg, sodium 160 mg

MARINATED ROASTED PEPPERS WITH THYME AND BALSAMIC VINEGAR *

SERVES 6

INGREDIENTS	AMOUNT/U.S.	METRIC
Red bell peppers, large	4	4
Yellow bell peppers, large	4	4
Balsamic vinegar	2.5 fl. oz.	75 ml
Olive oil, virgin	1 Tbsp.	15 ml
Lemon, juice of	2	2
Thyme, fresh snipped	1 tsp.	1 gm
Fresh, cracked white pepper	to taste	to taste
Kosher salt	to taste	to taste
Garnish:		
Feta cheese	2 oz.	56 gm
Kalamata olives, quartered	12	12

PREPARATION

1. Preheat oven to 375°F (190°C).
2. Wash whole peppers. Place on cookie sheet and gently roast until browned evenly. Remove from oven.
3. Place in large bowl covered with plastic wrap. Let rest for 10 minutes. Peel peppers. Remove stem and seeds and discard. Cut into quarters and place in shallow pan.
4. Drizzle with balsamic vinegar, olive oil, lemon juice, thyme, fresh cracked pepper, and salt. Marinate for several hours in the refrigerator.

PRESENTATION

Serve on plates garnished with feta cheese and kalamata olives.

NUTRITION PER SERVING
Calories 84, protein 2 gm, fat 6 gm, carbohydrates 8 gm, cholesterol 8 mg, sodium 162 mg

CRAB CAKES

SERVES 20

INGREDIENTS	AMOUNT/U.S.	METRIC
Olive oil	2 Tbsp.	30 ml
Celery, finely diced	12 oz.	336 gm
Egg substitute	6 fl. oz.	180 ml
Mayonnaise, nonfat	3 Tbsp.	45 gm
Fresh, cracked white pepper	¾ tsp.	2 gm
Curry powder	¾ tsp.	2 gm
Tabasco™ sauce	9 drops	9 drops
Lemon juice	3 Tbsp.	45 ml
Cloves, ground	⅜ tsp.	1 gm
Cayenne pepper	⅛ tsp.	.25 gm
English dry mustard	¼ tsp.	.5 gm
Kosher salt	to taste	to taste
Chives, minced	3 Tbsp.	15 gm
Miller's® Select lump crab meat, pasteurized, thoroughly drained	3 lb.	1350 gm
Bread crumbs, toasted	8 oz.	224 gm
Vegetable spray	as needed	as needed

PREPARATION

1. Heat olive oil; sweat celery until translucent. Remove from heat and cool thoroughly.

2. In separate bowl, combine egg substitute, mayonnaise, seasonings, and chives. Add completely drained crab meat and cooled celery. Combine mixture, but do not overmix.

3. Add toasted bread crumbs and combine. With plastic gloves, form into individual patties. Mixture should yield 20 2-oz. crab cakes. Rest cakes on parchment-covered sheet pan until ready to sauté. Do not wrap in plastic wrap, as this will create too much moisture.

4. Dry sauté crab cakes in nonstick pan using vegetable spray or olive oil, until golden brown on both sides.

NUTRITION PER SERVING

Calories 133, protein 16 gm, fat 3 gm, carbohydrates 10 gm, cholesterol 68 mg, sodium 249 mg

GNOCCHI TARTLETS WITH GRILLED VEGETABLES

SERVES 12

INGREDIENTS	AMOUNT/U.S.	METRIC
Zucchini, medium, sliced in ¼″ rounds, grilled	1	1
Eggplant, medium, sliced in ¼″ rounds, grilled	1	1
Olive oil	1 Tbsp.	15 ml
Kosher salt	to taste	to taste
Fresh, cracked white pepper	to taste	to taste
Onion, small, thinly sliced, sautéed	1	1
Red bell pepper roasted, peeled, and cut into strips	1	1
Yellow bell pepper roasted, peeled, and cut into strips	1	1
Reduced-fat milk (2%)	48 fl. oz.	720 ml
Semolina	24 oz.	672 gm
Egg substitute	6 oz.	180 ml
Parmesan cheese, grated	6 oz.	168 gm
Mozzarella cheese, thinly sliced	8 oz.	224 gm
Romano cheese, grated	1½ oz.	42 gm
Chili flakes	pinch	pinch

PREPARATION

VEGETABLES

1. Preheat grill and preheat oven to 375°F (190°C).
2. Lightly brush zucchini and eggplant slices with olive oil and season to taste with salt and pepper.
3. Place vegetable rounds on hot grill and allow to cook for 2 minutes; turn. Cook 2 additional minutes or until just tender. Set aside.
4. In hot, nonstick skillet, heat 1 tsp. olive oil. Add sliced onions and gently sauté until translucent and slightly brown. Set aside.
5. Wash peppers and leave whole. Place on cookie sheet and roast for approximately 10 minutes or until skin is darkened and blistering. Remove from oven.
6. Place in a bowl covered with plastic wrap, and allow to cool. Peel skin from peppers. Remove stem and seeds. Slice peppers into strips. Set aside.

TART BASES

1. In saucepan, bring milk, with a little salt and pepper, to a single boil.

2. Add semolina, stirring continuously and pressing out any lumps. Continue to cook over medium heat for about 15 minutes, stirring continuously.

3. Transfer semolina mixture to clean mixing bowl and, using electric mixer, beat in egg substitute and parmesan cheese. Beat until well combined.

4. Coat nonstick sheet pan with vegetable spray. With wet hands, form semolina mixture into twelve rounds about 6″ diameter; pat smooth.

ASSEMBLING AND BAKING

1. Preheat oven to 375°F (190°C).

2. Divide vegetables among tart bases, layering with mozzarella cheese. Sprinkle romano cheese on the top, then sprinkle with chili flakes.

3. Place tarts in oven and bake for approximately 15 minutes.

NUTRITION PER SERVING
Calories 341, protein 16 gm, fat 8 gm, carbohydrates 49 gm, cholesterol 23 mg, sodium 235 mg

SMOKED TROUT
WITH CUCUMBER RELISH

SERVES 8

INGREDIENTS	AMOUNT/U.S.	METRIC
Rainbow trout fillets, washed, boned, skinned; remove belly flap and tail about 4.5 oz. (126 gm) each	8	8
Thai basil, finely snipped	1 Tbsp.	15 gm
Mustard seed	1 tsp.	5 gm
Olive oil	1 Tbsp.	15 ml
Alder or hickory wood chips, fine	3 cups	500 gm
Cucumber Relish (below)		

PREPARATION

1. Wash, drain, and paper towel dry trout fillets.
2. In clean stainless steel bowl, combine basil, mustard seed, and olive oil. Marinate fillets in mixture for 30 minutes.
3. Remove with plastic gloves. Place fillets on foil-lined roasting rack.
4. Place wood chips on bottom of smoking pan and place over flame. Create a good, hot smoke. Remove pan from heat source, place rack in smoke pan, close lid, and allow flavors to develop for 4–6 minutes. Open lid and remove trout fillets.
5. Place on sheet pan and keep hot in 350°F (175°C) oven until ready to serve.
6. Serve trout fillets with Cucumber Relish.

CUCUMBER RELISH

INGREDIENTS	AMOUNT/U.S.	METRIC
English cucumber, peeled, seeded, diced	8 oz.	224 gm
Jicama, peeled, washed, diced	8 oz.	224 gm
OSO sweet onions, peeled, diced	4 oz.	112 gm
Olive oil	½ fl. oz.	15 ml
Rice wine vinegar	3 fl. oz.	90 ml
Oranges, juice of	2	2
Lemon grass, cleaned, finely chopped	2 tsp.	10 gm
Parsley, finely chopped	2 Tbsp.	30 gm
Cilantro, finely chopped	1 Tbsp.	15 gm
Kosher salt	to taste	to taste
Fresh, cracked white pepper	to taste	to taste

1. In clean stainless steel bowl, place cucumber, jicama, and onions. Add olive oil, vinegar, and orange juice. Add seasonings and adjust to taste with salt and pepper.
2. Marinate relish for 1 hour, and adjust seasonings prior to serving.

NUTRITION PER SERVING

Calories 230, protein 27 gm, fat 8 gm, carbohydrates 10 gm, cholesterol 73 mg, sodium 251 mg

WHITE BEAN SPREAD

SERVES 10

CHEF'S NOTES

Spread on toasted French bread points or toasted pita triangles.

INGREDIENTS	AMOUNT/U.S.	METRIC
Navy beans, dried	4 oz.	112 gm
Vegetable or chicken stock, high-quality	as needed	
Garlic cloves, roasted	5	5
Kosher salt	⅜ tsp.	2 gm
Fresh, cracked white pepper	⅜ tsp.	1 gm
Parmesan cheese, shredded	2 oz.	56 gm
Cilantro, chopped	1 Tbsp.	7 gm
Olive oil	3 Tbsp.	45 ml

PREPARATION

1. Sort and clean beans. Rinse in ample cold water. Drain. Cover with cold water and soak overnight.
2. Drain water and rinse beans.
3. In medium saucepan, place beans and cover with water. Bring to boil, reduce heat, and simmer until beans are tender.
4. Remove from heat and place in clean stainless steel bowl. Cool beans rapidly.
5. In a clean food processor, puree beans to a smooth puree. Use vegetable or chicken stock to achieve desired consistency.
6. Add roasted garlic and adjust seasoning with salt, fresh cracked pepper, Parmesan cheese, and cilantro.
7. Remove from food processor bowl, place in clean stainless steel container, fold in olive oil, wrap with plastic wrap, and place in refrigerator to allow flavors to mature.
8. Prior to serving, adjust seasoning.

NUTRITION PER SERVING

Calories 79, protein 3 gm, fat 4 gm, carbohydrates 8 gm, cholesterol 0 mg, sodium 116 mg

SCALLOPS WITH OKRA AND MANGO

SERVES 8

INGREDIENTS	AMOUNT/U.S.	METRIC
Sea scallops, medium, cleaned, muscle removed	21 oz.	588 gm
Olive oil	2 Tbsp.	30 ml
Red onion, finely minced	4 Tbsp.	60 gm
Garlic, finely minced	8 cloves	8 cloves
Sun-dried tomato, minced	2 Tbsp.	30 gm
Lemon, juice of	1	1
Dry white wine	2 fl. oz.	60 ml
Roma tomato, peeled, seeded, finely diced	4 oz.	112 gm
Okra, sliced on the bias	6 oz.	168 gm
Kosher salt	to taste	to taste
Fresh, cracked white pepper	to taste	to taste
Mango, fresh, peeled, diced	6 oz.	168 gm
Thai basil, fresh, chiffonade	12 leaves	12 leaves
Garnish:		
Chervil (optional)	to taste	to taste

CHEF'S NOTES
Sun-dried tomatoes should be a high-quality variety and not packed in oil.

PREPARATION

1. Rinse scallops in cold water and dry with paper towels.
2. Dry sauté scallops in nonstick skillet. Brown on both sides. Do not overcook. Keep warm.
3. In saucepan, heat olive oil. Add red onion and garlic; sweat for 1 minute. Add sun-dried tomato, lemon juice, and white wine, simmer for 1 minute.
4. Add diced tomato and okra and season to taste with salt and pepper.
5. Cook for 30 seconds, stirring continuously. Add any cooking liquid from the sautéed scallops. Remove from heat, and add diced mangos and chiffonade of basil, combining gently. Adjust seasoning.

PRESENTATION

Arrange okra and mango mixture in center of eight small serving plates and top with sautéed scallops. Garnish with chervil (optional) and serve at once.

NUTRITION PER SERVING

Calories 142, protein 14 gm, fat 4 gm, carbohydrates 12 gm, cholesterol 24 mg, sodium 200 mg

LINGUINE WITH ANDOUILLE-MUSHROOM BROTH AND SHAVED ASIAGO

SERVES 8

CHEF'S NOTES
Serve with toasted tomato bruschetta.

INGREDIENTS	AMOUNT/U.S.	METRIC
Linguine, fresh or dried (uncooked weight)	1 lb.	448 gm
Olive oil, virgin	2 Tbsp.	30 ml
Andouille sausage, finely diced	3 Tbsp.	45 gm
Red onion, finely diced	2 oz.	56 gm
Red bell pepper, seeded, diced	2 oz.	56 gm
Garlic, finely minced	3 cloves	3 cloves
Button mushrooms, fresh, clean, sliced	10 oz.	280 gm
Sherry	2 fl. oz.	60 ml
Chicken stock, high-quality	24 fl. oz.	720 ml
Basil, snipped	3 Tbsp.	21 gm
Cilantro, snipped	3 Tbsp.	21 gm
Roma tomatoes, peeled, seeded, finely diced	5 oz.	140 gm
Kosher salt	to taste	to taste
Fresh, cracked white pepper	to taste	to taste
Garnish:		
Asiago cheese, shaved	4 oz.	112 gm

PREPARATION

1. In large stock pot, cook linguine in ample boiling water, lightly salted, until firm to the bite but not hard. Drain and rinse thoroughly. Set aside.
2. In large saucepan, heat olive oil. Add andouille sausage and sauté for 1 minute. Add onion, pepper, and garlic and continue to sauté for 1 minute.
3. Add mushrooms and deglaze with sherry. Continue to cook for 4 minutes.
4. Add chicken stock; bring to rapid boil. Reduce and simmer for 5 minutes.
5. Add basil, cilantro, and tomatoes. Season to taste with salt and pepper. Simmer gently.
6. Add cooked linguine, combine mixture thoroughly, adjust seasonings, and heat.

PRESENTATION

Serve in hot, deep soup plates and divide shaved Asiago evenly on top.

NUTRITION PER SERVING

Calories 349, protein 15 gm, fat 10 gm, carbohydrates 48 gm, cholesterol 14 mg, sodium 330 mg

RISOTTO WITH SHRIMP, MUSHROOMS, AND ARUGULA

SERVES 10

INGREDIENTS	AMOUNT/U.S.	METRIC
Olive oil	1 Tbsp.	15 ml
Parma ham, finely diced	3 oz.	84 gm
Shallots, finely minced	2 oz.	56 gm
Arborio Italian rice, (uncooked weight)	6 oz.	168 gm
Chicken stock, hot	32 fl. oz.	960 ml
Porcine mushrooms, flash-frozen, diced	4 oz.	112 gm
White shrimp, 16–20 count, raw, headless, cleaned, peeled, deveined, washed, halved	20 oz.	560 gm
Chives, short-cut	3 Tbsp.	21 gm
Fresh, cracked white pepper	to taste	to taste
Kosher salt	to taste	to taste
Parmesan cheese, fresh, grated	2 oz.	56 gm
Garnish:		
Arugula leaves, young	½ lb.	227gm

CHEF'S NOTES
Serve risotto with garlic oregano toast points.

PREPARATION

1. In large saucepan, heat olive oil. Add ham; sauté gently to caramelize.
2. Add shallots; cook until translucent.
3. Add rice, stir thoroughly, and sauté for 2 minutes over low heat.
4. Add hot chicken stock, slowly (4 fl. oz. at a time), stirring frequently with wooden spoon. Mixture will become creamy and silken in appearance. This will take approximately 20 minutes. Rice is to be firm to the bite, but not raw.
5. Add diced porcine, shrimp, and chives. Return to low heat, cook gently, and add more hot stock to retain creamy texture. Heat thoroughly for 5 to 7 minutes.
6. Adjust seasoning with pepper and a little salt.
7. Finish risotto with parmesan.

PRESENTATION

Serve at once on deep plate, lined with cleaned arugula leaves.

NUTRITION PER SERVING

Calories 183, protein 18 gm, fat 5 gm, carbohydrates 16 gm, cholesterol 119 mg, sodium 337 mg

CHILI EMPANADAS WITH ROASTED POBLANO VEGETABLE SAUCE

YIELD: ABOUT 30 EMPANADAS

INGREDIENTS	AMOUNT/U.S.	METRIC
Fabricated Certified Angus Beef™, bottom sirloin butt flap, finely diced	1 lb.	448 gm
Serrano chilies, cleaned, seeded, membrane removed, finely minced	3	3
Ginger, fresh, minced	1 tsp.	2 gm
Garlic, minced	4 cloves	4 cloves
Onion, cleaned, finely diced	3 oz.	84 gm
Cumin powder	1 tsp.	5 gm
Teriyaki marinade, light	3 Tbsp.	45 ml
Vegetable spray	as needed	
Green olives, stuffed, finely diced	12	12
Roma tomatoes, peeled, seeded, diced	2 oz.	56 gm
Parsley, chopped	2 Tbsp.	15 gm
Lemon grass, finely minced	2 Tbsp.	15 gm
Fresh, cracked white pepper	to taste	to taste
Empanada Dough	to taste	to taste
Roasted Poblano Vegetable Sauce (p. 104)		

PREPARATION

1. In large mixing bowl, place cleaned, diced pieces of meat. Add chilies, ginger, garlic, onion, cumino powder, and marinade.
2. Combine mixture thoroughly and marinate in refrigerator for at least 1 hour, wrapped with plastic wrap.
3. Spray large, hot, nonstick pan with vegetable spray, wipe out the excess, and dry sauté meat mixture quickly, until evenly browned, stirring frequently.
4. Add olives and tomatoes. Adjust seasoning with parsley, lemon grass, and pepper to taste.
5. Remove mixture from heat and cool in refrigerator.

TO ASSEMBLE EMPANADA

1. Preheat oven to 350°F (175°C).
2. Roll out dough evenly to approximately ⅛" thick. Cut out circles of approximately 3–4" diameter with cutter.
3. Spoon equal amount of filling into center of each dough circle. Fold to form half moon. Moisten edges and seal gently with tines of a fork.
4. Place on sheet pan and bake for 15 minutes, until evenly browned.
5. Serve with Roasted Poblano Vegetable Sauce (p. 104).

Empanada Dough

INGREDIENTS	AMOUNT/U.S.	METRIC
All-purpose flour, sifted	16 oz.	448 gm
Kosher salt	1 tsp.	5 gm
Baking powder	2 oz.	56 gm
Ricotta cheese, part skim, cold	8 oz.	224 gm
Vegetable shortening	2 oz.	56 gm
Iced water	3 fl. oz.	90 ml

PREPARATION

1. In clean stainless steel mixing bowl, sift flour with salt and baking powder.
2. In food processor, place ricotta cheese and add shortening. Add flour mixture and combine with quick on-and-off pulse motion, just until the dough starts to form. Stop machine, scrape sides with rubber spatula, add iced water, and repeat until dough forms, approximately 30 seconds total time. Do not overwork dough in processor or it toughens and is not workable.
3. Remove dough from processor, form into ball, wrap tightly in plastic wrap, and refrigerate for at least 2 hours prior to use.

NUTRITION PER EMPANADA
Calories 109, protein 6 gm, fat 4 gm, carbohydrates 13 gm, cholesterol 11 mg, sodium 358 mg

ROASTED POBLANO VEGETABLE SAUCE

YIELD: 32 FL. OZ./960 ML
(2 OZ./60 ML SERVING)

CHEF'S NOTES

For this sauce recipe we opted for the Roasted Vegetable Sauce. However, a reduction of brown stock will also work well. This will affect the nutritional information, albeit minimally.

Replace half the poblano peppers with regular red, green, or yellow bell peppers for a less hot sauce. Use a high quality chicken stock to thin out consistency of sauce, as desired.

INGREDIENTS

INGREDIENTS	AMOUNT/U.S.	METRIC
Poblano peppers, fresh, washed, towel dry	2 lb.	900 gm
Olive oil	1 Tbsp.	15 ml
Roasted Vegetable Sauce (p. 174)	24 oz	720 ml
Lemon, juice of	1	1
Garlic, roasted, minced	5 cloves	5 cloves
Kosher salt	to taste	to taste
Fresh, cracked black pepper	to taste	to taste
Chives, short-cut	1 oz.	28 gm
Cilantro, short-cut	1 oz.	28 gm
Chicken stock, high-quality	as needed	as needed

PREPARATION

1. Brush peppers with olive oil and place on small sheet pan. Roast at 400°F (205°C) until nicely browned and skin is evenly blistered all around.
2. Remove from oven, place in bowl, and cover with plastic wrap. Allow to cool to room temperature.
3. Peel and remove seeds and core. Place pepper flesh in blender, add Roasted Vegetable Sauce, lemon juice, and roasted garlic, and puree.
4. Adjust seasoning with salt and pepper.
5. Place in saucepan; add chives and cilantro. If needed, adjust consistency with chicken stock until smooth.
6. Bring slowly to boil.

NUTRITION PER SERVING
Calories 51, protein 1 gm, fat 2 gm, carbohydrates 8 gm, cholesterol 0 mg, sodium 12 mg

ROASTED PEPPER
AND OLIVE SALAD *

SERVES 8

INGREDIENTS	AMOUNT/U.S.	METRIC
Red bell peppers, cleaned	1 lb.	450 gm
Green bell peppers, cleaned	1 lb.	450 gm
Yellow bell peppers, cleaned	1 lb.	450 gm
English cucumber, peeled, seeded, diced	4 oz.	112 gm
Roma tomatoes, peeled, seeded, julienned	8 oz.	224 gm
Red onion, julienned	4 oz.	112 gm
Black kalamata olives, pitted, quartered	30	30
Serrano pepper, seeded, membrane removed, finely minced	1	1
Cilantro, finely minced	1 oz.	28 gm
White rice wine vinegar	4 fl. oz.	120 ml
Olive oil	1 Tbsp.	15 ml
Sherry	1 fl. oz.	30 ml
Kosher salt	to taste	to taste
Fresh, cracked white pepper	to taste	to taste

PREPARATION

1. Preheat oven to 375°F (190°C).
2. Brush pepper skins with some olive oil. Roast peppers until evenly browned and the skins are blistered.
3. Place in bowl, cover with plastic wrap, and allow to cool until you can handle them comfortably.
4. Peel peppers, remove seeds and membrane, cut into strips, and place in large mixing bowl.
5. Add cucumber, tomato, onion, olives, serrano pepper, and cilantro; combine gently.
6. Add vinegar, olive oil, and sherry, and adjust seasoning with salt and pepper. Allow flavor to mature for at least 2 hours. Prior to serving, adjust seasoning and, allow to come to room temperature.

NUTRITION PER SERVING
Calories 109, protein 2 gm, fat 4 gm, carbohydrates 16 gm, cholesterol 0 mg, sodium 389 mg

CHICKEN AND FRUIT SALAD

SERVES 8

INGREDIENTS	AMOUNT/U.S.	METRIC
Chicken Salad:		
Chicken meat, roasted, skinless, diced	16 oz.	448 gm
Red grapes, seedless	6 oz.	168 gm
Celery, finely diced	6 oz.	168 gm
Apple, red-skinned, finely diced	6 oz.	168 gm
Mayonnaise, nonfat	4 tsp.	20 ml
Sour cream, light (40% less fat)	4 tsp.	20 ml
Yogurt, nonfat, plain	3 Tbsp.	45 ml
Mustard, Grey Poupon™	4 tsp.	20 ml
Italian salad dressing, fat-free	3 Tbsp.	45 ml
Basil, snipped	1 Tbsp.	5 gm
Garlic seasoning, salt-free	1 tsp.	3 gm
Lawry's™ seasoning, salt-free	1 tsp.	4 gm
Fruit:		
Cantaloupe, peeled and cubed	1½ lbs.	675 gm
Honeydew, peeled and cubed	1½ lbs.	675 gm
Pineapple, peeled and cubed	1½ lbs.	675 gm
Strawberries, trimmed, cut in half	1½ lbs.	675 gm
Garnish:		
Curly endive		

PREPARATION

1. In mixing bowl, combine all ingredients for chicken salad and mix well.
2. Place chicken salad on a bed of curly endive. Arrange cubed fruit around plate. Serve rye or sesame crackers on the side.

NUTRITION PER SERVING

Calories 271, protein 20 gm, fat 4 gm, carbohydrates 41 gm, cholesterol 49 mg, sodium 254 mg

ORANGE AND WATERMELON SALAD

SERVES 8

INGREDIENTS	AMOUNT/U.S.	METRIC
Watermelon, 1-inch cubes	1 lb. 8 oz.	675 gm
Oranges, fresh, cut into segments	4	4
Red onion, minced	3 oz.	80 gm
Cilantro, fresh snipped	2 Tbsp.	10 gm
Orange rind, grated (zest)	1 tsp.	6 gm
Vegetable stock	8 fl. oz.	240 ml
Cornstarch	2 tsp.	5 gm
Rice wine vinegar	2⅓ Tbsp. + 1 tsp.	35 ml
Lime juice, fresh	1 Tbsp.	15 ml
Orange juice, fresh	2 Tbsp.	30 ml
Fresh, cracked white pepper	to taste	to taste
Red oak leaf lettuce	4 oz.	112 gm
Red leaf lettuce	4 oz.	112 gm
Bibb lettuce	4 oz.	112 gm
Radicchio	8 leaves	8 leaves
Belgian endive	8 spears	8 spears
Cilantro sprigs for garnish		

PREPARATION

1. In large mixing bowl, combine prepared watermelon, orange segments, onion, cilantro, and orange zest. Marinate for 2 hours.
2. Bring vegetable stock to boil, and thicken with cornstarch that has been combined with a small amount of stock. Cool and whisk into vinegar and juices to form an emulsion.
3. Combine "dressing" with watermelon mixture; stir carefully. Add pepper to taste.
4. Prepare greens. Use whole leaf of radicchio per salad serving to form cup for watermelon. Place spear of Belgian endive sticking up for garnish.
5. Place a few ounces of greens in each radicchio cup and spoon in watermelon. Drizzle remaining dressing over the top, and garnish with a sprig of cilantro.

NUTRITION PER SERVING
Calories 84, protein 2 gm, fat 1 gm, carbohydrates 19 gm, cholesterol 0 mg, sodium 92 mg

CRAB MEAT SALAD
IN RED PLUM TOMATOES

SERVES 12

INGREDIENTS	AMOUNT/U.S.	METRIC
Plum tomatoes, peeled, halved; remove seeds and pulp	12	12
White balsamic vinegar	2 Tbsp.	30 ml
Olive oil	1 Tbsp.	15 ml
Marjoram, snipped	1 tsp.	1 gm
Parsley, chopped	1 tsp.	1 gm
Fresh, cracked white pepper	to taste	to taste
Kosher salt	to taste	to taste
Crab Meat Salad (below)		

PREPARATION

1. Preheat oven to 300°F (150°C)
2. Place tomatoes in bowl and toss with vinegar, olive oil, marjoram, parsley, and pepper and salt to taste.
3. Place tomatoes (pouring remaining liquid over them) on small sheet pan in oven and roast gently for 1½ hours. Rotate pan occasionally for consistent roasting.
4. Remove and cool completely.
5. Fill with Crab Meat Salad.

CRAB MEAT SALAD

INGREDIENTS	AMOUNT/U.S.	METRIC
Miller's® Select lump crab meat, pasteurized, cleaned, drained	8 oz.	224 gm
Red onion, finely diced	2 oz.	56 gm
Lemon, juice of	1	1
Celery, peeled, finely diced	2 oz.	56 gm
Basil, finely snipped	1 Tbsp.	5 gm
Chives, short-cut	1 Tbsp.	5 gm
Yogurt, nonfat, plain	2 oz.	56 gm
Kosher salt	to taste	to taste
Cayenne pepper	to taste	to taste
Fresh, cracked white pepper	to taste	to taste

PREPARATION

1. Clean crab meat, combine with onion, lemon juice, celery, basil, and chives.

2. Add yogurt, and adjust seasoning with salt, cayenne pepper, and white pepper.

3. Combine filling gently and marinate for 1 hour. Adjust seasoning.

NUTRITION PER SERVING OF CRAB MEAT SALAD ALONE

Calories 25, protein 4 gm, fat 0 gm, carbohydrates 1 gm, cholesterol 19 mg, sodium 61 mg

NUTRITION PER SERVING OF COMPLETE SALAD

Calories 49, protein 5 gm, fat 1 gm, carbohydrates 4 gm, cholesterol 19 mg, sodium 66 mg

MANGO APPLE SALAD

SERVES 6

INGREDIENTS	AMOUNT/U.S.	METRIC
Mangos, peeled, sliced into segments	1 lb.	448 gm
Apples, peeled, cored, sliced into segments	1 lb.	448 gm
Orange juice	4 fl. oz.	120 ml
Lime juice	2 fl. oz.	60 ml
Mint leaves, snipped	1 oz.	28 gm
Coriander seeds, toasted	1 Tbsp.	7 gm

CHEF'S NOTES

Serve as a dessert or afternoon snack.

PREPARATION

1. Place mangos and apples into clean stainless steel bowl, add orange and lime juice, then add mint and toasted coriander seeds.

2. Toss gently and marinate overnight in refrigerator.

NUTRITION PER SERVING

Calories 144, protein 1 gm, fat 1 gm, carbohydrates 37 gm, cholesterol 0 mg, sodium 3 mg

GREEN LENTIL SALAD
WITH BEAN SPROUTS

SERVES 8

INGREDIENTS	AMOUNT/U.S.	METRIC
Salad:		
Green lentils, dry weight French green, high quality	10 oz.	280 gm
Chicken stock	2 qt.	1920 ml
Bay leaf	2	2
Spring onions, cleaned, finely diced	6	6
Bean sprouts	5 oz.	140 gm
Pineapple, fresh, cleaned, diced	8 oz.	224 gm
Watercress leaves, cleaned, crisped	4 oz.	112 gm
Dressing:		
Olive oil	1 Tbsp.	15 ml
Rice vinegar	3 Tbsp.	45 ml
Dijon mustard	1 Tbsp.	15 ml
Honey	1 Tbsp.	15 ml
Kosher salt	to taste	to taste
Fresh, cracked white pepper	to taste	to taste
Garnish:		
Sunflower seeds, toasted	2 oz.	56 gm

PREPARATION

1. Place soaked, rinsed, and drained lentils in medium stockpot.
2. Add chicken stock and bay leaf; cook lentils until tender, yet still firm to the touch.
3. Remove bay leaf and drain lentils, retaining ⅓ of the cooking liquid.
4. Spread lentils on cookie sheet and cool.
5. Prepare dressing by combining olive oil, vinegar, mustard, honey, and cooled cooking liquid. Season to taste with salt and pepper.
6. Toss dressing with lentils, spring onions, bean sprouts, pineapple, and watercress.
7. Adjust seasoning and serve chilled, garnished with sunflower seeds.

NUTRITION PER SERVING

Calories 244, protein 13 gm, fat 8 gm, carbohydrates 33 gm, cholesterol 0 mg, sodium 221 mg

SOUTHWESTERN CAESAR SALAD

SERVES 8

INGREDIENTS	AMOUNT/U.S.	METRIC
Romaine lettuce	2 heads	2 heads
Red, yellow, and green bell peppers, cleaned, seeded, and trimmed	1 each	1 each
Vegetable spray	as needed	
Corn, fresh, cut from cob	2 ears	2 ears
Cornbread Croutons	6 oz.	168 gm
Parmesan cheese, grated	3 oz.	84 gm
Southwestern Caesar Dressing (p. 112)		

PREPARATION
1. Wash and trim lettuce. Remove tough outer leaves. Tear into bite-size pieces, about 1″ in size. Pat, spin, or drain dry.
2. Cut peppers into 1″ julienne strips. Add to lettuce in bowl.
3. Preheat oven to 375°F (190°C).
4. Lightly coat sheet pan with vegetable spray. Spread corn kernels evenly on pan. Place corn in hot oven and roast for 5 minutes, stirring once to ensure even roasting.
5. Remove corn from oven and allow to cool. Add to lettuce mixture.
6. Add cornbread croutons and toss salad well. Garnish with parmesan cheese.

PRESENTATION
Serve with Southwestern Caesar Dressing (p. 112).

Cornbread Croutons

1. Preheat oven to 350°F (175°C).
2. Prepare cornbread using your favorite recipe.
3. Lightly coat sheet pan with vegetable spray. Cut cooked cornbread into ½″ cubes and spread evenly on pan.
4. Roast croutons for approximately 5 minutes, stirring once to ensure even browning. Remove from oven and allow to cool.

NUTRITION PER SERVING FOR SALAD WITHOUT DRESSING
Calories 101, protein 4 gm, fat 3 gm, carbohydrates 16 gm, cholesterol 11 mg, sodium 69 mg

NUTRITION PER SERVING FOR SALAD WITH 1 OZ./30 ML OF DRESSING
Calories 136, protein 5 gm, fat 6 gm, carbohydrates 17 gm, cholesterol 11 mg, sodium 245 mg

SOUTHWESTERN CAESAR DRESSING

YIELD: 48 OZ./1440 ML
(1 OZ./30 ML SERVING)

CHEF'S NOTES

Dressing is best when pre-pared at least one day ahead.

INGREDIENTS	AMOUNT/U.S.	METRIC
Garlic, roasted	3 cloves	3 cloves
Shallot, minced	1	1
Jalapeño pepper, seeded, minced	1	1
Cilantro, cleaned, chopped	3 oz.	84 gm
Spinach, fresh, cleaned, chopped	5 oz.	140 gm
Dijon mustard	4 oz.	112 gm
Lemon, juice of	1	1
Lime, juice of	1	1
Anchovy fillets	4	4
Parmesan cheese, fresh, grated	2 Tbsp.	30 gm
Egg substitute	4 fl. oz.	120 ml
Champagne vinegar	8 fl. oz.	240 ml
Chicken stock, lied	9 fl. oz.	270 ml
Olive oil	4 fl. oz.	120 ml
Kosher salt	to taste	to taste
Fresh, cracked white pepper	to taste	to taste

PREPARATION

1. In blender, combine all ingredients except olive oil and half of the vine-gar and stock. Blend until smooth, approximately 1 minute. Add remaining vinegar and stock and blend for another 30 seconds.
2. Slowly add olive oil to mixture while blending on low speed. Once all the oil is incorporated, season with salt and pepper to taste. Place in stain-less steel container, cover tightly, and refrigerate.

PRESENTATION

Serve with Southwestern Caesar Salad (p. 111).

NUTRITION PER 1 OZ./30 ML SERVING

Calories 35, protein 1 gm, fat 3 gm, carbohydrates 1 gm, cholesterol 0 mg, sodium 176 mg.

CRACKED WHEAT SALAD WITH CITRUS AND GREEN ONIONS
SERVES 8

INGREDIENTS	AMOUNT/U.S.	METRIC
Bulgur wheat or couscous	12 oz.	336 gm
Chicken stock or water	21 fl. oz.	630 ml
Green onions, short-cut	4 oz.	112 gm
Garlic, oven-roasted, minced	2 cloves	2 cloves
Roma tomatoes, peeled, seeded, diced	16 oz.	448 gm
Celery, peeled, diced	8 oz.	224 gm
English cucumbers, peeled, seeded, diced	8 oz.	224 gm
Lemon juice	3 Tbsp.	45 ml
Orange, juice of	2	2
Kosher salt	to taste	to taste
Fresh, cracked white pepper	to taste	to taste
Parsley, chopped	3 Tbsp.	21 gm
Cilantro, chopped	1 Tbsp.	15 gm

CHEF'S NOTES

Use as a salad or serve as a filling for pita pocket sandwiches.

PREPARATION

1. Stir bulgur wheat or couscous into boiling stock or water, cover, remove from heat, and let rest for 5 minutes. Fluff mixture with fork and spread on sheet pan to cool.
2. Place in stainless steel mixing bowl with green onions, garlic, tomatoes, celery, and cucumbers and combine thoroughly.
3. Adjust seasoning with lemon and orange juice, salt, pepper, parsley, and cilantro.

NUTRITION PER SERVING
Calories 182, protein 7 gm, fat 1 gm, carbohydrates 41 gm, cholesterol 0 mg, sodium 41 mg

VEGETABLE AND EGGPLANT SALAD

SERVES 8

INGREDIENTS	AMOUNT/U.S.	METRIC
Zucchini squash, cleaned, peeled, coarsely diced	8 oz.	224 gm
Eggplant, cleaned, peeled, coarsely diced	8 oz.	224 gm
Red onion, cleaned, peeled, sliced	4 oz.	112 gm
Celery, cleaned, peeled, coarsely diced	8 oz.	224 gm
Olive oil	2 Tbsp.	30 ml
Garlic, minced	6 cloves	6 cloves
Tomato, cleaned, peeled, diced	8 oz.	224 gm
Capers, small	3 Tbsp.	45 gm
White balsamic vinegar or sherry wine vinegar	6 fl. oz.	180 ml
Chicken stock, high-quality	4 fl. oz.	120 ml
Black kalamata olives, pitted, quartered	12	12
Sugar	1 tsp.	5 gm
Fresh, cracked white pepper	to taste	to taste
Kosher salt	to taste	to taste
Cilantro, chopped	2 Tbsp.	30 gm
Vegetable spray	as needed	

Garnish:

Radicchio and endive

PREPARATION

1. Prepare all vegetables, by washing, cleaning, paper towel drying and cutting appropriately, evenly and consistently.
2. In large sauté pan, coated with vegetable spray, dry sauté zucchini, eggplant, onion, and celery. Vegetables are to be lightly browned and translucent. Place in large bowl and set aside.
3. Add olive oil to sauté pan. Add garlic and gently sweat over low heat. Add tomatoes, capers, vinegar, and stock.
4. Bring mixture to gentle boil. Add kalamata olives and sugar.
5. Adjust seasoning with salt and pepper.
6. Add sautéed vegetables to mixture and heat thoroughly. Adjust seasoning. Add chopped cilantro. Remove from heat.
7. Allow mixture to rest in large bowl, cool prior to serving, but allow flavor to mature.

PRESENTATION

Serve with radicchio and endive garnish (optional).

NUTRITION PER SERVING

Calories 77, protein 2 gm, fat 5 gm, carbohydrates 10 gm, cholesterol 0 mg, sodium 319 mg

VEGETABLE SALAD IN LIME VINAIGRETTE

SERVES 8

INGREDIENTS	AMOUNT/U.S.	METRIC
English cucumber, julienned	8 oz.	224 gm
Jicama, julienned	5 oz.	140 gm
Radishes, julienned	8	8
Red, yellow, and green peppers, seeded, julienned	½ each	½ each
Yellow pear tomatoes	16	16
Zucchini, peeled, sliced	5 oz.	140 gm
Red onion, thinly sliced	3 oz.	84 gm
Baby chicory or endive lettuce, small	2 heads	2 heads
Red oak leaf lettuce, small	2 heads	2 heads
Garnish:		
Chives, short-cut	2 oz.	56 gm
Cilantro sprigs	16	16
Lime Vinaigrette:		
Limes, grated, peel and juice of	5	5
Pink grapefruit, juice of	1	1
Rice vinegar	2 Tbsp.	30 ml
Cilantro, chopped	1 Tbsp.	15 gm
Olive oil	1 Tbsp.	15 ml
Cumin seeds	to taste	to taste
Cardamon	to taste	to taste
Kosher salt	to taste	to taste
Fresh, cracked white pepper	to taste	to taste

PREPARATION

1. In a clean stainless steel bowl, combine lime vinaigrette ingredients. Add cucumber, jicama, radishes, peppers, tomatoes, zucchini, and onion. Allow to marinate for 1 hour.

PRESENTATION

Arrange lettuce leaves on platter. Place vegetables in center of platter. Garnish with chives and cilantro sprigs.

NUTRITION PER SERVING

Calories 107, protein 5 gm, fat 3 gm, carbohydrates 20 gm, cholesterol 0 mg, sodium 115 mg

NAPA CABBAGE SLAW

SERVES 8

INGREDIENTS	AMOUNT/U.S.	METRIC
Ginger, fresh grated	¼ oz.	7 gm
Sesame oil	1 Tbsp.	15 ml
Chicken stock	1 fl. oz.	30 ml
Pink grapefruit, juice of	2 each	2 each
Napa cabbage, washed, cleaned, finely julienned	8 oz.	224 gm
Spinach leaves, cleaned, washed, julienned	6 oz.	168 gm
Red bell pepper, cleaned, seeded, membrane removed	3 oz.	84 gm
Yellow bell pepper, cleaned, seeded, membrane removed	3 oz.	84 gm
Kosher salt	to taste	to taste
Fresh, cracked white pepper	to taste	to taste

PREPARATION

1. In a clean stainless steel mixing bowl, place ginger, sesame oil, chicken stock, and grapefruit juice. Combine thoroughly.
2. Toss cabbage, spinach, and peppers with dressing.
3. Marinate mixture for 1 hour. Adjust seasoning with salt and fresh cracked white pepper.

NUTRITION PER SERVING

Calories 41, protein 1 gm, fat 2 gm, carbohydrates 5 gm, cholesterol 0 mg, sodium 23 mg

CUCUMBER SALAD

SERVES 8

INGREDIENTS	AMOUNT/U.S.	METRIC
English cucumber, peeled, cored, bias cut	2 lb.	908 gm
Red onion, julienned	6 oz.	168 gm
Basil, fresh, snipped	1 Tbsp.	7 gm
Chives, short-cut	1 Tbsp.	7 gm
Olive oil	1 Tbsp.	15 ml
Rice vinegar	3 fl. oz.	90 ml
Sugar, white	1 Tbsp.	15 gm
Kosher salt	to taste	to taste
Fresh, cracked white pepper	to taste	to taste

PREPARATION

1. Place cucumbers and onions in large stainless bowl. Toss with basil, chives, olive oil, vinegar, and sugar.
2. Season to taste with salt and pepper. Combine thoroughly and place in refrigerator to chill. Adjust seasoning prior to serving.

NUTRITION PER SERVING

Calories 58, protein 1 gm, fat 2 gm, carbohydrates 9 gm, cholesterol 0 mg, sodium 216 mg

FENNEL, CARROT, LEEK SALAD

SERVES 8

INGREDIENTS	AMOUNT/U.S.	METRIC
Fennel, fresh, julienned	1 lb.	448 gm
Carrots, peeled, julienned	5 oz.	140 gm
Leeks, trimmed, julienned	3 oz.	84 gm
Olive oil	1 Tbsp.	15 ml
White balsamic vinegar	2 fl. oz.	60 ml
Orange, juice of	1	1
Mint leaves, fresh, snipped	2 Tbsp.	14 gm
Kosher salt	to taste	to taste
Fresh, cracked white pepper	to taste	to taste

PREPARATION

1. Quickly blanch fennel, carrots, and leeks, separately, in lightly salted water, drain. Rinse in cold water and drain excess water off. Paper towel dry.
2. Place in large stainless steel bowl and toss with olive oil, vinegar, orange juice, and mint leaves, and adjust seasoning with salt and pepper.
3. Chill in refrigerator to allow flavors to fully develop before serving.

NUTRITION PER SERVING

Calories 53, protein 2 gm, fat 2 gm, carbohydrates 8 gm, cholesterol 0 mg, sodium 14 mg

SAUTÉED GINGERED SHRIMP WITH LENTIL BULGUR SALAD*

SERVES 10

INGREDIENTS	AMOUNT/U.S.	METRIC
Large brown shrimp, Compass® brand, 16/ to 0 peeled, deveined	40 pc.	40 pc.
Paprika powder	1 tsp.	2 gm
Fresh, cracked white pepper,	2 tsp.	4 gm
Tamari sauce, light	3 fl. oz.	90 ml
Olive oil	1 Tbsp.	15 ml
Lemon, juice of	1	1
Ginger, fresh, minced	1 oz.	28 gm
Mustard, dry	2 tsp.	4 gm
Tabasco	10 drops	10 drops
Cilantro, snipped	2 Tbsp.	15 gm
Lentil Bulgur Salad (below)		

Lentil Bulgur Salad:

Bulgur wheat, cooked	6 oz.	168 gm
Green lentils, cooked	8 oz.	224 gm
Red bell pepper, cleaned, seeded, diced	1 oz.	28 gm
Green bell pepper, cleaned, seeded, diced	1 oz.	28 gm
Yellow bell pepper, cleaned, seeded, diced	1 oz.	28 gm
Yellow onion, peeled finely diced	2 oz.	56 gm
Cumin powder	1 tsp.	2 gm
Cilantro, snipped	2 Tbsp.	15 gm
Lemon, juice of	1	1
Kosher salt	to taste	to taste
Rice vinegar	3 Tbsp.	45 ml
Olive oil, virgin	2 Tbsp.	30 ml

PREPARATION OF SHRIMP

1. Combine all ingredients except shrimp in stainless steel mixing bowl. Mix thoroughly; add cleaned shrimp. Marinate for 1 hour.
2. In large sauté pan, pan-sear shrimp quickly in two batches over medium-high heat to obtain even color on both sides (3–4 minutes).
3. Remove from heat. Serve shrimp with Lentil Bulgur Salad.

PREPARATION OF SALAD

1. For the salad, combine bulgur wheat with lentils, in a clean stainless steel mixing bowl. Add red, green, and yellow bell peppers and combine.
2. Add onion, cumin, cilantro, lemon juice, vinegar, and olive oil.

3. Adjust seasoning with ground pepper and a little salt. Combine thoroughly. Allow flavors to develop for 1 hour.
4. Before serving, adjust seasoning.

NUTRITION PER SERVING OF SHRIMP
Calories 104, protein 16 gm, fat 3 gm, carbohydrates 3 gm, cholesterol 110 mg, sodium 273 mg

NUTRITION PER SERVING OF SALAD
Calories 76, protein 3 gm, fat 3 gm, carbohydrates 10 gm, cholesterol 0 mg, sodium 88 mg

NUTRITION PER SERVING OF SHRIMP AND SALAD
Calories 180, protein 19 gm, fat 6 gm, carbohydrates 13 gm, cholesterol 110 mg, sodium 361 mg

ASPARAGUS SALAD

SERVES 12

INGREDIENTS	AMOUNT/U.S.	METRIC
Asparagus, fresh, peeled, trimmed, ends removed	2 lb.	908 gm
Olive oil	2 Tbsp.	30 ml
Kosher salt	to taste	to taste
Fresh, cracked white pepper	to taste	to taste

PREPARATION

1. Steam asparagus until fork goes in with ease. Cool in ice bath. Drain and paper towel dry. Cut asparagus in half lengthwise. Toss with olive oil. Season to taste with salt and pepper.

NUTRITION PER SERVING

Calories 38, protein 2 gm, fat 2 gm, carbohydrates 3 gm, cholesterol 0 mg, sodium 2 mg

SPICY FRUIT SALAD

SERVES 12

INGREDIENTS	AMOUNT/U.S.	METRIC
Simple syrup (sugar water)	5 fl. oz.	150 ml
Orange juice	12 fl. oz.	360 ml
Ginger, fresh, minced	1 oz.	28 gm
Sambal oelek (red pepper paste)	1 tsp.	5 gm
Honeydew and cantaloupe balls, fresh	1 lb.	448 gm
Orange segments, fresh	1 lb.	448 gm
Grapes, fresh, cleaned, washed	1 lb.	448 gm
Pineapple, fresh, diced	1 lb.	448 gm

PREPARATION

1. Combine simple syrup with orange juice, ginger, and sambal paste.
2. Combine with fruits. Marinate overnight in refrigerator.

NUTRITION PER SERVING

Calories 140, protein 1 gm, fat 1 gm, carbohydrates 36 gm, cholesterol 0 mg, sodium 34 mg

TOMATO SALAD

SERVES 8

INGREDIENTS	AMOUNT/U.S.	METRIC
Plum tomatoes, blanched, peeled	2 lb.	908 gm
Red onion, julienned	5 oz.	140 gm
Capers, small	2 oz.	56 gm
Olive oil	1 fl. oz.	30 ml
Rice vinegar	3 fl. oz.	90 ml
Kosher salt	to taste	to taste
Fresh, cracked white pepper	to taste	to taste
Arugula, chiffonade (optional)	1 bunch	1 bunch

PREPARATION

1. Cut tomatoes into segments. Remove pulp, using outside flesh only. Pulp can be used for making stocks.
2. In a clean stainless steel bowl, toss tomato segments with onions, capers, olive oil, and vinegar.
3. Adjust seasoning with a little salt and pepper. Cover with plastic wrap.
4. Refrigerate. Adjust seasoning prior to serving.
5. Sprinkle tomato salad with a chiffonade of arugula (optional).

NUTRITION PER SERVING

Calories 78, protein 1 gm, fat 4 gm, carbohydrates 9 gm, cholesterol 0 mg, sodium 665 mg

MUSHROOM SALAD

INGREDIENTS	AMOUNT/U.S.	METRIC
Olive oil	1 fl. oz.	30 ml
White onions, finely diced	5 oz.	140 gm
White mushrooms, cleaned, halved	2 lb.	908 gm
Chicken stock, high-quality	5 fl. oz.	150 ml
Rice vinegar	2 fl. oz.	60 ml
Bay leaves	2	2
Rosemary, needles only	½ oz.	14 gm
Mustard seeds	½ oz.	14 gm
Chives, short-cut	1 oz.	28 gm
Kosher salt	to taste	to taste
Fresh, cracked white pepper	to taste	to taste

PREPARATION

1. In sauté pan, heat olive oil. Sweat onions, add mushrooms, and sweat for 5 minutes.
2. Add stock, vinegar, bay leaves, rosemary, mustard seeds, and chives. Continue to cook for 5 minutes over low heat.
3. Remove from heat and place in clean stainless steel bowl. Cool thoroughly; marinate overnight. Adjust seasoning with salt and pepper.

NUTRITION PER SERVING

Calories 123, protein 4 gm, fat 6 gm, carbohydrates 14 gm, cholesterol 0 mg, sodium 198 mg

YOUNG BEET SALAD

SERVES 8

CHEF'S NOTES

Although the deep red color may discourage some cooks from using beets, beets make a superb alternative salad and are very refreshing.

INGREDIENTS	AMOUNT/U.S.	METRIC
Beets, young, fresh	2 lb.	980 gm
White onion, finely sliced	5 oz.	140 gm
Olive oil	1 Tbsp.	15 ml
Apple cider vinegar	3 fl. oz.	90 ml
Cilantro leaves, snipped	1 oz.	28 gm
Sugar	½ oz.	14 gm
Kosher salt	to taste	to taste
Fresh, cracked white pepper	to taste	to taste
Spring onions, short-cut	1 oz.	28 gm

PREPARATION

1. Clean and wash beets thoroughly under cold water. Remove tops, and place beets in boiling salted water. Cook until tender but still firm. Remove from heat and drain and rinse with cold water. Using gloves, peel beets (this works best when working under cold water).

2. Place peeled beets in stainless steel bowl. Using a mandolin, cut beets into small strips.

3. In separate bowl, combine onion, olive oil, vinegar, cilantro, and sugar. Add salt and pepper to taste. Add beets to the onion mixture.

4. Marinate salad for several hours in refrigerator. Adjust seasoning before serving.

5. Add spring onions just prior to serving.

NUTRITION PER SERVING

Calories 82, protein 2 gm, fat 2 gm, carbohydrates 15 gm, cholesterol 0 mg, sodium 91 mg

POTATO SALAD

SERVES 8

INGREDIENTS	AMOUNT/U.S.	METRIC
Fingerling potatoes, washed, thinly sliced, blanched	2 lb.	908 gm
Chicken stock	1 qt.	960 ml
White onions, julienned	8 oz.	224 gm
Mustard seeds, cracked	1 Tbsp.	15 gm
Champagne vinegar	3 fl. oz.	90 ml
Olive oil	1 fl. oz.	30 ml
Chives, short-cut	½ oz.	14 gm
Kosher salt	to taste	to taste
Fresh, cracked white pepper	to taste	to taste

PREPARATION

1. Place potatoes in boiling stock. Reduce heat and simmer until tender but still firm.
2. Remove from heat. Add onions and mustard seeds.
3. In separate bowl, combine vinegar, olive oil, and chives. Adjust seasoning with salt and pepper. Mix well. Pour over potatoes.
4. Cool in refrigerator. Adjust seasoning prior to serving.

NUTRITION PER SERVING

Calories 152, protein 3 gm, fat 5 gm, carbohydrates 25 gm, cholesterol 0 mg, sodium 10 mg

QUINOA AND VEGETABLE SALAD

SERVES 16

CHEF'S NOTE

To prepare the quinoa (keen'-wa), which is a grain high in protein and, botanically speaking, the dried fruit of an herb, should be washed thoroughly to remove the natural coating, which can taste bitter or soapy.

INGREDIENTS	AMOUNT/U.S.	METRIC
Couscous, dry, raw weight	1 lb.	448 gm
Quinoa, washed, cooked	½ lb.	227 gm
Cucumber, washed, seeded, diced	1 lb.	448 gm
Tomatoes, peeled, seeded, diced	8 oz.	224 gm
Red onion, diced	6 oz.	168 gm
Olive oil	1 fl. oz.	30 ml
Apple cider vinegar	3 fl. oz.	90 ml
Kosher salt	to taste	to taste
Fresh, cracked white pepper	to taste	to taste
Cilantro leaves, fresh, snipped	1 oz.	28 gm

PREPARATION

1. To prepare the couscous use 1 lb. (448 gm) couscous and 28 oz. (840 ml) of boiling water or stock and stir. Cover, remove from heat, and let rest for 5 minutes. Fluff with fork and spread on sheet pan to cool.

2. Add quinoa to 16 oz. (480 ml) of boiling water or stock and stir. Cook gently for 12 minutes. Drain, fluff, and spread on sheet pan to cool.

3. Wash, clean, and cut cucumber, tomatoes, and onions. Toss with olive oil and vinegar in large stainless steel bowl. Add couscous and quinoa.

4. Adjust seasoning with salt, pepper, and cilantro leaves.

5. Cool and marinate overnight. Adjust seasoning prior to serving.

NUTRITION PER SERVING

Calories 185, protein 6 gm, fat 3 gm, carbohydrates 34 gm, cholesterol 0 mg, sodium 15 mg

COUSCOUS SALAD

SERVES 10

INGREDIENTS	AMOUNT/U.S.	METRIC
Couscous, dry, raw weight	16 oz.	448 gm
Carrots, fresh, brunoise cut	4 oz.	112 gm
Zucchini squash, peeled, finely diced	3 oz.	84 gm
Red bell pepper, finely diced	4 oz.	112 gm
Green (spring) onions	3 oz.	84 gm
Parsley, fresh, snipped	2 Tbsp.	15 gm
Lemon, juice of	3	3
Olive oil	2 Tbsp.	30 ml
Rice wine vinegar	4 Tbsp.	60 ml
Kosher salt	to taste	to taste
Fresh, cracked white pepper	to taste	to taste

PREPARATION

1. To prepare the couscous use 16 oz. (448 gm) couscous and 28 oz. (840 ml) of boiling water or chicken stock and stir. Cover, remove from heat, and let rest covered for 5 minutes. Fluff mixture with a fork and spread on a sheet pan to cool.
2. Place carrots, zucchini, and pepper in clean stainless steel bowl. Add green onion, parsley, lemon juice, olive oil, and vinegar. Adjust seasoning with salt and fresh cracked pepper.
3. Refrigerate mixture. Prior to serving, adjust seasoning.

NUTRITION PER SERVING

Calories 217, protein 6 gm, fat 3 gm, carbohydrates 40 gm, cholesterol 0 mg, sodium 123 mg

SWEET AND SOUR CARROT SALAD

SERVES 8

INGREDIENTS	AMOUNT/U.S.	METRIC
Carrots, peeled, sliced	1 lb.	448 gm
Olive oil	1 Tbsp.	15 ml
White onion, julienned	8 oz.	224 gm
Rice vinegar	2 fl. oz.	60 ml
Chicken stock, high-quality	3 fl. oz.	90 ml
Honey	1 fl. oz.	30 ml
Sugar	½ oz.	14 gm
Kosher salt	to taste	to taste
Fresh, cracked white pepper	to taste	to taste

PREPARATION

1. Prepare and wash all vegetables. Blanch carrots quickly in slightly salted boiling water. Drain thoroughly and paper towel dry.
2. In saucepan, heat olive oil, add onion, and sweat quickly. Deglaze with vinegar. Add stock, honey, and sugar, and salt and pepper to taste.
3. Bring to a boil. Toss mixture with carrots and cool.
4. Adjust seasoning before serving. Serve chilled.

NUTRITION PER SERVING

Calories 84, protein 1 gm, fat 2 gm, carbohydrates 16 gm, cholesterol 0 mg, sodium 163 mg

CUCUMBER CABBAGE SALAD

SERVES 8

INGREDIENTS	AMOUNT/U.S.	METRIC
Napa cabbage, fresh, young	25 oz.	700 gm
Sambal oelek (red pepper paste)	1 tsp.	5 gm
Rice wine vinegar	3 fl. oz.	90 ml
Olive oil	1½ fl. oz.	45 ml
English cucumbers, peeled, seeded, diced	15 oz.	420 gm
Yellow onion, peeled, finely diced	3 oz.	84 gm
Green onions, cleaned, short-cut	3 oz.	84 gm
Kosher salt	to taste	to taste
Fresh, cracked white pepper	to taste	to taste

PREPARATION

1. Wash Napa cabbage heads. Remove core and cut into 2" pieces. Paper towel dry.
2. In a clean stainless steel mixing bowl, combine sambal oelek, vinegar, and olive oil.
3. Add cucumber, yellow and green onions. Add the thoroughly drained cabbage to mixture.
4. Toss salad gently, combining thoroughly. Adjust seasoning with salt and pepper.
5. Cover with plastic wrap and refrigerate for 1 hour to allow flavor to develop.

NUTRITION PER SERVING
Calories 95, protein 2 gm, fat 5 gm, carbohydrates 10 gm, cholesterol 0 mg, sodium 232 mg

TOMATO-BACON VINAIGRETTE *

INGREDIENTS	AMOUNT/U.S.	METRIC
Dijon mustard	1 Tbsp.	15 gm
Lemon juice	2 Tbsp.	30 ml
Olive oil	2½ fl. oz.	70 ml
Apple cider vinegar	2 Tbsp.	30 ml
Dry white wine	2 Tbsp.	30 ml
Garlic, minced	2 cloves	2 cloves
Red onion, finely diced	2 oz.	56 gm
Basil, fresh, snipped	1 Tbsp.	5 gm
Cilantro, fresh, snipped	1 Tbsp.	5 gm
Thyme, fresh, minced	2 Tbsp.	10 gm
Bacon, sautéed, minced	1 Tbsp.	15 gm
Honey	2 fl. oz.	56 ml
Chicken stock	6 fl. oz.	180 ml
Tomatoes, oven-roasted, chopped	12 oz.	336 gm
Kosher salt	to taste	to taste
Fresh, cracked white pepper	to taste	to taste

PREPARATION

1. Place all ingredients in stainless steel mixing bowl. Use submersible blender and blend until desired consistency. Adjust seasoning with salt and pepper.
2. Place in stainless steel container, cover tightly, and refrigerate.

NUTRITION PER 1 OZ./30 ML SERVING

Calories 43, protein 0 gm, fat 3 gm, carbohydrates 4 gm, cholesterol 1 mg, sodium 25 mg

APPLE CIDER VINAIGRETTE*

INGREDIENTS	AMOUNT/U.S.	METRIC
Apple cider	24 fl. oz.	720 ml
Hazelnut oil	2 fl. oz.	60 ml
Cider vinegar	3 fl. oz.	90 ml
Chives, short-cut	1 Tbsp.	5 gm
Basil, fresh, snipped	1 Tbsp.	5 gm
Kosher salt	to taste	to taste
Fresh, cracked white pepper	to taste	to taste

PREPARATION

1. In small stainless steel saucepan, heat apple cider, reducing it by one-third. Remove from heat and allow to cool.
2. Combine oil and vinegar with cooled cider. Mix well. Add chives and basil, and adjust seasoning with salt and pepper.
3. Place in stainless steel container, cover tightly, and refrigerate.

NUTRITION PER 1 OZ./30 ML SERVING
Calories 36, protein 0 gm, fat 3 gm, carbohydrates 3 gm, cholesterol 0 mg, sodium 1 mg

CREAMY BASIL MAYONNAISE

YIELD: 19 OZ./560 ML
(1 OZ./30 ML SERVING)

INGREDIENTS	AMOUNT/U.S.	METRIC
Arugula, fresh, snipped	1 oz.	28 gm
Basil, fresh, snipped	1 oz.	28 gm
Rice wine vinegar	4 fl. oz.	120 ml
Olive oil	2 Tbsp.	30 ml
Garlic, minced	1 clove	1 clove
Chicken stock, high-quality	4 fl. oz.	120 ml
Mayonnaise, fat-free, high-quality	8 oz.	224 gm
Kosher salt	to taste	to taste
Fresh, cracked white pepper	to taste	to taste

PREPARATION

1. Prepare and clean arugula and basil.
2. Place all ingredients except mayonnaise in blender and puree gently, approximately 2 minutes. Add mayonnaise and puree until smooth.
3. Adjust seasoning with salt and pepper.
4. Place in stainless steel container, cover tightly, and refrigerate.

NUTRITION PER 1 OZ./30 ML SERVING

Calories 33, protein 0 gm, fat 2 gm, carbohydrates 4 gm, cholesterol 0 mg, sodium 283 mg

RED ONION DRESSING

YIELD: 20 OZ./600 ML

(1 OZ./30 ML SERVING)

INGREDIENTS	AMOUNT/U.S.	METRIC
Red onion, finely minced	2 oz.	56 gm
Red wine vinegar	6 fl. oz.	180 ml
Basil leaves, dried	1½ tsp.	1.5 gm
Olive oil	2 Tbsp.	30 ml
Sugar	¼ tsp.	1.25 gm
Chicken stock	4 fl. oz.	120 ml
Mayonnaise, fat-free	8 oz.	224 gm
Kosher salt	¼ tsp.	1.25 gm
Fresh, cracked black pepper	¼ tsp.	.5 gm

PREPARATION

1. In mixing bowl, thoroughly combine all ingredients except mayonnaise.
2. Add mayonnaise, and whisk mixture until smooth. Adjust seasoning with salt and pepper.
3. Place in clean stainless steel container, cover tightly, and refrigerate.

NUTRITION PER 1 OZ./30 ML SERVING

Calories 25, protein 0 gm, fat 1 gm, carbohydrates 3 gm, cholesterol 0 mg, sodium 184 mg

SIMPLE VINAIGRETTE

YIELD: 15 OZ./450 ML
(1 OZ./30 ML SERVING)

Chopped herbs or pungents can be added for variety with minimal change in the calories.

INGREDIENTS	AMOUNT/U.S.	METRIC
Chicken or vegetable stock, high-quality	8 fl. oz.	240 ml
Cornstarch or arrowroot	1 tsp.	2.5 gm
Rice wine vinegar	4 fl. oz.	120 ml
Balsamic vinegar	2 Tbsp.	30 ml
Olive oil, virgin	2 fl. oz.	60 ml
Kosher salt	to taste	to taste
Fresh, cracked white pepper	to taste	to taste

PREPARATION

1. Bring stock to boil. Combine cornstarch or arrowroot with a little cold water, stir until smooth. Gradually stir cornstarch or arrowroot thickener into boiling stock until it is thick enough to coat back of spoon.
2. Remove from heat and cool stock. Whip remaining ingredients into cooled stock. Adjust seasoning with salt and pepper.
3. Place in stainless steel container, cover tightly, and refrigerate.

NUTRITION PER 1 OZ./30 ML SERVING

Calories 45, protein 0 gm, fat 4 gm, carbohydrates 2 gm, cholesterol 0 mg, sodium 152 mg

HONEY MUSTARD DRESSING

YIELD: 12 OZ./360 ML
(1 OZ./30 ML SERVING)

INGREDIENTS	AMOUNT/U.S.	METRIC
Dijon mustard	2 Tbsp.	30 gm
Lemon juice	1 Tbsp.	15 ml
Olive oil	1 fl. oz.	30 ml
Cider vinegar	4 Tbsp.	60 ml
Sherry	4 Tbsp.	60 ml
Honey	3 Tbsp.	45 ml
Garlic, minced	2 cloves	2 cloves
Red onion, minced	1 oz.	28 gm
Marjoram, snipped	1 Tbsp.	7 gm
Basil, fresh, snipped	1 Tbsp.	7 gm
Cilantro, fresh, snipped	1 Tbsp.	7 gm
Chicken stock, defatted	4 fl. oz.	120 ml
Kosher salt	to taste	to taste
Fresh, cracked black pepper	to taste	to taste
Thyme, fresh, snipped	3 tbsp.	21 gm

PREPARATION

1. In blender, blend all ingredients except thyme until thoroughly combined. Adjust seasoning with salt and pepper. Add snipped thyme leaves just before dressing a salad.
2. Place in stainless steel container, cover tightly, and refrigerate.

NUTRITION PER 1 OZ./30 ML SERVING

Calories 50, protein 0 gm, fat 3 gm, carbohydrates 6 gm, cholesterol 0 mg, sodium 105 mg

CREAMY CAPER DRESSING

YIELD: 40 OZ./1200 ML
(1 OZ./30 ML SERVING)

CHEF'S NOTES

For a salad dressing, add additional stock to make a creamy consistency. For a dip-style dressing, reduce vinegar and yogurt by one-half.

INGREDIENTS	AMOUNT/U.S.	METRIC
Ricotta cheese, low-fat, pureed	7 oz.	196 gm
Yogurt, nonfat	14 oz.	392 gm
Dijon mustard	2 oz.	56 gm
Rice wine vinegar	7 fl. oz.	210 ml
Capers, small, or caperberries, chopped	2 oz.	56 gm
Chives, short-cut	⅓ oz.	9 gm
Basil, snipped	1 Tbsp.	5 gm
Cilantro, snipped	⅓ oz.	9 gm
Red onion, finely minced	2 oz.	56 gm
Garlic, roasted, minced	2 cloves	2 cloves
Chicken stock	4 fl. oz.	120 ml
Kosher salt	to taste	to taste
Fresh, cracked white pepper	to taste	to taste

PREPARATION

1. Combine all ingredients in stainless steel bowl. Mix with rubber spatula or whisk until smooth. Adjust seasoning with salt and pepper.
2. Place in stainless steel container, cover tightly, and refrigerate.

NUTRITION PER 1 OZ./30 ML SERVING

Calories 22, protein 1 gm, fat 1 gm, carbohydrates 3 gm, cholesterol 2 mg, sodium 242 mg

SAVORY BLUE DRESSING

YIELD: 41 OZ./1230 ML
(1 OZ./30 ML SERVING)

INGREDIENTS	AMOUNT/U.S.	METRIC
Mayonnaise, fat-free, high-quality	8 oz.	224 gm
Ricotta cheese, fat-free	8 oz.	224 gm
Yogurt, nonfat, plain	8 oz.	224 gm
Buttermilk, low-fat (1%)	8 fl. oz.	240 ml
Maytag™ Blue cheese, crumbled	8 oz.	224 gm
Rice wine vinegar	2 Tbsp.	30 ml
Chives, fresh, short-cut	3 Tbsp.	15 gm
Kosher salt	¼ tsp.	1.25 gm
Fresh, cracked white pepper	½ tsp.	1 gm
Worcestershire sauce	1 tsp.	1 tsp.

PREPARATION

1. Combine mayonnaise, ricotta, and yogurt with buttermilk, add blue cheese crumbles, and combine thoroughly.
2. Add rice wine vinegar and fold in chives. Adjust seasoning with salt, pepper, and Worcestershire sauce.
3. Place in stainless steel container, cover tightly, and refrigerate.

NUTRITION PER 1 OZ./30 ML SERVING

Calories 34, protein 3 gm, fat 2 gm, carbohydrates 3 gm, cholesterol 5 mg, sodium 185 mg

SPICY REMOULADE

YIELD: 48 OZ./1440 ML
(1 OZ./30 ML SERVING)

CHEF'S NOTES

Serve with cold meats, seafood, or roasted vegetables. May also be served as a dip or sandwich spread.

INGREDIENTS	AMOUNT/U.S.	METRIC
Mayonnaise, fat-free, high-quality	8 oz.	224 gm
Ricotta cheese, fat-free	8 oz.	224 gm
Yogurt, nonfat, plain	8 oz.	224 gm
Buttermilk, low-fat (1 %)	8 fl. oz.	240 ml
Tomato puree	4 oz.	120 ml
Grey Poupon™ Dijon mustard	3 Tbsp.	45 gm
Rice wine vinegar	2 Tbsp.	30 ml
Parsley, fresh, minced	2 oz.	56 gm
Green olives, stuffed, finely chopped	2 oz.	56 gm
Dill pickles, finely chopped	6 oz.	168 gm
Tabasco™ Sauce	10 drops	10 drops
Worcestershire sauce	1½ tsp.	9 gm
Fresh, cracked white pepper	to taste	to taste

PREPARATION

1. Combine mayonnaise, ricotta, and yogurt with buttermilk. Add tomato puree and combine thoroughly.
2. Stir in mustard and vinegar.
3. Add parsley, olives, and pickles. Adjust seasoning with Tabasco and Worcestershire sauce and pepper to taste.
4. Place in stainless steel container, cover tightly, and refrigerate.

NUTRITION PER 1 OZ./30 ML SERVING

Calories 17, protein 1 gm, fat 0 gm, carbohydrates 3 gm, cholesterol 1 mg, sodium 181 mg

POBLANO CHILI DRESSING

YIELD: 54 OZ./1620 ML

(1 OZ./30 ML SERVING)

INGREDIENTS	AMOUNT/U.S.	METRIC
Plum tomatoes, cored, halved	1½ lb.	680 gm
Cooked yield	12 oz.	336 gm
Poblano peppers, washed and cleaned	2 lb.	908 gm
Cooked yield	7 oz.	196 gm
Olive oil	1 oz.	30 ml
Garlic, peeled, oven roasted, minced	4 cloves	4 cloves
Tomato puree	3 fl. oz.	90 ml
Mayonnaise, fat-free, high-quality	8 oz.	224 gm
Ricotta cheese, low-fat	8 oz.	224 gm
Yogurt, nonfat, plain	8 oz.	224 gm
Buttermilk, low-fat (1%)	8 fl. oz.	240 ml
Oregano, snipped	1 Tbsp.	5 gm
Chives, short-cut	1 oz.	28 gm
Tabasco™ sauce	10 drops	10 drops
Worcestershire sauce	⅓ tsp.	2 gm
Kosher salt	to taste	to taste
Fresh, cracked white pepper	to taste	to taste

PREPARATION

1. Clean tomatoes and peppers. Rub with olive oil and oven roast, along with garlic.
2. Remove from oven, peel garlic, and peel and seed tomatoes and peppers, reserving flesh. Cool and chop coarsely.
3. Combine these with tomato puree and puree in blender.
4. Remove and combine with mayonnaise, ricotta, yogurt, and buttermilk. Adjust seasoning with oregano, chives and Tabasco, Worcestershire sauce; add salt and fresh cracked pepper to taste. Combine mixture thoroughly.
5. Place in stainless steel container, cover tightly, and refrigerate.

NUTRITION PER 1 OZ./30 ML SERVING
Calories 21, protein 1 gm, fat 1 gm, carbohydrates 3 gm, cholesterol 1 mg, sodium 73 gm

SESAME-TERIYAKI DRESSING

YIELD: 48 OZ./1440 ML
(1 OZ./30 ML SERVING)

INGREDIENTS	AMOUNT/U.S.	METRIC
Onion, finely diced	10 oz.	280 gm
Ginger, fresh, finely diced	½ oz.	14 gm
Sesame oil, pure	2 Tbsp.	30 ml
Garlic, oven-roasted, minced	5 cloves	5 cloves
Mayonnaise, fat-free, high-quality	8 oz.	224 gm
Ricotta cheese, fat-free	8 oz.	224 gm
Yogurt, nonfat, plain	8 oz.	224 gm
Buttermilk, low-fat (1%)	4 fl. oz.	120 ml
Teriyaki marinade, light, and sauce	6 fl. oz.	180 ml
Chili sauce	4 Tbsp.	60 ml
Chives, fresh, short-cut	6 Tbsp.	30 gm
Cilantro, fresh, chopped	3 Tbsp.	15 gm
Rice wine vinegar	1 Tbsp.	15 ml
Fresh, cracked white pepper	1 tsp.	2 gm

PREPARATION

1. In sauté pan, sauté onion and ginger in sesame oil until translucent, approximately 10 minutes over low heat. Add roasted garlic. Remove from heat and cool thoroughly.
2. Combine mayonnaise, ricotta, yogurt, and buttermilk. Stir in teriyaki sauce, chili sauce, chives, cilantro, and rice vinegar. Blend in cooled onion mixture, and adjust seasoning with fresh cracked pepper.
3. Place in stainless steel container, cover tightly, and refrigerate.

NUTRITION PER 1 OZ./30 ML SERVING
Calories 23, protein 1 gm, fat 1 gm, carbohydrates 3 gm, cholesterol 2 mg, sodium 212 mg

ROASTED GARLIC VINAIGRETTE

INGREDIENTS	AMOUNT/U.S.	METRIC
Garlic	3 heads	3 heads
Olive oil	2½ fl. oz.	75 ml
Kosher salt	to taste	to taste
Dijon mustard	1 oz	28 gm
Red wine vinegar	1½ fl. oz.	45 ml
Balsamic vinegar	1 fl. oz.	30 ml
Chicken stock	4 fl. oz.	120 ml
Kosher salt	to taste	to taste
Fresh, cracked white pepper	to taste	to taste

PREPARATION

1. Place whole heads of garlic on small sheetpan or roasting pan. Drizzle with ½ fl. oz. (15 ml) olive oil, sprinkle with salt, and bake at 250°F (125°C) for about ¾ to 1 hour, until soft to the touch.
2. When slightly cooled, remove garlic cloves and squeeze garlic into bowl. Mash with fork. Add mustard and vinegars. Add 2 fl. oz. (60 ml) olive oil and whip well.
3. Thin with stock, and adjust seasoning with salt and pepper.

NUTRITION PER 1 OZ./30 ML SERVING

Calories 53, protein 0 gm, fat 5 gm, carbohydrates 2 gm, cholesterol 0 mg, sodium 60 mg

CREAMY TARRAGON DRESSING

YIELD: 22 OZ./660 ML
(1 OZ./30 ML SERVING)

INGREDIENTS	AMOUNT/U.S.	METRIC
Mayonnaise, nonfat	8 oz.	224 gm
Yogurt, nonfat, plain	4 oz.	112 gm
Buttermilk, low-fat (1%)	2 fl. oz.	60 ml
Red onion, finely diced	2 oz.	56 gm
Rice wine vinegar	4 fl. oz.	120 ml
Tarragon, fresh, snipped	1 Tbsp.	7 gm
Dijon mustard	2 oz.	56 gm
Fresh, cracked white pepper	1 tsp.	2 gm
Kosher salt	½ tsp.	2.5 gm

PREPARATION

1. Combine all ingredients. Mix well. Chill in refrigerator at least 1 hour before serving.

NUTRITION PER 1 OZ./30 ML SERVING

Calories 24, protein 1 gm, fat 0 gm, carbohydrates 4 gm, cholesterol 0 mg, sodium 361 mg

RASPBERRY DRESSING

YIELD: 32 OZ./960 ML
(1 OZ./30 ML SERVING)

INGREDIENTS	AMOUNT/U.S.	METRIC
Raspberries, frozen, thawed	16 oz.	448 gm
Red onions, finely diced	2	2
Raspberry vinegar	4 fl. oz.	120 ml
Chicken stock	4 fl. oz.	120 ml
Sesame oil	1 Tbsp.	15 ml
Cayenne pepper	1 pinch	1 pinch
Sugar	¼ tsp.	1.25 gm
Mayonnaise, fat free	8 oz.	224 gm

PREPARATION

1. Combine all ingredients except mayonnaise in blender and puree. Add mayonnaise and puree until smooth.

NUTRITION PER 1 OZ./30 ML SERVING

Calories 28, protein 0 gm, fat 1 gm, carbohydrates 6 gm, cholesterol 0 mg, sodium 84 mg

SHERRY VINAIGRETTE

YIELD: 16 OZ./480 ML

(1 OZ./30 ML SERVING)

INGREDIENTS	AMOUNT/U.S.	METRIC
Sherry vinegar, good quality	8 fl. oz.	240 ml
Grey Poupon Country French™ Dijon mustard	2 Tbsp.	30 gm
Mustard, dry	1 Tbsp.	15 gm
Garlic, minced	2 cloves	2 cloves
Chicken or vegetable stock	5 fl. oz.	150 ml
Cornstarch or arrowroot slurry	as needed	as needed
Kosher salt	to taste	to taste
Fresh, cracked white pepper	to taste	to taste
Olive oil	4 Tbsp.	60 ml

PREPARATION

1. In stainless steel mixing bowl, place vinegar, mustard, mustard powder, and garlic, and combine thoroughly.
2. Slightly thicken stock with cornstarch slurry for better consistency of dressing, and gently whisk into vinegar mixture.
3. Adjust seasoning with salt and pepper, and whisk in olive oil.

NUTRITION PER 1 OZ./30 ML SERVING

Calories 54, protein 0 gm, fat 4 gm, carbohydrate 1 gm, cholesterol 0 mg, sodium 146 mg

CHAPTER 9

STOCKS, SOUPS, SAUCES, RELISHES, AND SPREADS

@

THE CHEF'S TOOLS OF THE TRADE DON'T STOP WITH A KNIFE KIT, THEY MUST INCLUDE TIME MANAGEMENT SKILLS, FINANCIAL ACUMEN AND INTERPERSONAL SKILLS, JUST TO NAME A FEW.

Chef Ronald De Santis, CMC

YOUR REPUTATION AS A COOK STANDS ON THE LAST MEAL THAT YOU SERVED. IN COOKING DO THE SIMPLE THINGS WELL AND THE FOOD WILL BE SIMPLY DELICIOUS. COOKING IS HEAT TRANSFER, CULINARY ARTS IS THE INFLUENCE OF THE COOK.

Chef Noel C. Cullen, Ed.D., CMC

THERE IS NOTHING IN THIS WORLD AS BEAUTIFUL AS THE COLORS, SHAPES, AND TEXTURES OF THE FOODS WE HAVE TO WORK WITH. TO EAT HEALTHY MEANS TO FULLY UNDERSTAND FOODS OF ALL TYPES AND THEIR CONTRIBUTION TO OUR LIFESTYLE. IT REQUIRES EDUCATION, UNDERSTANDING, AND MODIFICATION, NOT JUST FOLLOWING RECIPES.

Chef Michael Robbins, CMC

*An asterisk following a recipe title indicates that the recipe also appears in another chapter.

Stocks are fundamental to good cooking. They are the backbone for our sauces and soups. In nutritional cooking, stocks are frequently used as flavor enhancers and as a cooking medium. As with any good cuisine, they should compliment the taste and flavor of the food served. The basic stock recipes provided in this book will work well with all the recipes where stock is utilized.

One of the main virtues of a recipe lies in its stock. Stock is sometimes known as a "free flavor" because of its ability to subtly enhance flavor, depth, and integrity, while adding very little fat and few calories, less than 5 calories per ounce. Stocks can be saved and reused, provided they are stored properly and safely.

Clearly one can intensify the flavor of these stock recipes to suit personal taste and liking, by adding other aromatics, pungents, and flavor enhancers, as well as reducing the strained stocks to create a higher level of concentration for the production of soups and sauces.

In the traditional kitchen, stocks are referred to as *fonds de cuisine,* the foundation of cooking, an essential component in major cooking techniques. In general, stocks may be used freely to add taste and flavor to foods during the cooking process. Stocks can also be lied, or "tightened," with root and tuber starches, such as arrowroot and potato, respectively, or with the cereal starch cornstarch.

Stocks are primarily used to make sauces and soups. The basic stocks are white, brown, fish, and vegetable.

White stock is a broth which, by its definition, has no color. It is produced with white meats, aromatics, and vegetables. White stock is used as a liquid in white-based sauces, in stews, and for poaching poultry.

Brown stock is produced with beef, veal, or poultry bones, depending on preference and recipe, along with aromatics and roasted vegetables. It is used as the liquid in brown sauces, in braising larger cuts of protein, as well as in stews.

Fish stock is produced with the cleaned bones and trimmings of flat fish. The liquid consists of water, wine, aromatics, and vegetables. This stock is used in the preparation of fine fish sauces and also as a cooking medium for poaching and shallow poaching.

Vegetable stock is produced by utilizing high-quality, cleaned vegetables and water, with aromatics and seasonings. This stock can be utilized for all preparations, particularly by reducing it, and using it as a seasoning agent for vegetables. Vegetable stock plays an important role in vegetarian cooking and may be used in many other dishes. Starchy vegetables, such as potatoes, sweet potatoes, and winter squash, make a stock cloudy, therefore if clarity is important, these vegetables should not be used when making the stock. Strong-flavored vegetables such as Brussels sprouts, cauliflower, and artichokes can overwhelm the stock with a strong flavor or odor and are best avoided, as are dark green leafy vegetables such as spinach. Remove skins from onions to avoid discoloring the stock. Using a small amount of olive oil and "sweating" the vegetables will produce a nice, subtle flavor.

Court Bouillon, or quick broth, is seasoned vegetable broth that includes wine and/or vinegar and is commonly used for poaching seafood.

Remouillage is the second stock made from the same bones, vegetables, and aromatics that were used for a first stock. This stock is usually not as strong or flavorful as the first drawn stock. However, it is used in soup production as a braising medium and can also be reduced for use as a glaze.

When preparing stocks, remember the following points to keep them as lean as possible, and always evaluate them on the basis of flavor, color, aroma, and clarity.

- Remove excess fat from the bones before beginning the cooking process. Also, remove excess fat from the pan after roasting the bones. Add none or use minimal fat to sauté the vegetables and pungents. Use stock, wine, or other liquids to sweat the vegetables.

- The addition of flavor comes from the techniques utilized in preparing stocks (caramelizing or roasting of bones and vegetables) and the addition of pungents and herbs or highly flavored liquids like wine.

- Skim excess fat, or refrigerate and then remove hardened fat from the top of the stock.

Stocks prepared with the recipes given, and which observe these guidelines, will produce a highly flavored, low-fat stock. Although exact nutritional information is not available for these recipes (because no data is available regarding the fat quantity in bones), it would be safe to assume that if the guidelines are followed, these stocks will be virtually fat-free and very low in calories. They will be comparable with high-quality commercial products. If using a high-quality commercial product, be sure to read the label and look for products that are natural and contain the least amount of additives.

CHEF'S NOTES

- *Always use the freshest ingredients available.*

- *Start with clean, pure, cold water.*

- *Never boil stock, always gently simmer.*

- *Remove impurities from stock frequently, as impurities will rise to the surface and collect around the edge.*

- *As fat collects along the edge of the pot, degrease the stock using a small ladle in a circular motion.*

- *Cook stocks only for the allotted time.*

- *Never add additional salt.*
- *Do not stir stocks.*
- *Strain and cool stocks properly, preferably in an ice bath to facilitate a safe and rapid cooldown.*
- *Remove excess fat when cold.*
- *Stocks are meant to be the substructure of the recipe, not the dominating flavor.*

SOUPS

THE SOUP SERVED AT A DINNER HAS EQUAL IMPORTANCE AS A UNIQUE

PORTE COCHERE ATTACHED TO A BUILDING.

Grimod de la Reyniere

In the traditional kitchen, when a menu does not include an appetizer, the soup generally becomes the introduction to the meal. When serving a soup, pay particular attention to the total composition of the menu for the taste and color choice of the soup.

We can categorize soups into two groups: clear soups and thick soups. Whereas today there are certainly many applications in the preparation of soups, they are clearly derived from the following classical formulations:

- Clear consommé, broth, or bouillon with the various garnitures and/or fumets
- Consommé lie
- Cream soups
- Velouté-style soups
- Vegetable and leguminous purees and coulis, as well as bisques
- Specialty soups

In preparing soups, it is good to keep in mind that a good soup is determined by its flavor, appearance, and texture. Flavors should be complimentary throughout.

Clear broths or consommés should be clear, not cloudy, and any additional ingredients should be attractively cut, colorful, and add to the eye appeal. Cream soups should be smooth and free of lumps.

CHEF'S NOTES

- *Use full-bodied, reduced stocks free of all fat as the base for soups and sauces.*
- *Thicken soups and sauces with purees of vegetables or legumes instead of the traditional roux.*

◎ *Reduce the amount of salt to no more than ⅓ tsp. (400 mg) per serving.*

◎ *Use fresh herbs, spices, citrus juices, or vinegars to enhance flavor.*

◎ *Base soups on vegetables and legumes.*

◎ *Keep soup portions appropriate: as a starter, a maximum of 6 oz.; as an entrée, a maximum of 10 oz.*

◎ *Sweat vegetables in wine, stock, or other liquid instead of fat.*

◎ *Limit the use of fat, and use only where it does the most justice to the flavor and texture of the soup or sauce.*

◎ *For more accurate control, measure the amount of fat used in sautéing garlic and onions. A small amount of fat can greatly add to the depth and flavor profile of a recipe.*

◎ *Garnish soups and sauces with small amounts of high-fat, high-flavor items, they will give the most impact to the dish while allowing the most control of the use of fats. For example, 1 tsp. of heavy cream or olive oil per portion added to soups just before serving will provide increased flavor depth, sheen, and richness.*

◎ *Use precooked, drained, and chopped bacon instead of rendering the fat into the soup when making such soups as bean and bacon.*

◎ *Be creative with the use of fresh vegetables, herbs, and fruits as a garnish. They add color, texture, and interesting flavors without adding a significant amount of unwanted calories.*

As an alternative to preparing stocks or sauce bases from scratch, there are several excellent products on the market today that one can use as an alternative to in-house produced stocks. These bases are frequently used to save time, maintain consistency in quality, and contain labor and equipment costs. If at all possible when using a commercial base, use one that is a natural product, with little or no chemical additives. When creating a stock made from a base, enhance the flavor profile by adding roasted vegetables, aromatics, and herbs.

Stocks made from a commercial base should be evaluated with the same quality standards as stocks made from scratch, such as flavor, balance of flavor, texture, and color.

Quality speed scratch products (high-quality products prepared from scratch and provided to the consumer in a ready-to-use form or shape) definitely have a future in food service. The foundation of good cooking will always be the use of solid, unadulterated ingredients. This concept coupled with the many techniques and fundamentals learned in the kitchen can result in the development of a skilled and discerning culinarian. However, we also understand that the reality today is an end-user consumer who demands taste, convenience, quality, and health-conscious offerings at a competitive price. Therefore the issue today is not the technology but what to do with it. Culinarians that source and utilize reliable, quality, and honest speed scratch products to enhance their operation's efficiency and productivity could exponentially gain the advantage over their competition. Today's food service manufacturers of speed scratch products certainly can deliver value in terms of improving our performance to the customer we serve.

Another issue when considering the application of speed scratch products is the concern over proper food-handling techniques, food safety, and sanitation. Safety and HACCP (hazard analysis and critical control points) issues are a global concern, in that a safe and reliable food source is demanded worldwide.

The food service professional of the future who can provide a proper balance in utilizing a variety of quality ingredients, such as fresh, frozen, and speed scratch, will ultimately be more effective and well positioned to meet the changing needs of the customer and society at large.

In our recipe development phase we tested such quality speed scratch products. For information on these ready-to-use quality stock and sauce products, see Appendix C, Speed Scratch Sauces and Stocks.

CHICKEN STOCK *

YIELD: 6 QT./5.75 L

INGREDIENTS	AMOUNT/U.S.	METRIC
Chicken carcass and bones	5 lb.	2270 gm
Turkey necks, skinless	5 lb.	2270 gm
Water	8 qt.	7.68 l
White onions, medium, cleaned, diced	3	3
Celery stalks, cleaned, diced	3	3
Leeks, cleaned, diced	3	3
White peppercorns, whole	1 Tbsp.	15 gm
Mustard seeds	1 Tbsp.	15 gm
Parsley, fresh, washed	1 bunch	1 bunch
Bay leaves	4	4
Thyme sprigs, fresh	2	2

PREPARATION

1. Wash chicken bones, carcass, and turkey necks to remove debris. Place into large stock pot with the water and bring to rapid boil. Reduce heat to simmer. Skim impurities as necessary.

2. Add cleaned and cut vegetables to stock; simmer for 1 hour.

3. Add peppercorns, mustard seeds, parsley, bay leaf, and thyme. Continue to simmer for an additional 3 hours.

4. Strain stock into clean stainless steel container and cool rapidly in ice bath.

CHEF'S NOTES

Spring or filtered water, instead of tap water, is recommended.

Adjust the seasoning when using the stock.

To intensify the stock, it can be reduced by half.

Turkey necks are very gelatineous and naturally clarify the stock.

Do not rapidly boil the stock, which will cause the proteins to break down and cloud the stock. Rather use a gentle simmer to extract all the nutrients from the vegetables and poultry products.

BROWN VEAL STOCK *

YIELD: 2 QUARTS/1.9 L

INGREDIENTS	AMOUNT/U.S	METRIC
Veal bones and shanks, fresh	10 lb.	4540 gm
Olive oil	⅓ cup	80 ml
Water	12 qt.	11.4 l
White onions, medium, diced	6	6
Horse carrots, cleaned, diced	6	6
Celeriac, cleaned, diced	1	1
Parsnips, cleaned, diced	5	5
Garlic, head, each bulb horizontally cut in half	1	1
Tomato paste	8 oz.	240 ml
Red wine, good quality	2 cups	480 ml
White peppercorns, fresh	25	25
Mustard seeds	1 Tbsp.	15 gm
Bay leaves	4	4
Rosemary sprig	1	1
Thyme sprigs	4	4

PREPARATION

1. Wash bones and shanks to remove excess blood and debris. Drain and paper towel dry thoroughly.

2. In large roasting pan, toss bones with olive oil. Place in a 450°C (230°C) oven. Roast bones until they give off a distinct aroma and begin to brown evenly. Stir occasionally. Roast until bones are thoroughly browned.

3. Remove bones from roasting pan and place in large (approx. 10-gallon) stock pot. Add the water and bring to boil. Reduce heat to simmer. Skim impurities before adding the mirepoix.

4. Remove all excess grease from roasting pan, and place cleaned and cut vegetables in pan. On stovetop, caramelize vegetables until nicely browned.

5. Add tomato paste, continue to cook until a rusty color develops, and deglaze with red wine. Make sure vegetable mixture browns but does not burn.

6. Add browned vegetable mixture to bones and water. Be sure to remove all caramelized product from roasting pan. Deglaze roasting pan with some liquid from stock pot.

7. Bring stock pot to boil once again, then reduce to simmer. Add small sachet of peppercorns, mustard seeds, bay leaf, rosemary, and thyme. Simmer stock for approximately 5 hours. Be sure to skim impurities.

8. Strain stock and place into clean stock pot. Reduce mixture to two quarts over gentle simmer.

9. Strain stock once again through a fine chinois into a clean stainless steel container, and place into an ice bath to cool rapidly.

@

FISH STOCK *

YIELD: 5 QT./4.8 L

INGREDIENTS	AMOUNT/U.S.	METRIC
Fish bones from white flat fish (preferably sole, turbot, halibut, snapper, or bass)	8 lb.	3632 gm
Celery stalks, cleaned, diced	4	4
Leeks, white part only, cleaned, diced	3	3
Fennel bulbs, cleaned, diced	2	2
White onion, medium, cleaned, diced	3	3
Mushrooms, button, cleaned	½ lb.	227 gm
Coriander seeds	1 Tbsp.	15 gm
Mustard seeds	½ Tbsp.	7 gm
Bay leaves	4	4
White peppercorns, fresh	25	25

CHEF'S NOTES

Spring or filtered water, instead of tap water, is recommended.

Adjust seasoning when using the stock.

To intensify the stock, it can be reduced by half.

Do not rapidly boil the stock, which will cause the proteins to break down and cloud the stock. Rather use a gentle simmer to extract all the nutrients from the vegetables and fish bones.

PREPARATION

1. Clean and wash the fish bones to remove excess blood and debris, and place in large stock pot. Add water (just enough to cover bones), and cleaned and cut vegetables, and bring to quick boil. Reduce heat to simmer. Skim impurities as necessary.

2. Add coriander seeds, mustard seeds, bay leaves, and peppercorns. Gently simmer stock for 45–50 minutes.

3. Strain stock into clean stainless steel container and cool rapidly in ice bath.

@

VEGETABLE STOCK *

YIELD: 4 QT/3.84 L

CHEF'S NOTES

Spring or filtered water, instead of tap water, is recommended.

Adjust the seasoning when using the stock.

To intensify the stock, it can be reduced by half.

Make sure the vegetables are cleaned and washed properly to avoid bitter undertones of flavor.

INGREDIENTS	AMOUNT/U.S.	METRIC
Onions, cleaned, diced	4	4
Fennel bulbs, cleaned, diced	4	4
Celery, cleaned, diced	4	4
Horse carrots, cleaned, diced	3	3
Leeks, cleaned, diced	4	4
Water	6 qt.	5.76 l
Roma tomatoes, cleaned, diced	6	6
Parsley, cleaned	½ bunch	½ bunch
Garlic, roasted	8 cloves	8 cloves
Thyme sprigs	3	3
Bay leaves	3	3
Mustard seeds	½ Tbsp.	7 gm
Kosher salt	1 Tbsp.	15 gm
Black peppercorns	1 Tbsp.	15 gm

PREPARATION

1. In large stock pot, bring water to rapid boil. Reduce heat. Add cleaned and cut vegetables, except tomatoes, herbs, and spices. Bring back to a boil, reduce heat, and simmer mixture for 1 hour.
2. Add tomatoes, parsley, garlic, thyme, bay leaves, mustard seeds, salt, and peppercorns. Continue to simmer additional 45 minutes.
3. Strain stock into clean stainless steel container and cool rapidly in ice bath.

ROOT VEGETABLE SOUP*

SERVES 8 (6 OZ./180 ML. SERVING)

INGREDIENTS	AMOUNT/U.S.	METRIC
Onions, cleaned, medium-diced	4 oz.	112 gm
Parsnips, cleaned, medium-diced	4 oz.	112 gm
Carrots, cleaned, medium-diced	4 oz.	112 gm
Celery, cleaned, medium-diced	4 oz.	112 gm
Garlic, minced	5 cloves	5 cloves
Olive oil	2 tsp.	10 ml
White wine	4 oz.	120 ml
Potatoes, peeled, large-diced	4 oz.	112 gm
Sugar	1 Tbsp.	7 gm
Thyme, fresh, snipped	1 Tbsp.	3 gm
V-8™ juice, low-sodium	6 fl. oz.	180 ml
Chicken stock, defatted, high-quality	48 fl. oz.	1440 ml
Worcestershire sauce	1 Tbsp.	15 ml
Tabasco™ sauce	to taste	to taste
Kosher salt	to taste	to taste
Fresh, cracked white pepper	to taste	to taste
Roma tomatoes, peeled, seeded, diced	10 oz.	280 gm

Garnish:
Basil chiffonade, fresh

CHEF'S NOTES

This soup can be served pureed, by using a submersible blender, or chunky style.

PREPARATION

1. Heat olive oil in large stock pot over medium heat. Add onions, parsnips, carrots, celery, and garlic. Combine thoroughly and sauté until tender and translucent.

2. Deglaze with white wine and reduce liquid by half. Add potatoes, sugar, and thyme. Mix well.

3. Add V–8 juice, chicken stock, Worcestershire sauce, and Tabasco sauce. Add kosher salt and cracked white pepper to taste, and stir gently. Bring to boil, then reduce to simmer. Gently cook for approximately 30 minutes.

4. Add tomatoes and continue to cook gently until vegetables and potatoes are tender.

5. Adjust seasoning prior to serving. Garnish soup with choice of fresh herb, such as chiffonade of fresh basil.

NUTRITION PER SERVING
Calories 97, protein 2 gm, fat 3 gm, carbohydrates 15 gm, cholesterol 0 mg, sodium 52 mg

CHILLED AVOCADO SOUP

SERVES 10 (4 OZ./120 ML SERVING)

NUTRITION NOTES

Avocados are high in fat for a vegetable (approx. 30 gm in one avocado), but it is monounsaturated fat, which a natural, more healthful option. To reduce the fat content you can serve half of a serving of the avocado soup and half of a serving of Roasted Vegetable Gazpacho (p. 170) together in one bowl. The two-tone pattern will create an interesting, flavorful, and compatible dish. Also, high-quality vegetable stock can be substituted for the chicken stock.

INGREDIENTS	AMOUNT/U.S.	METRIC
Yogurt, nonfat, plain	8 oz.	224 gm
Milk, nonfat, skim	8 fl. oz.	240 ml
Avocados, large, ripe	6	6
Lemon juice	3 Tbsp.	45 ml
Kosher salt	to taste	to taste
Fresh, cracked white pepper	to taste	to taste
Basil, fresh, snipped	1 Tbsp.	5 gm
Cilantro, fresh, snipped	1 Tbsp.	5 gm
Red bell peppers, seeded, finely diced	2	2
Chicken stock, high-quality	5 fl. oz.	150 ml
Spring onions, cleaned, finely diced	6	6

PREPARATION

1. In large stainless steel mixing bowl, combine yogurt and milk.
2. In food processor, puree avocado flesh with lemon juice, using pulse motion, alternating with scraping the sides to even the mix.
3. Combine avocado with yogurt mixture.
4. Add basil and cilantro, and adjust seasoning with pepper and salt.
5. Add bell peppers, and adjust consistency with chicken stock. Mix well. Add spring onions.
6. Chill thoroughly to let the flavor mature. Prior to serving, adjust seasoning.

NUTRITION PER SERVING

Calories 218, protein 5 gm, fat 19 gm, carbohydrates 13 gm, cholesterol 1 mg, sodium 44 mg

STEWED WHITE BEAN SOUP

SERVES 10 (6 OZ./180 ML SERVING)

INGREDIENTS	AMOUNT/U.S.	METRIC
White beans, dried, small, cleaned	26 oz.	728 gm
Olive oil	2 fl. oz.	60 ml
Smoked prosciutto, boneless, finely diced	4 oz.	112 gm
Garlic, fresh, minced	8 cloves	8 cloves
Carrots, cleaned, medium-diced	8 oz.	224 gm
Celery, cleaned medium-diced	8 oz.	224 gm
Onion, cleaned, medium-diced	4 oz.	112 gm
Leeks, cleaned, medium-diced	6 oz.	168 gm
Vegetable stock, high-quality	2 qt.	2 l
Chicken stock, high-quality	1 qt.	1 l
Potatoes, peeled, medium-diced	4 oz.	112 gm
Tomatoes, concasse	8 oz.	224 gm
Green beans, fresh, cleaned, cut in half	6 oz.	168 gm
Zucchini, peeled, medium-diced	6 oz.	168 gm
Basil leaves, fresh, snipped	1 oz.	28 gm
Kosher salt	to taste	to taste
Fresh, cracked white pepper	to taste	to taste

CHEF'S NOTES

This soup can be served as is for a hearty meal, or lightened with stock for a less filling soup. It can also be the base for a sauce to be used, for example, with roast pork.

PREPARATION

1. Sort beans. Rinse in cold water; drain. Place in large stainless steel container covered with water and soak overnight.
2. Drain liquid and rinse beans in colander.
3. Place olive oil in heavy stock pot, heat pot, and add smoked prosciutto. Gently caramelize prosciutto. Add garlic, carrots, celery, onion, and leeks. Continue to sauté until translucent. Add drained beans and both stocks.
4. Bring quickly to boil. Reduce heat and simmer gently for 45 minutes. Check frequently.
5. Add potatoes and continue cooking, adjusting seasoning with salt and pepper. Test beans for doneness.
6. During final stages of cooking add tomatoes, beans, and zucchini. Continue to simmer for 10–15 minutes. Adjust seasoning with fresh basil, salt, and pepper.
7. If needed, adjust consistency by adding stock.

NUTRITION PER SERVING
Calories 383, protein 20 gm, fat 9 gm, carbohydrates 60 gm, cholesterol 8 mg, sodium 57 mg

CHILLED TOMATO SOUP
WITH RICE AND BASIL

SERVES 6 (6 OZ./180 ML SERVING)

INGREDIENTS	AMOUNT/U.S.	METRIC
Olive oil	1 Tbsp.	15 ml
Garlic, minced	3 cloves	3 cloves
Red onion, medium, minced	1	1
Roma tomatoes, peeled, seeded, diced	2 lb.	900 gm
Chicken stock, defatted	24 fl. oz.	720 ml
Kosher salt	to taste	to taste
Fresh, cracked white pepper	to taste	to taste
Cilantro, minced	2 Tbsp.	10 gm
Garnish:		
White rice, cooked	2½ oz.	70 gm
Basil, fresh, chiffonade	3 Tbsp.	15 gm

PREPARATION

1. In saucepan, heat olive oil; add garlic and onion. Sauté gently until onion is translucent.
2. Add tomatoes. Cook gently for 5 minutes over medium heat.
3. Add stock and simmer for 15 minutes. Adjust seasoning with salt and pepper to taste.
4. Blend tomato mixture in blender or food processor for 30 seconds. Do not strain.
5. Add cilantro. Taste and adjust seasonings. Chill thoroughly. Serve chilled with garnish of cooked rice and chiffonade of basil.

NUTRITION PER SERVING

Calories 90, protein 2 gm, fat 4 gm, carbohydrates 14 gm, cholesterol 0 mg, sodium 18 mg

SEAFOOD SOUP

SERVES 10 (6 OZ./180 ML SERVING)

INGREDIENTS	AMOUNT/U.S.	METRIC
Olive oil	½ Tbsp.	7 ml
Pancetta, diced	2 oz.	56 gm
Onions, cleaned, finely diced	3 oz.	84 gm
Leeks, cleaned, finely diced	3 oz.	84 gm
Celery, cleaned, finely diced	3 oz.	84 gm
Garlic, minced	4 cloves	4 cloves
Tomato paste	8 oz.	224 gm
White wine	2 fl. oz.	60 ml
Clam juice, bottled	8 fl. oz.	240 ml
Fish stock, high-quality	2 qt.	2 l
Thyme, snipped	¾ tsp.	1 gm
Bay leaves	2	2
Rosemary needles, snipped	¾ tsp.	1 gm
Kosher salt	to taste	to taste
Fresh, cracked white pepper	to taste	to taste
Roma tomatoes, peeled, seeded, diced	8 oz.	224 gm
Shrimp, raw, peeled, diced	8 oz.	224 gm
Catfish, farm-raised, raw, cleaned, diced	8 oz.	224 gm
Lemon, juice of	1	1

CHEF'S NOTES

For a different flavor profile, one can add fresh oregano or marjoram.

PREPARATION

1. Heat heavy stock pot, and gently sauté pancetta in olive oil for 1 minute.
2. Add onion, leeks, celery, and garlic; sauté for 2 minutes. Add tomato paste. Continue to sauté until mixture takes on a rusty color and develops an aroma.
3. Deglaze mixture with white wine and clam juice, stirring gently.
4. Add fish stock and bring to boil. Return to simmer. Add thyme, bay leaf, and rosemary; simmer for 10 minutes until vegetables are tender but still firm.
5. Adjust seasoning with salt and pepper, add tomatoes.
6. Add shrimp and catfish; continue to simmer for additional 10 minutes. Adjust seasoning with lemon juice, salt, and pepper.
7. Serve soup piping hot, but never boil once the fish has been added.

NUTRITION PER SERVING

Calories 127, protein 12 gm, fat 4 gm, carbohydrates 10 gm, cholesterol 52 mg, sodium 184 mg

ACORN SQUASH SOUP

SERVES 10 (6 OZ./180 ML SERVING)

CHEF'S NOTES

This soup will also work using a West Indian pumpkin, calabaza winter squash, or butternut squash.

For smoother viscosity and fuller body, add finely diced potatoes half way through the cooking process.

INGREDIENTS

Ingredient	AMOUNT/U.S.	METRIC
Acorn squash (pureed, cooked weight)	40 oz.	1120 gm
Olive oil	2 Tbsp.	30 ml
Red onions, finely diced	3 oz.	84 gm
Celery, cleaned, diced	4 oz.	112 gm
Garlic, minced	3 cloves	3 cloves
Leeks, cleaned, diced	4 oz.	112 gm
Chicken or vegetable stock, high-quality	20 fl. oz.	600 ml
Honey	1 Tbsp.	15 ml
Nutmeg	1 tsp.	2 gm
Allspice	½ tsp.	1 gm
Cinnamon, ground	½ tsp.	1 gm
Fresh, cracked white pepper	1 Tbsp.	5 gm
Kosher salt	to taste	to taste
Garnish:		
Chives, short-cut	1 oz.	28 gm

PREPARATION

1. Preheat oven to 300°F (150°C). Quarter, seed, and brush acorn squash with 1 Tbsp. olive oil. Bake until evenly browned and tender. Cool, remove all pulp.

2. In nonstick stock pot, heat 1 Tbsp. olive oil and sauté onion, celery, garlic, and leeks until translucent. Add stock and bring to rapid boil. Add squash pulp, honey, nutmeg, allspice, cinnamon, and freshly ground white pepper, and adjust seasoning with salt.

3. Heat thoroughly and combine mixture well. Using submersible blender, puree mixture into fine, light, frothy consistency.

4. Simmer for 20 minutes. Adjust seasoning, and adjust consistency with additional stock.

5. Keep hot until served. Prior to serving, add chives.

NUTRITION PER SERVING

Calories 106, protein 2 gm, fat 2 gm, carbohydrates 23 gm, cholesterol 0 mg, sodium 19 mg

GREEN LENTIL AND PARSNIP SOUP

SERVES 10 (4 OZ./120 ML SERVING)

INGREDIENTS	AMOUNT/U.S.	METRIC
Olive oil	1 Tbsp.	15 ml
Parma ham, lean, diced	3 oz.	84 gm
Yellow onions, diced	7 oz.	196 gm
Garlic, minced	3 cloves	3 cloves
Carrots, cleaned, medium-diced	4 oz.	112 gm
Leeks, cleaned, medium-diced	5 oz.	140 gm
Parsnips, cleaned, medium-diced	4 oz.	112 gm
Caraway	½ tsp.	1.5 gm
Tomato paste	2 oz.	56 gm
Dry sherry	4 fl. oz.	120 ml
Chicken stock	2½ qt.	2½ l
Green lentils, French, dark green (Puy lentils), cleaned, soaked (dry weight)	10 oz.	280 gm
Bay leaves	2	2
Lemon thyme sprigs	3	3
White balsamic vinegar	1 fl. oz.	30 ml
Basil, snipped	1 Tbsp.	3 gm
Kosher salt	to taste	to taste
Fresh, cracked white pepper	to taste	to taste

CHEF'S NOTES

Cool properly after use. Soup can be blended with submersible blender if a smoother soup is desired. When blending, be sure to first remove bay leaves and thyme sprigs.

PREPARATION

1. In medium stock pot, heat olive oil and add Parma ham. Gently render until caramelized. Reduce heat.
2. Add onions and garlic; sweat until translucent.
3. Add carrots, leeks, parsnips, and caraway and continue to sauté for 2 minutes.
4. Add tomato paste and sauté until golden in color.
5. Deglaze vegetables with sherry and chicken stock.
6. Add cleaned, washed, and soaked lentils; bay leaves; and thyme, and simmer over medium heat 25–30 minutes. Add balsamic vinegar and basil, salt and pepper. Continue to simmer over medium heat until lentils and vegetables are tender.
7. Prior to serving, adjust seasoning if necessary. Serve soup hot.

NUTRTION PER SERVING

Calories 191, protein 11 gm, fat 4 gm, carbohydrates 27 gm, cholesterol 6 mg, sodium 106 mg

SWEET ONION BROTH *

SERVES 4 (4 OZ./120 ML SERVING)

INGREDIENTS	AMOUNT/U.S.	METRIC
OSO sweet onions, sliced	8 oz.	224 gm
Olive oil	1 tsp.	5 ml
Caraway seeds	5	5
White wine, dry	3 fl. oz.	90 ml
Lemon thyme, snipped	1 tsp.	2 gm
Chicken stock, high-quality	16 fl. oz.	480 ml
Kosher salt	to taste	to taste
Fresh, cracked white pepper	to taste	to taste

PREPARATION

1. Preheat oven to 325°F (165 °C).
2. Mix OSO sweet onions, olive oil, and caraway seeds. Place into a pre-heated, nonstick pan and slow-roast until browned.
3. Deglaze with white wine, reduce until almost dry.
4. Add thyme and chicken stock. Simmer for 15 minutes. Adjust seasoning with salt and pepper.

NUTRITION PER SERVING

Calories 62, protein 1 gm, fat 2 gm, carbohydrates 7 gm, cholesterol 0 mg, sodium 6 mg

GINGER-TARRAGON BROTH

SERVES 6 (4 OZ./120 ML SERVING)

INGREDIENTS	AMOUNT/U.S.	METRIC
Olive oil	2 tsp.	10 ml
Red onion, finely diced	3 oz.	84 gm
Garlic, minced	1 clove	1 clove
Ginger, fresh, grated	½ tsp.	2 gm
Tomato paste	2 Tbsp.	30 ml
Sherry, dry	2 fl. oz.	60 ml
Chicken stock, defatted, high-quality	1 qt.	1 l
Orange, zest of one large	1	1
Bay leaf	1	1
Tarragon leaves	2 tsp.	3 gm
Fresh, cracked white pepper	to taste	to taste
Kosher salt	to taste	to taste

PREPARATION

1. Heat large, deep saucepan. Add olive oil and onion. Sweat onions gently; add garlic and ginger, stirring continuously.
2. Add tomato paste; sauté until mixture is a rusty color. Deglaze pan with sherry and stock.
3. Add orange zest, bay leaf, and tarragon. Simmer gently for 4 minutes. Adjust seasoning with pepper and a little salt.

NUTRITION PER SERVING

Calories 56, protein 1 gm, fat 3 gm, carbohydrates 6 gm, cholesterol 0 mg, sodium 91 mg

TOMATO-BASIL BROTH *

SERVES 8 (4 OZ./120 ML SERVING)

INGREDIENTS	AMOUNT/U.S.	METRIC
Olive oil	1 Tbsp.	15 ml
Red onion, chopped	2 oz.	56 gm
Garlic, split in half, unpeeled	1 head	1 head
Roma tomatoes, peeled, seeded, diced	1 lb.	450 gm
White wine	¼ cup	60 ml
Chicken stock, defatted	1 qt.	1 l
Kosher salt	to taste	to taste
Fresh cracked white pepper	to taste	to taste

PREPARATION

1. Heat olive oil in 3-quart saucepan; sauté onions and garlic for 2–3 minutes over medium heat (do not brown).
2. Add tomatoes and continue to cook for 3–4 minutes.
3. Add white wine and chicken stock and simmer slowly for 20 minutes.
4. Pass broth through moulli mill, and season with salt and fresh cracked pepper to taste. Keep warm until serving.

NUTRITION PER SERVING

Calories 57, protein 1 gm, fat 3 gm, carbohydrates 7 gm, cholesterol 0 mg, sodium 9 mg

WHITE SHRIMP, BEAN, AND ROOT VEGETABLE SOUP

SERVES 10 (6 OZ./180 ML SERVING)

INGREDIENTS	AMOUNT/U.S.	METRIC
Olive oil, extra virgin	2 Tbsp.	30 ml
Red onion, diced	2 oz.	56 gm
Leeks, diced	4 oz.	112 gm
Garlic, minced	3 cloves	3 cloves
Tomato paste	1 Tbsp.	15 gm
White Italian beans, small, soft, soaked overnight, rinsed, drained	10 oz.	280 gm
Chicken stock, high-quality	80 fl. oz.	2400 ml
Bay leaves	2	2
Carrots, peeled, diced	3 oz.	84 gm
Celery, diced	3 oz.	84 gm
Bell pepper, red, green, and yellow, diced	1 each	1 each
Thyme leaves, fresh	2 sprigs	2 sprigs
Chives, fresh, short-cut	1 Tbsp.	7 gm
White shrimp, 16-20 count, peeled deveined, washed, paper towel dried, cut in half lengthwise	1 lb.	448 gm
Kosher salt	to taste	to taste
Fresh, cracked white pepper	to taste	to taste

CHEF'S NOTES

This soup can also be made with black beans, lentils, broad beans, or any leguminous vegetable.

PREPARATION

1. In heavy-bottomed, medium stock pot, heat olive oil, and gently sweat onions, leeks, and garlic until translucent (about 3 minutes).
2. Add tomato paste and cook until rusty in color. Add drained beans, along with high quality chicken stock, and bay leaves.
3. Simmer gently for 45 minutes; if needed, add additional stock.
4. Add carrots, celery, and bell peppers; continue to cook gently for additional 45 minutes.
5. Test beans for doneness. Beans should be soft yet still retain their shape.
6. Adjust seasoning. Add herbs and white shrimp; stew gently for 7 minutes. Taste and adjust seasoning. Serve hot with crunchy bread.

NUTRITION PER SERVING

Calories 154, protein 13 gm, fat 5 gm, carbohydrates 15 gm, cholesterol 88 mg, sodium 122 mg

ZUCCHINI SOUP WITH YOGURT AND DILL

SERVES 24 (5 OZ./150 ML SERVING)

INGREDIENTS	AMOUNT/U.S.	METRIC
Zucchini, fresh, peeled	2½–3 lb.	1135 gm
Olive oil	2 Tbsp.	30 ml
Onions, cleaned, chopped	24 oz.	672 gm
Garlic, minced	5 cloves	5 cloves
Roma tomatoes, peeled, seeded, diced	8 oz.	224 gm
Chicken stock	24 fl. oz.	720 ml
Kosher salt	to taste	to taste
Fresh, cracked white pepper	to taste	to taste
Tabasco™ sauce	to taste	to taste
Yogurt, nonfat, plain	16 fl. oz.	480 ml
Dill, fresh, snipped	1 oz.	28 gm

PREPARATION

1. Wash, trim and peel zucchini. Cut into ¼" pieces.
2. In medium stainless steel saucepan, heat olive oil and sweat onions and garlic. Cook until transparent. Add zucchini and tomatoes and simmer gently for 5 minutes.
3. Add chicken stock; bring mixture to boil. Reduce heat and simmer for 5–7 minutes.
4. Adjust seasoning with salt, pepper and Tabasco to taste. Remove from heat and puree mixture through food mill, food processor, or submersible blender.
5. Place mixture in clean stainless steel container and cool rapidly.
6. When cold, blend in yogurt and snipped dill. Adjust seasoning prior to serving, and serve soup chilled.

NUTRITION PER SERVING

Calories 44, protein 2 gm, fat 2 gm, carbohydrates 6 gm, cholesterol 0 mg, sodium 19 mg

ROAST TURKEY GUMBO

SERVES 8 (6 OZ./180 ML SERVING)

INGREDIENTS	AMOUNT/U.S.	METRIC
Olive oil	2 Tbsp.	30 ml
Andouille sausage, spicy, cubed	½ lb.	227 gm
Flour	3 Tbsp.	45 gm
Garlic, minced	3 cloves	3 cloves
Red onion, cleaned, diced	3 oz.	84 gm
Red bell pepper, cleaned diced	3 oz.	84 gm
Green bell pepper, cleaned, diced	3 oz.	84 gm
Celery stalks, cleaned, diced	2	2
Chicken stock	1¼ qt.	1200 ml
Tomatoes, seeded, diced	4	4
Fresh, cracked black pepper	⅛ tsp.	.25 gm
Roast turkey meat, pulled	½ lb.	227 gm
Okra, fresh or frozen, cut	5 oz.	140 gm
White rice, cooked	1 lb.	448 gm
Kosher salt	to taste	to taste

PREPARATION

1. In stock pot, heat olive oil and add sausage. Sauté until evenly browned, remove, and drain on paper towels.
2. Add flour to the oil in stock pot and cook until lightly browned.
3. Add garlic, onions, peppers, and celery to flour mixture. Gently cook for 3 minutes, stirring constantly.
4. Add chicken stock and bring mixture to a boil. Add tomatoes, and season with black pepper.
5. Add cooked sausage and turkey meat. Reduce heat and simmer gently for 15 minutes.
6. Add okra; continue to simmer for 5 minutes. Adjust seasoning. Serve over cooked white rice.

NUTRITION PER SERVING

Calories 323, protein 17 gm, fat 14 gm, carbohydrates 34 gm, cholesterol 34 mg, sodium 516 mg

ROASTED VEGETABLE GAZPACHO

SERVES 10 (6 OZ./180 ML SERVING)

INGREDIENTS	AMOUNT/U.S.	METRIC
Green peppers, roasted, peeled, seeded	8 oz.	224 gm
Yellow onions, peeled, sliced, roasted	8 oz.	224 gm
Olive oil	as needed	as needed
Jalapeño pepper, medium, seeded, membrane removed, finely diced	1	1
Roma tomatoes, peeled, seeded, diced	12 oz.	336 gm
English cucumbers, peeled, seeded, chopped	8 oz.	224 gm
Vegetable stock, high-quality, seasoned	1 qt.	1 l
Lemon, juice of	1	1
Olive oil, virgin	1 Tbsp.	15 ml
White balsamic vinegar	2 Tbsp.	30 ml
Kosher salt	to taste	to taste
Fresh, cracked white pepper	to taste	to taste

Garnish:

Tomato slice, green pepper, cucumber, or choice of herb

PREPARATION

1. Roast green peppers and onions. To roast peppers and onions, brush with some olive oil and place on small sheet pan. Roast peppers and onions in 350°F (175°C) oven until nicely browned and skin is evenly blistered all around. Carefully remove from oven, place in bowl, and cover with plastic wrap. When cool, peel skin and remove seeds.
2. In large blender or food processor, coarsely puree all ingredients except liquids. Place in chilled stainless steel bowl and combine with vegetable stock. Adjust seasoning with lemon juice, olive oil, and vinegar, and salt and fresh cracked white pepper to taste.
3. Adjust consistency with stock as desired.

PRESENTATION

Serve slightly chilled. Garnish soup with slice of tomato, green pepper, and cucumber, or choice of herb such as short-cut chives or sprig of chervil, parsley, or cilantro.

NUTRITION PER SERVING

Calories 44, protein 1 gm, fat 2 gm, carbohydrates 7 gm, cholesterol 0 mg, sodium 7 mg

ROASTED CORN BROTH

SERVES 8 (6 OZ./180 ML SERVING)

INGREDIENTS	AMOUNT/U.S.	METRIC
Corn on the cob, white, husked	5	5
Olive oil	1 fl. oz.	30 ml
Leeks, cleaned, diced	5 oz.	140 gm
Celery root, cleaned, diced	5 oz.	140 gm
Celery stalk, cleaned, diced	5 oz.	140 gm
Carrots, cleaned, peeled, diced	5 oz.	140 gm
White onions, cleaned, diced	5 oz.	140 gm
Shallots, cleaned, halved	4	4
Bay leaves	3	3
Mustard seeds	1 Tbsp.	9 gm
Parsley stems	½ bunch	½ bunch
Chicken stock, high-quality	64 fl. oz.	1920 ml
Garnish:		
Parsley, chopped, for garnish	1 oz.	28 gm
Tomato, peeled, diced	2 oz.	56 gm

PREPARATION

1. Brush corn on the cob with olive oil and place in preheated roasting pan in 350°F (175°C) oven. Roast for 25–30 minutes. When lightly browned, remove from oven and allow to cool.
2. Slice kernels from cobs. Reserve kernels from one cob for garnish.
3. Return stripped corn cobs to pan along with leeks, celery root, celery stalks, carrots, onions, and shallots. Return pan to oven and continue to roast for 30–45 minutes.
4. Combine browned cobs, corn kernels, vegetables, bay leaves, mustard seeds, and parsley with cold chicken stock in large, clean, stainless steel stock pot. Bring mixture slowly to simmer, and simmer gently for 1 to 1¼ hour.
5. Adjust seasoning as needed with a little salt and pepper. Remove corn cobs. Strain broth through double layer of dampened cheesecloth.

PRESENTATION

Serve with garnish of reserved corn kernels, chopped parsley, and diced tomato flesh.

NUTRITION PER SERVING

Calories 149, protein 4 gm, fat 6 gm, carbohydrates 23 gm, cholesterol 0 mg, sodium 71 mg

ROASTED PEPPER SOUP

SERVES 8 (6 OZ./180 ML SERVING)

CHEF'S NOTE

*By adjusting the consis-
tency, this soup can also
be used as a sauce.*

INGREDIENTS	AMOUNT/U.S.	METRIC
Green bell peppers, washed, paper towel dried	24 oz.	672 gm
Red bell peppers, wash, paper towel dry	24 oz.	672 gm
Poblano peppers, wash, paper towel dry	2	2
Olive oil	1 fl. oz.	30 ml
Garlic, minced	5 cloves	5 cloves
White onions, cleaned, diced	8 oz.	224 gm
Tomatoes, cleaned, peeled, seeded, diced	8 oz.	224 gm
Chipotle peppers, stewed (canned)	1 oz.	28 gm
Cumin powder	1 tsp.	2 gm
Chicken stock, high quality	26 fl. oz.	780 ml
Kosher salt	to taste	to taste
Fresh, cracked white pepper	to taste	to taste

PREPARATION

1. Preheat oven to 350°F (175°C). Wearing plastic gloves rub bell peppers and poblanos with some olive oil. Discard gloves.
2. Place on sheet pan in oven and roast until evenly browned and skins are blistered.
3. Remove from oven, place in clean stainless steel bowl, and cover with plastic wrap.
4. When cool, peel and seed peppers and coarsely dice. Set aside.
5. In medium, heavy-bottomed sauce pot, heat olive oil. Sweat garlic and onions until translucent, approximately 2 minutes, stirring frequently.
6. Add tomatoes, chipotles, and cumin. Combine thoroughly. Add roasted peppers and chicken stock. Bring mixture to boil.
7. Reduce to simmer, and with submersible blender puree mixture into smooth consistency. Adjust seasoning with salt and pepper. Allow mixture to simmer to reach desired consistency.

NUTRITION PER SERVING
Calories 91, protein 3 gm, fat 3 gm, carbohydrates 15 gm, cholesterol 0 mg, sodium 12 mg

Photo courtesy of Certified Angus Beef Program

Chili Empanadas with Roasted Poblano Vegetable Sauce

Photo courtesy of Ocean Garden Products, Inc.

Risotto with Shrimp, Mushroom, and Arugula

Photo courtesy of Ocean Garden Products, Inc.

White Shrimp, Bean, and Roasted Vegetable Soup

Photo courtesy of Zale Lipshy University Hospital

Chicken Breast in Herb Broth with Root Vegetables and Roasted Garlic

Photo courtesy of Ocean Garden Products, Inc.

Country Style Brown Shrimp Etouffee

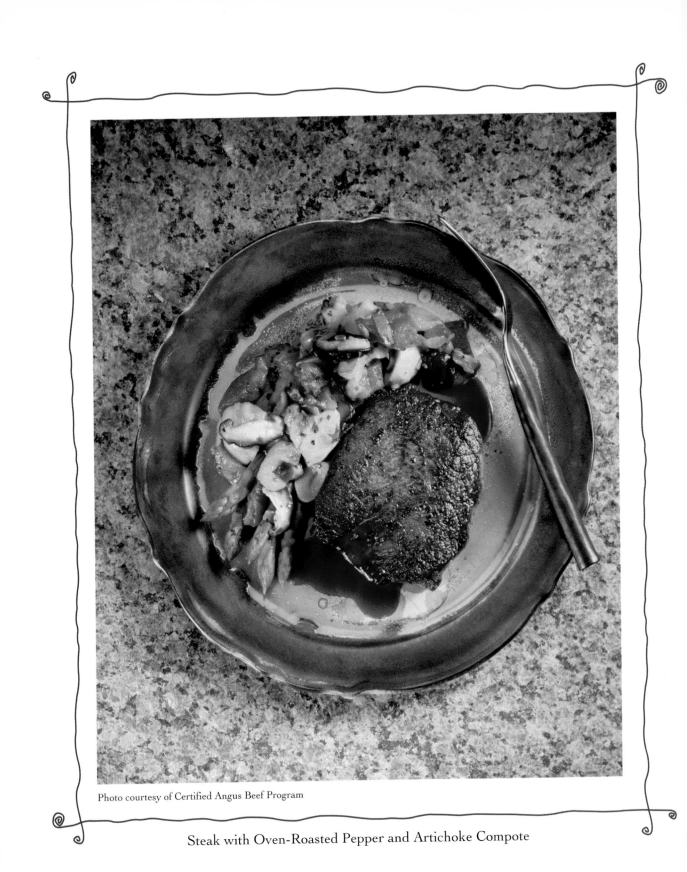

Photo courtesy of Certified Angus Beef Program

Steak with Oven-Roasted Pepper and Artichoke Compote

Photo courtesy of Certified Angus Beef Program

Grilled Flank Steak with Balsamic Glaze and Herbed Brown Rice

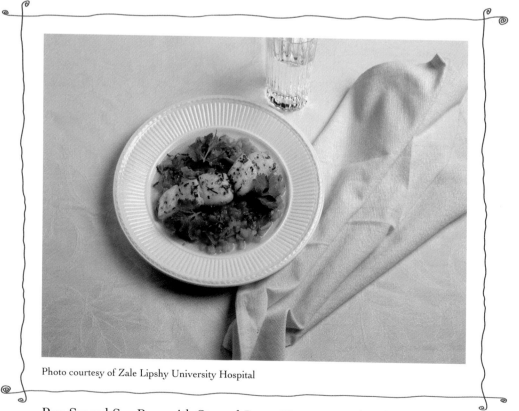

Photo courtesy of Zale Lipshy University Hospital

Pan-Seared Sea Bass with Stewed Roma Tomatoes and Kalamata Olives

Photo courtesy of Certified Angus Beef Program

Braised Sirloin with Green Lentil and White Bean Compote au Natural Jus

Photo courtesy of Ocean Garden Products, Inc.

Sauteed Gingered Shrimp with Lentil Bulgur Salad

Photo courtesy of Certified Angus Beef Program

Southwest-Style Wrap with Avocado Dip

Photo courtesy of Cervena Council & Cervena Company Ltd., © 1997

Pan-Seared Cervena on Fingerling Potato, Beet, and Onion Salad

PLUM SAUCE

YIELD: 20 FL. OZ./600 ML
(1 OZ./30 ML SERVING)

INGREDIENTS	AMOUNT/U.S.	METRIC
Peanut oil	1 Tbsp.	15 ml
Garlic, cleaned, minced	1 oz.	28 gm
Shallots, finely minced	5 oz.	140 gm
Plum wine	3 fl. oz.	90 ml
Roasted Vegetable Sauce (p. 174)	20 fl. oz.	600 ml
Plum sauce, bottled	3 fl. oz.	90 ml
Green onions, short-cut	1½ oz.	42 gm
Teriyaki, light	1 fl. oz.	30 ml
Arrowroot or cornstarch	2 Tbsp.	30 gm
Fresh, cracked white pepper	to taste	to taste

CHEF'S NOTES

For this sauce recipe we opted for the Roasted Vegetable Sauce. However, a reduction of high-quality brown stock or a top-quality speed scratch product will also work well. This will affect the nutritional information, albeit minimally.

PREPARATION

1. In stainless steel saucepan, heat peanut oil, add garlic and shallots, and sweat until translucent.
2. Deglaze with plum wine, reduce until sec.
3. Add Roasted Vegetable Sauce, bring to boil, and reduce heat. Add plum sauce, green onions, and teriyaki.
4. Simmer for 20 minutes. Adjust consistency with arrowroot or cornstarch mixed with a little cold water. Adjust seasoning with fresh, cracked white pepper.

NUTRITION PER 1 OZ./30 ML SERVING
Calories 44, protein 1 gm, fat 1 gm, carbohydrates 7 gm, cholesterol 0 mg, sodium 73 mg

ROASTED VEGETABLE SAUCE

YIELD: 1 1/2 QT./1440 ML/48 OZ.

CHEF'S NOTE

Crucial to this sauce is the roasting method necessary to achieve the desired color. This base jus can be used in place of the traditional protein-based jus to accompany a wide variety of dishes.

INGREDIENTS	AMOUNT/U.S.	METRIC
Olive oil	1 tsp.	5 ml
Parsnips, clean, medium-diced	4 oz.	112 gm
Carrots, clean, medium-diced	4 oz.	112 gm
Celery, clean, medium-diced	4 oz.	112 gm
Leeks, clean, medium-diced	4 oz.	112 gm
Onions, clean, diced	7 oz.	196 gm
Tomato paste	2½ oz.	70 gm
Garlic, minced	3 cloves	3 cloves
Red wine, dry	10 fl. oz.	300 ml
Bay leaves	2	2
Thyme sprigs	2	2
Mustard seeds	½ tsp.	1.5 gm
Peppercorns, white, fresh	½ tsp.	2 gm
Vegetable stock	2 qt.	2 l
Arrowroot	as needed	as needed
Kosher salt	to taste	to taste
Fresh, cracked white pepper	to taste	to taste

PREPARATION

1. In heavy-bottomed sauce pot, over medium heat, heat olive oil and sauté parsnips, carrots, and celery until they take on a golden color.
2. Remove from sauce pot and place on sheet pan. Roast in 350°F (175°C) oven.
3. Add leeks and onions. Continue to roast until vegetables take on a deep brown color. Stir occasionally for even browning.
4. Add tomato paste and garlic. Roast until tomato paste becomes rusty in color and has a sweet aroma. Remove mixture from sheet pan and return to heavy sauce pot.
5. Add half the red wine and allow to reduce completely. Add remaining red wine and allow to reduce.
6. Add bay leaves, thyme, mustard seeds, peppercorns, and stock. Bring to boil. Reduce heat and gently simmer until reduced by half, approximately 45–50 minutes. Skim surface frequently for impurities.
7. Remove bay leaves. Puree sauce with submersible blender. Adjust seasoning with salt and pepper.
8. If sauce is too thin, thicken with arrowroot mixed with cold water, just until it coats the back of the spoon. If sauce is too thick, add vegetable stock until desired consistency.
9. Cool sauce properly. This base can be frozen in airtight containers.

@

SAFFRON BROTH

SERVES 10 (3 OZ./90 ML. SERVING)

INGREDIENTS	AMOUNT/U.S.	METRIC	CHEF'S NOTE
Olive oil	1 Tbsp.	15 ml	*Serve as a broth-sauce for*
Red onion, peeled, finely diced	4 oz.	112 gm	*fish, vegetables, or pasta.*
Chicken stock, high-quality	33 fl. oz.	1 l	
Thyme leaves, snipped	1 tsp.	1 gm	
Spanish saffron, pure, steeped	1 tsp.	1 gm	
Roma tomatoes, peeled, seeded, finely diced	9 oz.	252 gm	
Kosher salt	to taste	to taste	
Fresh, cracked white pepper	to taste	to taste	
Arrowroot or cornstarch	as needed	as needed	

PREPARATION

1. In medium stainless steel saucepan, heat olive oil and sweat onion until translucent.
2. Add stock and snipped thyme. Bring to boil and reduce heat. Simmer for 4 minutes.
3. Add saffron and tomatoes. Adjust seasoning with salt and fresh, cracked white pepper. Gently simmer for 10 minutes.
4. Adjust consistency with slurry of arrowroot or cornstarch.

NUTRITION PER SERVING

Calories 43, protein 1 gm, fat 2 gm, carbohydrates 6 gm, cholesterol 0 mg, sodium 5 mg

@

TOMATO-PEPPER SAUCE

YIELD: 44 FL. OZ./1320 ML
(2 OZ./60 ML SERVINGS)

CHEF'S NOTES

For this sauce recipe we opted for the Roasted Vegetable Sauce. However, a reduction of brown stock will also work well. This will affect the nutritional information, albeit minimally.

INGREDIENTS	AMOUNT/U.S.	METRIC
Olive oil	1 Tbsp.	15 ml
Shallots, cleaned, finely minced	3½ oz.	98 gm
Garlic, cloves, cleaned, minced	1 oz.	28 gm
Roma tomatoes, peeled, seeded, diced	25 oz.	700 gm
Bell peppers, roasted, peeled, seeded, diced	10 oz.	280 gm
Roasted Vegetable Sauce (p. 174)	26 fl. oz.	780 ml
Thyme, fresh, snipped	1 tsp.	3 gm
Rosemary needles, fresh	1 tsp.	3 gm
Kosher salt	to taste	to taste
Fresh, cracked white pepper	to taste	to taste

PREPARATION

1. In medium stainless steel saucepan, heat olive oil and sweat shallots and garlic until translucent.

2. Add tomatoes and roasted peppers. Gently stew over low heat for 10 minutes, stirring occasionally.

3. Add Roasted Vegetable Sauce, bring to boil, and reduce heat to simmer. Add thyme and rosemary. Continue to simmer for 10 minutes. Allow flavors to mature.

4. Adjust seasoning with salt and pepper.

NUTRITION PER SERVING

Calories 42, protein 1 gm, fat 1 gm, carbohydrates 6 gm, cholesterol 0 mg, sodium 22 mg

BALSAMIC GLAZE

INGREDIENTS	AMOUNT/U.S.	METRIC
Olive oil	1 Tbsp.	15 ml
Shallots, cleaned, minced	3 oz.	84 gm
Balsamic vinegar, high-quality, less than 5% acidity	3 fl. oz.	90 ml
Roasted Vegetable Sauce (p. 174)	20 fl. oz.	600 ml
Kosher salt	to taste	to taste
Fresh, cracked white pepper	to taste	to taste

CHEF'S NOTES

For this recipe we opted for the Roasted Vegetable Sauce. However, a reduction of brown stock will also work well. This will affect the nutritional information, albeit minimally.

PREPARATION

1. In small stainless steel saucepan, heat olive oil and sweat shallots until translucent.
2. Deglaze with balsamic vinegar. Reduce for 1 minute.
3. Add Roasted Vegetable Sauce (p. 174) and simmer gently over low heat for 15 minutes.
4. Adjust seasoning with salt and pepper.

NUTRITION PER SERVING

Calories 34, protein 0 gm, fat 1 gm, carbohydrates 4 gm, cholesterol 0 mg, sodium 21 mg

APPLE CURRY SAUCE

SERVES 16 (2 OZ./60 ML SERVING)

INGREDIENTS	AMOUNT/U.S.	METRIC
Olive oil	2 Tbsp.	30 ml
Red onions, finely diced	3 oz.	84 gm
Apples, Granny Smith, peeled, cored, small-diced	20 oz.	560 gm
"Madras" curry powder, good-quality	1 oz.	28 gm
Bay leaves	2	2
Chicken stock, high-quality	24 fl. oz.	720 ml
Coconut milk	2 fl. oz.	60 ml
Lemon grass	1 Tbsp.	7 gm
Kosher salt	to taste	to taste
Fresh, cracked white pepper	to taste	to taste
Arrowroot or cornstarch	as needed	as needed

PREPARATION
1. In medium stainless steel saucepan, heat olive oil and sweat onions and apples for 5 minutes.
2. Add curry powder and bay leaves; combine thoroughly.
3. Add chicken stock; bring mixture to boil. Add coconut milk and lemon grass; simmer mixture for 20 minutes.
4. Adjust seasoning with salt and pepper. Adjust consistency, if needed, with slurry of arrowroot or cornstarch.
5. Remove bay leaves prior to serving.

NUTRITION PER SERVING
Calories 57, protein 1 gm, fat 3 gm, carbohydrates 8 gm, cholesterol 0 mg, sodium 3 mg

ROASTED POBLANO VEGETABLE SAUCE

YIELD: 32 FL. OZ./960 ML

(2 OZ./60 ML SERVING)

INGREDIENTS	AMOUNT/U.S.	METRIC
Poblano peppers, fresh, washed, towel dried	2 lb.	900 gm
Olive oil	1 Tbsp.	15 ml
Roasted Vegetable Sauce (p. 174)	24 oz	720 ml
Lemon, juice of	1	1
Garlic, roasted, minced	5 cloves	5 cloves
Kosher salt	to taste	to taste
Fresh, cracked black pepper	to taste	to taste
Chives, short-cut	1 oz.	28 gm
Cilantro, short-cut	1 oz.	28 gm
Chicken stock, high-quality	as needed	as needed

CHEF'S NOTES

For this sauce recipe we opted for the Roasted Vegetable Sauce. However, a reduction of brown stock will also work well. This will affect the nutritional information, albeit minimally.

Replace half the poblano peppers with regular red, green, or yellow bell peppers for a milder sauce. Use a high quality chicken stock to thin out consistency of sauce, as desired.

PREPARATION

1. Brush peppers with olive oil and place on small sheet pan. Roast at 350°F (175°C) until nicely browned and skin is evenly blistered all around.
2. Remove from oven, place in bowl, and cover with plastic wrap. Allow to cool to room temperature.
3. Peel and remove seeds and core. Place pepper flesh in blender, add Roasted Vegetable Sauce, lemon juice, and roasted garlic, and puree.
4. Adjust seasoning with salt and pepper.
5. Place in saucepan; add chives and cilantro. If needed, adjust consistency with chicken stock until smooth.
6. Bring slowly to boil.

NUTRITION PER SERVING

Calories 51, protein 1 gm, fat 2 gm, carbohydrates 8 gm, cholesterol 0 mg, sodium 17 mg

FISH SAUCE *

YIELD: 16 OZ./480 ML

(2 OZ./60 ML SERVING)

CHEF'S NOTES

This style of white sauce can be prepared with a variety of high-quality stocks, such as vegetable or chicken, and can certainly be a comparable substitute for a traditional velouté- or béchamel-style sauce. Enhance the flavor profile with a select variety of herbs.

INGREDIENTS	AMOUNT/U.S.	METRIC
Fish stock, high-quality	16 fl. oz.	480 ml
Cornstarch	1 Tbsp.	15 gm
Evaporated skim milk	4 fl. oz.	120 ml
Kosher salt	to taste	to taste
Fresh, cracked white pepper	to taste	to taste

PREPARATION

1. Bring stock to boil; reduce to simmer.
2. Mix cornstarch with a little cold evaporated skim milk to create a slurry; stir into simmering stock.
3. Slowly stir rest of evaporated skim milk into simmering stock, a little at a time. The stock should not be too thick, but it should coat the spoon.
4. Adjust to taste with salt and fresh cracked pepper.

NUTRITION PER SERVING

Calories 22, protein 1 gm, fat 0 gm, carbohydrates 3 gm, cholesterol 1 mg, sodium 20 mg

CHIPOTLE SAUCE

YIELD: 24 OZ./720 ML
(2 OZ./60 ML SERVING)

INGREDIENTS	AMOUNT/U.S.	METRIC
Olive oil	1 Tbsp.	15 ml
Red onion, finely diced	3 oz.	84 gm
Garlic, cloves, cleaned, minced	2 cloves	2 cloves
Chipotle peppers, seeded, minced	1 each	1 each
Honey	3 Tbsp.	45 ml
Tomato, peeled, seeded, diced	5 oz.	140 gm
Sherry	1 fl. oz.	30 ml
Roasted Vegetable Sauce (p. 174)	20 fl. oz.	600 ml
Vegetable stock	4 fl. oz.	120 ml
Kosher salt	to taste	to taste
Fresh, cracked white pepper	to taste	to taste

CHEF'S NOTES

For this sauce recipe we opted for the Roasted Vegetable Sauce. However, a reduction of brown stock will also work well. This will affect the nutritional information, albeit minimally.

PREPARATION

1. In a heavy-bottomed saucepan, heat olive oil and sauté red onion and garlic until translucent.
2. Add chipotle peppers and honey; cook for 3–4 minutes.
3. Add diced tomato and sherry. Continue cooking for 5 more minutes, then add Roasted Vegetable Sauce and stock.
4. Bring to boil, reduce heat, and simmer for 10–15 minutes. Adjust seasoning with salt and pepper. Keep sauce hot prior to serving.

NUTRITION PER SERVING
Calories 71, protein 1 gm, fat 2 gm, carbohydrates 11 gm, cholesterol 0 mg, sodium 32 mg

RED AND YELLOW TOMATO JUS

YIELD: 40 OZ./1200 ML

(2 OZ./60 ML SERVING)

CHEF'S NOTES

For this recipe we opted for the Roasted Vegetable Sauce. However, a reduction of brown stock will also work well. This will affect the nutritional information, albeit minimally.

INGREDIENTS	AMOUNT/U.S.	METRIC
Olive oil	2 Tbsp.	30 ml
Garlic, minced	1 oz.	28 gm
Shallots, minced	1½ oz.	42 gm
Yellow tomatoes, peeled, seeded, diced	5 oz.	140 gm
Red tomatoes, peeled, seeded, diced	5 oz.	140 gm
Roasted Vegetable Sauce (p. 174)	32 fl. oz.	960 ml
Chives, snipped	½ oz.	14 gm
Basil, fresh, julienned	⅛ oz.	3.5 gm
Black olives, seeded, cut into strips	2 oz.	56 mg
Kosher salt	to taste	to taste
Fresh, cracked white pepper	to taste	to taste

PREPARATION

1. In stainless steel saucepan, heat olive oil and sauté garlic and shallots over medium heat until translucent.

2. Add diced tomatoes and Roasted Vegetable Sauce. Bring slowly to simmer.

3. Add chives, basil, and black olives. Simmer gently for 10 minutes.

4. Adjust seasoning with salt and cracked white pepper.

NUTRITION PER SERVING

Calories 52, protein 1 gm, fat 2 gm, carbohydrates 6 gm, cholesterol 0 mg, sodium 44 mg

TARRAGON-TOMATO SAUCE

YIELD: 25 OZ./740 ML (2 OZ SERVING)

INGREDIENTS	AMOUNT/U.S.	METRIC
Olive oil	1 fl. oz.	30 ml
Shallots, cleaned, finely chopped	2½ oz.	70 gm
Garlic, cloves, cleaned, minced	1 oz.	28 gm
Roma tomatoes, peeled, seeded, diced	2 lb	896 gm
Tarragon, fresh, snipped	1 oz.	28 gm
Tomato paste	2 oz.	56 gm
White wine	3 fl. oz.	90 ml
Chicken stock, high-quality	4 fl. oz.	120 ml
Kosher salt	to taste	to taste
Fresh, cracked white pepper	to taste	to taste

PREPARATION

1. In a clean stainless steel saucepan, heat olive oil and sweat shallots and garlic gently until translucent.
2. Add diced tomatoes and tarragon. Sauté mixture gently for 3 minutes. Add tomato paste, stirring continuously until mixture takes on a rusty color.
3. Deglaze mixture with white wine and chicken stock. Simmer gently for 20 minutes over low heat. Remove from heat and adjust seasoning with salt and pepper.
4. Place mixture in a clean food processor bowl. Puree mixture in food processor or with submersible blender.
5. Return to saucepan, reheat, and adjust seasoning prior to serving.

NUTRITION PER SERVING
Calories 58, protein 2 gm, fat 3 gm, carbohydrates 7 gm, cholesterol 0 mg, sodium 32 mg

ROSEMARY JUS

SERVES 10 (2 OZ./60 ML SERVING)

CHEF'S NOTES

For this sauce recipe we opted for the Roasted Vegetable Sauce. However, a reduction of high-quality brown stock or a top-quality speed scratch product will also work well. This will affect the nutritional information, albeit minimally.

Rosemary is a very strong-flavored herb. To avoid an overpowering flavor, wrap the rosemary in a small piece of cheesecloth, and remove from the pot when the sauce reaches the desired flavor profile.

INGREDIENTS	AMOUNT/U.S.	METRIC
Olive oil	½ fl. oz.	15 ml
Red onions, finely diced	4 oz.	112 gm
Garlic, minced	1 oz.	28 gm
Celery root, finely diced	5 oz.	140 gm
Pinot Noir wine	3 fl. oz.	90 ml
Roasted Vegetable Sauce (p. 174)	16 fl. oz.	480 ml
Sherry wine vinegar	1 fl. oz.	30 ml
Rosemary, needles only, fresh	1 sprig	1 sprig
Fresh, cracked white pepper	to taste	to taste
Kosher salt	to taste	to taste

PREPARATION

1. In medium stainless steel saucepan, heat olive oil and sweat onions, garlic, and celery root for 2 minutes. Deglaze with Pinot Noir.
2. Add Roasted Vegetable Sauce; bring mixture to boil. Reduce heat and allow to summer for 10 minutes.
3. Add sherry wine vinegar and rosemary. Adjust seasoning with a little cracked pepper and salt. Simmer for an additional 10 minutes over low heat. Keep warm until serving.

NUTRITION PER SERVING
Calories 66, protein 1 gm, fat 2 gm, carbohydrates 9 gm, cholesterol 0 mg, sodium 30 mg

RHUBARB CHUTNEY

SERVES 8 (2 OZ./56 GM SERVING)

INGREDIENTS	AMOUNT/U.S.	METRIC
Rhubarb, cleaned, washed, stalks only, diced	1 lb.	450 gm
Apples, Granny Smith, peeled, cleaned, cored, diced	2	2
Red onions, cleaned, finely diced	6 oz.	168 gm
Ginger, fresh, grated	1 Tbsp.	9 gm
Raisins, plumped	3 oz.	84 gm
Brown sugar	4 oz.	112 gm
Red wine vinegar	2½ fl. oz.	75 ml
Cinnamon, ground	1 tsp.	2 gm
Cloves, ground	¼ tsp.	.5 gm
Mace	¼ tsp.	.5 gm
Kosher salt	to taste	to taste
Fresh, cracked white pepper	to taste	to taste

CHEF'S NOTES

Great with grilled seafood or chicken.

For variety, add herbs, such as mint, to chutney.

PREPARATION

1. In medium stock pot, place rhubarb, apples, and onions. Add ginger, raisins, sugar, red wine vinegar, and spices except salt and fresh, cracked white pepper.
2. Slowly stew all ingredients over medium heat until completely tender, approximately 40–45 minutes.
3. Adjust seasoning with salt and pepper. Heat thoroughly prior to storing in sterilized jars in refrigerator.

NUTRITION PER SERVING

Calories 128, protein 1 gm, fat 0 gm, carbohydrates 33 gm, cholesterol 0 mg, sodium 10 mg

ROASTED EGGPLANT AND BLACK OLIVE SPREAD

SERVES 24 (2 TBSP. SERVING)

INGREDIENTS	AMOUNT/U.S.	METRIC
Eggplant, purple, thick, cleaned, halved roasted (weight of roasted pulp)	20 oz.	560 gm
Olive oil	2 Tbsp.	30 ml
Sesame paste (tahini)	3 oz.	84 gm
Elephant garlic, roasted, pureed	8 cloves	8 cloves
Lime, juice of	2	2
Tabasco™ sauce	8 drops	8 drops
Kalamata black olives, finely diced	30	30
Chives, short-cut	3 Tbsp.	10 gm
Kosher salt	to taste	to taste
Fresh, cracked black pepper	to taste	to taste

PREPARATION

1. Brush eggplant with 1 Tbsp. olive oil. Oven-roast at 350° F(175°C) until completely soft. Cool.
2. Remove skin and excessive seeds to avoid bitter taste.
3. Place pulp in mixing bowl. Combine with smooth sesame paste, roasted garlic puree, and lime juice.
4. Place mixture in food processor and puree until smooth.
5. Return to mixing bowl, and finish mixture with 1 Tbsp. olive oil, Tabasco sauce, Kalamata olives, and chives. Adjust seasoning.

PRESENTATION

Serve spread as an hors d'oeuvre on toasted brioche, semolina bread, pita chips, or raw vegetables.

NUTRITION PER SERVING

Calories 44, protein 1 gm, fat 3 gm, carbohydrates 3 gm, cholesterol 0 mg, sodium 38 mg

MANGO–WHITE BEAN RELISH

SERVES 24 (2 TBSP. SERVING)

INGREDIENTS	AMOUNT/U.S.	METRIC
White Italian beans, small, sorted, soaked (cooked weight)	8 oz.	224 gm
Mango, ripe, peeled, finely diced	10 oz.	280 gm
Red bell pepper, flesh only, finely diced	6 oz.	168 gm
Poblano pepper, flesh only, minced	2 Tbsp.	30 gm
Lemon, juice of	2	2
Ginger root, fresh, peeled, finely minced	1 Tbsp.	10 gm
Cilantro, snipped	2 Tbsp.	10 gm
Tabasco™ sauce	3–4 drops	3–4 drops
Olive oil	1 Tbsp.	15 ml
Kosher salt	to taste	to taste
Fresh, cracked black pepper	to taste	to taste

PREPARATION

1. Soak beans overnight. Drain water. Rinse. Cook beans in ample water until tender but still firm to the bite. Drain, rinse, and cool.
2. Place in large stainless steel mixing bowl. Gently toss with mango, bell pepper, poblano, lemon juice, ginger, and cilantro.
3. Adjust seasoning with Tabasco, olive oil, salt, and cracked black pepper.
4. Combine ingredients gently and marinate for 2 hours. Adjust seasoning prior to serving.

PRESENTATION

Serve as an hors d'oeuvre on toasted brioche or semolina bread, or as a relish with grilled meats. Also works well as a salad.

NUTRITION PER SERVING

Calories 29, protein 1 gm, fat 1 gm, carbohydrates 5 gm, cholesterol 0 mg, sodium 3 mg

PICANTE TOMATO RELISH

SERVES 16 (2 TBSP. SERVING)

INGREDIENTS	AMOUNT/U.S.	METRIC
Roma tomatoes, red, cleaned, peeled, seeded, flesh only	12 oz.	336 gm
Red onion, finely diced	4 oz.	112 gm
Spring onions, short-cut	2 Tbsp.	10 gm
Jalapeño pepper, seeded, finely minced, membrane removed	1	1
Lemon, juice of	1	1
Lime, juice of	1	1
Cilantro, snipped	2 Tbsp.	10 gm
Fresh, cracked white pepper	to taste	to taste
Kosher salt	to taste	to taste

PREPARATION

1. In mixing bowl, combine tomatoes, red onions, spring onions, jalapeño peppers, and lemon and lime juice.
2. Adjust seasoning with cilantro, fresh, cracked white pepper, and salt. Place in refrigerator for ½ hour. Remove and allow to rest for ½ hour prior to serving. Adjust seasoning as needed.

PRESENTATION

Serve on toasted semolina bread points for an hors d'oeuvre, or served with grilled fish.

NUTRITION PER SERVING

Calories 9, protein 0 gm, fat 0 gm, carbohydrates 2 gm, cholesterol 0 mg, sodium 3 mg

CITRUS TOMATILLO RELISH

SERVES 32 (4 TBSP. SERVING)

INGREDIENTS	AMOUNT/U.S.	METRIC
Tomatillos, cleaned, small-diced	32 oz.	896 gm
Cucumber, seeded, small-diced	8 oz.	224 gm
Tomatoes, peeled, seeded, small-diced	16 oz.	448 gm
Yellow bell pepper, seeded, small-diced	8 oz.	224 gm
Jalapeño pepper, seeded, minced	2	2
Orange juice, fresh	12 fl. oz.	360 ml
Lime juice, fresh	2 fl. oz.	60 ml
Rice wine vinegar	2 fl. oz.	60 ml
Cilantro, fresh, snipped	4 Tbsp.	20 gm
Fresh, cracked black pepper	½ tsp.	1 gm
Kosher salt	½ tsp.	2.5 gm
Garnish:		
Orange segments	45	45

PREPARATION

1. Combine all ingredients except orange segments in bowl. Refrigerate overnight for best flavor development.

PRESENTATION

Serve on bottom of plate with choice of poultry, game, or fish. Garnish with orange segments, and drizzle a small amount of the liquid over the top.

NUTRITION PER SERVING

Calories 32, protein 1 gm, fat 0 gm, carbohydrates 7 gm, cholesterol 0 mg, sodium 74 mg

TOMATILLO-PAPAYA SALSA

SERVES 10 (4 TBSP. SERVING)

INGREDIENTS	AMOUNT/U.S.	METRIC
Tomatillos, cleaned, small-diced	16 oz.	448 gm
Papaya, peeled, seeded, small-diced	8 oz.	224 gm
Tomatoes, peeled, seeded, small-diced	4 oz.	112 gm
Red bell pepper, seeded, brunoise	2 oz.	56 gm
Green bell pepper, seeded, brunoise	4 oz.	112 gm
Jalapeño pepper, seeded, brunoise	1	1
Cilantro, fresh, snipped	2 Tbsp.	10 gm
Chives, fresh, short-cut	1 Tbsp.	5 gm
Orange juice, fresh	4 fl. oz.	120 ml
Lime juice, fresh	2 fl. oz.	60 ml
Fresh, cracked black pepper	½ tsp.	1 gm
Kosher salt	½ tsp.	2.5 gm

PREPARATION

1. Combine all ingredients and refrigerate for a minimum of 1 hour. Best if made the day before and refrigerated overnight to allow flavors to develop.

PRESENTATION

Serve with seafood or game meats.

NUTRITION PER SERVING

Calories 38, protein 1 gm, fat 1 gm, carbohydrates 8 gm, cholesterol 0 mg, sodium 121 mg

CAPER BERRY–TOMATO COMPOTE

SERVES 12 (4 TBSP. SERVING)

INGREDIENTS	AMOUNT/U.S.	METRIC
Red onion, finely diced	3 Tbsp.	45 gm
Parsley, finely chopped	3 Tbsp.	15 gm
Tomato, red, peeled, seeded, diced	16 oz.	448 gm
Caper berries, stemmed, quartered	30	30
Eggs, hard-boiled, white only, chopped	3	3
Red wine vinegar	5 Tbsp.	75 ml
Olive oil	2 Tbsp.	30 ml
Chicken stock, lightly thickened with cornstarch slurry	6 fl. oz.	180 ml
Kosher salt	to taste	to taste
Fresh, cracked white pepper	to taste	to taste

CHEF'S NOTES

If caper berries cannot be found, regular nonpareil small capers can be substituted.

PREPARATION

1. Combine onion, parsley, tomatoes, caper berries, and eggs in mixing bowl.
2. Add vinegar, olive oil, and chicken stock slurry; combine thoroughly. Adjust seasoning with a little salt and cracked pepper.

NUTRITION PER SERVING

Calories 38, protein 1 gm, fat 3 gm, carbohydrates 3 gm, cholesterol 0 mg, sodium 240 mg

PICKLED MUSHROOMS

SERVES 8

CHEF'S NOTES

Serve with Filo Triangles (p. 89) or as a condiment.

INGREDIENTS	AMOUNT/U.S.	METRIC
Mushrooms, fresh	12 oz.	336 gm
Olive oil	1 Tbsp.	15 ml
Garlic, minced	3 cloves	3 cloves
Chicken stock	2½ fl. oz.	75 ml
Rosemary needles, cracked	½ Tbsp.	2.5 gm
Chives, short-cut	1 Tbsp.	5 gm
Parsley, fresh, chopped	½ Tbsp.	2.5 gm
White balsamic vinegar	1 Tbsp.	15 ml
Lime, juice of	1	1
Kosher salt	to taste	to taste
Fresh, cracked white pepper	to taste	to taste

PREPARATION

1. Clean and quarter mushrooms. Heat oil with garlic, add quartered mushrooms, and sauté for 3 minutes.
2. Add stock, reduce by one-third.
3. Add herbs, vinegar, and lime juice. Adjust seasoning with salt and cracked white pepper.

NUTRITION PER SERVING

Calories 30, protein 1 gm, fat 2 gm, carbohydrates 3 gm, cholesterol 0 mg, sodium 2 mg

FIG RELISH

SERVES 24 (1 OZ./28 GM SERVING)

INGREDIENTS	AMOUNT/U.S.	METRIC
Figs, fresh, small-diced	2 lb.	896 gm
or		
Figs, dried, small-diced	1 lb.	448 gm
Red onions, finely diced	8 oz.	224 gm
Garlic, cleaned, minced	3 cloves	3 cloves
Sherry	4 fl. oz.	120 ml
Honey	4 fl. oz.	120 ml
Balsamic vinegar, white	2 fl. oz.	60 ml
Bay leaves	2	2
Black peppercorns, cracked	1 tsp.	3 gm
Pears, fresh, peeled, cored, diced	1 lb.	448 gm
Lemon peel, grated	2 tsp.	10 gm
Mint, fresh, snipped	1 oz.	28 gm

CHEF'S NOTES

This relish goes well with game birds, pork, and chicken.

PREPARATION

1. In medium stainless steel saucepan, combine figs, onion, garlic, sherry, honey, vinegar, bay leaves, and peppercorns. Simmer over low heat for 30 minutes, stirring frequently.

2. Add diced pear and continue to simmer for an additional 15 minutes. Adjust seasoning with lemon zest and mint. Allow mixture to cool.

NUTRITION PER SERVING

Calories 92, protein 1 gm, fat 0 gm, carbohydrates 23 gm, cholesterol 0 mg, sodium 33 mg

CORN-PANCETTA RELISH

SERVES 12 (1 OZ./28 GM SERVING)

INGREDIENTS	AMOUNT/U.S.	METRIC
Pancetta, medium-diced	4 oz.	112 gm
Onion, finely diced	2 oz.	56 gm
Garlic, minced	3 cloves	3 cloves
Corn kernels, fresh (blanched) or frozen	10 oz.	280 gm
Red bell pepper, small-diced	2 oz.	56 gm
Parsley, fresh, snipped	1 Tbsp.	7 gm
Lemon, juice of	1	1
Kosher salt	to taste	to taste
Fresh, cracked white pepper	to taste	to taste

PREPARATION

1. In sauté pan, heat diced pancetta thoroughly and sauté until translucent. Add onions and garlic, and sauté until pancetta takes on a brown color, stirring frequently.

2. Add corn kernels and peppers; sauté gently. Adjust seasoning with parsley, lemon juice, salt, and fresh cracked pepper.

PRESENTATION

Serve with poultry or pork or toss warm over salad greens.

NUTRITION PER 1 OZ./28 GM SERVING

Calories 46, protein 4 gm, fat 1 gm, carbohydrates 6 gm, cholesterol 9 mg, sodium 10 mg

YELLOW TOMATO–CAPER SALSA

SERVES 12 (2 OZ./56 GM SERVING)

INGREDIENTS	AMOUNT/U.S.	METRIC
Yellow tomatoes, peeled, seeded, finely diced	1 lb.	448 gm
Capers, small	4 oz.	112 gm
Chives, short-cut	1 oz.	28 gm
White onion, diced	4 oz.	112 gm
Apple cider vinegar	2 fl. oz.	60 ml
Kosher salt	to taste	to taste
Fresh, cracked white pepper	to taste	to taste

PREPARATION

1. Place tomatoes, capers, chives, and onions in clean stainless steel mixing bowl.
2. Toss with vinegar. Adjust seasoning with salt and pepper.
3. Chill in refrigerator to allow flavors to fully develop.

NUTRITION PER SERVING

Calories 16, protein 1 gm, fat 0 gm, carbohydrates 4 gm, cholesterol 0 mg, sodium 592 mg

STEWED CRANBERRY, APPLE, AND ONION COMPOTE *

SERVES 10 (2 OZ./56 GM SERVING)

CHEF'S NOTES

Compote may be served with a variety of roasted meats, as well as fish.

INGREDIENTS	AMOUNT/U.S.	METRIC
Cranberries, dried	4 oz.	112 gm
Port wine	2 fl. oz.	60 ml
Olive oil	1 tsp.	5 ml
Red onions, finely sliced	8 oz.	224 gm
Balsamic vinegar	2 fl. oz.	60 ml
Red wine	2 fl. oz.	60 ml
Green apples, medium, peeled, cored, julienned	2	2
Chicken stock, defatted	2 fl. oz.	60 ml
Kosher salt	to taste	to taste
Fresh, cracked white pepper	to taste	to taste

PREPARATION

1. In small sauté pan, heat dried cranberries and port wine. Allow cranberries to bloom over low heat. Cranberries should be plump and the liquid should be reduced.

2. In 2-quart saucepan, heat olive oil over medium heat. Add onions and sauté gently for 3 minutes, until onions begin to turn brown. Stir occasionally.

3. Deglaze with vinegar and reduce until dry. Gradually add red wine at two intervals. Add apples, chicken stock, and cranberries. Simmer gently for 20 minutes, stirring occasionally.

4. Season with salt and pepper. Remove from heat and keep warm.

NUTRITION PER SERVING

Calories 50, protein 0 gm, fat 1 gm, carbohydrates 9 gm, cholesterol 0 mg, sodium 2 mg

ROASTED TRI-PEPPER RELISH

SERVES 8 (2 OZ./56 GM SERVING)

INGREDIENTS	AMOUNT/U.S.	METRIC
Red, yellow, and green bell peppers, roasted, peeled, seeded (cleaned weight)	8 oz. each	224 gm each
Red onion, julienned	8 oz.	224 gm
Chives, snipped	1 oz.	28 gm
Olive oil	1 Tbsp.	15 ml
Rice vinegar	1 fl. oz.	30 ml
Kosher salt	to taste	to taste
Fresh, cracked white pepper	to taste	to taste

PREPARATION

1. Clean, wash, and dry peppers. To roast peppers, brush with a little olive oil and place on small sheet pan. Roast at 350°F (175°C) until nicely browned and skin is evenly blistered all around.
2. Carefully remove from oven, place in bowl, and cover with plastic wrap. Allow to cool to room temperature.
3. When peppers cool, using plastic gloves, peel skins and remove seeds and core. Cut in julienne strips. Place in large stainless steel bowl.
4. Toss with onions, chives, olive oil, and vinegar. Season with salt and pepper. Rest mixture in refrigerator.
5. Adjust seasoning prior to serving.

NUTRITION PER SERVING

Calories 53, protein 1 gm, fat 2 gm, carbohydrates 8 gm, cholesterol 0 mg, sodium 74 mg

PINEAPPLE, APPLE, AND MANGO RELISH

SERVES 8 (2 OZ./56 GM SERVING)

INGREDIENTS	AMOUNT/U.S.	METRIC
Lime, juice of	2	2
Orange, juice of	1	1
Cilantro, cleaned, chopped	½ oz.	14 gm
Ginger, peeled, minced	½ oz.	14 gm
Pineapple, fresh, peeled, cored, finely diced	4 oz.	112 gm
Green apples, peeled, cored, finely diced	5 oz.	140 gm
Mango, fresh, ripe, pitted, diced	4 oz.	112 gm
Tomato, fresh, peeled, seeded, diced	2 oz.	56 gm
Red onion, finely minced	½ oz.	14 gm
Jalapeño pepper, seeded, membrane removed, finely minced	½	½

PREPARATION

1. In clean stainless steel mixing bowl combine lime and orange juices with cilantro and ginger.
2. Gently mix in pineapple, apple, mango, tomato, onion, and jalapeño pepper.
3. Cover with plastic wrap, refrigerate, and allow flavors to develop for 1 hour.

NUTRITION PER SERVING

Calories 38, protein 0 gm, fat 0 gm, carbohydrates 10 gm, cholesterol 0 mg, sodium 3 mg

FOUR-FRUIT CHUTNEY

INGREDIENTS	AMOUNT/U.S.	METRIC
Olive oil	2 Tbsp.	30 ml
Apple slices, dried, high-quality	6 oz.	168 gm
Cranberries, dried	4 oz.	112 gm
Cherries, dried	4 oz.	112 gm
Golden raisins	2 oz.	56 gm
Red onion, peeled, finely diced	5 oz.	140 gm
Yellow bell pepper, cleaned, seeded, finely diced	3 oz.	84 gm
Brown sugar	2 oz.	56 gm
Orange juice	5 fl. oz.	150 ml
Lemon, juice of	1	1
Rice wine vinegar	4 fl. oz.	120 ml
Lemon grass, cleaned, finely chopped	1 Tbsp.	7 gm
Kosher salt	to taste	to taste
Fresh, cracked white pepper	to taste	to taste

PREPARATION

1. In heavy saucepan, heat olive oil, add onions, and sweat until translucent, 2–3 minutes.
2. Add apples, cranberries, cherries, and raisins; cook gently over low heat for 3–4 minutes.
3. Add bell pepper, brown sugar, and orange juice. Bring mixture to boil, reduce heat, and simmer for 10–15 minutes, stirring occasionally. Check frequently to prevent sticking.
4. Remove from heat, place in stainless steel container, and cool in ice water bath. When cold, add lemon juice, vinegar, and lemon grass. Adjust seasoning with salt and pepper.

NUTRITION PER SERVING
Calories 125, protein 1 gm, fat 3 gm, carbohydrates 25 gm, cholesterol 0 mg, sodium 212 mg

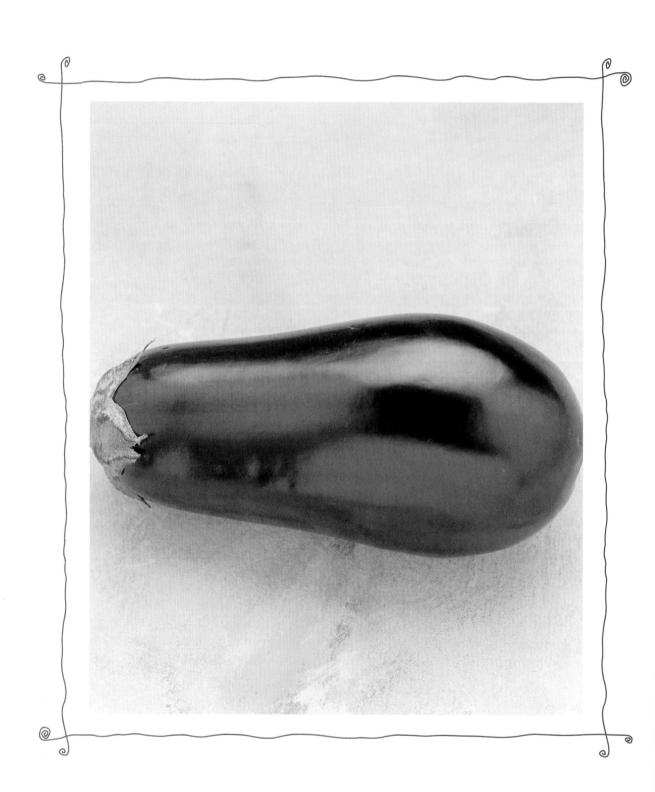

CHAPTER 10

MAIN COURSE SELECTIONS

CHEFS SHOULD BE CREATING A MINDSET OF TEAM DEVELOPMENT

WITH A SPECIAL ATTITUDE IN ORDER TO ENDURE,

AN ATTITUDE OF GRATEFULNESS.

Chef John M. Shoop CMC

IT IS THE HOPE OF A GOOD DINNER THAT BEGUILES YOU.

juvenal

THE ONLY REASON WE COOK FOOD IS TO MAKE IT TASTE GOOD.

Chef Ronald De Santis, CMC

*An asterisk following a recipe indicates that the recipe also appears in another chapter.

The purchase, handling, and preparation of fish and shellfish is not only an art but a science. Over the years, fish and shellfish prices have steadily increased. Demand is increasing as fish and shellfish are appearing more frequently on restaurant menus and in home kitchens.

In addition to the annual U.S. seafood production of approximately 11 billion pounds, aquaculture contributes some 12 million tons annually. This is particularly important since some of the world's fish stocks are becoming depleted. The National Fishery Institute expects the aquaculture industry to continue growing at the rate of about 11 percent per year. At this rate, farm-raised seafood could reach at least 20 percent of the world's total production.

This controlled-environment culture, improved methods of shipping and handling, rising international trade, and health concerns have all added to the increased popularity of seafood items in the American diet. The consumer's concern for health and nutrition in the marketplace is evidenced by the surge in availability of low-fat, low-cholesterol, and reduced-sodium foods. Demographic studies in the area of health and nutrition have shown that consumers with the greatest concern for restricting their intake of foods high in fat, sodium, and cholesterol are those who also frequently dine in restaurants. This underscores the probability that health, and nutrition-conscious offerings on the menu will broaden the customer base of a restaurant and could provide a competitive advantage over other facilities.

We are in the era of a keen, educated consumer who is hungry for taste and high-quality, lower-fat food products, sensibly and consistently well executed. Seafood provides culinarians with endless possibilities to develop stellar dishes.

However, the various environmental issues such as high mercury levels and pollution can cause great concern to those who purchase and prepare seafood. Therefore, the culinarian and seafood buyer must continually stay abreast of the fish market if the operation is to serve a quality product with integrity at an acceptable price to the consumer. Although we cannot be responsible for what the consumer chooses to eat, it is our responsibility to guarantee that what we offer to the customer is safe, cooked correctly, and nutritionally sound. It must consistently meet high standards in taste, quality, and safe food-handling practices.

The selection of your fresh seafood suppliers is critical to the overall success of your fresh fish program. As with all suppliers, a partnership must be developed with your seafood suppliers, as they too should have a shared interest in the success of your program. Make a point to visit the seafood supplier's facility in order to observe fish handling procedures and sanitation.

We know that fish and shellfish are excellent sources of protein, minerals, and vitamins. Given the variety of fresh seafood available today, a chef has the opportunity for great versatility in menu and recipe planning. Always utilize fish at the peak of its freshness to capture the firmness of the flesh and the pure taste.

Within your seafood program there can also be a place for fresh frozen seafood products, provided you place an emphasis on quality and purchase only top-quality products. Before the product reaches you, many steps have occurred, including handling by the fisherman, processor, wholesaler, and distributor.

Fish markets today are flooded with underutilized seafood products such as skate, shark, tile fish, squid, angel fish, and roughy, to mention only a few. Success with these lesser-known varieties depends greatly on their correct preparation. Some species may be unfamiliar to culinarians, but this should not be a reason to avoid these products. Armed with sound product knowledge and simple preparation and presentation, the culinarian can create a flavorful and nutritionally balanced dish.

Fresh fish does not have a fishy odor. This distinctive odor develops as the product remains "on hold" in refrigerator storage. In general it takes three to four days for this odor to develop and for the product to be deemed unacceptable for food service. Obviously, any fresh fish will have an odor, but it should be a clean, mild, sea-like smell. All fish should feel firm to the touch, never soft or mushy, and the flesh should spring back from a light touch. The gills of a fish should always be a bright pinkish-red color, and the scales should also be bright. Eyes should not be sunken.

The water content of fish varies from 60 to 80 percent. Therefore, the flesh of fish is very different from that of land animals. The meat of land animals is colored by a greater contribution of blood, hemoglobin, and myoglobin. Blood vessels of fish are much less numerous, thus fish flesh retains its whiteness. When it is colored or tinted, it is due to the feeding habits of the fish.

Also, the presence of fatty matter is less in fish than in land animals, and fat content is variable in assorted species. Fat that is present in fish does not present itself as a subcutaneous layer, except in the eel, but rather it is distributed in the muscular tissue (intramuscular fat). Fat content is also indicated by the color of the flesh. As a rule, the darker the flesh the fattier the fish. Unlike land animal meat, fish has no need to be tenderized by aging. The sooner fish is prepared after being harvested from the sea, the better.

Before fabricating a fish of a larger size such as turbot, halibut, or brill, it should be allowed to drain of blood completely. To do this, the fish is cut near the tail and refrigerated in an upright position.

One of the most popular seafoods today is the striped bass, or seabass. This fish is offered throughout the country in many restaurants. Striped bass should not be confused with its freshwater relative, yellow or white bass. The flesh of the striped bass is of high quality, white and flaky, rich in nutritional value, and lends itself extremely well to baking, grilling, sautéing, and poaching.

The black or striped mullet is another tender fish with firm-textured flesh and a mild nutty flavor. Preparation methods for this fish include grilling, pan-smoking, and baking.

Other popular favorites incude cod, salmon, sole, brill, flounder, turbot, and bass. Although many cooking methods may apply to these selections, the moist-heat cooking technique does the most justice to the delicate texture of these sea delicacies.

Seafood cookery is indeed a specialization and demands from the culinarian expertise, accuracy, and excellent cooking skills. In the traditional kitchen, the individual responsible for seafood cookery was the *chef poissonnier*; he or she was specifically charged with the preparation of all fish dishes. *Poissonnier* was also the term used for the fish purveyor.

The preparation of saltwater and freshwater fish differs somewhat, although the most common methods of seafood preparation are poaching, braising, grilling, sautéing, deep-frying, smoking, and au gratin.

We believe that food tastes best, and contains the most benefit for the body, in its simplest form. As culinarians we should not assume that we must have a multitude of ingredients to create good food.

The culinary profession is really about doing ordinary things extraordinarily well, and understanding food with all of its important values.

Moist-heat cooking techniques include steaming, poaching, and shallow poaching. Poaching is a wonderful cooking technique and is defined as submerging a food product into a flavored cooking liquid that is held at a constant temperature, below the boiling point. The use of flavored cooking liquids can be a phenomenally creative outlet for the culinarian, from creating a simple court bouillon to the use of more exotic seasonings indigenous to the different regions of the world. The culinarian can experiment with various stocks, wines, and even beers. However, always use ingredients that are supportive of each other, have harmonious flavors, and do the most justice to your food product. Focus on herbs, pungents, citrus fruits, spices, and aromatics, while developing an understanding of the critical part they play in food preparation.

Poached and shallow poached foods should never be undercooked or overcooked. The fish should be cooked to the point that it flakes to the touch of a fork (indicating cooked protein fibers) and appears opaque. Watch out for distinctive albumen separation, which is a clear sign of overheated liquid and overcooking. It is important to use an appropriate amount of liquid for the amount of fish to be prepared. Too much liquid, no matter how good, as well as overcooking both contribute to a great loss of flavor in the end product.

Upon completion of the cooking process, it is critical that the food product be served immediately. Therefore, in an a la carte restaurant, selecting the shallow poaching method is perhaps the most appropriate. Using this method, the aromatics and flavor enhancers are combined with the poaching liquid in a cooking vessel. The food product is added to the liquid. The vessel is placed on a heat source and allowed to reach the necessary temperature. The food product is commonly covered with a piece of buttered or olive-oiled parchment, or aluminum foil. The food product is finished over the heat source and checked for doneness. The item is then removed from the cooking liquid and kept warm until service. The remaining liquid, classically called cuisson, can be used to prepare an accompanying sauce or broth.

Steaming can be achieved in a covered colander or stacked bamboo steamer over a flavor-infused liquid, where vapors and steam not only cook the product but also infuse the flavor from the cooking liquid. Again, it is imperative with this cooking method that upon completion of the cooking process the food is served immediately.

In steaming, poaching, and shallow poaching, it is critical to use restraint when working with seasonings and flavor enhancers, because the foods prepared in this manner are extremely delicate, and one can unintentionally over-season and mask the flavor of the food product being prepared.

SEAFOOD TERMINOLOGY

Drawn fish. A whole fish with bones but with the entrails removed.

Dressed Fish. A whole fish that has been scaled and has entrails, head, tail, and fins removed.

Fillet of fish. Boneless fish fillet, skinless, cut lengthwise from the backbone with the bloodline removed.

Fish steak. A cross-cut section of a large dressed fish.

CHEF'S NOTES

⊚ *Purchase the finest-quality product available.*

⊚ *When purchasing fresh fish, the following can be used as a guide to approximate the amounts needed per serving:*

   ⊚ *One pound per person for whole fish.*

   ⊚ *One-half pound per person for dressed fish.*

   ⊚ *One-third pound per person for fillets.*

⊚ *To store fish, use perforated pans over cracked ice, exchange ice frequently, and provide for adequate drainage.*

⊚ *Do not refreeze fish; this will contribute greatly to the loss of texture, flavor, and moisture, as ice crystals once again form in the flesh.*

⊚ *Decide on the cooking method.*

⊚ *Always cook fish for the shortest possible holding time.*

⊚ *Focus on perfecting cooking skill, taste, and flavor profile enhancement.*

⊚ *Don't force creativity; keep it simple and elegant.*

MEATS AND POULTRY

There are many healthful cooking methods available for the preparation of lean meats. In fact, almost all cooking methods except those that add fat, such as deep-frying and pan frying, can be used in nutritional cooking.

@

The goal in preparing lean meat items is to reduce the amount of fat in the dish by removing as much visible fat before cooking, not adding additional sources of fat, and utilizing cooking techniques that allow the fat to melt away and be discarded.

The popularity of poultry is very evident as one views restaurant menus and sales across the country. The tender, moist meat lends itself to all cooking methods, particularly roasting, broiling, grilling, poaching, and sautéing. Poultry is very versatile. It is also the mainstay of many ethnic cuisines, from simple to elegant.

By far the most popular chicken is the broiler/fryer, which is usually up to 2 months old and weighs from 2½ to 4 pounds. This bird is used for roasting, poaching, grilling, and spit-roasting.

Removing the skin from chicken reduces the amount of fat found in the meat, since most of the fat is found in the skin. This fat adds flavor and moisture to the meat; therefore, if removed prior to the cooking process, it is necessary to evaluate the dish to determine when additional flavor and moisture can be added, either before or during the cooking process. A high-quality chicken stock or a marinade can serve this dual role in many dishes. Braising, poaching, and stewing are excellent cooking methods to help retain flavor and tenderness.

For some cooking methods, especially dry-heat methods such as roasting, it is desirable to leave the skin intact. The fat from the skin protects the meat so that it remains moist during the cooking process. Some fat will drain from the meat into the pan and can be removed from the pan before utilizing the pan drippings.

Dark leg meat is higher in fat and calories than white meat and represents a product conducive to the braising and simmering procedures.

One of the most common causes of foodborne illness is infection by salmonella bacteria. This bacteria is present in approximately 30 to 50 percent of the raw poultry sold in the United States. Therefore, we must take care to observe proper storage, handling, preparation, and cooking of poultry, in order to prevent, minimize, or eliminate a health hazard. Some simple tips will help to prevent the spread and growth of salmonella.

CHEF'S NOTES ON SAFE POULTRY HANDLING PRACTICES

◉ *Thoroughly rinse poultry products in running cold water prior to cooking (the "dilution method" of controlling salmonella count).*

◉ *After handling raw poultry, always wash hands in hot soapy water before handling any other food.*

◉ *Thoroughly wash and sanitize all utensils and cutting boards, and use different utensils for raw and cooked poultry in order to prevent cross-contamination.*

◉ *Never stuff any poultry ahead of time, but rather, stuff it just before the cooking procedure. It is best to cook the stuffing separately.*

- ⑥ *Don't undercook chicken. Thorough cooking to high heat (165° F/74° C) will kill the bacteria.*

- ⑥ *Uncooked chicken if left at room temperature for any length of time can multiply salmonella bacteria. Always cover and store washed chicken in the refrigerator at 35° F (2° C) prior to cooking, or wrap properly and store in the freezer.*

- ⑥ *Thaw frozen chicken in the refrigerator in a perforated container which allows juices to drain into a pan; never thaw at room temperature. Dispose of drained liquid properly, so that it does not contaminate other foods or work surfaces.*

CHEF'S NOTES

- ⑥ *Choose the appropriate portions of lean, high-quality cuts of meat and poultry.*

- ⑥ *Utilize the leanest meat and poultry, but don't substitute less-lean meats when it will compromise the integrity of the dish.*

- ⑥ *Alternate your selection of meats to include products that are naturally raised to be leaner, such as Brangus, a cross-breed of Angus and Brahman cattle from Texas. This breed is raised without the use of hormones or steroids and fed a natural feed. Also, a good alternate choice is Chianina beef, an Italian breed of cattle raised for its low fat content.*

- ⑥ *Follow the Food Guide Pyramid guidelines for appropriate portion size. Select a 4- to 5-ounce raw weight to produce a 3- to 3½ ounce cooked portion of meat.*

- ⑥ *Trim all excess fat from meat.*

- ⑥ *Remove skin from poultry before or after cooking, depending of the method of preparation chosen.*

- ⑥ *Purchase alternative meats when appropriate for inclusion in a recipe. Look for reduced-fat versions of high-fat meats that will still offer the flavor depth needed, or precook and drain excess fat before adding to a recipe, as can be done with bacon and sausage.*

- ⑥ *Balance meat portions with additional vegetables and starches to extend the portion size while reducing the fat, calories, and cholesterol found in the overall recipe.*

- ⑥ *To create the illusion of a large portion when serving meat items, utilize the following techniques:*

  - ⑥ *Slice roasted meats thinly and fan on top of grains or a vegetable medley.*

  - ⑥ *Shave meat when preparing sandwich fillings so it can be stacked to give the appearance of a larger portion. Utilize vegetables, like slaws, in sandwiches to extend the portion.*

  - ⑥ *Utilize a meat or poultry item as a flavor enhancer rather than as the main component in dishes such as stir-fry, pasta, and stew.*

  - ⑥ *Utilize sauces such as vegetable coulis, stock reductions, fruit or vegetable relishes to give additional plate coverage and eye appeal.*

OVEN-ROASTED PORK LOIN WITH LENTIL BULGUR SALAD *

SERVES 8 (3 OZ./84 GM PORK PER SERVING)

CHEF'S NOTES

Thoroughly marinating the pork loin plays an important role in this recipe, for a number of reasons. Even though the cooking process uses dry heat, you can fearlessly trim excess fat before roasting and still keep the meat juicy and tender.

For an alternative flavor, experiment with different spice rubs, such as roasted cumin and roasted coriander.

INGREDIENTS	AMOUNT/U.S.	METRIC
Pork loin roast, boneless, center-cut, cleaned, excess fat and sinew removed	30 oz.	840 gm
Garlic, minced	3 cloves	3 cloves
Teriyaki light marinade	2 Tbsp.	30 ml
Ginger, minced	1 tsp.	3 gm
Chicken broth	3 fl. oz.	90 ml
Salad:		
Bulgur wheat, cooked weight	8 oz.	225 gm
Green lentils, cooked weight	8 oz.	225 gm
Tomatoes, peeled, seeded, and diced	6 oz.	168 gm
Yellow onion, finely diced	2 oz.	56 gm
Red bell pepper, cleaned, seeded, diced	1 oz.	28 gm
Green bell pepper, cleaned, seeded, diced	1 oz.	28 gm
Yellow bell pepper, cleaned, seeded, diced	1 oz.	28 gm
Cilantro, chopped	2 Tbsp.	10 gm
Rice vinegar	2 Tbsp.	30 ml
Olive oil, light	1 Tbsp.	15 ml
Lemon, juice of	1 ea.	1 ea.
Cumin powder	1 tsp.	2 gm
Kosher salt	pinch	pinch
Fresh, cracked white pepper	to taste	to taste

PREPARATION

1. Marinate pork with garlic, teriyaki, and ginger. Pan-sear on all sides until evenly browned. Place in roasting pan in 375°F (190°C) oven and roast until internal temperature reaches 145°F (63°C). Turn roast occasionally utilizing tongs (do not spear with a fork).

2. Remove from oven and set pork aside to rest. Deglaze roasting pan with chicken stock on stove, stirring continuously; reduce by one-third. Remove jus and set aside to mix with salad.

3. Prepare Lentil Bulgur Salad by combining all salad ingredients. Add cooled jus drippings and combine thoroughly with salad to allow flavors to fully develop.

4. Just before serving, taste and adjust seasoning as needed. Slice pork loin in even portions (approx. 3 oz.); serve on top of Lentil Bulgur Salad.

NUTRITION PER SERVING

Calories 316, protein 31 gm, fat 14 gm, carbohydrates 16 gm, cholesterol 84 mg, sodium 264 mg

FILLET OF HALIBUT WITH AROMATICS AND RICE VINEGAR

SERVES 6

INGREDIENTS	AMOUNT/U.S.	METRIC
Halibut, center-cut steaks	6 @ 5 oz. ea.	6 @ 140 gm ea.
Kosher salt	to taste	to taste
Flour	1 Tbsp.	7 gm
Vegetable spray	as needed	as needed
Lime, sliced	1	1
Fresh, cracked white pepper	to taste	to taste
Bay leaves	4	4
Parsley sprigs or cilantro leaves	1 oz.	28 gm
Olive oil	2 Tbsp.	30 ml
Garlic, minced	3 cloves	3 cloves
Red onion, julienned	1 lg.	1 lg.
Leek, white part, julienned	1 lg.	1 lg.
Carrot, sliced	1 lg.	1 lg.
Madras curry powder	1 tsp.	2 gm
Rice wine vinegar	6 fl. oz.	180 ml
White wine	2½ fl. oz.	75 ml
Chicken stock, high-quality	6 fl. oz.	180 ml
Garnish:		
Arugula, snipped	⅓ bunch	⅓ bunch

CHEF'S NOTES

This dish holds very well in the refrigerator for up to 3 days. Remove from refrigerator and let sit at room temperature for 15 minutes before serving. The flavor comes through better if the dish is not very, very cold. Also, experiment with different vinegars to adjust flavor profile.

In days past, this preparation method was frequently used to preserve food; however, harsher vinegars were used. This method is very popular with the Portuguese and Spanish

Halibut can be replaced with swordfish, seabass, snapper, etc.

PREPARATION

1. Sprinkle fish steaks with a little salt, dust with flour, and dry sauté in hot nonstick pan sprayed with vegetable spray until golden brown, about 2 minutes each side.
2. Remove from sauté pan and place in casserole. Add lime slices, cracked pepper, bay leaves, and parsley or cilantro.
3. In stainless steel saucepan, heat olive oil and sweat garlic, onions, leeks, and carrots gently over low heat until translucent.
4. Add curry powder, rice vinegar, and white wine and reduce for 1 minute. Add chicken stock and simmer for 3 minutes. Adjust seasoning with salt and pepper.
5. Remove from heat and cool. Pour over fish. Rest for 5 minutes. Store in refrigerator to allow flavors to mature. Serve cold garnished with arugula.

NUTRITION PER SERVING
Calories 288, protein 31 gm, fat 9 gm, carbohydrates 16 gm, cholesterol 66 mg, sodium 656 mg

CHICKEN BREAST IN GINGER-
TARRAGON BROTH*,
WITH BARLEY
AND VEGETABLE MEDLEY*

SERVES 10

INGREDIENTS	AMOUNT/U.S.	METRIC
Chicken breasts (all visible fat trimmed)	10 @ 4 oz. ea.	10 @ 112 gm ea.
Vegetables:		
Carrots, peeled, washed, bias-cut	10 oz.	280 gm
Celery, peeled, washed, bias-cut	10 oz.	280 gm
Broccoli florets, small, cleaned, washed	10 oz.	280 gm
Shiitaki mushrooms, sliced fine	5 oz.	140 gm
Leeks, green part, julienned	5 oz.	140 gm
Barley, cooked, seasoned (keep warm) (cooked weight)	10 oz.	280 gm
Olive oil	1 Tbsp.	15 ml
Chicken stock, defatted	½ cup	120 ml
Kosher salt	to taste	to taste
Fresh, cracked white pepper	to taste	to taste
Broth:		
Olive oil	2 tsp.	10 ml
Red onion, finely diced	3 oz.	84 gm
Garlic, minced	1 clove	1 clove
Ginger, fresh, grated	½ tsp.	1.5 gm
Tomato paste	2 oz.	56 gm
Dry sherry	2 fl. oz.	60 ml
Chicken stock, defatted	1 qt.	1 l
Orange zest	1 lg. pc.	1 lg. pc.
Bay leaf	1	1
Tarragon leaves	2 tsp.	3 gm
Fresh, cracked white pepper	to taste	to taste
Kosher salt	to taste	to taste

PREPARATION
1. Preheat oven to 350°F (175°C).

VEGETABLES

2. Blanch or steam carrots, celery, and broccoli florets until tender. (Be sure to retain the bright vegetable color.) Cold shock, drain, and set aside, wash mushrooms and leeks. Drain thoroughly. Reserve, keeping warm.

3. In large saucepan, sauté mushrooms and leeks in olive oil. Add stock; adjust seasoning with salt and pepper to taste. Add carrots, celery, and broccoli florets; reheat.

4. Toss mixture with cooked and seasoned barley.

BROTH

1. Heat large, deep saucepan. Add oil and onion. Sweat onions gently; add garlic and ginger, stirring continuously.

2. Add the tomato paste; sauté until the mixture is a rusty color. Deglaze pan with sherry and stock. Add orange zest, bay leaf, and tarragon. Simmer gently for 4 minutes.

3. Taste and adjust seasoning with pepper and a little salt.

CHICKEN BREASTS

5. Place cleaned chicken breasts in baking dish and cover with hot Ginger-Tarragon Broth. Cover dish with parchment or foil and place in hot oven for 5–7 minutes.

6. Remove from oven and test chicken for doneness, making sure chicken is firm to the touch.

7. Place chicken on serving platter and keep warm. Bring broth to a gentle boil and adjust seasoning. Remove bay leaf and orange zest.

PRESENTATION

Serve chicken in a deep dish with barley-vegetable mixture. Ladle broth over the top.

NUTRITION PER SERVING
Calories 250, protein 30 gm, fat 5 gm, carbohydrates 21 gm, cholesterol 67 mg, sodium 175 mg

WHITE BEAN CASSOULET

SERVES 8 (6–8 OZ. SERVING)

CHEF'S NOTES

Garnish with pico de gallo and baked julienned corn tortillas. Can also be served with a slice of warm cornbread.

NUTRITION NOTES

Prepared mustard contains a high level of sodium, however this adds substantial flavor to the recipe. Additional salt may need to be added for flavor balance. (See Chapter 7 for additional discussion of sodium.)

INGREDIENTS	AMOUNT/U.S.	METRIC
Parma ham, small-diced	4 oz.	112 gm
Onion, peeled, washed, small-diced	3 oz.	84 gm
Celery, peeled, washed, small-diced	3 oz.	84 gm
Carrot, peeled, washed, small-diced	3 oz.	84 gm
Garlic, minced	2 cloves	2 cloves
Jalapeño pepper, seeded, minced	1	1
Dijon mustard	8 oz.	224 gm
White beans, soaked overnight, rinsed (raw weight)	24 oz.	670 gm
Chicken stock, defatted	42 fl. oz.	1260 ml
Kosher salt	to taste	to taste
Fresh, cracked white pepper	to taste	to taste
Chicken meat, roasted, pulled off the bone, skinless, coarsely chopped	1 lb.	450 gm
Green pepper, cleaned, seeded, small-diced	4 oz.	112 gm
Red pepper, cleaned, seeded, small-diced	4 oz.	112 gm
Yellow pepper, cleaned, seeded, small-diced	4 oz.	112 gm
Cilantro, fresh, chopped	1 bunch	1 bunch

PREPARATION

1. Preheat oven to 350°F (175°C).
2. In large stainless steel saucepan, render Parma ham for approximately 2 minutes.
3. Add onion, celery, and carrots, mix well, and cook until tender.
4. Add garlic and jalapeño, mix well. Continue to cook for 5 minutes.
5. Add Dijon mustard, stirring well so that mustard does not burn on the bottom of the pan. Add beans and chicken stock. Mix well. Adjust seasoning with salt and pepper.
6. Bring to boil and cover, then place in preheated oven for 45 minutes.
7. Remove from oven and remove cover. Add chicken meat and peppers, place back in oven, and reheat thoroughly, for 10–15 minutes.
8. Remove from oven. Add cilantro, taste, and adjust seasoning. Cover and rest for 10 more minutes.
9. Taste and adjust seasoning as needed.

NUTRITION PER SERVING

Calories 479, protein 40 gm, fat 8 gm, carbohydrates 61 gm, cholesterol 56 mg, sodium 1111 mg

SALMON FILLET WITH ARUGULA AND FENNEL

SERVES 8

INGREDIENTS	AMOUNT/U.S.	METRIC
Salmon fillet, fabricated, cleaned, rinsed, cut into steaks	8 @ 5 oz.	8 @ 140 gm
Kosher salt	to taste	to taste
Fresh ground black pepper	to taste	to taste
Fennel, cleaned, washed, sliced	16 oz.	448 gm
Chicken stock	8 oz.	240 ml
Arugula greens, cleaned, washed	16 oz.	448 gm
Onion and Potato Puree (p. 296)		
Tomato-Bacon Vinaigrette (p. 216)	8 oz.	240 ml

PREPARATION

1. Season each steak with salt and pepper. In hot nonstick pan, sear steaks on both sides using the dry sauté method. Finish in oven at 350°F (175°C) for 3–5 minutes.
2. Cook fennel slices slowly in chicken stock until tender. Remove fennel slices from stock; save stock to reuse or use in Tomato-Bacon Vinaigrette.
3. Place drained fennel slices with arugula greens in hot sauté pan and sauté quickly, until greens are slightly wilted. Adjust seasoning and set aside.

PRESENTATION

Use a pastry bag to pipe the Onion and Potato Puree, following the curvature of the plate. Center the greens and fennel on the plate; top with the salmon. Dress the plate with 1 oz. Tomato-Bacon Vinaigrette per serving.

NUTRITION PER SERVING OF SALMON

Calories 234, protein 31 gm, fat 10 gm, carbohydrates 5 gm, cholesterol 78 mg, sodium 83 mg

NUTRITION PER COMPLETE ENTREE SERVING

Calories 386, protein 35 gm, fat 14 gm, carbohydrates 31 gm, cholesterol 82 mg, sodium 136 mg

TOMATO-BACON VINAIGRETTE *

INGREDIENTS	AMOUNT/U.S.	METRIC
Dijon mustard	1 Tbsp.	15 gm
Lemon juice	2 Tbsp.	30 ml
Olive oil	2½ fl. oz.	70 ml
Apple cider vinegar	2 Tbsp.	30 ml
Dry white wine	2 Tbsp.	30 ml
Garlic, minced	2 cloves	2 cloves
Red onion, finely diced	2 oz.	56 gm
Basil, fresh, snipped	1 Tbsp.	5 gm
Cilantro, fresh, snipped	1 Tbsp.	5 gm
Thyme, fresh, minced	2 Tbsp.	10 gm
Bacon, sautéed, minced	1 Tbsp.	15 gm
Honey	2 fl. oz.	56 ml
Chicken stock	6 fl. oz.	180 ml
Tomatoes, oven-roasted, chopped	12 oz.	336 gm
Kosher salt	to taste	to taste
Fresh, cracked white pepper	to taste	to taste

PREPARATION

1. Place all ingredients in stainless steel mixing bowl. Use submersible blender and blend until desired consistency. Adjust seasoning with salt and pepper.
2. Place in stainless steel container, cover tightly, and refrigerate.

NUTRITION PER 1 OZ./30 ML SERVING
Calories 43, protein 0 gm, fat 3 gm, carbohydrates 4 gm, cholesterol 1 mg, sodium 25 mg

GRILLED FLANK STEAK WITH SWEET ONION BROTH

INGREDIENTS	AMOUNT/U.S.	METRIC
Flank steak (all visible fat trimmed)	2 lb.	896 gm
Orange juice	8 fl. oz.	240 ml
Apple juice	8 fl. oz.	240 ml
Red onion, cleaned, peeled, thinly sliced	3 oz.	84 gm
San-J™ teriyaki sauce, low-sodium	3 Tbsp.	45 ml
Orange, zest of	1	1
Sherry vinegar	1 Tbsp.	15 ml
Olive oil	1 Tbsp.	15 ml
Lime, sliced	1	1
Cilantro, fresh, snipped	5 sprigs	5 sprigs
Garlic, minced	3 cloves	3 cloves
Jalapeño pepper, seeded, minced	1 tsp.	3 gm
Chili powder	1 tsp.	2 gm
Sweet Onion Broth (p. 218)		
Orzo Vegetable Medley (p. 219)		

PREPARATION

1. Combine orange and apple juice, onion, teriyaki sauce, orange zest, vinegar, olive oil, lime slices, cilantro, garlic, jalapeño, and chili powder; mix well. Place flank steaks in marinade and marinate for at least 2 hours.
2. Remove flank steaks from marinade and discard marinade.
3. Preferably, grill flank steaks over hardwood grill, but a brick char-broiler will accomplish the task just fine. Grill flanks until evenly browned on both sides.

PRESENTATION

Reheat broth and vegetables. Arrange a serving of vegetables on each plate, place a sliced flank steak on Orzo Vegetable Medley, surround with 2 oz. of Sweet Onion Broth.

NUTRITION PER SERVING OF STEAK
Calories 250, protein 23 gm, fat 13 gm, carbohydrates 10 gm, cholesterol 57 mg, sodium 275 mg

NUTRITION PER COMPLETE ENTREE SERVING
Calories 449, protein 31 gm, fat 16 gm, carbohydrates 46 gm, cholesterol 57 mg, sodium 354 mg

SWEET ONION BROTH *

SERVES 8

INGREDIENTS	AMOUNT/U.S.	METRIC
Oso sweet onions, cleaned, peeled, finely diced	8 oz.	224 gm
Olive oil	1 tsp.	5 ml
Caraway seeds	5 ea	5 ea
Dry white wine	3 fl. oz.	90 ml
Lemon thyme, snipped	1 tsp.	1 gm
Chicken stock, high quality	16 fl. oz.	480 ml
Kosher salt	to taste	to taste
Fresh, cracked white pepper	to taste	to taste

PREPARATION
1. Preheat oven to 325°F (165°C).
2. Mix the onions, oil, and caraway seeds. Place into a preheated, nonstick pan and panroast over medium heat until browned.
3. Deglaze with white wine, reduce until almost dry.
4. Add lemon thyme and chicken stock. Simmer for 15 minutes.
5. Adjust seasoning with salt and pepper.

NUTRITION PER 2 OZ./60 ML SERVING

Calories 31, protein 1 gm, fat 1 gm, carbohydrates 4 gm, cholesterol 0 mg, sodium 3 mg

ORZO VEGETABLE MEDLEY *

SERVES 8

INGREDIENTS	AMOUNT/U.S.	METRIC
Orzo, raw	6 oz.	168 gm
Artichokes, large	5 each	5 each
Water	1 qt.	960 ml
Baby carrots, cleaned, trimmed, halved	5 oz.	140 gm
Olive oil	1 Tbsp.	15 ml
Fava beans, fresh, cleaned, cooked, drained	6 oz.	168 gm
Tarragon, snipped	2 Tbsp.	10 gm
Kosher salt	to taste	to taste
Fresh, cracked white pepper	to taste	to taste

PREPARATION

1. Cook orzo in 1 quart of slightly salted boiling water until tender. Drain and rinse. Adjust seasoning. Place in a clean stainless steel insert pan and keep warm.
2. Trim artichoke hearts. Slice hearts and simmer in 1½ cups salted water. Remove from water. Reserve artichokes and broth.
3. Sweat carrots in olive oil until tender.
4. Add artichokes, fava beans, cooked orzo, artichoke broth, and tarragon to carrots. Bring to a simmer and season with pepper and salt, as needed.
5. Portion vegetable in dish; arrange flank steak on top.

NUTRITION PER SERVING
Calories 168, protein 7 gm, fat 2 gm, carbohydrates 32 gm, cholesterol 0 mg, sodium 76 mg

SAUTÉED CHICKEN BREAST WITH APPLE CIDER VINAIGRETTE

SERVES 8

CHEF'S NOTES

To prevent cut apples from turning brown, place in stainless steel bowl with ice water and lemon juice.

NUTRITION NOTES

When adding the optional toasted pecans, the following nutritional values will be added for each ½ ounce. Calories 94, protein 1 gm, fat 3 gm, carbohydrates 10 gm, cholesterol 0 mg, sodium 2 mg

INGREDIENTS	AMOUNT/U.S.	METRIC
Apple Cider Vinaigrette (p. 221)		
Chicken breasts, cleaned, washed, fat trimmed	8 @ 5 oz. ea.	8 @ 140 gm. ea.
Arugula greens, cleaned, washed, drained	6 oz.	168 gm
Mesclun greens, cleaned, washed, drained	6 oz.	168 gm
Garnish:		
Granny smith apples, peeled, cored, julienned	8 oz.	224 gm
Pecans, toasted (optional)	4 oz.	112 gm

PREPARATION

1. Prepare Apple Cider Vinaigrette.
2. Remove all fat and sinew from the chicken breasts.
3. Dry sauté chicken breasts on both sides until golden brown. Place on rack in 375°F (190°C) oven; cook for 4–5 minutes. Remove from oven and cool slightly to allow the juices to set. Slice chicken and arrange on plates.
4. In a clean stainless steel bowl, combine the two greens and toss gently with warm vinaigrette. Arrange on plates next to the chicken.
5. Garnish with julienned apples and optional toasted pecans.

NUTRITION PER COMPLETE ENTREE SERVING
Calories 275, protein 34 gm, fat 9 gm, carbohydrates 13 gm, cholesterol 82 mg, sodium 107 mg

APPLE CIDER VINAIGRETTE *

SERVES 8

INGREDIENTS	AMOUNT/U.S.	METRIC
Apple cider	14 fl. oz	420 ml
Hazelnut oil	2 fl. oz.	60 ml
Cider vinegar	3 fl. oz.	90 ml
Chives, short cut	1 Tbsp.	5 gm
Basil, snipped	1 Tbsp.	5 gm
Kosher salt	to taste	to taste
Fresh, cracked white pepper	to taste	to taste

PREPARATION

1. Heat the apple cider in a small stainless saucepan, reducing it by two-thirds. Remove the cider from the heat and allow to cool.
2. Combine the oil and vinegar with the cooled cider. Mix well. Add the chives, basil, salt, and pepper. Reserve.
3. Place in stainless steel container, cover tightly, and store in refrigerator.

NUTRITION PER SERVING

Calories 90, protein 0 gm, fat 7 gm, carbohydrates 7 gm, cholesterol 0 mg, sodium 2 mg

CRISPY SEARED HALIBUT WITH ORZO, STEWED TOMATOES, CAPERS, AND BLACK OLIVES

SERVES 8

CHEF'S NOTES

Halibut cooks quickly; fish should flake, be firm, but not fall apart.

NUTRITION NOTES

The optional addition of the Asiago cheese is to intensify the flavors in this dish. The Asiago is meant to be a garnish, therefore, use it judiciously as it will increase the amount of fat and calories in the dish. If you include the Asiago, it will add the following nutritional values: Calories 220, fat 14 gm to the total recipe.

INGREDIENTS	AMOUNT/U.S.	METRIC
Halibut fillets, center-cut, skin off, cleaned, washed, paper towel dried	8 @ 5 oz. ea.	8 @ 140 gm ea.
Orzo pasta	½ lb.	224 gm
Olive oil	2 Tbsp.	30 ml
Garlic, minced	4 cloves	4 cloves
Red onion, finely diced	4 oz.	112 gm
Yellow peppers, cleaned, seeded, finely diced	2	2
Anchovy fillets, minced	2	2
Chicken stock	12 fl. oz.	360 ml
Roma tomatoes, peeled, seeded, finely diced	1 lb.	450 gm
Basil, chiffonade	3 Tbsp.	15 gm
Tarragon, fresh, snipped	2 Tbsp.	10 gm
Kalamata olives, quartered	2 oz.	56 gm
Capers, fine	1 oz.	28 gm
Kosher salt	to taste	to taste
Fresh, cracked white pepper	to taste	to taste
Garnish:		
Asiago cheese, grated	2 oz.	56 gm
Cilantro	1 bunch	1 bunch

PREPARATION

1. Prepare and dress halibut. Season with salt and fresh cracked pepper; set aside.

2. Cook orzo in 1 quart of slightly salted boiling water until tender. Drain and rinse. Adjust seasoning. Place in stainless steel insert pan and keep warm.

3. In a nonstick sauté pan, heat olive oil, and sweat garlic, onions, and yellow peppers, for 2 minutes over gentle heat.

4. Add anchovy, and deglaze with chicken stock. Add tomatoes, and simmer mixture gently over low heat for 15 minutes.

5. Season with basil and tarragon. Add olives and capers, and simmer gently for an additional 5 minutes. Adjust seasoning with salt and fresh, cracked white pepper.

6. In a sauté pan, dry sauté halibut until brown on both sides. Remove from pan and finish in oven at 350°F (175°C) for 3 minutes.

Place a large serving spoon full of prepared orzo in center of plate; top and surround with stewed tomato mixture. Place crispy halibut on top, garnish with cilantro leaves, and sprinkle with Asiago cheese. Serve at once.

NUTRITION PER SERVING
Calories 349, protein 37 gm, fat 9 gm, carbohydrates 29 gm, cholesterol 67 mg, sodium 632 mg

CARAMELIZED RED SNAPPER FILLET

SERVES 10

INGREDIENTS	AMOUNT/U.S.	METRIC
Red snapper fillets, dressed, skin on	10 @ 4 oz. ea.	10 @ 112 gm ea.
Kosher salt	to taste	to taste
Fresh, cracked white pepper	to taste	to taste
Olive oil	3 Tbsp.	45 ml
Garlic, minced	3 cloves	3 cloves
Leeks, cleaned, washed, julienned	3 oz.	84 gm
Yellow squash, peeled, cleaned, julienned (not seeded)	7 oz.	196 gm
Zucchini, peeled, cleaned, julienned (not seeded)	7 oz.	196 gm
Idaho potatoes, boiled, large-diced	20 oz.	560 gm
Haricot verts, cleaned, blanched	10 oz.	280 gm
Tomatoes, sundried, chopped	12 oz.	336 gm
Kalamata olives, sliced	30	30
White wine	10 fl. oz.	300 ml
Vegetable stock (high-quality)	1½ qt.	1½ l
Basil leaves, fresh, chiffonade	1 bunch	1 bunch

PREPARATION

1. Preheat oven to 375°F (190°C).
2. Season fish fillets with salt and pepper. Heat oven-safe sauté pan; add oil. Place fish fillets, skin side down, in hot pan and sauté until skin is crisp and fillet is browned. Remove from pan; keep warm.
3. Using same pan, add garlic and leeks, and cook until tender. Add squash, zucchini, and potatoes. Sauté lightly and adjust seasoning with salt and white pepper.
4. Place sauté pan in the oven for 3 minutes.
5. Add tomatoes, haricot verts, and olives to pan; sauté lightly. Deglaze pan with white wine. Add vegetable stock and simmer gently on top of the stove. Adjust seasoning; add basil chiffonade.

PRESENTATION

Place warm vegetable-potato mixture into large soup bowls and top with fish fillet.

NUTRITION PER SERVING

Calories 342, protein 30 gm, fat 8 gm, carbohydrates 36 gm, cholesterol 41 mg, sodium 863 mg

TURKEY SCALLOPINI WITH STEWED CRANBERRY, APPLE, AND ONION COMPOTE

SERVES 10

INGREDIENTS	AMOUNT/U.S.	METRIC
Turkey scallopini, fat and sinew trimmed	20 @ 3 oz. ea.	20 @ 84 gm ea.
Kosher salt	to taste	to taste
Fresh, cracked white pepper	to taste	to taste
Flour	as needed	as needed
Vegetable spray	as needed	as needed
Stewed Cranberry, Apple, Onion Compote (p. 226)		

PREPARATION

1. Preheat oven to 350°F (175°C).
2. Season turkey scallopini with salt and white pepper and dust with flour.
3. Heat nonstick sauté pan over medium heat. Spray with vegetable spray and wipe out excess.
4. Place turkey scallopini in skillet and quickly sear on both sides until golden brown.
5. Remove from pan and place in baking dish. Finish cooking in oven for approximately 3–4 minutes.

PRESENTATION

Place two turkey scallopini on each plate and serve with Stewed Cranberry, Apple, and Onion Compote (p. 226).

NUTRITION PER SERVING OF TURKEY
Calories 263, protein 38 gm, fat 11 gm, carbohydrates 0 gm, cholesterol 88 mg, sodium 81 mg

NUTRITION PER COMPLETE ENTREE SERVING
Calories 313, protein 38 gm, fat 12 gm, carbohydrates 9 gm, cholesterol 88 mg, sodium 83 mg

STEWED CRANBERRY, APPLE, ONION COMPOTE *

SERVES 10

INGREDIENTS	AMOUNT/U.S.	METRIC
Red onions, cleaned, finely sliced	8 oz.	224 gm
Cranberries, dried	4 oz.	112 gm
Green apples, peeled, cored, julienned	2 med.	2 med.
Balsamic vinegar	2 fl. oz.	60 ml
Red wine	2 fl. oz.	60 ml
Chicken stock, defatted	2 fl. oz.	60 ml
Port wine	2 fl. oz.	60 ml
Olive oil	1 tsp.	5 ml
Kosher salt	to taste	to taste
Fresh, cracked white pepper	to taste	to taste

PREPARATION

1. In a small sauté pan, place dried cranberries and port wine. Allow cranberries to bloom over low heat. Cranberries should be plump and liquid should be reduced.
2. In a two-quart saucepan, heat 1 tsp. olive oil over medium heat. Add onions and sauté gently for 3 minutes. Stir occasionally.
3. Cook gently until onions begin to turn brown. Deglaze with vinegar and reduce until dry. Gradually add wine at two intervals. Add apples, chicken stock, and cranberries. Simmer gently for 20 minutes, stirring occasionally.
4. Season with salt and cracked white pepper. Remove from heat and keep warm. Set aside.

NUTRITION PER SERVING

Calories 50, protein 0 gm, fat 1 gm, carbohydrates 9 gm, cholesterol 0 mg, sodium 2 mg

CHICKEN SHANKS WITH ORIENTAL APPLE RICE

SERVES 6 (2 LEGS EACH)

INGREDIENTS	AMOUNT/U.S.	METRIC
Chicken legs, washed	12	12
Scallions, cleaned, minced	5	5
Garlic, peeled, minced	4 cloves	4 cloves
Jalapeño pepper, seeded, minced	½	½
Ginger, peeled, minced	1 tsp.	3 gm
Onion, cleaned, peeled, small-diced	4 oz.	112 gm
Celery, cleaned, peeled, small-diced	4 oz.	112 gm
Carrots, cleaned, peeled, small-diced	4 oz.	112 gm
Shiitaki mushrooms, cleaned, small-diced	3 oz.	84 gm
White rice, long-grain, raw	12 oz.	336 gm
Chicken stock	1 qt.	1 l
Apple juice	8 fl. oz.	240 ml
Soy sauce, light	2 fl. oz.	60 ml
Szechwan sauce	1 Tbsp.	15 ml
Green peas, fresh or frozen	4 oz.	112 gm
Yellow, red, and green bell peppers, large, cleaned, seeded, small-diced	1 each	1 each
Vegetable spray	as needed	as needed
Kosher salt	to taste	to taste
Fresh, cracked white pepper	to taste	to taste

NUTRITION NOTES

The skin can be removed from the chicken legs to reduce fat and calories.

PREPARATION

1. Preheat oven to 375°F (190°C). Spray medium, oven-safe stainless steel saucepan with vegetable spray and heat over medium heat.
2. Place chicken legs in pan. Brown evenly on all sides. Remove from pan and keep warm.
3. Add scallions, garlic, jalapeño pepper, and ginger to hot pan, mix well. Sauté gently for 1 minute.
4. Add onions, celery, carrots, and Shiitake mushrooms, mix well. Sauté for 2 minutes.
5. Add rice, stock, apple juice, soy sauce, and Szechwan sauce.
6. Place chicken in rice mixture, bring to light boil. Remove from heat. Cover saucepan and place in oven for 30–40 minutes.
7. Remove from oven and uncover. Add peas and peppers. Let stand for 10 minutes. Fluff mixture gently, add scallions, and adjust seasoning with kosher salt and cracked white pepper.

8. Re-cover and place back in oven for 5 more minutes. Remove from oven and rest for 10 minutes prior to service. Fluff rice with fork.

PRESENTATION

Place an even layer of rice around the bottom of warm dinner plate. Cross two chicken legs in the center of the plate.

NUTRITION PER SERVING

Calories 496, protein 38 gm, fat 8 gm, carbohydrates 66 gm, cholesterol 121 mg, sodium 545 mg

SAUTÉED CURRY SEA SCALLOPS
WITH COUSCOUS
AND TOMATO-BASIL BROTH

SERVES 8

INGREDIENTS	AMOUNT/U.S.	METRIC
Scallops:		
Sea scallops, large, cleaned, muscles removed	2 lb.	896 gm
Curry powder	¼ cup	20 gm
Mustard, dry	1½ tsp.	3 gm
Cayenne pepper	½ tsp.	1 gm
Hungarian paprika	1 tsp.	2 gm
Oregano, fresh, snipped	½ tsp.	14 gm
Thyme, fresh, snipped	½ tsp.	14 gm
Cinnamon	1½ tsp.	7 gm
Lemon juice	6 fl. oz.	180 ml
Olive oil	4 fl. oz.	120 ml
Kosher salt	to taste	to taste
Fresh, cracked white pepper	to taste	to taste
Tomato-Basil Broth:		
Olive oil	1 Tbsp.	15 ml
Garlic, split in half	1 head	1 head
Red onions, peeled, chopped	2 oz.	56 gm
Roma tomatoes, peeled, seeded, diced	1 lb.	450 gm
White wine	¼ cup	60 ml
Chicken stock, defatted	1 qt.	1 l
Couscous:		
Water	24 fl. oz.	720 ml
Butter	1 Tbsp.	15 gm
Lemon, zest of, grated	½	½
Kosher salt	½ tsp.	2.5 gm
Couscous	2 lb.	896 gm
Kalamata olives, sliced	30	30
Pinenuts, toasted	2 Tbsp.	15 gm
Raisins, plumped in boiling water	1 oz.	28 gm
Garnish:		
Parsley sprigs	4	4
Chives, chopped	2 Tbsp.	14 gm

CHEF'S NOTES

To achieve the best flavor profile, more marinade is made than will be used in this recipe. However, the remaining marinade, which in not used in marinating the scallops, can be stored in the refrigerator for up to 2 weeks and used to flavor other meats and vegetables.

PREPARATION OF SCALLOPS

1. In a clean stainless steel bowl, combine all spices, lemon juice, and olive oil to form the marinade; adjust seasoning with kosher salt and cracked

white pepper. Mix well. In a second bowl, place scallops and ¼ of the curry marinade. Gently toss scallops to cover with marinade, place in refrigerator, and allow to marinate for 2–3 hours.

PREPARATION FOR THE TOMATO-BASIL BROTH

2. Place 1 tablespoon of olive oil in a 3-quart saucepan. In the hot pan, sauté the garlic and onions for 2–3 minutes over medium heat (do not brown). Add the tomatoes and continue to cook for 3–4 minutes. Add the white wine. Add the chicken stock and simmer slowly for 20 minutes. Pass broth through a moulli mill and season with salt and fresh, cracked pepper to taste. Set aside and keep warm.

PREPARATION OF COUSCOUS

3. Place water, butter, lemon zest, and salt in 2-quart saucepan; bring to boil. Stir in couscous; remove from heat. Cover pan with plastic wrap. Let stand 5 minutes, uncover, and fluff with fork to separate the grains.
4. Stir in chopped olives, pinenuts, and raisins. Adjust seasoning. Cover and set aside.

5. Remove scallops from marinade and discard excess marinade. Allow scallops to drain on plate for a few minutes. Place scallops in hot, nonstick sauté pan over medium heat. Sauté for approximately 2 minutes on each side. Remove from heat.

PRESENTATION

Place a portion of the couscous in a bowl. Ladle warm Tomato-Basil Broth around the couscous, then arrange scallops. Sprinkle each serving with chopped chives and a parsley sprig.

NUTRITION PER SERVING
Calories 710, protein 36 gm, fat 16 gm, carbohydrates 105 gm, cholesterol 41 mg, sodium 398 mg

GRILLED SALMON WITH ROASTED PEPPER AND OLIVE SALAD

SERVES 8

INGREDIENTS	AMOUNT/U.S.	METRIC
Lemon or lime, thinly sliced	1	1
Red onion, peeled, minced	1 oz.	28 gm
Rice wine vinegar	1 Tbsp.	15 ml
Maple syrup	1 tsp.	5 ml
Fresh, cracked black pepper	dash	dash
Salmon fillets, cleaned, trimmed, cut into steaks	8 @ 4 oz. ea.	8 @ 112 gm ea.
Balsamic vinegar or lemon juice	2 Tbsp.	30 ml
Roasted Pepper and Olive Salad (p. 232)		

PREPARATION

1. Heat grill; preheat oven to 350°F (175°C).
2. Clean and trim fresh salmon. Remove all bones. Cut salmon into 4 oz. steaks. Place into a small insert pan.
3. Combine lemon, onion, vinegar, maple syrup, and black pepper; mix well. Rub mixture evenly onto salmon steaks. Allow salmon to marinate for about 15 minutes.
4. Remove lemon slices from salmon. Grill salmon until evenly marked and browned on both sides.
5. Place salmon steaks on slightly oiled sheet pan and finish in oven for approximately 3 minutes.
6. Remove salmon from oven and test for doneness. Salmon should be firm to the touch and flake.
7. Serve grilled salmon with Roasted Pepper and Olive Salad. Drizzle with balsamic vinegar or lemon juice.

NUTRITION PER SERVING OF SALMON
Calories 170, protein 23 gm, fat 7 gm, carbohydrates 3 gm, cholesterol 62 mg, sodium 86 mg

NUTRITION PER COMPLETE ENTREE SERVING
Calories 279, protein 25 gm, fat 11 gm, carbohydrates 19 gm, cholesterol 62 mg, sodium 475 mg

ROASTED PEPPER
AND OLIVE SALAD *

SERVES 8

CHEF'S NOTE

*Do not serve directly from
the refrigerator; allow to
come to room temperature.*

INGREDIENTS	AMOUNT/U.S.	METRIC
Red, green, yellow bell peppers, cleaned	1 lb. of each	450 gm of each
English cucumber, peeled, seeded, diced	4 oz.	112 gm
Roma tomatoes, peeled, seeded, julienne	8 oz.	224 gm
Red onion, peeled, julienned	4 oz.	112 gm
Black kalamata olives, pitted, quartered	30 each	30 each
Serrano pepper, seeded, membrane removed, finely minced	1	1
Cilantro, snipped	1 oz.	28 gm
Sherry	1 fl. oz.	30 ml
Olive oil	1 Tbsp.	15 ml
White rice wine vinegar	4 fl. oz.	120 ml
Kosher salt	to taste	to taste
Fresh, cracked white pepper	to taste	to taste

PREPARATION

1. Brush the pepper skins with olive oil. In a 375°F (190°C). oven, roast the peppers until they are evenly browned and the skins are blistered.
2. Place peppers into a bowl, cover with plastic wrap, and allow to cool until you can handle them comfortably.
3. Peel peppers, remove seeds and membrane, cut peppers into strips, and place into large mixing bowl.
4. Clean, peel, and dice English cucumbers; add to peppers.
5. Add the tomatoes, onions, olives, serrano, and cilantro to the peppers. Combine ingredients gently. Add sherry, oil, and vinegar and adjust seasoning with salt and pepper. Allow flavor to mature for at least 2 hours. Adjust seasoning prior to serving.

NUTRITION PER SERVING
Calories 109, protein 2 gm, fat 4 gm, carbohydrates 16 gm, cholesterol 0 mg, sodium 389 mg

PAN-SEARED SEABASS WITH STEWED ROMA TOMATOES AND KALAMATA OLIVES

SERVES 6

INGREDIENTS	AMOUNT/U.S.	METRIC
Olive oil	1 Tbsp.	15 ml
Garlic, peeled, minced	3 cloves	3 cloves
Red onion, peeled, finely diced	4 oz.	112 gm
Black kalamata olives, julienned	3 Tbsp.	25 gm
Chicken stock, defatted	4 fl. oz.	120 ml
Red Roma tomatoes, peeled, seeded, finely diced	1 lb.	450 gm
Basil, fresh, chiffonade	3 Tbsp.	15 gm
Tarragon, snipped	1 Tbsp.	5 gm
Fresh, cracked white pepper	to taste	to taste
Kosher salt	to taste	to taste
Seabass fillets, boneless, cleaned, dressed, skinned	6 @ 5 oz. ea.	6 @ 140 gm ea.
Chives, short-cut	1 Tbsp.	5 gm

Garnish:
Cilantro or parsley sprigs

CHEF'S NOTES

The use of a well-seasoned nonstick pan is one of the essential elements for success with this procedure. For variety, you may want to experiment with different herbs and spices. The sauce adds moisture and lends a hearty, robust flavor.

PREPARATION

1. In saucepan, heat olive oil and sauté garlic, onion, and olives for 1 minute over medium heat. Deglaze pan with chicken stock.
2. Add tomatoes; stew mixture gently over low heat for 20 minutes. Season with basil and tarragon. Adjust seasoning with cracked white pepper and kosher salt.
3. Wash seabass and pat dry. Season with salt, pepper, and chives.
4. In hot nonstick pan, dry sauté gently. Remove from pan and keep warm.

PRESENTATION

Dress plate with stewed tomato and olive mixture. Top with sautéed seabass, and garnish plates with cilantro or parsley sprigs.

NUTRITION PER SERVING

Calories 187, protein 23 gm, fat 8 gm, carbohydrates 7 gm, cholesterol 77 mg, sodium 149 mg

BRAISED CHICKEN THIGHS WITH STEWED ZUCCHINI, PEPPERS, AND TOMATOES

SERVES 12

NUTRITION NOTES	INGREDIENTS	AMOUNT/U.S.	METRIC
To reduce the overall fat in this dish, the chicken skin can be removed prior to browning, but this will affect the flavor of the dish.	Chicken thighs, trimmed, cleaned, washed, excess sinew removed	24	24
	Olive oil	1 Tbsp.	15 ml
	Fresh, cracked white pepper	1 Tbsp.	7 gm
	Cloves, ground	1 tsp.	2 gm
	Nutmeg	½ tsp.	1 gm
	Kosher salt	to taste	to taste
	Chicken stock, dark, high-quality	1 qt.	960 ml
	Garlic, minced	5 cloves	5 cloves
	Red onion, peeled, cleaned, finely diced	4 oz.	112 gm
	Carrot, peeled, cleaned, finely diced	4 oz.	112 gm
	Parma ham, lean, finely diced	3 oz.	84 gm
	Red wine	8 fl. oz.	240 ml
	Cinnamon stick	1	1
	Tomatoes, cleaned, peeled, diced	5 oz.	140 gm
	Parsley, chopped	2 Tbsp.	10 gm
	Spring onions, short-cut	½ bunch	½ bunch
	Tabasco™ sauce	to taste	to taste
	Stewed Zucchini with Peppers and Tomatoes (p. 236)		

PREPARATION

1. Clean chicken thighs using plastic gloves. Rub with olive oil, pepper, cloves, and nutmeg, and salt if desired. Marinate for 30 minutes.

2. In a hot sauté pan, dry sauté thighs for even browning. Remove from pan and place in stainless steel saucepot or casserole. Deglaze sauté pan with a little stock. Pour juices over chicken.

3. Wipe sauté pan clean, reheat, and sauté garlic, onions, carrots, and ham until gently brown.

4. Add browned vegetables to chicken, deglaze sauté pan with wine, and reduce until sec.

5. Add remaining stock to sauté pan and bring to boil. Add cinnamon stick and tomatoes.

6. Pour mixture over chicken thighs. Cover saucepot and slowly simmer for 40–50 minutes, checking frequently.

7. Add parsley and spring onions, and adjust seasoning to taste with Tabasco and salt. Remove cinnamon stick.

8. Test chicken for tenderness—tip of knife should go in with ease. Remove skin, and serve over Stewed Zucchini with Peppers and Tomatoes.

9. Pass remaining cooking liquid and vegetables through food mill and use as a sauce over chicken and zucchini.

NUTRITION PER SERVING OF CHICKEN
Calories 237, protein 31 gm, fat 8 gm, carbohydrates 5 gm, cholesterol 117 mg, sodium 219 mg

NUTRITION PER COMPLETE ENTREE SERVING
Calories 276, protein 32 gm, fat 10 gm, carbohydrates 11 gm, cholesterol 117 mg, sodium 225 mg

STEWED ZUCCHINI WITH PEPPERS AND TOMATOES *

SERVES 12

INGREDIENTS	AMOUNT/U.S.	METRIC
Green bell pepper, roasted, peeled, seeded, diced	8 oz.	224 gm
Zucchini squash, peeled, coarsely diced	8 oz.	224 gm
Roma tomatoes, peeled, seeded, coarsely diced	1 lb.	448 gm
Yellow onions, peeled, coarsely diced	10 oz.	280 gm
Garlic, peeled, minced	4 cloves	4 cloves
Basil, snipped	2 Tbsp.	10 gm
Lemon thyme, snipped	1 Tbsp.	5 gm
Olive oil	1 Tbsp.	15 ml
Chicken stock	6 fl. oz.	180 ml
Kosher salt	to taste	to taste
Cayenne pepper	to taste	to taste
Fresh, cracked white pepper	to taste	to taste

PREPARATION

1. Oven roast peppers; peel, seed, and dice.
2. Prepare zucchini, tomato, and onion.
3. Peel garlic; snip basil and lemon thyme.
4. In a saucepan heat oil and gently sweat garlic and onion for 2 minutes.
5. Over low heat add zucchini, sauté gently, toss mixture gently.
6. Add tomatoes and peppers. Add stock and continue to cook gently for 5 minutes.
7. Adjust seasoning with basil, thyme, salt, cayenne pepper, and cracked white pepper.
8. Add additional stock to achieve desired consistency.

NUTRITION PER SERVING

Calories 39, protein 1 gm, fat 2 gm, carbohydrates 6 gm, cholesterol 0 mg, sodium 6 mg

BRAISED VEAL SHANK

SERVES 8

INGREDIENTS	AMOUNT/U.S.	METRIC
Veal shank boneless steaks, fabricated and trimmed	8 @ 5 oz. ea.	8 @ 140 gm ea.
Flour	as needed	as needed
Olive oil	1 Tbsp.	15 ml
Celery, cleaned, small-diced	7 oz.	196 gm
Red onions, peeled, small-diced	7 oz.	196 gm
Carrots, peeled, cleaned, small-diced	7 oz.	196 gm
Red wine, high-quality	7 fl. oz.	210 ml
Roasted Vegetable Sauce (p. 174) or high-quality brown stock	2 qt.	1920 ml
Basil, fresh, snipped	1 Tbsp.	7 gm
Rosemary, needles only	2 sprigs	2 sprigs
Bay leaves	2	2
Parsley, cleaned, chopped	1 Tbsp.	15 gm
White peppercorns, fresh	20	20
Kosher salt	to taste	to taste
Fresh, cracked white pepper	to taste	to taste

CHEF'S NOTES

If using brown stock, one can add a tomato product to intensify the flavor profile.

PREPARATION

1. Season veal shank steaks as desired with kosher salt and cracked white pepper. Dust lightly with flour and dry sauté in nonstick skillet until browned on each side. Remove from skillet and keep warm.

2. In medium stock pot, heat olive oil and sweat celery, onions, and carrots for 5 minutes. Deglaze with red wine; reduce for 1 minute.

3. Add Roasted Vegetable Sauce or brown stock, basil, rosemary, bay leaves, parsley, and peppercorns.

4. Bring to boil, reduce heat, add browned veal shank steaks, and simmer gently for 45–60 minutes, covered, until veal shank steaks are fork-tender but still firm.

5. Adjust seasoning with salt and pepper, remove bay leaves, and serve veal shank steaks with the cooking liquid and vegetables. If desired, remove veal shanks from cooking liquid and blend sauce with a submersible blender for a smooth consistency.

NUTRITION PER SERVING
Calories 373, protein 32 gm, fat 9 gm, carbohydrates 29 gm, cholesterol 113 mg, sodium 212 mg

CHICKEN BREAST IN HERB BROTH
WITH ROOT VEGETABLES
AND ROASTED GARLIC

YIELD 6 SERVINGS

CHEF'S NOTES

One of the main virtues of this recipe lies in its stock. Sometimes known as a "free flavor" because of its ability to subtly enhance taste while adding very little fat and few calories, stocks can be saved and reused.

INGREDIENTS	AMOUNT/U.S.	METRIC
Chicken in Herb Broth:		
Red onion, peeled, minced	1 med.	1 med.
Garlic, minced	1 clove	1 clove
Orange, peel of	1	1
Ginger, fresh, peeled, sliced	½ tsp.	1.5 gm
Bay leaf	1	1
Chicken broth, defatted, high-quality	18 fl. oz.	540 ml
Chicken breasts, fat and sinew trimmed	6 @ 5 oz. ea.	6 @ 140 gm ea.
Fresh, cracked white pepper	½ tsp.	1 gm
Kosher salt	to taste	to taste
Root Vegetables:		
Carrots, turned (approx. ½ oz. each)	18	18
Pearl onions, fresh, whole	18	18
Potatoes, turned (approx. ½ oz. each)	18	18
Asparagus tips	18	18
Leeks, cleaned, washed, bias-cut	12	12
Chicken stock, defatted, high-quality	8 fl. oz.	240 ml
Garnish:		
Garlic cloves, peeled, oven-roasted	18	18
Chives, short-cut	2 Tbsp.	10 gm
Dill sprigs	6	6

PREPARATION OF CHICKEN IN HERB BROTH

1. Preheat oven to 375°F (190°C). In large saucepan, place onions, garlic, orange peel, ginger, bay leaf, and chicken broth. Bring to rapid boil. Reduce heat, keep warm on simmer.

2. In nonstick sauté pan, dry sauté chicken breasts on both sides until evenly browned but not cooked.

3. Place chicken breasts in baking dish with broth and cover with foil or parchment paper. Place in oven until done, approximately 10 minutes. Do not allow broth to boil. Remove chicken from oven, taste broth, and adjust seasoning with pepper and kosher salt if desired.

4. Prepare vegetables, cut and trim to appropriate size.
5. Blanch all vegetables until tender in lightly salted boiling water. Drain vegetables in colander and cold-shock in a container of iced water. Drain properly and set aside.
6. In saucepan, toss vegetables with chicken stock. Adjust seasoning. Heat thoroughly.

PRESENTATION

Arrange vegetables in a deep dish surrounding the chicken breasts. Generously ladle herb broth over vegetables and chicken. Garnish with roasted garlic, chives, and dill sprigs.

NUTRITION PER SERVING

Calories 247, protein 31 gm, fat 3 gm, carbohydrates 27 gm, cholesterol 66 mg, sodium 151 mg

PORK TENDERLOIN WITH ANGEL HAIR PASTA, STRING VEGETABLES, AND OVEN-ROASTED TOMATO COULIS

SERVES 8 (4 OZ./112 GM PORK PER SERVING)

INGREDIENTS	AMOUNT/U.S.	METRIC
Pork:		
Pork tenderloin, fat and sinew trimmed	2 @ 1 lb	896 gm
Sage, fresh, snipped	2 tsp.	10 gm
Fresh, cracked black pepper	½ tsp.	1 gm
Pasta and Vegetables:		
Angel hair pasta	11 oz.	308 gm
Olive oil	1 Tbsp.	15 ml
Zucchini, peeled, seeded, julienned	10 oz.	280 gm
Carrots, peeled, julienned	10 oz.	280 gm
Chives, short-cut	2 Tbsp.	10 gm
Kosher salt	1 tsp.	5 gm
Fresh, cracked black pepper	1 tsp.	2 gm
Coulis:		
Roma tomatoes, cut in half, seeded	1½ lb.	675 gm
Olive oil	1 Tbsp.	15 ml
Oregano, fresh, snipped	2 tsp.	3 gm
Basil, fresh, snipped	1 Tbsp.	5 gm
Fresh, cracked black pepper	1 tsp.	2 gm
Vegetable stock, high-quality, hot	8 fl. oz.	240 ml
Garnish:		
Basil, fresh, chiffonade	3 Tbsp.	21 gm

PREPARATION OF THE COULIS

1. Place prepared tomatoes in mixing bowl. Toss with olive oil, herbs, cracked black pepper, and kosher salt if desired.
2. Lightly spray sheet pan with nonstick coating. Place tomatoes cut side down on sheet pan. Slowly roast tomatoes in 225°F (110°C) oven for 5–6 hours.
3. Remove from oven, place in blender with hot vegetable stock. Blend for only a few seconds to maintain texture in the coulis. Strain through a china cap to remove skins.

PREPARATION OF THE PORK

4. Rub sage and pepper into pork. Spray sauté pan lightly with nonstick coating and bring to very high heat. Sear pork on all sides until golden brown.

5. Remove from heat and place in roasting pan. Finish cooking in convection oven at 375°F (190°C) for 10–15 minutes and rest for 2–3 minutes.

PREPARATION OF THE PASTA
AND VEGETABLES

6. Cook pasta until tender in slightly salted water. Drain and rinse; toss with olive oil. Set aside and keep warm.
7. Quickly blanch julienned vegetables in slightly salted water. Drain; add to pasta and adjust seasoning with chives, salt, and pepper. Combine mixture gently and keep warm.

PRESENTATION

Place one portion of the vegetables and pasta in center of plate. Top with pork thinly sliced on the diagonal and fanned out. Surround with the oven-roasted tomato coulis. Garnish with fresh basil chiffonade or a sprinkle of chopped herbs.

NUTRITION PER SERVING

Calories 343, protein 31 gm, fat 7 gm, carbohydrates 38 gm, cholesterol 74 mg, sodium 374 mg

SPICED BRAISED BEEF BRISKET WITH WILD MUSHROOM RISOTTO

SERVES 16 (3 OZ./84 GM BEEF PER SERVING)

CHEF'S NOTES

Arborio rice, because of its texture and flavor, is considered the premium rice. The use of Arborio rice results in a creamy texture and viscosity that we have come to expect from a great risotto. The rice has the ability to absorb a great deal of moisture while still maintaining its firmness. Risotto is a famous Northern Italian specialty, and today we find many varieties featuring vegetables, shellfish, country sausages, cheeses, and even desserts.

INGREDIENTS	AMOUNT/U.S.	METRIC
Fabricated Certified Angus Beef™ brisket, excess fat and deckle trimmed	5 lb. trimmed	2240 gm trimmed
Cumin seeds, toasted	1 Tbsp.	15 gm
Kosher salt	½ oz.	14 gm
Fresh, cracked white pepper	1 Tbsp.	15 gm
Olive oil	1 fl. oz.	30 ml
Carrot, cleaned, peeled, diced	1	1
Celery stalk, cleaned, peeled, diced	1	1
Elephant garlic, peeled, diced	1 head	1 head
Onion, white, cleaned, peeled, diced	1	1
Tomato paste	2 oz.	56 gm
Madeira wine	4 fl. oz	120 ml
Red wine	4 fl. oz.	120 ml
Beef or veal stock, high-quality	2 qt.-3 oz.	2 l
Thyme sprigs	2	2
Mustard seeds	1 tsp.	5 gm
Bay leaves	4	4

PREPARATION

1. Preheat oven to 350°F (175°C).
2. On a clean surface place trimmed brisket. Mix cumin seeds, salt, and cracked white pepper; rub evenly onto surface of brisket.
3. Heat large casserole, add olive oil, and heat thoroughly. Brown brisket evenly on all sides.
4. Remove brisket, set aside.
5. Add carrots, celery, garlic, and onion to casserole. Roast gently until golden brown. Add tomato paste and gently caramelize.
6. Deglaze with Madeira and red wine, and reduce by one-third.
7. Add beef or veal stock, thyme, mustard seeds, and bay leaves, and return brisket to braising liquid; cover.
8. Place casserole in oven and braise gently for 2½–3 hours.
9. Test for doneness. Remove brisket from liquid; keep warm on serving platter.
10. Skim excess fat from braising liquid. Pass braising liquid through Mouli mill to strain jus into saucepan.
11. Adjust seasoning of the sauce. Slice brisket and serve over Wild Mushroom Risotto drizzled with jus.

WILD MUSHROOM RISOTTO

INGREDIENTS	AMOUNT/U.S.	METRIC
Olive oil	1 Tbsp.	15 gm
Red onion, cleaned, finely minced	2 med.	2 med.
Arborio Italian rice	8 oz.	224 gm
Chicken stock, hot	1½ qt.	1440 ml
Porcine mushrooms, flash-frozen, diced	5 oz.	140gm
Chives, short-cut	4 Tbsp.	20 gm
Kosher salt	to taste	to taste
Fresh, cracked white pepper	to taste	to taste
Asiago cheese	2 oz.	56 gm
Arugula leaves, washed, julienned	½ lb.	227 gm
Butter	1 Tbsp.	15 gm

PREPARATION

1. In medium stainless steel saucepan, heat olive oil and add onions; cook until translucent. Add rice, stir thoroughly, and sauté for 2 minutes over low heat.

2. Add hot chicken stock slowly, 3 oz. at a time, while stirring continuously with wooden spoon. Mixture will become creamy and have a silken appearance, firm to the bite but not raw. This procedure will take +/- 20 minutes.

3. Add mushrooms and chives, return to low heat, and add more stock to retain creamy texture. Heat thoroughly; adjust seasoning with fresh cracked white pepper and a dash of kosher salt. Fold Asiago cheese and arugula into rice mixture. Combine well, and stir in butter. Serve at once.

NUTRITION PER SERVING OF BEEF
Calories 260, protein 26 gm, fat 14 gm, carbohydrates 5 gm, cholesterol 79 mg, sodium 520 mg

NUTRITION PER SERVING OF RISOTTO
Calories 99, protein 3 gm, fat 3 gm, carbohydrates 15 gm, cholesterol 4 mg, sodium 63 mg

NUTRITION PER COMPLETE ENTREE SERVING
Calories 359, protein 29 gm, fat 17 gm, carbohydrates 20 gm, cholesterol 83 mg, sodium 583 mg

MARINATED CHUCK STEAK WITH BASIL-NUT PESTO AND PIQUANT TOMATO SAUCE

SERVES 8

INGREDIENTS

Ingredient	AMOUNT/U.S.	METRIC
Fabricated Certified Angus Beef™ chuck, top blade muscle steaks, fat and sinew trimmed	8 @ 4 oz. ea.	8 @ 112 gm ea.
Thyme, fresh, snipped	½ tsp.	3 gm
Olive oil	1 Tbsp.	15 ml
Kosher salt	½ tsp.	2.5 gm
Fresh, cracked white pepper	1 tsp.	2 gm
Orange, zest of	1	1

PREPARATION

1. Place prepared and trimmed steaks into a clean insert pan. Combine thyme, oil, salt, pepper, and orange zest. Rub mixture into steaks. Cover pan with plastic wrap and place in refrigerator to marinate for one hour.
2. Remove steaks from marinade and pan-sauté in hot nonstick skillet until golden brown on both sides and to desired doneness.

PRESENTATION

Drizzle each steak with 1 tsp. of Basil-Nut Pesto and serve with Piquant Tomato Sauce.

BASIL-NUT PESTO

INGREDIENTS

Ingredient	AMOUNT/U.S.	METRIC
Jalapeño peppers, seeded, minced, no seeds or membrane	2	2
Ginger, fresh, minced	1 Tbsp.	15 gm
Garlic, cloves, cleaned	6 cloves	6 cloves
Chicken stock	4 fl. oz.	120 ml
Olive oil	3 Tbsp.	45 ml
Basil leaves, fresh, cleaned	2 bunches	2 bunches
Cilantro, fresh, cleaned	2 oz.	56 gm
Parsley, fresh, cleaned	1 oz.	28 gm
Limes, juice of	3	3
Brown sugar	1 tsp.	5 gm
Hazelnuts, roasted, peeled, finely chopped	1½ oz.	42 gm

1. In food processor, place jalapeño, ginger, garlic, and half the chicken stock; puree mixture gently. Add remaining chicken stock, olive oil, herbs, lime juice, and sugar to the mixture. Continue on pulse motion until smooth in consistency.
2. Remove pureed mixture from food processor and fold in roasted, finely chopped hazelnuts.
3. Set mixture aside in a clean container. Drizzle one teaspoon per serving over steak.

PIQUANT TOMATO SAUCE

INGREDIENTS	AMOUNT/U.S.	METRIC
Chicken stock, high-quality	6 fl. oz.	180 ml
Onion, cleaned, finely diced	3 oz.	84 gm
Garlic, cloves, cleaned, minced	8 cloves	8 cloves
Sherry	3 fl. oz.	90 ml
Coriander seeds, toasted	2 tsp.	10 gm
Roma tomatoes, large, ripe, cleaned, quartered, seeded	10	10
Fresh, cracked, black pepper,	1 tsp.	5 gm
Cinnamon stick	1	1

PREPARATION
1. Preheat oven to 375°F (190°C).
2. In saucepan, place 1 Tbsp. chicken stock, add onion and garlic, and sweat gently for 2 minutes. Deglaze saucepan with sherry. Add toasted coriander seeds and remaining chicken stock and keep warm.
3. On sheet pan, place tomatoes and sprinkle with black pepper. Place in oven and roast for 8 minutes, or until tomato skins blister.
4. Remove tomatoes from oven and add to stock mixture. Add cinnamon stick and bring to boil. Reduce heat and simmer gently for 5 minutes.
5. Remove cinnamon stick and with submersible blender blend sauce carefully. Add additional chicken stock to adjust consistency if needed. Adjust seasoning.

NUTRITION PER SERVING
Calories 323, protein 29 gm, fat 17 gm, carbohydrates 14 gm, cholesterol 67 mg, sodium 304 mg

SLOW-COOKED SHOULDER ROAST
"POT ON THE FIRE"

SERVES 16 (3 OZ./84 GM BEEF PER SERVING)

INGREDIENTS	AMOUNT/U.S.	METRIC
Fabricated Certified Angus Beef™, shoulder clod roast, tied	4 lb.	1792 gm
Olive oil	3 Tbsp.	45 ml
Onions, cleaned, diced	3 oz.	84 gm
Carrots, cleaned, diced	3 oz.	84 gm
Celery root, cleaned, diced	3 oz.	84 gm
Parsnips, cleaned, diced	3 oz.	84 gm
Garlic, cloves, cleaned, minced	6 cloves	6 cloves
Roma tomatoes, washed, seeded, diced	6 oz.	168 gm
Sherry	3 fl. oz.	90 ml
Beef or veal stock, dark, high-quality	70 fl. oz.	2100 ml
Thyme sprigs	2	2
White peppercorns	24	24
Bay leaves	4	4
Kosher salt	1 tsp.	5 gm
Vegetable Medley:		
Asparagus spears, 2" pieces, cleaned, peeled, end removed	12 oz.	336 gm
Green beans, cleaned	12 oz.	336 gm
Carrots, cleaned, cut into 2" sticks	12 oz.	336 gm
Potatoes, cleaned, cut into 2" sticks	16 oz.	448 gm
Chicken stock, high-quality, hot	6 fl. oz.	180 ml
Kosher salt	to taste	to taste
Fresh, cracked white pepper	to taste	to taste

PREPARATION

1. In 12-quart saucepan, heat olive oil and sauté onions, carrots, celery, parsnips, and garlic gently until mixture takes on a rusty color and develops an aroma.

2. Add tomatoes and deglaze with sherry. Add beef or veal stock, thyme, peppercorns, bay leaves, and salt.

3. Add cleaned fabricated tied clod roast to liquid. Stock should cover the meat; add additional stock if needed. When mixture comes to a boil, reduce heat, skim off impurities, and partially cover casserole.

4. Simmer gently over low heat for 2½–3 hours. Baste meat occasionally. Beef is ready when the tip of a sharp knife pierces meat with ease.

5. Remove beef and place on platter, slice, and keep warm. Strain stock through a fine sieve. Degrease stock and bring back to a boil; reduce by

one-third. Adjust seasoning, and return beef to the stock to reheat. Some stock will be used as jus; leftover stock can be frozen for later use.

PREPARATION OF THE VEGETABLE MEDLEY
1. Clean and appropriately cut all vegetables and potatoes. Steam or blanch in salted water. Drain and cold-shock to maintain color. Drain properly.
2. Thoroughly reheat vegetables by tossing in hot chicken stock; drain and save chicken stock for reuse. Adjust seasoning with salt and pepper. Heat thoroughly prior to serving.

PRESENTATION
Place serving of vegetable in center of plate, top with sliced beef, coat freely with jus, and just prior to serving drizzle with $\frac{1}{2}$ Tbsp. Caper Berry Dressing to enhance overall flavor.

CAPER BERRY DRESSING

INGREDIENTS	AMOUNT/U.S.	METRIC
Olive oil	2 fl. oz.	60 ml
Chicken stock, high-quality	4 fl. oz.	120 ml
Balsamic vinegar	3 Tbsp.	45 ml
Parsley, finely chopped	2 Tbsp.	14 gm
Gherkins, finely chopped	2 oz.	56 gm
Caper berries, sliced, or small capers	2 oz.	56 gm
Lemon, juice of	1	1
Lemon, zest of (grated)	1	1
Fresh, cracked white pepper	to taste	to taste

PREPARATION
1. In a clean, small stainless steel mixing bowl, place olive oil, stock, and vinegar; combine vigorously.
2. Add parsley, gherkins, and caper berries.
3. Adjust seasoning with lemon juice, lemon zest, and cracked white pepper to taste.
4. Wrap with plastic wrap, chill, and allow flavors to mature.

NUTRITION PER SERVING OF BEEF
Calories 284, protein 27 gm, fat 16 gm, carbohydrates 5 gm, cholesterol 90 mg, sodium 251 mg

NUTRITION PER SERVING OF VEGETABLE MEDLEY

Calories 43, protein 2 gm, fat 0 gm, carbohydrates 10 gm, cholesterol 0 mg, sodium 11 mg

NUTRITION PER ½ TBSP. OF CAPER BERRY DRESSING

Calories 39, protein 0 gm, fat 4 gm, carbohydrates 2 gm, cholesterol 0 mg, sodium 246 mg

NUTRITION PER COMPLETE ENTREE SERVING

Calories 366, protein 85 gm, fat 20 gm, carbohydrates 17 gm, cholesterol 90 mg, sodium 508 mg

HALIBUT WITH FETTUCCINE AND STEWED ROMA TOMATOES

SERVES 6

INGREDIENTS	AMOUNT/U.S.	METRIC
Halibut fillets, cleaned, washed, paper towel dried	6 @ 4 oz. ea.	6 @ 112 gm ea.
Cilantro, snipped	1 Tbsp.	7 gm
Kosher salt	1 tsp.	5 gm
Fresh, cracked white pepper	1 tsp.	2 gm
Fettuccine pasta, dry, high-quality	12 oz.	336 gm
Vegetable oil	1 Tbsp.	15 ml
Olive oil	1 Tbsp.	15 ml
Garlic, peeled, minced	3 cloves	3 cloves
Red onion, peeled, finely diced	3 oz.	84 gm
Kalamata olives, black, julienned	3 Tbsp.	45 gm
Fish stock, high-quality	8 fl. oz.	340 ml
Roma tomatoes, peeled, seeded, diced	1 lb.	448 gm
Basil, chiffonade	3 Tbsp.	21 gm
Tarragon, snipped	1 Tbsp.	7 gm

PREPARATION

1. Prepare halibut with cilantro and kosher salt and cracked white pepper as desired. Heat and prepare grill and preheat oven to 350°F (175°C).
2. Cook pasta al dente in 1 gallon of lightly salted water. Drain, rinse, and toss with vegetable oil. Adjust seasoning with salt and pepper and keep warm.
3. In stainless steel saucepan, heat olive oil and sweat garlic, onions, and olives for 1 minute. Deglaze with fish stock. Add tomatoes; stew mixture gently over low heat for 20 minutes. Season with basil and tarragon. Adjust seasoning with salt and pepper, if needed.
4. Grill mark halibut fillets on both sides. Finish in oven for 3–4 minutes.
5. Toss, warm pasta with stewed tomatoes.

PRESENTATION

Dress plate with fettuccine and stewed tomatoes and top with halibut; serve at once.

NUTRITION PER SERVING

Calories 269, protein 28 gm, fat 11 gm, carbohydrates 15 gm, cholesterol 59 mg, sodium 910 mg

ROAST BEEF WITH SHERRY–BELL PEPPER VINAIGRETTE

SERVES 16 (3 OZ./84 GM BEEF PER SERVING)

CHEF'S NOTES

If desired use caramelized roasted vegetables to enhance the flavor, and catch pan drippings to make a natural jus to accompany the vinaigrette.

INGREDIENTS	AMOUNT/U.S.	METRIC
Fabricated Certified Angus Beef™, round flat roast, cleaned, trimmed and tied	4 lb.	1792 gm
Fennel seeds	1 Tbsp.	10 gm
Coriander seeds	1 Tbsp.	10 gm
Turmeric	2 tsp.	5 gm
Cinnamon	1 tsp.	5 gm
Red pepper flakes	2 tsp.	5 gm
Kosher salt	1 Tbsp.	15 gm
Fresh, cracked white pepper	1 Tbsp.	15 gm
Orange, zest of (grated)	2	2
Olive oil	2 Tbsp.	30 ml

PREPARATION

1. Prepare a roasting rack. Preheat oven to 350°F (175°C).
2. Place fennel, coriander, turmeric, cinnamon, and red pepper flakes in mortar. Grind coarsely with pestle. Place in large stainless steel bowl, add salt, pepper, orange zest, and olive oil, and combine mixture thoroughly.
3. Rub all the marinade evenly into meat using plastic gloves, cover with plastic wrap, and refrigerate for 1 hour. Use all the marinade.
4. Remove roast from refrigerator, place roast on roasting rack and roast in oven to an internal temperature of 135°F (58°C), or to desired doneness (check with a clean, sanitized instant reading thermometer).
5. Allow to rest for ½ hour prior to slicing. Serve with 2 Tbsp. of Sherry–Bell Pepper Vinaigrette per serving.

SHERRY–BELL PEPPER VINAIGRETTE

INGREDIENTS	AMOUNT/U.S.	METRIC
Red bell peppers, roasted, peeled, seeded	8	8
Garlic, roasted	4 cloves	4 cloves
Rice wine vinegar	4 fl. oz.	120 ml
Chicken stock	4 fl. oz.	120 ml
Sherry	3 Tbsp.	45 ml
Cumin powder	1 tsp.	2 gm
Paprika	1 Tbsp.	15 gm
Red pepper, ground	1 tsp.	2 gm
Kosher salt	to taste	to taste
Fresh, cracked white pepper	to taste	to taste
Olive oil	2 Tbsp.	30 ml

PREPARATION

1. Prepare all ingredients. Place roasted peppers and garlic in food processor or blender with vinegar, stock, and sherry and puree finely.
2. Remove from bowl and place in a clean stainless steel mixing bowl and add cumin, paprika, and red pepper, and salt and white pepper to taste. Incorporate the mixture well.
3. Add olive oil, whisking vigorously to thoroughly combine all ingredients. Clean sides of bowl, wrap with plastic wrap, and allow flavors to mature.
4. Serve Roasted Beef with 2 tablespoons of vinaigrette.

NUTRITION PER SERVING OF BEEF

Calories 208, protein 27 gm, fat 10 gm, carbohydrates 1 gm, cholesterol 82 mg, sodium 483 mg

NUTRITION PER SERVING OF SHERRY–BELL PEPPER VINAIGRETTE

Calories 45, protein 1 gm, fat 2 gm, carbohydrates 5 gm, cholesterol 0 mg, sodium 144 mg

NUTRITION PER COMPLETE ENTREE SERVING

Calories 253, protein 28 gm, fat 12 gm, carbohydrates 6 gm, cholesterol 82 mg, sodium 627 mg

GRILLED FLANK STEAK WITH BALSAMIC GLAZE AND HERBED BROWN RICE

SERVES 8 (4 OZ./112 GM BEEF PER SERVING)

INGREDIENTS

INGREDIENTS	AMOUNT/U.S.	METRIC
Fabricated Certified Angus Beef™ flank steaks	3 @ 1 lb. ea.	3 @ 448 gm ea.
Rosemary, fresh, snipped	2 sprigs	2 sprigs
Sage, fresh, snipped	12 leaves	12 leaves
Thyme, fresh, snipped	1 sprig	1 sprig
Fresh, cracked white pepper	1 tsp.	2 gm
Garlic, cleaned, minced	6 cloves	6 cloves
Dry red wine	¼ cup	60 ml
Olive oil	2 Tbsp.	30 ml

PREPARATION

1. Place fabricated flank steaks in sheet pan.
2. In bowl, combine rosemary, sage, thyme, and pepper with garlic, wine, and olive oil.
3. Using plastic gloves, rub marinade into flank steaks. Marinate for a minimum of 1 hour to allow flavor to develop.
4. Remove flank steaks from marinade and discard marinade.
5. Preferably, grill flank steaks over hardwood grill, but a brick char-broiler will accomplish the task just fine. Grill flanks until evenly browned on both sides before basting. Baste flanks two or three times with Balsamic Glaze.

PRESENTATION

Serve with Herbed Brown Rice, and provide cups of glaze for dipping.

BALSAMIC GLAZE

INGREDIENTS	AMOUNT/U.S.	METRIC
Brown sugar	2 Tbsp.	18 gm
Red wine	4 Tbsp.	60 ml
Roasted Vegetable Sauce (p. 174)	8 oz.	240 ml
Balsamic vinegar, red, high-quality	4 oz.	120 ml
Balsamic vinegar, white	2 Tbsp.	30 ml
Kosher salt	to taste	to taste
Fresh, cracked white pepper	to taste	to taste

1. In small saucepan, heat brown sugar, swirling frequently until sugar caramelizes. Be careful not to burn the sugar.
2. Deglaze pan with red wine. Add Roasted Vegetable Sauce and bring to a boil.
3. Add vinegars and gently reduce by one-third. Season to taste with kosher salt and cracked white pepper.

HERBED BROWN RICE

INGREDIENTS	AMOUNT/U.S.	METRIC
Converted brown or Basmati rice	18 oz.	504 gm
Olive oil	2 Tbsp.	30 ml
Chicken stock, high-quality	1 qt.	960 ml
Kosher salt	to taste	to taste
Cranberries, dried	2 oz.	56 gm
Raisins, plumped in boiling water	2 oz.	56 gm
Parsley, finely chopped	1 Tbsp.	10 gm
Thyme, snipped	1 Tbsp.	10 gm
Filberts, roasted, peeled, chopped	2 oz.	56 gm
Fresh, cracked white pepper	to taste	to taste

PREPARATION

1. Preheat oven to 350°F (175°C).
2. Heat two tablespoons of olive oil in medium, oven-safe stock pot, add the cleaned and sorted rice. Sauté gently over high heat.
3. Add chicken stock and salt. Cover pot and place in oven for 20–25 minutes.
4. Remove rice from oven; rice should be firm but tender. Fluff with a large fork.
5. Add cranberries, raisins, fresh herbs, and roasted filberts, and adjust seasoning with a little kosher salt and cracked white pepper. Combine mixture gently.
6. Serve with Grilled Flank Steak and Balsamic glaze.

NUTRITION PER SERVING OF BEEF AND 1 OZ./30 ML DIPPING GLAZE
Calories 303, protein 29 gm, fat 15 gm, carbohydrates 8 gm, cholesterol 71 mg, sodium 113 mg

NUTRITION PER SERVING OF HERBED BROWN RICE
Calories 340, protein 7 gm, fat 9 gm, carbohydrates 58 gm, cholesterol 0 mg, sodium 10 mg

NUTRITION PER COMPLETE ENTREE SERVING
Calories 643, protein 36 gm, fat 24 gm, carbohydrates 66 gm, cholesterol 71 mg, sodium 123 mg

GRILLED SEABASS
WITH RED PEPPER ROUILLE
AND POTATO SALAD

SERVES 8

INGREDIENTS	AMOUNT/U.S.	METRIC
Seabass fillets, washed, boned, skinned	8 @ 5 oz. ea.	8 @ 140 gm ea.
Lemon, juice of	1	1
Garlic, peeled, minced	3 cloves	3 cloves
Fresh, cracked white pepper	1 tsp.	2 gm
Olive oil	1 tsp.	5 ml

PREPARATION

1. Heat grill.
2. In stainless steel mixing bowl, combine lemon juice with garlic, pepper, and olive oil.
3. Place cleaned seabass fillets on a clean platter. With plastic gloves, spread marinade evenly over fish, rub gently. Marinate for one-half hour.
4. Grill seabass fillets on a clean, hot grill for approximately 2 minutes per side.
5. Serve with Potato Salad and with 2 Tbsp. of Red Pepper Rouille per serving.

RED PEPPER ROUILLE

INGREDIENTS	AMOUNT/U.S.	METRIC
Red peppers, roasted, peeled, seeded	6	6
Elephant garlic, peeled, minced	6 cloves	6 cloves
Lime, juice of	2	2
Egg substitute, pasteurized	4 fl. oz.	120 ml
Fresh, cracked white pepper	½ tsp.	1 gm
Kosher salt	to taste	to taste
Olive oil	1 Tbsp.	15 ml

PREPARATION

1. Place roasted peppers, garlic, and lime juice in food processor and puree until smooth.
2. Add egg substitute and continue to puree until silken in appearance. Remove mixture from processor bowl and place in stainless steel mixing bowl.
3. Season mixture with fresh cracked pepper and add kosher salt to taste. Whisk in olive oil. Allow mixture to rest.
4. Serve two tablespoons per serving with the seabass fillets.

POTATO SALAD

INGREDIENTS	AMOUNT/U.S.	METRIC
Potatoes, fresh young fingerling new, cleaned, washed, sliced	1 lb.	450 gm
Vegetable or chicken stock, hot	8 fl. oz.	240 ml
OSO sweet onions, cleaned, finely sliced	4 oz.	112 gm
Chives, fresh, short-cut	1 oz.	28 gm
Kalamata olives, pitted, quartered	30	30
Sherry Vinaigrette (below)	4 fl. oz.	120 ml
Kosher salt	to taste	to taste
Fresh, cracked white pepper	to taste	to taste

PREPARATION

1. Place potatoes in large nonstick skillet. Add hot stock and slowly simmer until potatoes are cooked but still firm.
2. Drain stock and cool properly, and keep for future use.
3. Spread potatoes on sheet pan and cool quickly. Potatoes should maintain their shape.
4. In a clean stainless steel mixing bowl, combine onions, chives, olives, and Sherry Vinaigrette. Combine well, add cooled potato slices.
5. Marinate salad for at least 1 hour to allow the flavors to mature.
6. Prior to serving, adjust seasoning with salt and pepper.

SHERRY VINAIGRETTE

YIELD: 16 OZ./480 ML

INGREDIENTS	AMOUNT/U.S.	METRIC
Sherry vinegar, good-quality	8 fl. oz.	240 ml
Grey Poupon Country French™ Dijon mustard	2 Tbsp.	30 gm
Mustard, dry	1 Tbsp.	15 gm
Garlic, peeled, minced	2 cloves	2 cloves
Chicken or vegetable stock (can use stock from potato preparation)	5 fl. oz.	150 ml
Cornstarch or arrowroot slurry	as needed	as needed
Kosher salt	to taste	to taste
Fresh, cracked white pepper	to taste	to taste
Olive oil	4 Tbsp.	60 ml

PREPARATION

1. In a clean stainless steel mixing bowl, place vinegar, mustard, mustard powder, and garlic, and combine thoroughly.

2. Slightly thicken stock with cornstarch slurry for better consistency of dressing, and gently whisk into vinegar mixture.

3. Adjust seasoning with kosher salt and cracked white pepper, and whisk in olive oil.

NUTRITION PER SERVING OF SEABASS AND ROUILLE
Calories 216, protein 29 gm, fat 8 gm, carbohydrates 6 gm, cholesterol 96 mg, sodium 124 mg

NUTRITION PER SERVING OF POTATO SALAD WITH VINAIGRETTE
Calories 90, protein 2 gm, fat 3 gm, carbohydrates 12 gm, cholesterol 0 mg, sodium 171 mg

NUTRITION PER COMPLETE ENTREE SERVING
Calories 306, protein 31 gm, fat 11 gm, carbohydrates 18 gm, cholesterol 96 mg, sodium 295 mg

HONEY-BANANA PORK TENDERLOIN

SERVES 12

INGREDIENTS	AMOUNT/U.S.	METRIC
Bananas	2 lb.	896 gm
Garlic, fresh, peeled, minced	1½ oz.	42 gm
Canola oil	6 fl. oz.	180 ml
Clove	1½ tsp.	8 gm
Allspice	1½ tsp.	8 gm
Cinnamon	2 tsp.	10 gm
Sweet onion, peeled, chopped	6 oz.	168 gm
Cayenne pepper	1½ tsp.	8 gm
Fresh, cracked white pepper	3 Tbsp.	45 ml
Kosher salt	to taste	to taste
Honey	3 fl. oz.	90 ml
Pork tenderloin, trimmed, sinew removed	60 oz.	1680 gm

CHEF'S NOTES

The leftover honey-banana marinade should be discarded.

PREPARATION

1. Preheat oven to 350°F (175°C).
2. Leave peels on bananas and arrange on sheet pan. Bake for 25–30 minutes or until soft to the touch. Peel bananas and blend in food processor until smooth.
3. Add all other ingredients except tenderloins in food processor with the bananas and blend until smooth.
4. Trim the pork tenderloins of all fat, silver skin, and sinew. Wearing plastic gloves, rub banana mixture over exterior of tenderloins. Place tenderloins in a clean flat stainless steel insert pan, discard gloves, and wrap pan with plastic wrap. Refrigerate tenderloins for up to 12 hours.
5. Preheat oven to 400°F (205°C).
6. Scrape tenderloins to remove any excess banana mixture. Place the tenderloins in hot, oven-safe nonstick pan and sear on all sides until browned.
7. Place pan in oven for 8–10 minutes, until internal temperature reaches at least 145°F (62°C) or to desired doneness.
8. Remove from oven and allow meat to rest. Slice tenderloin into thin slices, approximately 4 oz. per person.

NUTRITION PER SERVING
Calories 231, protein 31 gm, fat 6 gm, carbohydrates 13 gm, cholesterol 92 mg, sodium 73 mg

PARMESAN-CRUSTED VEAL STEAK
WITH BRAISED BOK CHOY
AND ROASTED POTATOES

SERVES 8

INGREDIENTS	AMOUNT/U.S.	METRIC
Veal steak, fabricated from the loin, sinew and fat trimmed	8 @ 2 oz. ea.	8 @ 56 gm ea.
Egg substitute, pasteurized	6 oz.	180 ml
Parmesan cheese, low-fat, fresh grated	2½ oz.	70 gm
Kosher salt	to taste	to taste
Fresh, cracked white pepper	to taste	to taste
Flour for dusting	as needed	as needed

PREPARATION

1. Preheat oven to 350°F (175°C).
2. Pound veal steaks lightly under plastic wrap.
3. In a clean stainless steel mixing bowl, whip eggs until frothy, add parmesan.
4. Season veal as desired with kosher salt and fresh, cracked white pepper. Dust with flour and dip into egg wash with parmesan.
5. Place in hot nonstick skillet and dry sauté until golden brown on both sides.
6. Place veal on sheet pan and finish cooking in oven for 2 minutes.
7. Serve at once with Braised Bok Choy and Roasted Potatoes.

BRAISED BOK CHOY

INGREDIENTS	AMOUNT/U.S.	METRIC
Bok Choy, baby, cleaned, washed, trimmed, cored	9 oz.	252 gm
Carrots, peeled, washed, cut into strips	10 oz.	280 gm
Tomatoes, peeled, seeded, cut into strips	10 oz.	280 gm
Chicken stock	2 fl. oz.	60 ml
Kosher salt	to taste	to taste
Fresh, cracked white pepper	to taste	to taste
Parsley, chopped	1 Tbsp.	15 gm

PREPARATION

1. Clean and prepare bok choy and carrots. Blanch bok choy and carrots separately in lightly salted boiling water. Quickly cold-shock in an ice bath, to retain color.
2. Peel and deseed tomatoes and cut into strips.

3. In large sauté pan, bring chicken stock to boil. Add bok choy and carrot strips; heat thoroughly. Reduce liquid by one-half. Add tomato strips.

4. Adjust seasoning to taste with kosher salt, cracked white pepper, and parsley.

ROASTED POTATOES

INGREDIENTS	AMOUNT/U.S.	METRIC
Potatoes, washed, peeled, cut into balls with large melon scooper	1½ lb.	672 gm
Olive oil	1 Tbsp.	15 ml
Kosher salt	to taste	to taste
Fresh, cracked white pepper	to taste	to taste

PREPARATION

1. Blanch potato balls in salted water, drain, and cool on large sheet pan. With plastic gloves, rub in olive oil and kosher salt and cracked white pepper as desired, and toss gently.

2. In hot nonstick skillet, sauté potatoes until golden brown.

NUTRITION PER SERVING OF VEAL

Calories 133, protein 17 gm, fat 4 gm, carbohydrates 5 gm, cholesterol 51 mg, sodium 226 mg

NUTRITION PER SERVING OF BOK CHOY

Calories 27, protein 1 gm, fat 0 gm, carbohydrates 6 gm, cholesterol 0 mg, sodium 37 mg

NUTRITION PER SERVING OF POTATOES

Calories 74, protein 2 gm, fat 2 gm, carbohydrates 14 gm, cholesterol 0 mg, sodium 5 mg

NUTRITION PER COMPLETE ENTREE SERVING

Calories 234, protein 20 gm, fat 6 gm, carbohydrates 25 gm, cholesterol 51 mg, sodium 268 mg

SMOKED SALMON STEAKS WITH CELERIAC, BELL PEPPER, AND CUCUMBER RELISH AND TOMATO SALSA

SERVES 6

CHEF'S NOTES

Pan-smoking is a wonderful way to introduce an exciting flavor profile. Use fine wood chips to give salmon a distinctive flavor.

INGREDIENTS	AMOUNT/U.S.	METRIC
Salmon steaks, Norwegian-farmed, center-cut, skinless, boneless	6 @ 4 oz. ea.	6 @ 112 gm ea.
Basil, snipped	½ Tbsp.	3 gm
Cilantro, snipped	½ Tbsp.	3 gm
Mustard seeds	½ tsp.	1.5 gm
Olive oil	1 tsp.	5 ml
Fresh, cracked white pepper	to taste	to taste
Alder, hickory, or mesquite wood chips, fine-cut	8 oz.	224 gm

PREPARATION

1. Place salmon in a large bowl. Combine basil, cilantro, mustard seeds, olive oil, and cracked white pepper to taste. Using plastic gloves, rub mixture evenly into salmon steaks. Allow steaks to marinate for 15–30 minutes.

2. Prepare smoking pan. Place chips on bottom of pan. Place roasting rack on top of chips. Place smoking pan over direct heat until smoke aroma becomes apparent. Also preheat oven to 350°F (175°C).

3. Place salmon steaks on roasting rack, close lid, and let flavor develop for 3 minutes. Remove salmon steaks. (Use caution when opening the smoking pan.)

4. Finish cooking in oven for 5–7 minutes, until steaks reach the desired doneness.

PRESENTATION

Dress plate with Celeriac, Bell Pepper, and Cucumber Relish. Top with salmon, and garnish with Tomato Salsa.

CELERIAC, BELL PEPPER, AND CUCUMBER RELISH

CHEF'S NOTES
Relish can be prepared the day before to allow the flavors to develop.

INGREDIENTS	AMOUNT/U.S.	METRIC
Celeriac, cleaned, washed, julienned; cooked but still firm, drained and cooled	8 oz.	224 gm
Orange, juice of	4	4
Lemon, juice of	1	1
Olive oil	1 Tbsp.	15 ml
Rice wine vinegar	2 Tbsp.	30 ml
Cilantro, chopped	1 oz.	28 gm

INGREDIENTS	AMOUNT/U.S.	METRIC
Chives, snipped	1 oz.	28 gm
Yellow bell pepper, cleaned, julienned	4 oz.	112 gm
Red bell pepper, cleaned, julienned	4 oz.	112 gm
Cucumber, cleaned, washed, peeled, seeded, julienned	12 oz.	336 gm
Serrano pepper, cleaned, seeded, membrane removed, minced	1	1
Green apple, cleaned, cored, julienned	4 oz.	112 gm
Fresh, cracked white pepper	to taste	to taste
Kosher salt	to taste	to taste

PREPARATION

1. Blanch celeriac in boiling water, drain, and cold-shock. Drain well and allow to cool.

2. In a mixing bowl, combine citrus juices, olive oil, vinegar, and herbs. Add all other ingredients, and toss thoroughly but gently. Season with a little kosher salt and cracked white pepper to taste.

TOMATO SALSA

INGREDIENTS	AMOUNT/U.S.	METRIC
Roma tomatoes, peeled, diced	8 oz.	224 gm
Red onion, peeled, diced	3 oz.	84 gm
Garlic, roasted, finely minced	2 cloves	2 cloves
Olive oil	1 tsp.	5 ml
Red wine vinegar	2 Tbsp.	30 ml
Parsley, snipped	2 tsp.	2 tsp.
Fresh, cracked white pepper	to taste	to taste
Kosher salt	to taste	to taste

PREPARATION

1. Combine ingredients in stainless steel mixing bowl and allow to marinate at least 1 hour. Taste and adjust seasoning with kosher salt and cracked white pepper.

NUTRITION PER SERVING OF SALMON

Calories 167, protein 22 gm, fat 8 gm, carbohydrates 0 gm, cholesterol 62 mg, sodium 49 mg

NUTRITION PER SERVING OF SALSA

Calories 28, protein 1 gm, fat 1 gm, carbohydrates 4 gm, cholesterol 0 mg, sodium 99 mg

NUTRITION PER SERVING OF RELISH

Calories 106, protein 2 gm, fat 3 gm, carbohydrates 19 gm, cholesterol 0 mg, sodium 138 mg

NUTRITION PER SERVING OF COMPLETE ENTREE

Calories 285, protein 25 gm, fat 12 gm, carbohydrates 22 gm, cholesterol 62 mg, sodium 249 mg

PAN-SEARED CERVENA™ VENISON ON FINGERLING POTATO, BEET, AND ONION SALAD

SERVES 6

INGREDIENTS	AMOUNT/U.S.	METRIC
Cervena™ venison loin, mignons	12 @ 2 oz. ea.	12 @ 56 gm ea.
Garlic, peeled, minced	1 clove	1 clove
Olive oil	1 Tbsp.	15 ml
Lemon thyme, snipped	1 Tbsp.	7 gm
Fresh, cracked pepper	1 tsp.	2 gm

Garnish:
Apple, julienned
Tortilla strips

PREPARATION

1. Combine garlic, olive oil, thyme, and pepper. Using plastic gloves, rub marinade into venison mignons. Place under wrap in refrigerator for 1 hour.
2. Heat sauté pan and pan-sear mignons on both sides until evenly browned. Finish sautéing over low heat; serve mignons medium.

PRESENTATION

Place warm potato salad on each dinner plate; place two venison mignons on top and serve. Optional: Garnish with julienned apple and crispy tortilla strips.

FINGERLING POTATO, BEET, AND ONION SALAD

INGREDIENTS	AMOUNT/U.S.	METRIC
Fingerling potatoes, medium, washed	10	10
Red beets, medium, trimmed, cleaned, washed	4	4
Parma ham, genuine, finely diced	4 oz.	112 gm
Garlic, peeled, minced	1 clove	1 clove
Red onions, cleaned, peeled, julienned	2	2
Dijon mustard	1 tsp.	5 gm
Chicken stock, hot	3 fl. oz.	90 ml
Rice wine vinegar	6 fl. oz.	180 ml
Virgin olive oil	1 fl. oz.	30 ml
Chives, short-cut	2 Tbsp.	14 gm
Cilantro, snipped	2 Tbsp.	14 gm

INGREDIENTS	AMOUNT/U.S.	METRIC
Arugula, chiffonnade	3 oz.	84 gm
Fresh, cracked white pepper	to taste	to taste
Kosher salt	to taste	to taste

PREPARATION

1. Boil potatoes to the point of being cooked but still firm; drain and cool. Slice thinly; leave skin on. Boil beets to the point cooked but still firm; drain and cool. Peel and cut into sticks. Set beets and potatoes aside in separate bowls.

2. In a small heated stainless steel saucepan, sauté Parma ham for 1 minute, stirring continuously. Add garlic and onions; sweat until onions become translucent. Add mustard, stir thoroughly, and add hot chicken stock and vinegar.

3. Remove from heat, stir in olive oil, and season with chives, cilantro, and kosher salt and cracked white pepper to taste.

4. Fold dressing into beets, add sliced potatoes, and toss gently. Fold in arugula last. Adjust seasoning and keep warm until serving.

NUTRITION PER SERVING OF VENISON

Calories 156, protein 27 gm, fat 5 gm, carbohydrates 0 gm, cholesterol 96 mg, sodium 58 mg

NUTRITION PER SERVING OF FINGERLING POTATO, BEET, AND ONION SALAD

Calories 343, protein 11 gm, fat 6 gm, carbohydrates 59 gm, cholesterol 10 mg, sodium 884 mg.

NUTRITION PER COMPLETE ENTREE SERVING

Calories 499, protein 38 gm, fat 11 gm, carbohydrates 59 gm, cholesterol 106 mg, sodium 942 mg

Recipe courtesy of Cervena Plates Culinary Competition, organized by the Cervena Council.

COUNTRY-STYLE BROWN
SHRIMP ETOUFFÉE

SERVES 10

CHEF'S NOTES	INGREDIENTS	AMOUNT/U.S.	METRIC
This item can be frozen, reheats very well, and tastes even better the second day.	Olive oil	2 Tbsp.	30 ml
	Garlic, peeled, minced	5 cloves	5 cloves
	Red onion, cleaned, peeled, diced	4 oz.	112 gm
	Brown rice, uncooked	6 oz.	168 gm
	Tomato paste	3 Tbsp.	45 gm
	Dry white wine	3 fl. oz.	90 ml
	Chicken stock	64 fl. oz.	1920 ml
	Heinz® chili sauce	5 Tbsp.	75 gm
	Bay leaves	3	3
	Celery stalk, cleaned, washed, diced	4 oz.	112 gm
	Red and green bell pepper, cleaned, washed, diced	4 oz. ea.	112 gm ea.
	Tomatoes, skinned, seeded, diced	8	8
	Cilantro, chopped	3 Tbsp.	22 gm
	Gumbo filé powder	2 Tbsp.	15 gm
	Basil, fresh, snipped	2 Tbsp.	15 gm
	Okra, diced, fresh or frozen	10 oz.	280 gm
	Brown shrimp, 16/20 count, raw, headless, cleaned, peeled, deveined, washed & diced	20 oz.	560 gm
	Kosher salt	to taste	to taste
	Fresh, cracked pepper	to taste	to taste
	Garnish:		
	Cilantro sprigs	10 sprigs	10 sprigs

PREPARATION

1. In large, double-bottom stainless steel stock pot, heat olive oil over medium heat. Add garlic and onions, sweat for 1 minute.

2. Add brown rice and tomato paste and combine thoroughly. Heat thoroughly and gently pan roast tomato paste and rice, stirring frequently, approximately 3 minutes.

3. Deglaze the stock pot with white wine; continue cooking until dry.

4. Add chicken stock, chili sauce, and bay leaves. Bring to rapid boil, reduce heat, and simmer for 20 minutes.

5. Add celery and peppers; cook for 10 minutes. Add diced tomatoes, cilantro, and filé powder. Continue to simmer gently for 5 minutes.

6. Add basil, stir, and continue to simmer for 20 minutes. Add okra and shrimp; cook gently over reduced heat.

7. Adjust seasoning with salt and fresh cracked pepper to taste. Simmer for an additional 10 minutes before serving to allow flavors to mature.

PRESENTATION
Serve in large crocks or soup plates, piping hot, garnished with fresh cilantro sprigs.

NUTRITION PER SERVING
Calories 231, protein 16 gm, fat 6 gm, carbohydrates 29 gm, cholesterol 85 mg, sodium 238 mg

PAN-SEARED CHICKEN WITH GREEN BEANS AND COUSCOUS

SERVES 12

CHEF'S NOTES

When marinating chicken breasts, one can also use a large plastic ziplock bag. Place cleaned chicken breasts in bag and add marinade (no more than six to eight pieces to a gallon-size bag for maximum flavor distribution), close bag, and place in refrigerator overnight.

These chicken breasts can also be frozen ahead and thawed in the refrigerator when ready to use.

INGREDIENTS	AMOUNT/U.S.	METRIC
Chicken:		
Chicken breasts, boneless, skinless, rinsed, paper towel dry	12 @ 4 oz. ea.	12 @ 112 gm ea.
Olive oil	2 Tbsp.	30 ml
Cumin, ground	1 Tbsp.	15 gm
Turmeric, ground	1 tsp.	5 gm
Lemon, juice of	1	1
Fresh cracked pepper	1 Tbsp.	15 gm
Couscous:		
Couscous	1 lb.	448 gm
Water or chicken stock	25 fl. oz.	840 ml
Olive oil	2 Tbsp.	30 ml
Red onions, finely diced	4 oz.	112 gm
Red bell peppers, cleaned, seeded, diced	2	2
Tomatoes, peeled, seeded, diced	6	6
Cayenne pepper	½ tsp.	3 gm
Kosher salt	to taste	to taste
Fresh, cracked white pepper	to taste	to taste
Beans:		
Green beans, fine, cleaned, washed, blanched, cold-shocked, drained	1 lb.	448 gm
Olive oil	1 Tbsp.	15 ml
Nutmeg	to taste	to taste

PREPARATION

1. For the chicken, combine olive oil, cumin, turmeric, lemon juice, and pepper in mixing bowl. Add chicken breasts, toss gently, and marinate for 1 hour.

2. For the couscous: Put couscous in boiling water or chicken stock, stir, cover, remove from heat, and rest covered for 5 minutes. Fluff with fork and spread on sheet pan to cool.

Or, steam couscous over water or stock in a perforated pan or fine mesh colander for 6–8 minutes. Fluff occasionally with fork. Keep warm.

3. In large stainless steel saucepan, heat olive oil, add onions and pepper, and sauté gently for 2 minutes.

4. Add tomatoes; season mixture with cayenne and kosher salt and fresh cracked white pepper to taste. Combine mixture with couscous, stir thoroughly, adjust seasoning, and set aside. Keep warm.

5. For the beans, in nonstick skillet, heat olive oil and sauté blanched beans. Seasoned to taste with kosher salt, pepper, and a touch of nutmeg. Set aside.

6. To finish chicken, in separate nonstick skillet, pan-sear chicken breasts for 2–3 minutes each side. Place in oven-proof dish and finish in 375°F (190°C) oven for approximately 4 minutes. Do not overcook; chicken should be firm but still moist.

PRESENTATION

Place mound of couscous in center of plate, arrange sautéed beans around couscous, and place chicken breast on top. Serve at once, with optional Red and Yellow Tomato Jus (p. 182).

NUTRITION PER SERVING

Calories 348, protein 33 gm, fat 7 gm, carbohydrates 38 gm, cholesterol 66 mg, sodium 89 mg

BRISKET OF BEEF WITH HERB BROTH AND ROOT VEGETABLES

SERVES 16

INGREDIENTS	AMOUNT/U.S.	METRIC
Horse carrots, cleaned, peeled, diced	2 lg.	2 lg.
Celeriac, peeled, diced	1 lg.	1 lg.
Red onion, cleaned, diced	2 med.	2 med.
Leeks, cleaned, trimmed, diced	2	2
Parsley stems, washed	2 oz.	56 gm
Cilantro stems, washed	2 oz.	56 gm
Bay leaves	3	3
White peppercorns	1 Tbsp.	15 gm
Mustard seeds	½ Tbsp.	7 gm
Chicken stock	64 fl. oz.	1920 ml
Beef brisket, boneless, deckle off, visible fat trimmed	5 lb.	2240 gm

PREPARATION

1. In large stock pot, place all cleaned and prepared vegetables, herbs, and spices. Fill pot half full with water. Add chicken stock and bring to boil, reduce to simmer, and add brisket . Slowly cook until brisket is tender, 2–2½ hours. Check for doneness with a baking needle. It should go in and out of meat with ease when it is tender.

2. Remove meat and keep warm in 2 quarts of the stock to cover the meat. This stock will be used to prepare the Herb Broth. Strain remainder of stock, place in container, and freeze for future use.

PRESENTATION

In deep soup plates, place turned potato–vegetable mixture. Top with sliced brisket, 3 oz. cooked per portion. Top with 4 oz. of Herb Broth.

HERB BROTH

INGREDIENTS	AMOUNT/U.S.	METRIC
Stock, strained and defatted	64 fl. oz.	1920 ml
Basil, snipped	1 Tbsp.	7 gm
Chives, snipped	1 Tbsp.	7 gm
Roma tomatoes, peeled, seeded, julienned	6 oz.	168 gm
Fresh, cracked white pepper	to taste	to taste
Kosher salt	to taste	to taste
Virgin olive oil	1 Tbsp.	15 ml

1. Place stock in a stainless steel saucepan. Heat thoroughly, add herbs, tomatoes and adjust seasoning with kosher salt and cracked white pepper.
2. Finish with olive oil. Remove from heat.

ROOT VEGETABLES AND POTATOES

INGREDIENTS	AMOUNT/U.S.	METRIC
Potatoes, turned	32 @ ½ oz. each	32 @ ½ oz. each
Carrots, turned	32 @ ½ oz. each	32 @ ½ oz. each
Celery, turned	32 @ ½ oz. each	32 @ ½ oz. each
Yellow turnips, turned	32 @ ½ oz. each	32 @ ½ oz. each
Chicken stock	as needed	as needed
Kosher salt	to taste	to taste
Fresh, cracked black pepper	to taste	to taste

PREPARATION
1. Clean and wash all vegetables.
2. Cook all vegetables separately in salted water until tender. Drain properly.
3. Place all vegetables in large saucepan, moisten with chicken stock, and adjust seasoning with kosher salt and cracked white pepper. Simmer gently until well heated.

NUTRITION PER SERVING
Calories 408, protein 35 gm, fat 12 gm, carbohydrates 40 gm, cholesterol 86 mg, sodium 208 mg

STEAK WITH OVEN-ROASTED PEPPER AND ARTICHOKE COMPOTE

SERVES 8

INGREDIENTS	AMOUNT/U.S.	METRIC
Steaks:		
Certified Angus Beef™ steaks cut from sirloin ball tip	8 @ 4 oz. ea.	8 @ 112 gm ea.
Olive oil	1 Tbsp.	15 ml
Dijon mustard	1 Tbsp.	15 gm
Fresh, cracked white pepper	½ Tbsp.	7 gm
Serrano pepper, seeded, minced	½	½
Rosemary sprig, needles only	1	1
For the Compote:		
Red, yellow, and green bell peppers, cleaned, washed, roasted, peeled, large-diced	4 lg. ea.	4 lg. ea.
Artichokes, whole, cleaned, peeled, completely trimmed, use bottoms only, fresh, quartered	6	6
Olive oil	2 Tbsp.	30 ml
Red onions, peeled, diced	3 oz.	84 gm
Garlic, peeled, minced	4 cloves	4 cloves
Shiitake mushrooms, cleaned, sliced	8 oz.	224 gm
Red wine, high-quality	8 fl. oz.	240 ml
Roasted Vegetable Sauce (p. 174)	8 fl. oz.	240 ml
Kosher salt	to taste	to taste
Fresh, cracked white pepper	to taste	to taste
Chives, finely snipped	1 oz.	28 gm

PREPARATION

1. To marinate steaks: Place steaks on a sheet pan. In small stainless steel bowl, combine olive oil, mustard, pepper, serrano, and rosemary. Brush steaks with this mixture and marinate for 1 hour.
2. For the compote: Clean, wash, roast, and peel all bell peppers; core and seed. Cut in large dice, using flesh only; set aside.
3. Brush artichoke bottoms with 1 Tbsp. olive oil, place in hot skillet, and roast in 350°F (175°C) oven until evenly browned. Toss frequently.
4. In large sauté pan, heat remaining olive oil and sweat red onions and garlic until translucent. Add mushrooms; sauté over medium heat. Deglaze with red wine and reduce by one-half.
5. Add Roasted Vegetable Sauce; simmer gently. Add peppers and artichokes; simmer for 20 minutes. Adjust seasoning with kosher salt and cracked white pepper. Finish with chives.
6. To finish steaks: In large nonstick skillet over medium-high heat, pan-sear steaks until evenly browned and to desired doneness. Serve steaks with the compote.

SEAFOOD STEW

SERVES 8

INGREDIENTS	AMOUNT/U.S.	METRIC
Olive oil	2 Tbsp.	30 ml
Onions, cleaned, finely diced	6 oz.	168 gm
Green bell pepper, cleaned, finely diced	5 oz.	140 gm
Scallions, cleaned, short-cut	10	10
Fennel, fresh, cleaned, finely diced	4 oz.	112 gm
Garlic, peeled, minced	4 cloves	4 cloves
Tomatoes, cleaned, peeled, seeded, diced	1 lb.	448 gm
Tomato puree	8 fl. oz.	240 ml
Fish stock	8 fl. oz.	240 ml
Dry white wine	2 fl. oz.	60 ml
Thyme sprigs	2	2
Oregano sprig	1	1
Bay leaves	2	2
Kosher salt	to taste	to taste
Fresh, cracked white pepper	to taste	to taste
Shrimp, 16 to 20 count, peeled, deveined	16	16
Snapper fillets, cleaned, diced	1 lb.	448 gm
Parsley, cleaned, finely chopped	1 Tbsp.	14 gm

CHEF'S NOTES

The consistency of the tomato base can be adjusted according to preference. Also, a favorite fish or shellfish, such as clams, crab, or angler fish, can be substituted for the seafood.

PREPARATION

1. Heat olive oil in heavy sauce pot and sweat onions, peppers, and scallions until translucent. Add fennel, garlic, diced tomatoes, tomato puree, stock and white wine. Bring mixture to boil and simmer gently for 30 minutes.

2. Add thyme, oregano, and bay leaves, and adjust seasoning with a little kosher salt and cracked white pepper. Reduce tomato base to desired consistency.

3. Cut the cleaned seafood into bite-sized chunks. Add seafood into the tomato base. Simmer gently for 6–8 minutes.

4. Adjust seasoning with chopped parsley. Serve in hot, deep bowls with crusty French bread.

NUTRITION PER SERVING

Calories 225, protein 24 gm, fat 6 gm, carbohydrates 22 gm, cholesterol 76 mg,
sodium 130 mg

COUNTRY-STYLE BEEF STEW

SERVES 16

CHEF'S NOTES

Great with crunchy bread or served over rice, noodles, or garlic mashed potatoes.

INGREDIENTS	AMOUNT/U.S.	METRIC
Certified Angus Beef™ round, knuckle peeled, cut into 1½″ cubes	4 lb.	1792 gm
Fresh, cracked white pepper	1 Tbsp.	15 gm
Flour	3 oz.	84 gm
Brown stock, high-quality	36 fl. oz.	1080 ml
Olive oil	2 Tbsp.	30 ml
Red onions, diced	1½ lb.	681 gm
Garlic, peeled, minced	10 cloves	10 cloves
Tomato paste	8 oz.	224 gm
Madeira	8 fl. oz.	240 ml
Pinot Noir wine	8 fl. oz.	240 ml
Bay leaves	3	3
Orange peel	2 tsp.	4 gm
Lemon thyme sprigs	2	2
Carrots, cleaned, peeled diced	8 oz.	224 gm
Celery, cleaned, diced	8 oz.	224 gm
Fennel, cleaned, diced	8 oz.	224 gm
Roma tomatoes, peeled, seeded, diced	1 lb.	448 gm
Cilantro, snipped	2 Tbsp.	14 gm
Vegetable spray	as needed	as needed
Garnish:		
Spring onions	16	16

PREPARATION

1. Dust beef cubes with mixture of pepper and flour.

2. Spray 14″ nonstick skillet with vegetable spray and pan-sear meat in two batches until lightly browned on all sides. Remove meat and keep warm.

3. Deglaze pan with ½ cup stock. Pour liquid over beef cubes.

4. In large stainless steel saucepan or rondeau, heat oil and sweat onions and garlic until translucent. Add tomato paste and pan roast until rusty in color.

5. Deglaze with Madeira and Pinot Noir wine. Add remaining stock, bay leaves, orange peel, thyme, carrots, celery, and fennel.

6. Bring to boil then reduce to simmer. Add pan-seared beef cubes. Stir, and cook over low heat for 1 hour. Stir gently occasionally. Add diced tomatoes, and adjust seasoning with cracked white pepper and kosher salt. Add additional stock if needed.

7. Simmer for additional 20–30 minutes. Remove bay leaves; add snipped cilantro. Garnish with spring onions.

PAN-SEARED CHICKEN WITH ADOBO HONEY CHIPOTLE SAUCE

SERVES 6

INGREDIENTS	AMOUNT/U.S.	METRIC
Olive oil	1 Tbsp.	15 ml
Red onion, peeled, finely diced	1 med.	1 med.
Garlic, peeled, minced	2 cloves	2 cloves
Chilies Chipotle, canned in tomato sauce	3	3
Marsala	3 oz.	90 ml
Brown stock, high-quality	12 oz.	360 ml
Tomato concassée	12 oz.	336 gm
Honey	4 tsp.	20 ml
Cilantro, snipped	1 Tbsp.	10 gm
Kosher salt	to taste	to taste
Fresh, cracked pepper	to taste	to taste
Vegetable spray	as needed	as needed
Chicken breasts, cleaned, fat and excess sinew removed	6 @ 4 oz. ea.	6 @ 112 gm ea.

PREPARATION

1. In stainless steel saucepan, heat olive oil and gently sweat red onion and garlic over low heat.
2. Add chipotles and cook until mixture takes on a rusty appearance and aroma develops.
3. Deglaze with marsala. Add brown stock and simmer for 5–10 minutes.
4. Add tomato concassée and honey. Adjust seasoning with a little salt and pepper. Finish with cilantro. Simmer for an additional 5–10 minutes over low heat to mature flavor. Keep warm.
5. Meanwhile, dry sauté chicken breasts until golden brown. Place on roasting rack and finish in oven at 375°F (190°C) for 5–7 minutes.

PRESENATION

Serve chicken breasts with sauce, garnished with cilantro sprigs.

BRAISED SIRLOIN WITH GREEN LENTIL AND WHITE BEAN COMPOTE AND NATURAL JUS

SERVES 12

INGREDIENTS	AMOUNT/U.S.	METRIC
Certified Angus Beef™ bottom sirloin butt tri-tip, trimmed	4 lb.	1816 gm
Olive oil	2 Tbsp.	30 ml
Carrots, cleaned, peeled, diced	4 oz.	112 gm
Red onion, peeled, diced	4 oz.	112 gm
Leek, green part only, cleaned, diced	3 oz.	84 gm
Garlic, cleaned, peeled, minced	6 cloves	6 cloves
Parsnips, cleaned, diced	3	3
Tomato paste	3 Tbsp.	45 gm
Red wine	8 fl. oz.	240 ml
Brown stock	2 qt.	1920 ml
Bay leaves	2	2
Lemon thyme sprigs	2	2
Cilantro, cleaned, washed	½ bunch	½ bunch
Rosemary sprigs, needles only	2	2
Roma tomatoes, cleaned, peeled, seeded, diced	6	6
Chives, short-cut	1 oz.	28 gm
Fresh, cracked pepper	to taste	to taste
Kosher salt	to taste	to taste
Green Lentil and White Bean Compote (p. 276)		

PREPARATION

1. Clean and fabricate beef. Remove excessive fat. Rinse in cold water, and paper towel dry. Season with kosher salt and cracked white pepper as desired.

2. Heat olive oil in large sauté pan and pan-sear beef until golden brown on all sides. Remove from pan and place in large rondeau or stainless steel saucepot.

3. Place carrots, onions, leeks, garlic, and parsnips in sauté pan. Sauté for 5 minutes, stirring frequently. Add tomato paste. Sauté until rusty in color and desired aroma develops. Place vegetables with beef. Deglaze sauté pan with wine, and pour all drippings over beef.

4. Add stock to beef. Add bay leaves, thyme, cilantro, and rosemary. Bring to rapid boil, then place saucepot in oven at 375°F (190°C) for 45–60 minutes. Check, turn, and baste beef occasionally. Test for doneness; baking needle should go in with ease, indicating tenderness.

5. Remove beef from oven, place on platter, keep warm, and allow to rest for 10 minutes. Remove bay leaves, strain jus into saucepan. Keep vegetables from jus. Place jus over medium heat; deglaze frequently.

6. Puree the vegetables into the jus for appropriate consistency. Finish jus with diced tomatoes and chives. Heat thoroughly, and adjust seasoning with kosher salt and cracked white pepper.

7. Slice beef and serve with jus on top of Green Lentil and White Bean Compote.

NUTRITION PER SERVING OF BEEF AND JUS

Calories 295, protein 34 gm, fat 11 gm, carbohydrates 11 gm, cholesterol 92 mg, sodium 116 mg

NUTRITION PER COMPLETE ENTREE SERVING

Calories 397, protein 39 gm, fat 14 gm, carbohydrates 25 gm, cholesterol 92 mg, sodium 128 mg

GREEN LENTIL AND WHITE BEAN COMPOTE

SERVES 12

INGREDIENTS	AMOUNT/U.S.	METRIC
Virgin olive oil	2 Tbsp.	30 ml
Red onions, peeled, finely minced	2 oz.	56 gm
Carrots, cleaned, peeled, finely diced	2 oz.	56 gm
Serrano chili, cleaned, seeded, minced	1	1
Garlic, peeled, minced	2 cloves	2 cloves
Celery, cleaned, finely diced	2 oz.	56 gm
White beans, small, hulled, soaked overnight in water	6 oz.	168 gm
Chicken stock	48 fl. oz.	1440 ml
Cilantro, snipped	1 oz.	28 gm
Chives, short-cut	1 oz.	28 gm
Kosher salt	to taste	to taste
Fresh, cracked white pepper	to taste	to taste
Green lentils, cooked, drained but still firm (cooked weight)	6 oz.	168 gm

PREPARATION

1. In medium stainless steel saucepan, heat olive oil and sauté onions, carrots, serrano, garlic, and celery for 3 minutes over low heat.
2. Add soaked and rinsed white beans and add stock and bring to rapid boil. Reduce heat and simmer gently until beans are tender.
3. Add cilantro and chives; adjust seasoning with a little kosher salt and fresh, cracked white pepper.
4. Just prior to serving, fold cooked lentils into beans and stew mixture gently over low heat. Add additional stock if necessary. Adjust seasoning.
5. Dress with natural jus, if desired.

NUTRITION PER SERVING
Calories 102, protein 5 gm, fat 3 gm, carbohydrates 14 gm, cholesterol 0 mg, sodium 13 mg

ROASTED VEGETABLE WRAP

SERVES 10

INGREDIENTS	AMOUNT/U.S.	METRIC
Black beans, dry	8 oz.	224 gm
Garlic, roasted	10 cloves	10 cloves
Zucchini, cleaned, peeled, cut into sticks	1 lb.	448 gm
Yellow squash, cleaned, peeled, cut into sticks	1 lb.	448 gm
Carrots, cleaned, peeled, cut into sticks	1 lb.	448 gm
Onion, cleaned, peeled, coarsely diced	6 oz.	168 gm
Corn kernels, frozen or fresh	6 oz.	168 gm
Olive oil	4 Tbsp.	60 ml
Kosher salt	to taste	to taste
Fresh, cracked white pepper	to taste	to taste
Flour tortilla, 10″	10	10
Vegetable or chicken stock	as needed	as needed

CHEF'S NOTES

This item goes great with Picante Tomato Relish (p. 188).

PREPARATION

1. Sort and clean beans. Rinse in ample cold water, drain. Cover with cold water and soak overnight. Drain water and rinse beans.
2. Place beans in medium saucepan and cover with water. Bring to boil, reduce heat, and simmer until beans are tender.
3. Remove from heat, drain, and place in clean stainless steel bowl. Cool beans rapidly.
4. In a clean food processor, puree beans until smooth. Add roasted garlic and puree. Use vegetable or chicken stock to achieve desired consistency.
5. Remove from food processor bowl, place in clean stainless steel container, wrap with plastic wrap, and keep warm.
6. Clean and wash all vegetables. Cut appropriately.
7. Place vegetables in a clean stainless steel bowl, add olive oil, and toss thoroughly. Add a little kosher salt and cracked white pepper.
8. Place vegetables on a clean sheet pan and roast in preheated oven at 375°F (190°C). Check vegetables during the cooking process for doneness and even roasting. Allow vegetables to color, but not become too soft.
9. Remove from oven, adjust seasoning, with salt and fresh, cracked pepper and toss thoroughly.
10. Equally spread black bean spread over flour tortillas. Add roasted vegetable mixture, and wrap and roll tortillas into cylindrical shape.
11. Cut into halves, and serve at once.

NUTRITION PER WRAP

Calories 350, protein 12 gm, fat 9 gm, carbohydrates 58 gm, cholesterol 0 mg, sodium 285 mg

SOUTHWEST-STYLE WRAP WITH AVOCADO DIP

SERVES 12

NUTRITION NOTES

For a lower-fat option, use a chunky and spicy tomato salsa for the dip.

INGREDIENTS	AMOUNT/U.S.	METRIC
Certified Angus Beef™ flank steak, all visible fat and sinew trimmed	4 lb.	1792 gm
Mustard seeds	1 tsp.	3 gm
Bay leaves	3	3
Peppercorns	1 tsp.	3 gm
Chicken broth	64 fl. oz.	1920 ml
Olive oil	2 Tbsp.	30 ml
Red onion, peeled, finely minced	4 oz.	112 gm
Jalapeño chilies, seeded, minced	1	1
Garlic, peeled, finely minced	5 cloves	5 cloves
Roma tomatoes, peeled, seeded, diced	1 lb.	448 gm
Fennel seeds	1 tsp.	3 gm
Cilantro, snipped	1 Tbsp.	7 gm
Cumin seeds, crushed	1 tsp.	3 gm
Oregano, snipped	1 Tbsp.	7 gm
Kosher salt	to taste	to taste
Fresh, cracked white pepper	to taste	to taste
Kalamata olives, diced	3 oz.	84 gm
Flour tortillas, 8", thin, high-quality	24	24

PREPARATION

1. In large (4 qt.) stock pot, place flank steak with mustard seed, bay leaves, peppercorns, and stock. Bring to quick boil and reduce to simmer gently. Cook flank steak until tender. Remove from heat and cool.

2. Cut flank steak into small juliennes. Set aside. Strain stock and freeze for future use.

3. In large nonstick skillet, heat olive oil and sweat onion, jalapeño, and garlic until translucent. Add tomatoes, simmer gently over low heat for 10 minutes. Add fennel seed, cilantro, cumin seed, and oregano. Combine mixture thoroughly with julienned flank steak.

4. Adjust seasoning with cracked white pepper and a little kosher salt. Add kalamata olives.

5. Heat thoroughly, remove from heat. Place equal amounts of flank steak filling into flour tortillas. Wrap and fold into cylinder shape, and serve with Avocado Dip.

Avocado Dip

INGREDIENTS	AMOUNT/U.S.	METRIC
Avocados, ripe, peeled, pitted, chopped	2	2
Buttermilk, low-fat	4 oz.	120 ml
Lemon, juice of	1	1
Rice vinegar	1½ Tbsp.	21 ml
Cilantro, fresh, snipped	1 Tbsp.	7 gm
Red onion, peeled, finely chopped	2 oz.	56 gm
Spring onions, minced	2 oz.	56 gm
Kosher salt	to taste	to taste
Fresh cracked white pepper, milled	to taste	to taste

PREPARATION

1. Combine all ingredients thoroughly, season to taste with kosher salt and cracked white pepper, and keep mixture chunky.

NUTRITION PER 2 TORTILLA WRAPS
Calories 543, protein 37 gm, fat 22 gm, carbohydrates 44 gm, cholesterol 76 mg, sodium 514 mg

NUTRITION PER SERVING OF AVOCADO DIP
Calories 61, protein 1 gm, fat 5 gm, carbohydrates 4 gm, cholesterol 0 mg, sodium 48 mg

NUTRITION PER 2 WRAPS
Calories 604, protein 38 gm, fat 27 gm, carbohydrates 48 gm, cholesterol 76 mg, sodium 562 mg

PAN-SMOKED SALMON WITH ITALIAN WHITE BEANS AND SAFFRON BROTH

SERVES 8

CHEF'S NOTES

The purpose of pan-smoking is to infuse the smoke flavor without drying out, or overcooking, the fish.

INGREDIENTS	AMOUNT/U.S.	METRIC
Alder, hickory, or mesquite wood chips, fine-cut	8 oz.	224 gm
Pickling spice	1 Tbsp.	15 gm
Kosher salt	1 Tbsp.	15 gm
Salmon fillets, center-cut	8 @ 4 oz. ea.	8 @ 112 gm ea.
Olive oil	1 Tbsp.	15 ml

PREPARATION OF SALMON

1. Soak wood chips in water for 2 hours. Remove and drain.
2. Combine pickling spice with salt and rub into salmon steaks. Cover with plastic wrap and refrigerate for 1 hour to allow salmon to absorb flavors.
3. Rinse salmon in cold water to remove salt and pickling spice. Paper-towel dry. Rub with olive oil and set aside.
4. Prepare smoking pan. Place chips on bottom of pan. Place roasting rack on top of chips. Cover and place smoking pan over direct heat until smoke aroma becomes apparent.
5. Place salmon on roasting rack, close lid, and let flavor develop for 3 minutes. Remove salmon. (Note: Use caution when opening smoking pan.)
6. Finish cooking in 350°F (175°C) oven for 5–7 minutes, until salmon reaches desired doneness.

ITALIAN WHITE BEANS AND SAFFRON BROTH

INGREDIENTS	AMOUNT/U.S.	METRIC
Italian White Beans:		
Cannellini beans, cooked (cooked weight)	6 oz.	168 gm
Garlic, peeled, minced	3 cloves	3 cloves
Onions, peeled, finely diced	4 oz.	112 gm
Olive oil	1 Tbsp.	15 ml
Porcini mushrooms, fresh or flash frozen, sliced	4 oz.	112 gm
Bowtie pasta, cooked (cooked weight)	1 lb.	448 gm
Saffron Broth	24 fl. oz.	720 ml
Fresh, cracked white pepper	to taste	to taste
Kosher salt	to taste	to taste

Saffron Broth:

Fish stock, hot	64 fl. oz.	1920 ml
Saffron	2 tsp.	2 gm
Fennel, cleaned, washed, diced	2 bulbs	2 bulbs
Celery stalks, cleaned, diced	2	2
Leek, white part only, diced	1	1
White wine	4 fl. oz.	120 ml
Bay leaf	1	1

PREPARATION OF BEANS

1. In stainless steel saucepan, heat olive oil and sweat garlic and onions gently over low heat for 3 minutes, until onions are translucent.
2. Add porcine mushrooms, continue to cook gently. Add Saffron Broth and bring mixture to boil, then reduce to simmer.
3. Add cooked cannellini beans to broth, heat thoroughly, add cooked bowtie pasta. Adjust seasongin with cracked white pepper and kosher salt.

PREPARATION OF BROTH

1. Combine 2 fl. oz. of fish stock with saffron. Set aside and allow to steep.
2. In medium stock pot, place remaining fish stock, fennel, celery, and leeks. Allow mixture to come to boil, reduce to simmer. Add white wine and bay leaf, simmer for 45 minutes.
3. Strain stock through fine-mesh sieve and return stock to heat. Add steeped saffron and adjust seasoning with kosher salt and cracked white pepper.

PRESENTATION

Ladle Italian White Beans and Saffron Broth into deep soup plates and serve with pan-smoked salmon on top.

NUTRITION PER COMPLETE ENTREE SERVING

Calories 347, protein 29 gm, fat 12 gm, carbohydrates 29 gm, cholesterol 62 mg, sodium 372 mg

MARINATED ROAST PORK LOIN WITH SAVOY CABBAGE AND LENTILS

SERVES 8

INGREDIENTS	AMOUNT/U.S.	METRIC
Pork loin, boneless, center-cut, cleaned, excessive fat and sinew removed	40 oz.	1120 gm
Apple cider	16 fl. oz.	480 ml
Honey	1 Tbsp.	15 gm
Garlic, peeled, minced	2 cloves	2 cloves
Shallots, peeled, minced	2 oz.	56 gm
Ginger, fresh, minced	1 Tbsp.	15 gm
Pommery® mustard	1 Tbsp.	15 gm
Fresh, cracked white pepper	1½ tsp.	7 gm
Cilantro, washed, cleaned	2 Tbsp.	30 gm

PREPARATION

1. Place fabricated pork loin in a clean stainless steel insert pan.
2. In a clean stainless steel mixing bowl, place cider, honey, garlic, shallots, ginger, mustard, pepper, and cilantro. Combine mixture thoroughly.
3. Marinate pork loin in marinade, refrigerated, for at least 24 hours.
4. Remove pork loin from marinade, drain properly. In large nonstick skillet, using the dry sauté method, pan-sear on all sides until evenly browned.
5. Place in roasting pan in 375°F (190°C) oven and roast until internal temperature reaches 145°F (63°C). Turn roast occasionally utilizing a tong (do not spear with a fork, as meat juices and perception of tenderness are lost).
6. Remove from oven and set pork aside to rest. Deglaze roasting pan with chicken stock over medium heat, stirring continuously. Reduce by one-third.
7. Remove jus and mix with Savoy Cabbage or Lentils.

PRESENTATION

Serve roast pork with Savoy Cabbage and Lentils.

SAVOY CABBAGE

INGREDIENTS	AMOUNT/U.S.	METRIC
Savoy cabbage, medium head, cleaned, washed, cut into thin strips	1	1
Bacon, cut into small dice	4 slices	4 slices
Chicken stock	16 fl. oz.	480 ml
Caraway seeds	½ Tbsp.	7 gm
Kosher salt	to taste	to taste
Fresh, cracked white pepper	to taste	to taste

1. In a saucepan, gently caramelize bacon over low heat.
2. Gradually add Savoy cabbage while stirring continuously. Deglaze with stock.
3. Add caraway seeds; cook cabbage until tender. Adjust seasoning to taste with kosher salt and cracked white pepper.

LENTILS

INGREDIENTS	AMOUNT/U.S.	METRIC
Green French Lentils, dry	8 oz.	224 gm
Chicken stock	16 fl. oz.	480 ml
Carrots,peeled, peeled, finely diced	4 oz.	112 gm
Onions, peeled, finely diced	4 oz.	112 gm
Shallots, peeled, finely diced	2 oz.	56 gm
Garlic, peeled, minced	2 cloves	2 cloves
Balsamic vinegar	2 fl. oz.	60 ml
Olive oil	1 Tbsp.	15 ml
Chives, short-cut	½ oz.	14 gm

PREPARATION
1. Sort and soak lentils in cold water for 1 hour.
2. Drain and rinse lentils. Place in a stock pot with chicken stock, bring to a boil, reduce heat, and simmer for 15 minutes.
3. Add carrots, onions, shallots, and garlic. Cook gently for an additional 15 minutes.
4. Adjust seasoning with Balsamic vinegar and kosher salt and cracked white pepper to taste. Lentils should be tender but still firm.
5. Just before serving, add olive oil to enhance flavor and give a sheen to the lentils, and stir in chives.

NUTRITION PER SERVING OF PORK
Calories 234, protein 30 gm, fat 11 gm, carbohydrates 3 gm, cholesterol 85 mg, sodium 132 mg

NUTRITION PER SERVING OF SAVOY CABBAGE
Calories 44, protein 2 gm, fat 2 gm, carbohydrates 4 gm, cholesterol 3 mg, sodium 71 mg

NUTRITION PER SERVING OF LENTILS
Calories 133, protein 9 gm, fat 2 gm, carbohydrates 21 gm, cholesterol 0 mg, sodium 22 mg

NUTRITION PER COMPLETE ENTREE SERVING
Calories 411, protein 40 gm, fat 16 gm, carbohydrates 27 gm, cholesterol 88 mg, sodium 225 mg

SAUTÉED GINGERED SHRIMP WITH LENTIL BULGUR SALAD*

SERVES 10

INGREDIENTS	AMOUNT/U.S.	METRIC
Large brown shrimp, Compass® brand, 16 to 20 peeled, deveined	40 pc.	40 pc.
Paprika powder	1 tsp.	2 gm
Fresh, cracked white pepper	2 tsp.	4 gm
Tamari sauce, light	3 fl. oz.	90 ml
Olive oil	1 Tbsp.	15 ml
Lemon, juice of	1	1
Ginger, fresh, minced	1 oz.	28 gm
Mustard, dry	2 tsp.	4 gm
Tabasco	10 drops	10 drops
Cilantro, snipped	2 Tbsp.	15 gm
Lentil Bulgur Salad (below)		
Lentil Bulgur Salad:		
Bulgur wheat, cooked	6 oz.	168 gm
Green lentils, cooked	8 oz.	224 gm
Red bell pepper, cleaned, seeded, diced	1 oz.	28 gm
Green bell pepper, cleaned, seeded, diced	1 oz.	28 gm
Yellow bell pepper, cleaned, seeded, diced	1 oz.	28 gm
Yellow onion, peeled finely diced	2 oz.	56 gm
Cumin powder	1 tsp.	2 gm
Cilantro, snipped	2 Tbsp.	15 gm
Lemon, juice of	1	1
Kosher salt	to taste	to taste
Rice vinegar	3 Tbsp.	45 ml
Olive oil, virgin	2 Tbsp.	30 ml

PREPARATION OF SHRIMP

1. Combine all ingredients except shrimp in stainless steel mixing bowl. Mix thoroughly; add cleaned shrimp. Marinate for 1 hour.
2. In large sauté pan, pan-sear shrimp quickly in two batches over medium-high heat to obtain even color on both sides (3–4 minutes).
3. Remove from heat. Serve shrimp with Lentil Bulgur Salad.

PREPARATION OF SALAD

1. For the salad, combine bulgur wheat with lentils, in a clean stainless steel mixing bowl. Add red, green, and yellow bell peppers and combine.
2. Add onion, cumin, cilantro, lemon juice, vinegar, and olive oil.

3. Adjust seasoning with ground pepper and a little salt. Combine thoroughly. Allow flavors to develop for 1 hour.
4. Before serving, adjust seasoning.

NUTRITION PER SERVING OF SHRIMP
Calories 104, protein 16 gm, fat 3 gm, carbohydrates 3 gm, cholesterol 110 mg, sodium 273 mg

NUTRITION PER SERVING OF SALAD
Calories 76, protein 3 gm, fat 3 gm, carbohydrates 10 gm, cholesterol 0 mg, sodium 88 mg

NUTRITION PER SERVING OF SHRIMP AND SALAD
Calories 180, protein 19 gm, fat 6 gm, carbohydrates 13 gm, cholesterol 110 mg, sodium 361 mg

CHAPTER 11

VEGETABLES, POTATOES, GRAINS, AND LEGUMES

❦

HAPPINESS RARELY KEEPS COMPANY WITH AN EMPTY STOMACH.

Japanese proverb

WINE IS BOTTLED POETRY.

R. L. Stevenson

TOO MUCH OF A GOOD THING CAN BE WONDERFUL.

Mae West

EVERYONE EATS, BUT FEW KNOW FLAVOR.

Confucius

TO EAT IS HEAVEN!

Confucius

NO MATTER HOW WELL ITS NUTRITIONAL ANALYSIS READS, IF A DISH
DOESN'T TASTE GOOD IT ISN'T NUTRITIOUS.

Chef Mark V. Erickson, CMC

IT'S NOT JUST ABOUT FOOD, IT'S ABOUT PEOPLE ENJOYING ALL THE
ELEMENTS OF FOOD!

Chef Eric Kopelow, CEC

ALL GOOD COOKS, LIKE ALL GREAT ARTISTS, MUST HAVE AN AUDIENCE
WORTH COOKING FOR.

André Simon

IN COOKING, AS IN ALL THE ARTS, SIMPLICITY IS THE SIGN OF
PERFECTION.

Curnonsky

SMALL CHEER AND GREAT WELCOME MAKE A MERRY FEAST.

William Shakespeare

*An asterisk following a recipe title indicates that the recipe also appears in another chapter.

VEGETABLES, POTATOES, GRAINS, AND LEGUMES

Vegetables are rich in health-promoting qualities, therefore increased consumption of vegetables contributes necessary nutrients for a person's well-being.

Perhaps an area often overlooked in planning is that of an appropriate accompaniment to be served with a main course. However today, vegetables, potatoes, grains, and legumes are no longer just considered an accompaniment, they are often the main focal point of a dish.

Vegetables offer unlimited variations in texture, taste, and color. By definition, vegetables are any edible portions of plants with soft green stems. They are classified according to the part of the plant from which they come. For instance, beets and potatoes are roots and tubers; varieties of onions are bulbs; asparagus and kohlrabi are stems; spinach greens and lettuce are leaves; celery, rhubarb, and fennel are leaf stalks; cauliflower and broccoli are immature flowers; and legumes, peas, and beans are seeds and seed pods.

Another classification of vegetables is the fruit vegetable. Botanically speaking, these are actually fruits because they contain one or more seeds surrounded by the flesh of the plant. From a culinary viewpoint, they qualify as vegetables, primarily because they are not sweet as are fruits and they are not typically eaten alone as is a piece of fruit. Included in this group are bell peppers, eggplants, tomatoes, avocados, cucumbers, corn, and squashes.

Although mushrooms are generally considered a vegetable, they are really a fungus.

Many of today's vegetables are domesticated descendants of ancient wild plants.

Vegetables, potatoes, grains, and legumes play an important role in our daily consumption of foods. Grains and legumes are great sources of complex carbohydrates and benefit good health. In vegetarian dishes, combining legumes, nuts, and grains will raise the protein value of the meal.

For variety, a combination of vegetables, potatoes, grains, and legumes can be used as the main item in a meal, such as a paella. This lavish, multicolored dish centers around rice, saffron, olives, and vegetables and is merely seasoned by including fish, shellfish, or a meat product.

The Mediterranean cuisine relies on a daily diet of fresh greens and vegetables. Fruits, pasta, grains, legumes, potatoes, nuts, cheese, yogurt, fish, poultry, and always garlic, olive oil, and aromatics are present to enhance and vary the taste of foods. The popularity of this cuisine is attributed to the healthfulness and flavor of its ever-present ingredient, olive oil.

Ideally, vegetables and fruits should be purchased as fresh as possible. Always select crisp and firm vegetables. Avoid small or immature vegetables, as well as overgrown ones; the first will lack substantial flavor and the latter are usually coarse. Vegetables, potatoes, grains, and legumes are by far the most widely available, versatile, flavorful, and simple-to-prepare foods.

Proper selection, purchasing, handling (including storage), and preparation of vegetables, potatoes, grains, and legumes will complement the natural taste and give the maximum benefit of the nutritional value of the product.

Cooking vegetables improves palatability and digestibility. Several changes occur during the cooking process. The texture changes, the flavor develops, and the water content is affected.

When cooking green vegetables, utilize plenty of liquid and do not cover the cooking vessel. The exception is spinach leaves which can be cooked in a covered saucepan using relatively little liquid. Also, avoid acids as they will have an effect on the green color of the vegetables.

When cooking beets, it is not necessary to peel the beets prior to cooking. Adding acid to the cooking liquid will intensify the red color of the beets. Acid will also assist in brightening and intensifying the color of white or yellow vegetables.

It is important to avoid overcooking vegetables. Overcooking will result in the loss of texture, loss of colors, and loss of the natural nutrients and vitamins. In some cases, flavors become objectionable (e.g., Brussel sprouts).

When cooking vegetables, prepare only the amount that you are going to use. Cook vegetables as quickly as possible with the shortest possible holding time.

When seasoning vegetables, use seasonings or aromatics that bring out the natural flavor of the foods.

When working with potatoes, remove potatoes from plastic storage bags and store in a dark, cool, and dry place. Do not store potatoes under refrigeration, as this will cause the potato starch to convert to sugar. Sort potatoes, and do not use potatoes with spots, sprouting eyes, or greenish skin (solanine) (caused by overexposure to artificial light).

There are virtually hundreds of potato varieties available today. The four basic types are Long Whites, Round Whites, Round Reds, and Russets. Experiment with the more unique potatoes available, such as Gold or Red Fingerling. The taste and texture vary greatly, and the variety can increase the creative use of potatoes.

Although the American palate is perhaps not as familiar with root vegetables as is that of some other cultures, try revisiting the use of these simple and delicious foods. When planning meals, plan ways to incorporate root vegetables such as celeriac, parsnips, kohlrabi, carrots, sunchokes, radishes, sweet potatoes, turnips, and beets.

Dried beans, lentils, and peas are found in practically every kitchen, yet these venerable foods are too often treated with little imagination, simply because they seem so ordinary that many chefs and cooks overlook their possibilities.

All dried beans and peas should be sorted to remove any foreign substances such as rocks, and are soaked in cold water for at least eight hours, or overnight. Because beans, lentils, and peas vary in size, texture, and form, the method by which they are cooked can range from steaming to simmering to boiling. Whether fresh or dried, all bean seeds must be cooked before eating. One cup of cooked bean seeds provides approximately 200 calories, 1 gram of fat, and 15 grams of protein.

Today pasta is available in many forms (e.g., wheat-free and egg-free formulations) from good-quality sources. Be selective in the purchasing decision. Whether you prefer dried or fresh, high quality determines good pasta. Pasta is very versatile and nutritious, and provides a great creative outlet for chef and cooks. It may be created containing vegetables such as tomatoes, beets, carrots, legumes, pureed beans, herbs, spices, or cheeses.

When making fresh pasta it is best to use hard-wheat flour, such as milled durum wheat, known as semolina flour, in addition to an egg product and olive oil.

CORN-POBLANO-POTATO PANCAKES

SERVES 12 (3 OZ. PATTIES)

INGREDIENTS	AMOUNT/U.S.	METRIC
Potatoes, washed, cleaned, peeled, 1″ diced	2 lb.	900 gm
Olive oil	1 fl. oz.	30 ml
Corn kernels, fresh	8 oz.	224 gm
Poblano pepper, washed, cored, seeded, membrane removed, finely minced	1	1
Egg substitute	5 oz.	150 ml
Butter, soft	1 Tbsp.	15 gm
Kosher salt	¼ tsp.	1.25 gm
Fresh, cracked white pepper	dash	dash
Milk, skim	8 fl. oz.	240 ml
Cilantro, chopped	3 Tbsp.	15 gm

PREPARATION

1. Boil potatoes until tender, drain, and allow to dry off. Pass potatoes through food mill or ricer into stainless mixing bowl.
2. In large skillet, heat olive oil and gently sauté corn kernels until lightly browned. Add minced poblano and heat thoroughly. Remove from heat.
3. To potato mixture, add egg substitute, butter, salt, a dash of cracked white pepper, and enough milk for desired consistency, and gently combine.
4. Fold in sautéed corn, and pepper mixture and cilantro. Place mixture on sheet pan and cool prior to shaping.
5. Shape potato mixture into patties. In nonstick pan, brown patties on both sides, and serve hot.

NUTRITION PER SERVING
Calories 115, protein 4 gm, fat 4 gm, carbohydrates 17 gm, cholesterol 3 mg, sodium 102 mg

WILD RICE AND SWEET CORN PANCAKES

SERVES 20 (1 OZ. PANCAKES)

INGREDIENTS	AMOUNT/U.S.	METRIC
Flour, all-purpose	4 oz.	112 gm
Yellow cornmeal	1 Tbsp.	15 gm
Baking powder	1½ tsp.	7 gm
Egg substitute	2 fl. oz.	60 ml
Milk, whole	4 fl. oz.	120 ml
Club soda	4 fl. oz.	120 ml
Sweet corn kernels, fresh, cooked	3 oz.	84 gm
Wild rice, cooked (cooked weight)	3 oz.	84 gm
Green peppercorn, lightly crushed	1 Tbsp.	15 gm
Butter, browned	1 Tbsp.	15 ml
Kosher salt	to taste	to taste
Fresh, cracked white pepper	to taste	to taste
Vegetable spray	as needed	as needed

PREPARATION

1. Mix flour, cornmeal, and baking powder in mixing bowl. In separate bowl, mix egg and milk; add to dry ingredients. Stir in club soda. Fold in corn, rice, peppercorns, browned butter, kosher salt and fresh cracked pepper to taste. Stir just until combined.
2. Coat hot nonstick griddle or skillet with vegetable spray. Spoon pancake batter onto griddle (pancakes should be about 3″ in diameter), and brown pancakes on both sides and then remove from skillet.

NUTRITION PER PANCAKE

Calories 44, protein 2 gm, fat 1 gm, carbohydrates 8 gm, cholesterol 2 mg, sodium 31 mg

WHITE BEAN AND TOMATO RAGOUT

SERVES 12

INGREDIENTS	AMOUNT/U.S.	METRIC
White beans, small, washed, soaked for 12 hours, rinsed, drained	8 oz.	224 gm
Chicken stock	1½ qt.	1½ l
Garlic, peeled, finely minced	2 cloves	2 cloves
Savory	½ Tbsp.	5 gm
Red onion, peeled, finely diced	3 oz.	84 gm
Paprika powder	1 tsp.	2 gm
Cayenne powder	⅛ tsp.	.5 gm
Kosher salt	to taste	to taste
Fresh, cracked white pepper	to taste	to taste
Chives, short-cut	3 Tbsp.	15 gm
Parsley, snipped	2 Tbsp.	10 gm
Olive oil	1 Tbsp.	15ml
Red and green bell pepper, cleaned, washed, seeded, diced	1 each	1 each
Roma tomatoes, red, cleaned, blanched, peeled, seeded, diced	12 oz.	336 gm

CHEF'S NOTES

Serve over couscous, rice, or any cooked grain.

PREPARATION

1. In medium stock pot, place white beans and chicken stock. Bring to rapid boil, reduce to simmer.

2. Add garlic, savory, and onions. Cook over medium heat until beans are tender and cooked, approximately 40–45 minutes, stirring occasionally. Add paprika and cayenne. Adjust seasoning to taste with kosher salt, cracked white pepper, chives, and parsley.

3. In separate sauté pan, heat olive oil and sauté red and green bell peppers for 1 minute. Add diced tomato and sauté for an additional 3 minutes. Add this to bean mixture and combine gently. Taste and adjust seasoning.

NUTRITION PER SERVING

Calories 100, protein 5 gm, fat 2 gm, carbohydrates 16 gm, cholesterol 0 mg, sodium 9 mg

ONION AND POTATO PUREE *

SERVES 8

INGREDIENTS	AMOUNT/U.S.	METRIC
Red onion, peeled, small-diced	6 oz.	168 gm
Idaho potatoes, peeled, quartered	2 lb.	896 gm
Buttermilk, low-fat	4 fl. oz.	120 ml
Half & half	2 fl. oz.	60ml
Kosher salt	to taste	to taste
Fresh, cracked white pepper	to taste	to taste
Vegetable spray	as needed	as needed

PREPARATION

1. Preheat oven to 350°F (175°C).
2. Place a sheet of parchment paper on a sheet pan. Spray paper with vegetable spray. Spread onions on paper and bake until onions are caramelized and dry. Allow to cool.
3. Place potatoes in saucepan and barely cover with salted cold water. Bring to boil and simmer until fork-tender, drain. Allow most of the moisture to evaporate so that the potatoes are dry.
4. Run dried potatoes through a ricer.
5. In small saucepan, heat buttermilk and half & half; do not boil. Adjust seasoning with kosher salt and cracked white pepper.
6. Stir buttermilk mixture into potatoes; keep hot.
7. Just before serving, fold caramelized onions into potato mixture.

NUTRITION PER SERVING

Calories 109, protein 4 gm, fat 1 gm, carbohydrates 22 gm, cholesterol 3 gm, sodium 28 mg

BAKED POTATO PUREE

INGREDIENTS	AMOUNT/U.S.	METRIC
Potatoes, large, baking, washed	2 lb.	896 gm
Buttermilk, hot	4 fl. oz.	120 ml
Milk, reduced fat (2%), hot	4 fl. oz.	120 ml
Parsley, fresh, snipped	2 Tbsp.	14 gm
Fresh, cracked white pepper	to taste	to taste
Kosher salt	to taste	to taste
Olive oil	1 Tbsp.	15 ml

PREPARATION

1. Preheat oven to 375°F (190°C).
2. Wrap potatoes in foil and place on baking sheet. Bake potatoes in oven until tender.
3. Remove from oven and scoop the pulp into stainless steel mixing bowl.
4. With wire whisk mix gently until potatoes are pureed. Add hot buttermilk and milk. Mix ingredients thoroughly.
5. Add parsley, and adjust seasoning to taste with kosher salt and cracked white pepper. Last, fold in olive oil.

NUTRITION PER SERVING
Calories 113, protein 4 gm, fat 2 gm, carbohydrates 21 gm, cholesterol 1 mg, sodium 32 mg

CHEF'S NOTES

For variations of this recipe, experiment with flavor enhancers such as pureed oven roasted garlic, shallots, bell peppers, or leeks. Also, various herbs such as basil, parsley, chives, or lemon thyme add interesting flavor characteristics to mashed potatoes.

ORZO VEGETABLE MEDLEY *

SERVES 8

INGREDIENTS	AMOUNT/U.S.	METRIC
Orzo	6 oz.	168 gm
Artichokes, large, fresh, cleaned, trimmed, sliced	5	5
Baby carrots, cleaned, trimmed, halved	5 oz.	140 gm
Olive oil	1 Tbsp.	15 ml
Fava beans, fresh, cleaned, cooked, drained (cooked weight)	6 oz.	168 gm
Tarragon, snipped	2 Tbsp.	10 gm
Fresh, cracked white pepper	to taste	to taste
Kosher salt	½ tsp.	2.5 gm
Water	1 qt.	960 ml

PREPARATION

1. In medium stock pot, cook orzo in 1 quart (1 liter) of slightly salted (½ tsp.) boiling water until tender. Drain and rinse. Place in stainless steel insert pan and keep warm.

2. In stock pot, simmer sliced artichoke hearts in 2½ cups salted (1 tsp.) water until tender. Remove from water; reserve broth in pot.

3. In sauté pan, sweat carrots in olive oil until tender. Add to artichoke broth along with artichokes, fava beans, cooked orzo, and tarragon. Bring to simmer, and adjust seasoning with pepper and salt, as needed.

NUTRITION PER SERVING

Calories 168, protein 7 gm, fat 2 gm, carbohydrates 32 gm, cholesterol 0 mg, sodium 296 mg

SOUTHWEST LENTIL RAGOUT

SERVES 12

INGREDIENTS	AMOUNT/U.S.	METRIC
Olive oil	3 Tbsp.	45 ml
Corn kernels, fresh	16 oz.	448 gm
Garlic, peeled, minced	2 Tbsp.	20 gm
Yellow onions, peeled, small-diced	8 oz.	224 gm
Celery, peeled, small-diced	8 oz.	224 gm
Carrots, peeled, small-diced	8 oz.	224 gm
Jalapeño pepper, seeded, minced	1	1
Shiitaki mushrooms, cleaned, small-diced	8 oz.	224 gm
Vegetable stock, high-quality	4½ qt.	4.25 l
Tomato paste	2 Tbsp.	20 gm
Dry white wine	4 fl. oz.	120 ml
Lentils, French Green, soaked for 1 hour	12 oz.	336 gm
Basil, fresh, snipped	1 Tbsp.	5 gm
Kosher salt	⅔ tsp.	3 gm
Fresh, cracked black pepper	½ tsp.	1 gm
Garnish:		
Tomatoes, peel on, cut into strips	8 oz.	224 gm
Cilantro, fresh, snipped	4 Tbsp.	20 gm

PREPARATION

1. Heat olive oil over medium heat in sauté pan. Sauté corn and until light brown. Add garlic, onions, celery, carrots, and jalapeño. Reduce heat and gently sauté until translucent.
2. Add mushrooms and cook gently. Deglaze pan with a little stock and reduce. Stir in tomato paste and cook until rusty in color. Deglaze again with a small amount of vegetable stock.
3. Add white wine, cleaned and rinsed lentils, and remainder of vegetable stock. Bring to boil, reduce heat, and simmer until lentils are tender, approximately 30–40 minutes. (Do not cook until dry; there should be a small amount of liquid with the lentils.)
4. Add basil, salt, and pepper; combine. Garnish with strips of tomato and fresh cilantro.

NUTRITION PER SERVING
Calories 232, protein 11 gm, fat 6 gm, carbohydrates 35 gm, cholesterol 0 mg, sodium 179 mg

STEWED VEGETABLE MEDLEY *

SERVES 8

INGREDIENTS	AMOUNT/U.S.	METRIC
Olive oil	3 Tbsp.	45 ml
Red onion, peeled, julienned	6 oz.	168 gm
Potatoes, cleaned, washed, peeled, cut in batonnets*	1 lb.	448 gm
Carrots, peeled, cleaned, washed, cut in batonnets	8 oz.	224 gm
Haricot verts, cleaned, washed	8 oz.	224 gm
Chicken stock, high-quality	16 fl. oz.	480 ml
Yellow squash, peeled, cut in batonnets	8 oz	224 gm
Zucchini, peeled, cut in batonnets	8 oz.	224 gm
Basil, fresh, snipped	1 Tbsp.	5 gm
Chives, fresh, short-cut	1 Tbsp.	5 gm
Kosher salt	to taste	to taste
Fresh, cracked white pepper	to taste	to taste

PREPARATION

1. In large saucepan, heat olive oil and sweat red onion gently for 1 minute or until translucent. Add potatoes, carrots and haricot verts; continue to sauté gently for 2 minutes.
2. Add stock, bring to simmer and cook for 5 minutes. Add yellow squash and zucchini; cook gently for an additional 10 minutes. (Vegetables should be tender but not overcooked.)
3. Just before serving, add fresh herbs and kosher salt and fresh, cracked white pepper to taste.

NUTRITION PER SERVING

Calories 131, protein 3 gm, fat 6 gm, carbohydrates 19 gm, cholesterol 0 mg, sodium 20 gm

*Batonnets are small sticks cut about ¼″ × ¼″ x 2″.

Photo courtesy of Certified Angus Beef Program

Marinated Chuck Steak with Basil-Nut Pesto and Piquant Tomato Sauce

Photo courtesy of Zale Lipshy University Hospital

Smoked Salmon Steaks with Celeriac, Bell Pepper, Cucumber Relish, and
Tomato Salsa and Oven-Roasted Pork Loin with Lentil Bulgur Salad

Photo courtesy of Certified Angus Beef Program

Country-Style Beef Stew

Photo courtesy of Certified Angus Beef Program

Spiced Braised Beef Brisket with Wild Mushroom Risotto

Photo courtesy of Certified Angus Beef Program

Roast Beef with Sherry–Bell Pepper Vinaigrette

Photo courtesy of Certified Angus Beef Program

Slow-Cooked Shoulder Roast "Pot on the Fire"

Photo courtesy of Idaho Potato Commission

Corn-Poblano-Potato Pancakes

Photo courtesy of Zale Lipshy University Hospital

Halibut with Fettucine and Stewed Roma Tomatoes

Photo courtesy of Certified Angus Beef Program

Brisket of Beef with Herb Broth and Root Vegetables

Photo courtesy of California Fig Advisory Board

California Fig and Grape Strudel

STEWED ZUCCHINI WITH PEPPERS AND TOMATOES *

INGREDIENTS	AMOUNT/U.S.	METRIC
Olive oil	1 Tbsp.	15 ml
Garlic, peeled, minced	4 cloves	4 cloves
Yellow onions, peeled, coarsely diced	10 oz.	280 gm
Zucchini squash, peeled, coarsely diced	8 oz.	224 gm
Roma tomatoes, peeled, seeded, coarsely diced	1 lb.	448 gm
Green bell pepper, roasted, peeled, seeded, diced	8 oz.	224 gm
Chicken stock	6 fl. oz.	180 ml
Basil, snipped	2 Tbsp.	10 gm
Lemon thyme, snipped	1 Tbsp.	5 gm
Kosher salt	to taste	to taste
Cayenne pepper	to taste	to taste
Fresh, cracked white pepper	to taste	to taste

PREPARATION

1. In a saucepan heat oil and gently sweat garlic and onion for 2 minutes.
2. Over low heat add zucchini, sauté gently, toss mixture gently.
3. Add tomatoes and peppers. Add stock and continue to cook gently for 5 minutes.
4. Adjust seasoning with basil, thyme, salt, cayenne pepper, and cracked white pepper.
5. Add additional stock to achieve desired consistency.

NUTRITION PER SERVING

Calories 39, protein 1 gm, fat 2 gm, carbohydrates 6 gm, cholesterol 0 mg, sodium 6 mg

SAUTÉED WILD MUSHROOMS

SERVES 12

INGREDIENTS	AMOUNT/U.S.	METRIC
Assorted mushrooms, cleaned, sliced (e.g., Shiitaki, Cepes, Oyster, or Crimini, depending on the season)	2 lb.	896 gm
Olive oil	1 Tbsp.	15 ml
Thyme, fresh, snipped	1 tsp.	1 gm
Tarragon, fresh, snipped	1 tsp.	1 gm
Chicken stock	8 fl. oz.	240 ml
Kosher salt	to taste	to taste
Fresh, cracked white pepper	to taste	to taste

PREPARATION

1. Place cleaned mushrooms in mixing bowl; toss with olive oil and herbs.
2. In sauté pan, dry sauté mushrooms, mix gently. Deglaze pan with stock at intervals.
3. Continue to sauté for approximately 10 minutes. Adjust seasoning to taste with kosher salt and cracked white pepper.

NUTRITION PER SERVING

Calories 56, protein 1 gm, fat 2 gm, carbohydrates 12 gm, cholesterol 0 mg, sodium 4 mg

WILD MUSHROOM RAGOUT

SERVES 8

INGREDIENTS	AMOUNT/U.S.	METRIC
Olive oil	1 Tbsp.	15 ml
Yellow onion, peeled, finely diced	1	1
Garlic, roasted, minced	3 cloves	3 cloves
White mushrooms, cleaned, sliced	1 lb.	448 gm
Shiitaki mushrooms, cleaned, sliced	¼ lb.	112 gm
Oyster mushrooms, cleaned, sliced	¼ lb.	112 gm
Vegetable stock	¾ cup	180 ml
Sherry wine vinegar	1 fl. oz.	30 ml
Basil, fresh, snipped	1 Tbsp.	10 gm
Parsley, fresh, snipped	1 Tbsp.	10 gm
Kosher salt	to taste	to taste
Fresh, cracked white pepper	to taste	to taste

CHEF'S NOTES

Serve ragout in herb crepes or over mashed potatoes or herbed polenta.

PREPARATION

1. Heat olive oil in large nonstick skillet and sweat onion until translucent. Add garlic and mushrooms and sauté gently for 2 minutes. Deglaze with stock. Cook mushrooms gently over low heat for 5 minutes.
2. Add vinegar, basil, and parsley, and adjust seasoning to taste with kosher salt and cracked white pepper.

NUTRITION PER SERVING

Calories 54, Protein 2 gm, Fat 2 gm, Carbohydrates 7 gm, Cholesterol 0 mg, Sodium 28 mg

STEWED EGGPLANT
AND ZUCCHINI

SERVES 8

INGREDIENTS	AMOUNT/U.S.	METRIC
Eggplant, peeled, diced	28 oz.	780 gm
Zucchini, peeled, diced	16 oz.	448 gm
Olive oil	1 Tbsp.	15 ml
Bell peppers, assorted cleaned, seeded, diced	8 oz.	224 gm
Onion, diced	6 oz.	168 gm
Celery, diced	2 oz.	56 gm
Vegetable stock	2 fl. oz.	60 ml
Tomato, peeled, seeded, diced	4 oz.	160 gm
Capers, small	2 tsp.	10 gm
Black olives, pitted, diced	2 tsp.	10 gm
Balsamic vinegar	2 Tbsp.	30 ml
Sugar	½ tsp.	2.25 gm
Kosher salt	to taste	to taste
Fresh, cracked white pepper	to taste	to taste

PREPARATION

1. Heat olive oil in large nonstick skillet, add eggplant and zucchini, and sauté until browned. Reduce heat.

2. Add peppers, onion, and celery. Deglaze pan with vegetable stock. Simmer until almost tender.

3. Add tomato and cook over medium heat for 5 minutes.

4. Finish with capers, olives, vinegar, and sugar. Continue to simmer mixture gently for 10 minutes. Adjust seasoning to taste with salt and pepper.

NUTRITION PER SERVING

Calories 72, protein 3 gm, fat 2 gm, carbohydrates 13 gm, cholesterol 0 mg, sodium 77 mg

POTATO PANCAKES
WITH APPLESAUCE

SERVES 12

INGREDIENTS	AMOUNT/U.S.	METRIC
Idaho potatoes, peeled	2 lb.	896 gm
Yellow onions, peeled, grated	1 lg.	1 lg.
Egg substitute	4 fl. oz.	120 ml
All-purpose flour	2 Tbsp.	15 gm
Spring onions, short-cut	1 oz.	28 gm
Kosher salt	to taste	to taste
Fresh, cracked white pepper	to taste	to taste
Nutmeg, fresh-grated	to taste	to taste
Applesauce:		
Red MacIntosh apples, cored, sliced	3 lb.	1362 gm
Apple cider	8 fl. oz.	240 ml
Maple syrup	3 Tbsp.	45 ml
Cinnamon sticks	2	2

CHEF'S NOTES

White wine can be used in place of the apple cider to give applesauce a different flavor.

PREPARATION FOR PANCAKES

1. Preheat oven to 350°F (175°C).
2. Grate potatoes into a bowl of cold water to prevent them from turning brown. Grate onion, and set aside.
3. In medium stainless steel bowl, beat eggs, add onions, flour, and spring onions, and add salt, pepper, and nutmeg; combine mixture thoroughly.
4. Drain grated potatoes, pat dry with paper towels, and add to egg mixture. Combine thoroughly.
5. In hot nonstick skillet using the dry sauté method, place a spoonful of potato mixture into mounds to form pancakes. Make two or three at a time. Keep space between pancakes to prevent running together. Cook until golden brown and crisp on each side.
6. Place on sheet pan and finish cooking in 350°F (175°C) oven. Serve hot with warm applesauce.

PREPARATION FOR APPLESAUCE

1. Place apples into medium stainless steel stock pot, and add apple cider, maple syrup, and cinnamon sticks. Cook gently over medium heat until apples are soft, approximately 15–20 minutes.
2. Remove cinnamon sticks and pass apple mixture through food mill.
3. Serve warm.

NUTRITION PER SERVING OF POTATO PANCAKES
Calories 76, protein 3 gm, fat 0 gm, carbohydrates 16 gm, cholesterol 0 mg, sodium 20 mg

NUTRITION PER SERVING OF APPLESAUCE

Calories 91, protein 0 gm, fat 0 gm, carbohydrates 23 gm, cholesterol 0 mg, sodium 1 mg

NUTRITION PER COMPLETE ENTREE SERVING

Calories 167, protein 3 gm, fat 0 gm, carbohydrates 39 gm, cholesterol 0 mg, sodium 21 mg

BLUE CHEESE POLENTA MOONS

SERVES 6

CHEF'S NOTES

Polenta shapes may be dry sautéed until lightly browned for added flavor and texture.

INGREDIENTS	AMOUNT/U.S.	METRIC
Chicken stock, high-quality, defatted	16 fl. oz.	480 ml
Garlic, peeled, minced	1 clove	1 clove
Polenta meal or cornmeal	8 oz.	224 gm
Egg substitute (or 2 egg whites)	2 oz.	60 ml
Blue cheese, crumbled	2 oz.	56 gm
Kosher salt	to taste	to taste
Fresh, cracked white pepper	to taste	to taste
Basil, snipped	2 tsp.	2 gm
Thyme, snipped	1 tsp.	1 gm
Vegetable spray	as needed	as needed

PREPARATION

1. Preheat oven to 325°F (165°C).
2. In heavy saucepan, bring chicken stock and minced garlic to rapid boil. Quickly whisk in polenta meal or cornmeal. Lower heat to medium-low and stir constantly with wooden spoon for approximately 20 minutes; mixture should be firm.
3. Remove from heat. Gradually stir in egg substitute and blue cheese.
4. Return pan to low heat and cook, stirring until blue cheese melts. Season with salt and pepper to taste and stir in basil and thyme.
5. Grease lightly or coat with vegetable spray a 9″ nonstick pie pan. Place polenta mixture evenly into pie pan; smooth mixture in pan. Cover polenta with wax paper or parchment paper that has been coated with vegetable spray.
6. Bake in center of oven for 30 minutes.
7. Remove from oven, and allow to cool. Invert onto cutting board. Using a cookie cutter, cut into moons or any distinct shape you prefer.

NUTRITION PER SERVING

Calories 131, protein 5 gm, fat 4 gm, carbohydrates 19 gm, cholesterol 7 mg, sodium 149 mg

STIR-FRY VEGETABLES

SERVES 8

INGREDIENTS	ANOUNT/U.S.	METRIC
Lotus roots, canned, drained, sliced	5 oz.	140 gm
Celery, blanched, sliced	5 oz.	140 gm
Asparagus, peeled, cut on bias	5 oz.	140 gm
Carrots, peeled, diced	5 oz.	140 gm
Zucchini, peeled, diced	5 oz.	140 gm
Bok choy, washed, diced	5 oz.	140 gm
Sesame oil	1 fl. oz.	30 ml
Cilantro, snipped	½ oz.	14 gm
Thyme, snipped	½ oz.	14 gm
Kosher salt	to taste	to taste
Fresh, cracked white pepper	to taste	to taste

PREPARATION

1. Blanch all fresh vegetables, shock in cold water, drain thoroughly, paper towel dry.
2. In large hot skillet, quickly sauté vegetable medley in sesame oil.
3. Add cilantro and thyme, and adjust seasoning with salt and pepper.

NUTRITION PER SERVING

Calories 60, protein 2 gm, fat 4 gm, carbohydrates 7 gm, cholesterol 0 mg, sodium 30 mg

GREEN LENTIL AND WHITE BEAN COMPOTE *

SERVES 12

INGREDIENTS	AMOUNT/U.S.	METRIC
Virgin olive oil	2 Tbsp.	30 ml
Red onions, peeled, finely minced	2 oz.	56 gm
Carrots, peeled, finely diced	2 oz.	56 gm
Serrano chili, cleaned, seeded, minced	1	1
Garlic, peeled, minced	2 cloves	2 cloves
Celery, finely diced	2 oz.	56 gm
White beans, small, hulled, soaked overnight in water	6 oz.	168 gm
Chicken stock	48 fl. oz.	1440 ml
Cilantro, snipped	1 oz.	28 gm
Chives, short-cut	1 oz.	28 gm
Kosher salt	to taste	to taste
Fresh, cracked white pepper	to taste	to taste
Green lentils, cooked, drained but still firm (cooked weight)	6 oz.	168 gm

PREPARATION

1. In medium stainless steel saucepan, heat olive oil and sauté onions, carrots, serrano, garlic, and celery for 3 minutes over low heat.
2. Add soaked and rinsed white beans and stock and bring to rapid boil. Reduce heat and simmer gently until beans are tender.
3. Add cilantro and chives; adjust seasoning with a little kosher salt and fresh, cracked white pepper
4. Just prior to serving, fold cooked lentils into beans and stew mixture gently over low heat. Add additional stock if necessary. Adjust seasoning.

NUTRITION PER SERVING
Calories 102, protein 5 gm, fat 3 gm, carbohydrates 14 gm, cholesterol 0 mg, sodium 12 mg

BROWN RICE AND BARLEY

SERVES 10

INGREDIENTS	AMOUNT/U.S.	METRIC
Olive oil	2 Tbsp.	224 ml
Garlic, peeled, minced	6 cloves	6 cloves
Red onion, peeled, finely diced	3 oz.	84 gm
Long-grain brown rice and barley	½ lb. of each	224 gm of each
Chicken stock, high-quality, hot	30 fl. oz.	900 ml
Bay leaves	2	2
Chives, short-cut	2 oz.	56 gm
Kosher salt	to taste	to taste
Fresh, cracked white pepper	to taste	to taste

PREPARATION

1. In heavy sauce pot, heat olive oil and sweat garlic and onions gently for 3 minutes, until onions are translucent.
2. Add rice and barley mixture, stirring gently over low heat for 2 minutes. Add hot chicken stock and bay leaves, cover sauce pot, and simmer gently for 35 minutes.
3. Remove from heat and rest covered for 10 minutes.
4. Remove cover, test mixture for doneness, fluff gently with a fork.
5. Add chives and adjust seasoning to taste with salt, and pepper.
6. Prior to serving remove bay leaves.

NUTRITION PER SERVING

Calories 205, protein 5 gm, fat 5 gm, carbohydrates 37 gm, cholesterol 0 mg, sodium 7 mg

SAVORY POTATOES

SERVES 10

CHEF'S NOTES

To roast poblano peppers, wash and dry 3 or 4 medium poblanos. Brush with olive oil. Oven-roast until golden brown with blistered skins. Remove from oven and place in clean stainless steel bowl covered with plastic wrap. When cool, peel and seed. Pureed roasted poblano peppers also make a great addition to mashed potato puree.

INGREDIENTS	AMOUNT/U.S.	METRIC
Potatoes, peeled, medium-diced	20 oz.	560 gm
Shallots, cleaned, peeled and cut into quarters	12 oz.	336 gm
Olive oil	1 Tbsp.	15 ml
Kosher salt	to taste	to taste
Fresh, cracked white pepper	to taste	to taste
Poblano peppers, cleaned, oven roasted, peeled, seeded, minced (cooked weight of flesh only)	4 oz.	112 gm
Oven-Roasted Tomatoes (p. 311), diced (prepared weight)	4 oz.	112 gm
Thyme, fresh, snipped	¾ oz.	21 gm

PREPARATION

1. Preheat oven to 375°F (190°C).
2. Blanch potatoes, drain in colander, and place on sheet pan. Add shallot quarters and toss mixture with olive oil.
3. Place sheet pan in oven and roast potato mixture until golden brown.
4. Remove from oven, adjust seasoning to taste with salt and pepper. Add roasted poblanos, Oven- Roasted Tomatoes, and thyme. Serve at once.

NUTRITION PER SERVING

Calories 67, protein 2 gm, fat 1 gm, carbohydrates 13 gm, cholesterol 0 mg, sodium 65 mg

OVEN-ROASTED TOMATOES

SERVES 36 (½ TOMATO PER SERVING)

INGREDIENTS	AMOUNT/U.S.	METRIC
Olive oil	2 oz.	60 ml
Garlic, cleaned, minced	1 oz.	28 gm
Basil, finely snipped	¼ oz.	7 gm
Oregano, finely snipped	¼ oz.	7 gm
Parsley, chopped	¼ oz.	7 gm
Fresh, cracked white pepper	¾ tsp.	2 gm
Roma plum tomatoes, cleaned, halved, cored, seeds removed	18	18

CHEF'S NOTES

This recipe yields more than is required for the Savory Potatoes recipe. The rest can be used in or pureed for use in a sauce or soup or as a salad condiment.

PREPARATION

1. Preheat oven to 225°F (110°C).
2. In stainless steel mixing bowl, combine olive oil, garlic, basil, oregano, parsley, and pepper. Combine thoroughly.
3. Using plastic gloves add tomato halves to herb mix and coat well. Place on glazing rack on sheet pan with flesh side up. Roast in oven for a minimum of 3 hours.
4. Depending on the oven calibration, rotate rack occasionally to achieve even roasting and browning.
5. Remove from oven to cool.

NUTRITION PER ½ TOMATO

Calories 21, protein 1 gm, fat 1 gm, carbohydrates 3 gm, cholesterol 0 mg, sodium 6 mg

BOUILLON POTATOES

SERVES 8

INGREDIENTS	AMOUNT/U.S.	METRIC
Olive oil	1 fl. oz.	30 ml
Shallots, cleaned, peeled, minced	4 oz.	112 gm
Leeks, cleaned, diced	6 oz.	168 gm
Carrots, cleaned, peeled, diced	6 oz.	168 gm
Celery stalks, cleaned, peeled, diced	6 oz.	168 gm
Idaho potatoes, peeled, ½" diced	1 lb.	448 gm
Chicken or vegetable stock, high-quality	32 fl. oz.	960 ml
Parsley, cleaned, chopped	1 oz.	28 gm
Kosher salt	to taste	to taste
Fresh, cracked white pepper	to taste	to taste

PREPARATION

1. In a clean stainless steel medium saucepan, heat olive oil and sweat shallots until translucent.

2. Add leeks, carrots, and celery and continue to cook gently for 2 minutes, stirring continuously.

3. Add diced potatoes and cover with chicken or vegetable stock. Cook over low heat until tender. Adjust seasoning with parsley and salt and pepper to taste.

NUTRITION PER SERVING
Calories 113, protein 2 gm, fat 4 gm, carbohydrates 17 gm, cholesterol 0 mg, sodium 63 mg

CRUNCHY VEGETABLE SLAW

SERVES 8

INGREDIENTS	AMOUNT/U.S.	METRIC
English cucumbers, cleaned, peeled	10 oz.	280 gm
Diakon radish, cleaned, peeled	10 oz.	280 gm
Zucchini, cleaned, peeled	10 oz.	280 gm
Hazelnut oil	1 fl. oz.	30 ml
Rice wine vinegar	3 fl. oz.	90 ml
Chives, short-cut	½ oz.	14 gm
Kosher salt	to taste	to taste
Fresh, cracked white pepper	to taste	to taste

CHEF'S NOTES

Serve chilled as a salad or as an accompaniment to lunch or dinner.

PREPARATION

1. Using a small Japanese mandolin, cut cucumber, diakon, and zucchini into long, spaghetti-like strips. Use extreme care with the mandolin as it has very sharp edges. Place julienned strips in a clean stainless steel bowl.
2. Toss with hazelnut oil, vinegar, and chives, and add salt and pepper to taste. Chill.

NUTRITION PER SERVING

Calories 61, protein 1 gm, fat 4 gm, carbohydrates 6 gm, cholesterol 0 mg, sodium 223 mg

PAN-ROASTED CORN
AND VEGETABLES

SERVES 8

INGREDIENTS	AMOUNT/U.S.	METRIC
Corn on the cob, fresh (kernel weight)	10 oz.	280 gm
Olive oil	1 Tbsp.	15 ml
Celery stalks, cleaned, peeled, finely diced	6 oz.	168 gm
Carrots, cleaned, peeled, finely diced	6 oz.	168 gm
White onions, cleaned, peeled, finely diced	6 oz.	168 gm
Button mushrooms, cleaned, quartered	6 oz.	168 gm
Vegetable stock	3 fl. oz.	90 ml
Kosher salt	to taste	to taste
Fresh, cracked white pepper	to taste	to taste

PREPARATION

1. Remove corn kernels from the cob and set aside. Scrape cobs to extract the milk/starch. Keep in separate dish.

2. In clean stainless steel saucepan, heat olive oil and sauté corn kernels sauté until corn begins to take on color.

3. Add celery, carrots, and onions and continue to cook over low heat

4. Add mushrooms; deglaze pan with stock. Reduce liquids by one-half.

5. Add reserved corn milk/starch. Combine mixture thoroughly.

6. Adjust seasoning with salt and pepper to taste.

NUTRITION PER SERVING

Calories 87, protein 2 gm, fat 4 gm, carbohydrates 12 gm, cholesterol 0 mg, sodium 33 mg

POTATO-VEGETABLE HASH

SERVES 8

INGREDIENTS	AMOUNT/U.S.	METRIC
Idaho potatoes, cleaned, peeled, medium-diced	12 oz.	336 gm
Carrots, cleaned, peeled, medium-diced	4 oz.	112 gm
Olive oil	1 fl. oz.	30 ml
White onions, peeled, small-diced	5 oz.	140 gm
Garlic, peeled, minced	½ oz.	14 gm
Red bell pepper, cleaned, finely diced	4 oz.	112 gm
Zucchini, cleaned, peeled, medium-diced	4 oz.	112 gm
Thyme, snipped	⅛ oz.	4 gm
Kosher salt	to taste	to taste
Fresh, cracked white pepper	to taste	to taste
Chives, short-cut	¼ oz.	7 gm

PREPARATION

1. In stainless steel saucepan, quickly blanch potatoes in boiling water (do not overcook). Drain in colander and quickly rinse with cold water. Spread on sheet pan to cool.
2. Repeat procedure with carrots.
3. In large nonstick sauté pan, heat olive oil and sweat onions and garlic until translucent.
4. Add red bell pepper and zucchini and continue to sauté for 1 minute. Add paper-towel-dried blanched potatoes and carrots. Sauté mixture until potatoes take on golden-brown color. Add thyme and adjust seasoning with salt and pepper.
5. Just before serving, add chives.

NUTRITION PER SERVING
Calories 83, protein 2 gm, fat 4 gm, carbohydrates 12 gm, cholesterol 0 mg, sodium 10 mg

YELLOW RICE

SERVES 8

CHEF'S NOTES

Saffron can be increased depending on personal taste.

NUTRITION NOTE

Adding vegetables to this recipe increases the nutritional value of this starch. Chopped spinach will increase the iron content and chopped carrots will increase the vitamin A content.

INGREDIENTS	AMOUNT/U.S.	METRIC
Olive oil	1 fl. oz.	30 ml
Shallots, cleaned, peeled, finely sliced	5 oz.	140 gm
Red bell pepper, cleaned, seeded, diced	2 oz.	56 gm
Garlic, cloves, cleaned, peeled, minced	1½ oz.	42 gm
Shiitaki mushrooms, cleaned, sliced	2 oz.	56 gm
White rice	12 oz.	336 gm
White wine	2 fl. oz.	60 ml
Chicken stock, high-quality, hot	15 fl. oz.	450 ml
Saffron	pinch	pinch
Kosher salt	to taste	to taste
Fresh, cracked white pepper	to taste	to taste

PREPARATION

1. In stainless steel sauce pot, heat olive oil and sweat shallots, red bell pepper, and garlic until translucent.
2. Add Shiitaki mushrooms and continue to sauté for 1 minute, stirring continuously. Add rice and stir.
3. Deglaze with white wine, and reduce.
4. Add hot chicken stock and saffron. Stir rice mixture and cover.
5. Reduce heat to low and cook for 20 minutes. Check rice for doneness and fluff with a fork. Adjust seasoning with salt and pepper.

NUTRITION PER SERVING

Calories 212, protein 4 gm, fat 4 gm, carbohydrates 38 gm, cholesterol 0 mg, sodium 36 mg

LEEKS AND MUSHROOMS

SERVES 8

INGREDIENTS	AMOUNT/U.S.	METRIC
Olive oil	1 Tbsp.	15 ml
White onions, cleaned, peeled, finely sliced	3 oz.	84 gm
Crimini mushrooms, cleaned, sliced	6 oz.	168 gm
Leeks, cleaned, diced	15 oz.	420 gm
Chicken stock, high-quality	4 fl. oz.	120 ml
Parsley, snipped	¼ oz.	7 gm
Kosher salt	to taste	to taste
Fresh, cracked white pepper	to taste	to taste

PREPARATION

1. In a clean stainless steel saucepan, heat olive oil and sauté onions and mushrooms for 1 minute.

2. Add leeks and continue to sauté for 1 minute. Add chicken stock and reduce heat. Simmer mixture gently over low heat for approximately 15 minutes. Leeks should be tender but not mushy. Depending on desired consistency, additional stock can be added.

3. Add snipped parsley and adjust seasoning with salt, and pepper.

NUTRITION PER SERVING

Calories 58, protein 1 gm, fat 2 gm, carbohydrates 10 gm, cholesterol 0 mg, sodium 12 mg

SPINACH WITH LEMON

SERVES 8

INGREDIENTS	AMOUNT/U.S.	METRIC
Olive oil	1 tsp.	5 ml
Pancetta, diced	1 oz.	28 gm
Leeks, cleaned, julienned	2 oz.	56 gm
Garlic, cloves, peeled, minced	½ oz.	14 gm
Mushrooms, white, cleaned, sliced	2 oz.	56 gm
Spinach, leaves, fresh, cleaned, washed	2 lb.	896 gm
Lemon, zest of (finely grated)	1	1
Kosher salt	to taste	to taste
Fresh, cracked white pepper	to taste	to taste

PREPARATION

1. In large nonstick sauté pan, combine olive oil and pancetta. Gently sauté until pancetta starts to take on color.
2. Add leeks, garlic, and mushrooms. Continue to sauté for 1 minute, stirring continuously.
3. Add spinach, combine mixture thoroughly. Sauté only until spinach wilts (do not overcook).
4. Add lemon zest, and adjust seasoning with salt and pepper. Serve at once.

NUTRITION PER SERVING

Calories 48, protein 5 gm, fat 2 gm, carbohydrates 6 gm, cholesterol 3 mg, sodium 93 mg

APPLE-COOKED LENTILS

SERVES 8

INGREDIENTS	AMOUNT/U.S.	METRIC
Parma ham, finely diced	2 oz.	56 gm
Garlic, peeled, finely minced	5 cloves	5 cloves
Onions, cleaned, peeled, finely diced	4 oz.	112 gm
Celery, cleaned, finely diced	4 oz.	112 gm
Leeks, cleaned, finely diced	4 oz.	112 gm
Carrots, cleaned, peeled, finely diced	4 oz.	112 gm
Tomato paste	4 oz.	112 gm
Apple juice concentrate	4 fl. oz.	120 ml
Lentils, tiny green French, soaked	1 lb.	448 gm
Chicken stock, high-quality	32 fl. oz.	960 ml
Thyme, fresh, snipped	1 tsp.	1 gm
Rosemary sprigs	1	1
Apples, peeled, cored, finely diced	6 oz.	168 gm
Kosher salt	to taste	to taste
Fresh, cracked white pepper	to taste	to taste

CHEF'S NOTES

Don't overcook. It is important for this item to simmer gently so that the flavors can fully develop. For best results, use French green (puy) lentils.

PREPARATION

1. In medium saucepan, sauté Parma ham. Add garlic, onion, celery, leeks, and carrots, and sweat for 3 minutes.
2. Add tomato paste, stirring continuously until mixture takes on a rusty color and an aroma develops. Deglaze with apple juice, and reduce by half.
3. Add lentils and stock to cover. Simmer until lentils are tender, approximately 30 minutes. Add herbs and diced apple and simmer for an additional 20 minutes.
4. Adjust seasoning with salt and pepper. Remove rosemary sprig and serve.

NUTRITION PER SERVING
Calories 287, protein 19 gm, fat 2 gm, carbohydrates 51 gm, cholesterol 4 mg, sodium 136 mg

ROASTED PARSNIP PUREE

SERVES 8

For variety, experiment with the different root vegetables by roasting carrots or celery root in place of the parsnips.

INGREDIENTS	AMOUNT/U.S.	METRIC
Potatoes, russet, cleaned, peeled, diced	8 oz.	224 gm
Parsnips, cleaned, peeled, diced	1 lb.	448 gm
White onions, cleaned, peeled, finely sliced	1 oz.	28 gm
Olive oil	1 fl. oz.	30 ml
Vegetable stock	6 fl. oz.	180 ml
Kosher salt	to taste	to taste
Fresh, cracked white pepper	to taste	to taste

PREPARATION

1. Steam potatoes until tender, and puree through a ricer or food mill. Keep warm.
2. Steam parsnips until slightly softened.
3. In shallow, oven-safe saucepan, sweat onions in olive oil. Add stock and bring mixture to boil.
4. Add parsnips to saucepan and stir mixture to distribute the onions.
5. Place in 375°F (190°C) oven and allow to bake gently, occasionally tossing and basting the parsnips in the reducing stock until parsnips are tender and stock is reduced to a glaze.
6. Puree parsnip and onion mixture and combine with potato puree. Adjust seasoning with salt and pepper.

NUTRITION PER SERVING

Calories 96, protein 1 gm, fat 4 gm, carbohydrates 15 gm, cholesterol 0 mg, sodium 8 mg

PEARL PASTA WITH PEAS AND CORN

INGREDIENTS	AMOUNT/U.S.	METRIC
Israeli couscous/pearl pasta	14 oz.	392 gm
Vegetable stock	26 fl. oz.	780 ml
Peas, fresh or frozen	8 oz.	224 gm
Corn, fresh or frozen	8 oz.	224 gm
Roma tomatoes, peeled, seeded, diced	6 oz.	112 gm
Flatleaf parsley, chopped	½ oz.	14 gm
Kosher salt	to taste	to taste
Fresh, cracked white pepper	to taste	to taste

PREPARATION

1. Rinse couscous and place in a clean oven-safe stainless steel saucepan. Add stock, bring to boil, and cover.
2. Place in 325°F (165°C) oven for 5 minutes.
3. Remove from oven, and add peas, corn, and tomatoes. Stir mixture gently with fork to incorporate vegetables.
4. Return to oven for an additional 5 minutes, until almost all the stock is absorbed and couscous is tender.
5. Rmove from oven. Add parsley and adjust seasoning with salt and pepper.

NUTRITION PER SERVING

Calories 242, protein 9 gm, fat 1 gm, carbohydrates 49 gm, cholesterol 0 mg, sodium 45 mg

YELLOW SQUASH
WITH CUCUMBERS

SERVES 8

INGREDIENTS	AMOUNT/U.S.	METRIC
Olive oil	1 Tbsp.	15 ml
Leeks, cleaned, julienned	2 oz.	56 gm
Red bell pepper, cleaned, seeded, julienned	2 oz.	56 gm
Green bell pepper, cleaned, seeded, julienned	2 oz.	56 gm
English cucumbers, peeled, seeded, cut into batonnets*	14 oz.	392 gm
Yellow squash, cleaned, peeled, cut into batonnets	6 oz.	168 gm
Parsley, chopped	½ oz	14 gm
Kosher salt	to taste	to taste
Fresh, cracked white pepper	to taste	to taste

PREPARATION

1. In large nonstick sauté pan, heat olive oil and sweat leeks and bell peppers for 1 minute. Add cucumbers and yellow squash and sauté gently for 3 minutes. Add chopped parsley and adjust seasoning with salt and pepper.

NUTRITION PER SERVING

Calories 34, protein 1 gm, fat 2 gm, carbohydrates 4 gm, cholesterol 0 mg, sodium 5 mg

*Batonnets are small sticks cut about ¼" × ¼" × 2".

JICAMA, CORN, AND TOMATILLO

SERVES 8

INGREDIENTS	AMOUNT/U.S.	METRIC
Olive oil	1 Tbsp.	15 ml
Garlic, cloves, cleaned, peeled, minced	½ oz.	14 gm
Corn kernels, fresh or frozen	16 oz.	448 gm
Jicama, cleaned, peeled, finely diced	3 oz.	84 gm
Tomatillos, cleaned, cored, finely diced	3 oz.	84 gm
Red bell peppers, cleaned, seeded, diced	3 oz.	84 gm
Jalapeño pepper, cleaned, seeded, minced	½	½
Spring onions, short-cut	1 oz.	28 gm
Cilantro, snipped	2 tsp.	2 gm
Kosher salt	to taste	to taste
Fresh, cracked white pepper	to taste	to taste

PREPARATION

1. In medium nonstick sauté pan, heat olive oil and sweat garlic over low heat until it takes on color. Add corn kernels, sauté gently for 3 minutes.
2. Add jicama, tomatillos, bell peppers, and jalapeños and continue to sauté for an additional 2 minutes. Combine mixture thoroughly.
3. Add spring onions and cilantro, and adjust seasoning with salt and pepper.

NUTRITION PER SERVING

Calories 78, protein 2 gm, fat 3 gm, carbohydrates 14 gm, cholesterol 0 mg, sodium 10 mg

WHEATBERRY PILAF

SERVES 8

CHEF'S NOTES

*Wheatberries are some-
what chewy in texture
even when cooked properly.
Wheatberry Pilaf can be
combined with other veg-
etables and served as an
entree.*

INGREDIENTS	AMOUNT/U.S.	METRIC
Wheatberries, sorted	8 oz.	224 gm
Olive oil	2 Tbsp.	30 ml
Leeks, cleaned, finely diced	3 oz.	84 gm
Red onions, peeled, finely diced	3 oz.	84 gm
Carrots, cleaned, peeled, finely diced	3 oz.	84 gm
Chicken stock, high-quality	48 fl. oz.	1440 ml
Parsley, cleaned, finely chopped	1 oz.	28 gm
Kosher salt	to taste	to taste
Fresh, cracked white pepper	to taste	to taste

PREPARATION

1. Place wheatberries in clean stainless steel container, cover with water, and soak overnight. Drain the berries and rinse well.
2. In medium saucepan, heat olive oil and sweat leeks, red onion, and carrots for 1 minute.
3. Add wheatberries and chicken stock, bring to boil. Reduce heat, cover saucepan, and simmer gently until tender, approximately 45 minutes.
4. Add parsley and adjust seasoning with salt and pepper.
5. Continue to simmer gently until berries are tender and all liquid is absorbed.

NUTRITION PER SERVING

Calories 124, protein 5 gm, fat 6 gm, carbohydrates 23 gm, cholesterol 0 mg, sodium 12 mg

QUINOA WITH PECANS

SERVES 8

INGREDIENTS	AMOUNT/U.S.	METRIC
Pecans	3 oz.	84 gm
Quinoa	8 oz.	224 gm
Chicken stock or water	40 fl. oz.	1200 ml
Bulgur wheat	8 oz.	224 gm
Olive oil	1 fl. oz.	30 ml
Red bell pepper, cleaned, seeded, finely diced	3 oz.	84 gm
Green bell pepper, cleaned, seeded, finely diced	3 oz.	84 gm
Chives, cleaned, short-cut	2 oz.	56 gm
Kosher salt	to taste	to taste
Fresh, cracked white pepper	to taste	to taste

CHEF'S NOTES

For better flavor, first wash quinoa, remove gritty residue, and place on sheet pan to dry and toast in oven.

PREPARATION

1. Oven-toast pecans in 350°F (175°C) oven. Remove, cool, and finely chop.
2. Add quinoa to 16 fl. oz. (480 ml) of boiling chicken stock or water; cook gently for 12 minutes. Drain, fluff, and spread on sheet pan to cool.
3. Add bulgur wheat to 24 fl. oz. (720 ml) of boiling chicken stock or water; cook gently for 15–20 minutes. Drain, fluff, and spread on sheet pan to cool.
4. In large nonstick sauté pan, heat olive oil and sauté bell peppers until translucent.
5. Add quinoa and bulgur wheat and combine thoroughly.
6. Add pecans and chives. Adjust seasoning with salt and pepper. Heat mixture thoroughly while fluffing with a fork, and serve.

NUTRITION PER SERVING
Calories 308, protein 8 gm, fat 13 gm, carbohydrates 44 gm, cholesterol 0 mg, sodium 23 mg

CHAPTER 12

DESSERTS, BREADS, AND QUICK BREADS

THE ESSENCE OF TASTE, SMELL, SIGHT, AND SOUND ARE INDISPENSABLE TO LIFE'S MANY PLEASURES. THE PREPARATION OF FOOD IS AN ART FORM CREATED BY THE SKILLFUL HANDS OF THE CULINARIAN, BLENDING A WEALTH OF INGREDIENTS TO CREATE DISHES THAT ARE A FEAST FOR THE EYES, AND AN EXPERIENCE FOR THE SENSES.

unknown

A GOOD COOK IS THE PECULIAR GIFT OF THE GODS. HE MUST BE A PERFECT CREATURE FROM THE BRAIN TO THE PALATE, FROM THE PALATE TO THE FINGER'S END.

Walter Savage Landor

THE NOBLEST OF ALL DOGS IS THE HOT DOG; IT FEEDS THE HAND THAT BITES IT.

Laurence J. Peter

@

FRUITS

In the nutritional kitchen, recipes made with fruits are a delicious source of vitamins, particularly A and C, micronutrients, and minerals. In addition to their nutritional value, the sugar and acid content in fruit contributes greatly to the flavor profile of the recipe being prepared.

Fresh and dried fruits can have a variety of applications in healthful cooking. Fruits can be consumed solo, raw; added to salads; cooked in sauces; used in simple desserts; poached in aromatic liquids; and baked in pies and cobblers.

Soft fruits such as currants, strawberries, raspberries, blackberries, and blueberries are excellent in strudel, pie, and cobbler. Berries can also be utilized as fruit purees to enhance low-fat desserts and to make berry yogurts.

Top, or hard, fruits such as apples, peaches, plums, pears, apricots, and cherries are all best when in season. Dessert apples and pears are available yearround in many varieties. The most common types of apples include Golden and Red Delicious, McIntosh, and Rome Beauty. The most common types of pears include Anjou, Comice, and Bosc. Fruits such as these make a refreshing dessert when simply poached in a sweetened liquid, or oven-roasted and served chilled. These fruits can also be used to create fruit soups.

The other fruits, including pineapple, mangoes, guava, passion fruit, kiwi fruit, figs, and papaya, also have excellent application for creative use in salsas, dressings, fruit slaws, chutneys, purees, preserved fruits, granitas, and marinades (e.g., the enzymes in papaya and pineapple assist in tenderizing meat products in that they break down protein). When serving papayas or melons raw, served chilled and enhance the flavor with a generous sprinkle of lemon or lime juice.

Citrus fruits such as oranges, mandarins, kumquats, tangelos, lemons, grapefruit, and limes are all rich in vitamin C. Although these fruits are most widely served fresh, they offer many applications in the kitchen and as flavoring agents. Some seasonal varieties have an attractive appeal and high quality, such as blood oranges and pink grapefruit.

PIES

Pies are suitable for many occasions, and the secret to a great crust is the dough. The dough is made of four ingredients, flour, salt, fat, and water. For best results, measure ingredients accurately. Use cold margarine and iced water to reduce fat coating the flour and to produce flakes. Blend in the margarine until the mixture resembles tiny peas or a coarse meal. Bits of solid shortening will melt between flour layers during the baking, giving the dough its flakiness. Do not add the iced water all at once, only a tablespoon at a time, as needed. Dough should be moist but not wet or sticky. Too much water will make the crust hard; too little will cause it to crack when rolled out. For health purposes, oil may be used in pie crust preparation in place of solid fat, although this prevents the formation of the desired flakes because it does not melt between the flour layers.

Some pastry chefs add eggs to pie dough for extra richness or a touch of vinegar for flakiness. Do not overwork the dough or gluten may develop, resulting in toughness. Chill the dough for at least 1 hour prior to use to allow the gluten strands to relax. This makes the dough easier to handle and prevents shrinkage.

Pie dough can be prepared ahead of time, wrapped, and refrigerated for approximately 1 week (not frozen). Prior to use and rolling, bring dough to room temperature.

The freezer becomes an invaluable time saver when making other doughs. Most doughs can be made ahead in bulk and frozen. Take out pieces as you need them and thaw in the refrigerator. Most doughs can be held frozen 3 to 4 weeks.

BAKING

The following overview highlights some basic steps that are of prime importance to success in the baking process.

Bread is made by baking dough (flour and liquid) that has been raised with a leavening agent. Yeast bread requires a yeast for leavening. Yeast is a living organism that produces carbon dioxide bubbles biologically in the dough, causing it to rise. Quick breads are relatively quick to prepare and are raised by carbon dioxide produced chemically by baking powder or baking soda.

The three common types of yeast are dry, compressed, and rapid-rise, which are interchangeable. Always use yeast prior to the expiration date on the package.

Active dry yeast should be dissolved in liquid at 80 to 115 degrees Fahrenheit (35 to 46 degrees Celsius). A thermometer is the best way to determine temperature. If the liquid is too hot, it will kill the yeast. If the liquid is too cold, the dough will take longer to rise, or it will not rise at all.

To determine whether the yeast is still active, dissolve one envelope in 2 fluid ounces of warm water with 1 teaspoon of sugar. Let it stand in a warm place for 5 minutes. An active yeast will form a bubbly froth on the surface. The proper rising temperature for completed dough is also 80 to 115 degrees Fahrenheit (35 to 46 degrees Celsius).

Baking powder is a leavening agent that consists of an acid and an alkaline material (plus starch filler to prevent premature reaction in storage) which react with one another in the presence of moisture to form carbon dioxide gas. The carbon dioxide produces tiny bubbles in the batter. In baking, oven heat causes these bubbles to quickly expand the batter, which is then set by the heat to make light-textured crumb.

Baking soda is the alkaline ingredient of baking powder, and it requires an acid ingredient, such as (liquids) buttermilk or molasses or (dry) cream of tartar (tartaric acid) to react.

A sourdough starter also biologically produces carbon dioxide, by bacteria and yeast. It requires days of fermentation at room temperature prior to addition to a flour mixture.

There is a great variety of flour types on the market today. The following are among the more common types used for desserts and breads:

- **All-purpose flour** is a mixture of hard and soft wheat flours. It is available bleached or unbleached and works well for many baking needs except fine and delicate cakes, which require the use of cake or pastry flour. One pound of all-purpose flour equals about 4 cups sifted and about 3½ cups unsifted.

- **Bread flour** is hard wheat flour. It has a high gluten potential and is essential in creating the elastic structure for yeast dough products. It is not a successful substitute when used for cake, pie, or cookie recipes. Bread flour recipes require 10 minutes of kneading to develop gluten, longer rising times, and 15 minutes of resting time prior to final shaping and baking.

- **Cake flour** is made from soft wheat and contains 7 to 8½ percent protein. It should be sifted before measuring.

- **Pastry flour** is made from soft wheat and is ideal for pie doughs.

- **Instant flour** or **agglomerated flour** has been processed so that it has a granular texture. It disperses quickly in cold water, which aids in making sauces and jus lump-free.

- **Self-rising flour** contains baking powder and salt so that the dough rises without requiring yeast. It is excellent for the preparation of biscuits, muffins, and some cakes. (Make your own self-rising flour by adding 1½ teaspoons baking powder and ½ teaspoon salt to 1 cup all-purpose flour.)

- **Potato "flour" or starch** is a good thickening agent. Compared to arrowroot, this may be preferred, particularly in sauce production, as it gives a natural glossy sheen to the product. In baking, it is used in combination with other flours.

- **Cornmeal** is made from yellow or white corn and is used in a variety of recipes, such as breads, puddings, and breadings. It is usually combined with a wheat flour in order to form gluten, since it does not form gluten.

- **Rye flour** produces a sticky dough, is slow to rise, and requires longer kneading. Rye breads are best served the day after baking.

- **Semolina flour** is made from the grain-like portions of durum wheat remaining in the bolting machine after the fine flour has been sifted through. It is a hard wheat flour, ideal for making pasta.

- **Whole-wheat flour** is a dark flour that contains the whole grain, including the germ, endosperm, and bran of the kernel. It is thought to be the most nutritious of flours, and is often stone ground and unsifted. Whole-wheat flour, as well as other whole-grain flours such as rye, should be mixed with all-purpose or bread flour for high volume and finer texture, since the bran and germ limit structural development.

When making breads or pastries, dust the work surface lightly with flour. If you use more flour than necessary, the dough will toughen, due to an insufficient liquid-to-flour ratio.

When purchasing flour, always purchase the freshest flour available. Check the package for date of expiration. All-purpose and bread flour keep well for 6 months or more at room temperature. They must be well sealed and stored in a cool, dry place away from strong food odors.

Whole-wheat and other whole-grain flours are perishable because the natural oils within the flour (especially germ) can become rancid. Buy whole grains in small quantities and store at room temperature for no more than 1 month. If refrigerated, they will keep for up to 2 months.

You can freeze flour for longer storage. It is best to place it in an airtight container or seal the package in a double plastic bag.

Self-rising flour should not be stored longer than 2 to 3 months as the leavening agent loses it potency.

Since baking is a precise science, recipes often specify sifting the flour before measuring. Sifting aerates the flour and lessens the weight per cup, and therefore the quantity needed in the finished product. If sifting is required, always sift the flour shortly before measuring so that it does not settle or pack down in volume. Pastry and cake flour always need to be sifted to break up the clumps. Do not shake or pack the flour down into the cup before leveling. Do not sift whole-grain flours; simply stir lightly with a fork to loosen the mix.

Often recipes for yeast breads do not specify precise amounts of flour to use, because the ability of flour to absorb liquid varies. For example, in very dry climates, or under dry storage conditions, flour loses moisture to the atmosphere and requires more water/less flour in preparation. Begin by adding the amount specified, then gradually add more until the dough is the proper consistency.

There are a multitude of recipes defining the perfect biscuit. In order to serve piping hot, tender, and flaky biscuits, following are some tips that can help you achieve the best possible product.

First, combine or sift flour, baking powder, and salt in a bowl. Then cut shortening into the flour mixture with a pastry blender, until the mixture resembles a coarse meal. Make a "well" in the dry ingredients mixture. Pour in the liquid and mix only until well blended.

Turn the mixture out onto a lightly floured surface. Form into a ball and knead for a few moments. If you knead the dough too much it will overdevelop gluten strands and become hard and stiff. Under-kneading does not allow proper gluten structure development. In either case the biscuits will not rise properly or become flaky.

Flatten dough lightly with your hands or rolling pin until even. For high biscuits, roll the dough to ½-inch thickness. For thinner biscuits, roll out to ¼-inch thickness.

Place biscuits on an ungreased baking sheet. Brush tops with either beaten eggs or milk. Bake in a preheated 450°F (230°C) oven on the middle rack, for about 10 minutes for thinner biscuits and 15 minutes for thicker biscuits.

LOW-FAT CHOCOLATE BROWNIES

SERVES 8

CHEF'S NOTES

If desired, brownies can also be baked in an 8" nonstick cake pan.

INGREDIENTS	AMOUNT/U.S.	METRIC
Chocolate, unsweetened	1 oz.	28 gm
Sweet potato puree	2 oz.	56 gm
Nonfat, skim milk	2 Tbsp.	30 ml
Egg whites	2	2
Vanilla	1 tsp.	5 ml
Brown sugar	4 oz.	112 gm
Kosher salt	¼ tsp.	1.25 gm
Cocoa powder	2 Tbsp.	30 gm
All-purpose flour	¼ cup	32 gm
Walnuts, chopped	2 Tbsp.	30 gm

PREPARATION

1. Preheat oven to 350°F (175°C).
2. Melt chocolate gently over low heat.
3. Cook and puree sweet potato to the measured amount. (A canned sweet potato puree can be substituted.)
4. Combine sweet potato puree with skim milk, egg whites, vanilla, brown sugar, and salt. Mix thoroughly.
5. Sift cocoa and flour together in a clean stainless steel bowl and add to batter. Add chopped walnuts and melted chocolate.
6. Spray eight stainless steel or ceramic oyster cups or ovenproof molds with vegetable spray.
7. Bake for approximately 20–25 minutes. Brownie should feel firm to the touch.

PRESENTATION

Serve with low-fat Yogurt-Ricotta Ice (p. 349).

NUTRITION PER SERVING

Calories 119, protein 3 gm, fat 4 gm, carbohydrates 22 gm, cholesterol 0 mg, sodium 100 mg

PUMPKIN AND APPLE POUND CAKE

YIELD: 2 CAKES (24 SERVINGS)

INGREDIENTS	AMOUNT/U.S.	METRIC
Butter	4 oz.	112 gm
Granulated sugar	16 oz.	448 gm
Egg substitute	5 fl. oz.	180 ml
Applesauce	5 oz.	140 gm
All-purpose flour	3 cups	380 gm
Baking powder	2 tsp.	8 gm
Cinnamon	2 tsp.	4 gm
Baking soda	½ tsp.	2 gm
Ginger, ground	½ tsp.	1 gm
Pumpkin puree	2 cups	448 gm
Rum	⅓ cup	80 ml
Granny Smith apples, peeled, chopped, sautéed	12 oz.	336 gm

PREPARATION

1. Preheat oven to 350°F (175°C).
2. Combine butter and sugar, cream until light and fluffy. Add egg substitute (at room temperature) to butter mixture in three parts. Allow each addition to be well incorporated. Fold in the applesauce in similar fashion.
3. Sift dry ingredients together. Add to butter mixture, alternating with pumpkin puree, until all three mixtures are incorporated.
4. Add rum and sautéed and cooled apples.
5. Divide batter evenly between two nonstick, sprayed, and flour-dusted tube pans.
6. Bake 50–60 minutes, until cake springs back when touched.
7. Remove from oven and let cake cool prior to unmolding.

PRESENTATION

Dust with powdered sugar and cinnamon.

NUTRITION PER SERVING

Calories 196, protein 3 gm, fat 4 gm, carbohydrates 36 gm, cholesterol 10 mg, sodium 65 gm

CALIFORNIA FIG
AND GRAPE STRUDEL

SERVES 8

INGREDIENTS	AMOUNT/U.S.	METRIC
Gamay wine	⅓ cup	80 ml
Lime, zest and juice of	1	1
Orange, zest and juice of	1	1
Maple syrup	4 Tbsp.	60 ml
California dried figs, diced	¼ lb.	114 gm
Black grapes, seedless, cut in quarters	¼ lb.	114 gm
Pears, peeled, finely diced	2	2
Filo dough	6 sheets	6 sheets
Vegetable spray	as needed	as needed
Filberts, roasted, chopped	1 oz.	28 gm
Clarified butter	1 Tbsp.	15 ml

PREPARATION

1. Preheat oven to 375°F (190°C).
2. In stainless steel saucepan, place wine, citrus juices, and maple syrup and bring to boil. Reduce heat, add figs, grapes, and pears.
3. Add zests and steep mixture slowly over low heat, stirring frequently until sec. Remove from heat and place in a mixing bowl to cool.
4. On clean working surface spread out two sheets of filo dough, overlapping one-third at edges. Spray lightly with vegetable spray. Repeat twice (making a total of three layers). Do not spray the third layer.
5. Spread fig mixture evenly over dough. Sprinkle with roasted filberts.
6. Roll into cylinder shape to form a strudel. Brush top and edges with clarified butter, fold edges over.
7. Place on lightly greased cookie sheet and bake until golden brown.
8. Remove from oven and rest before slicing into 8 pieces.

PRESENTATION

Dust with powdered sugar and cinnamon. Serve with a dollop of mascarpone cheese.

NUTRITION PER SERVING

Calories 192, protein 2 gm, fat 5 gm, carbohydrates 35 gm, cholesterol 4 mg, sodium 73 mg

KILN-DRIED CHERRY
RICE PUDDING

SERVES 12

INGREDIENTS	AMOUNT/U.S.	METRIC
Nonfat, skim milk	48 fl oz.	1440 ml
Sugar	1 cup	224 gm
Rice, short-grain	8 oz.	224 gm
Orange peel, grated	1 tsp.	2 gm
Vanilla bean, seeds from	1	1
Nutmeg	⅛ tsp.	.25 gm
Dried cherries, quality, chopped	8 oz.	224 gm

CHEF'S NOTES

Serve with carmelized sugar on top and fruit puree.

PREPARATION

1. Preheat oven to 350°F (175°C). In oven-safe saucepan with tight lid, bring milk and sugar to boil.
2. Add rice, orange peel, vanilla, and nutmeg. Return to boil.
3. Cover with lid and bake for approximately 1¼ hour, stirring every 20 minutes, until rice is very tender.
4. Remove from oven and add chopped cherries. Let mixture set for 20 minutes, or until cherries are soft.
5. Check consistency; add a little milk if needed. Pudding will stiffen somewhat as it cools.
6. Spoon into custard cups to the top, and cover with plastic wrap to prevent drying. Refrigerate.

NUTRITION PER SERVING
Calories 199, protein 6 gm, fat 1 gm, carbohydrates 43 gm, cholesterol 2 mg, sodium 66 mg

ANGEL FOOD CAKE
WITH CHOCOLATE GLACÉ
AND WARM DRIED CHERRY SAUCE

SERVES 20

INGREDIENTS	AMOUNT/U.S.	METRIC
Sugar	16 oz.	448 gm
Cake flour	6 oz.	168 gm
Egg whites	16 oz.	480 ml
Cream of tartar	⅛ tsp.	60 mg
Kosher salt	½ tsp.	2.5 gm
Vanilla	1 tsp.	5 ml
Orange extract	1 tsp.	5 ml
Orange, rind of, finely grated	1	1
Vegetable spray	as needed	as needed

PREPARATION

1. Preheat oven to 350°F (175°C).
2. In a clean stainless steel mixing bowl, sift together half the sugar and the flour, set aside.
3. In clean bowl, whip egg whites, cream of tartar, salt, and remaining sugar into very soft peaks.
4. Stir vanilla, orange extract, and orange rind into dry sugar and flour mixture.
5. Fold whipped egg whites into sugar and flour mixture.
6. Spray 20 savarin molds or individual angel food cake molds with vegetable spray. Pipe mixture into molds.
7. Bake for 15–20 minutes. Invert on wire rack to cool.

PRESENTATION

Hold sauce warm for service. Place a small pool (about 1 oz.) of Warm Dried Cherry Sauce in center of plate. Dust cake with powdered sugar and place in center of sauce. Scoop about 1½ oz. of Chocolate Glacé into center.

Optional: Sprinkle on a few white chocolate shavings or drizzle with chocolate sauce.

CHOCOLATE GLACÉ

INGREDIENTS	AMOUNT/U.S.	METRIC
Water	19 fl. oz.	570 ml
Milk powder, nonfat	4 oz.	112 gm
Cocoa powder	2 oz.	56 gm
Sugar	¾ cup	168 gm
Vanilla extract (or seeds of ¼ of a vanilla bean	1 tsp.	5 ml

1. In food processor or blender, combine all ingredients and blend gently for 3–5 minutes to incorporate mixture smoothly.
2. Remove from processor bowl. Freeze mixture in ice cream machine.
3. Place in clean deep stainless steel insert. Cover with plastic wrap and place in freezer until ready to use.

WARM DRIED CHERRY SAUCE

INGREDIENTS	AMOUNT/U.S.	METRIC
Red wine	8 fl. oz.	240 ml
Water	16 fl. oz.	480 ml
Sugar	8 oz.	224 gm
Cinnamon stick	1	1
Dried cherries, quality	12 oz.	336 gm
Cornstarch slurry to thicken	as needed	as needed

P R E P A R A T I O N
1. In saucepan, place wine, water, sugar, and cinnamon stick. Bring to rapid boil. Add dried cherries and allow to bloom.
2. Reduce heat and steep for 20 minutes.
3. Reduce by one-fourth, and thicken with a little cornstarch slurry. Serve warm.

NUTRITION PER SERVING OF CAKE
Calories 131, protein 3 gm, fat 0 gm, carbohydrates 29 gm, cholesterol 0 mg, sodium 99 mg

NUTRITION PER SERVING OF GLACÉ
Calories 61, protein 3 gm, fat 0 gm, carbohydrates 13 gm, cholesterol 0 mg, sodium 31 mg

NUTRITION PER SERVING OF SAUCE
Calories 65, protein 0 gm, fat 0 gm, carbohydrates 15 gm, cholesterol 0 mg, sodium 1 mg

NUTRITION PER COMPLETE DESSERT SERVING
Calories 257, protein 6 gm, fat 0 gm, carbohydrates 57 gm, cholesterol 0 mg, sodium 131 mg

CARAMEL-BANANA CUSTARD TART

SERVES 12

INGREDIENTS	AMOUNT/U.S.	METRIC
Crust:		
Graham cracker crumbs	12 oz.	336 gm
Sugar	2 oz.	56 gm
Egg white	1 fl. oz.	30 ml
Bananas, fresh, sliced	2	2
Lemon, juice of	½	5 ml
Apricot jam	2 oz.	56 gm
Custard Filling:		
Sugar	4 oz.	112 gm
Lemon juice	1 tsp.	1 tsp.
Nonfat, skim milk	8 fl. oz.	240 ml
Nonfat, skim milk (for the slurry)	6 fl. oz.	180 ml
Cornstarch	2½ Tbsp.	20 gm
Egg yolks	3	3
Banana paste or puree	1 Tbsp.	15 gm

PREPARATION OF CRUST

1. Preheat oven to 350°F (175°C). In stainless steel mixing bowl, combine crumbs, sugar, and egg white. Press crumb mixture into 9″ × 1″ flan pan with a removable bottom.
2. Bake for 10 minutes to set. Cool.
3. Slice bananas and toss with lemon juice to prevent discoloring.
4. On cooled crust, spread a thin layer of apricot jam. Line with sliced bananas.

PREPARATION OF CUSTARD FILLING

1. In a clean saucepan, combine sugar and lemon juice. Gently heat and caramelize, stirring continuously.
2. When sugar is a light caramel color, stir in skim milk and bring to boil. All the sugar should be dissolved.
3. In another saucepan, make a slurry of 6 fl. oz. (180 ml) of skim milk, cornstarch, and egg yolks. Stir and temper the slurry over low heat for 1 minute.
4. Add mixture to the caramel milk. Bring combined mixture to boil and reduce heat to thicken, stirring constantly.
5. Add banana paste or puree to mixture, combine thoroughly.
6. Pour banana custard into crust lined with apricot jam and bananas. Chill to set.

Serve on sugar-dusted plate with fresh fruit garnish.

NUTRITION PER SERVING
Calories 230, protein 5 gm, fat 4 gm, carbohydrates 48 gm, cholesterol 55 mg, sodium 215 mg

LOW-FAT PIE CRUST

YIELD: ONE 8″ CRUST

INGREDIENTS	AMOUNT/U.S.	METRIC
Margarine	2 Tbsp.	30 gm
Unbleached flour	2¼ oz.	65 gm
Whole-wheat flour	2¼ oz.	65 gm
Kosher salt	pinch	pinch
Ice water	approx. 8 Tbsp.	approx. 120 ml

PREPARATION
1. In medium bowl, combine margarine, flours, and salt. Slowly add water, a tablespoon at a time, mixing, just enough to make dough hold together. Do not overmix.
2. On lightly floured surface, use rolling pin to flatten dough to ⅛″ thickness.
3. Place dough into an 8″ pie pan. The crust is now ready for filling.

NUTRITION PER ⅛ OF CRUST
Calories 83, protein 2 gm, fat 3 gm, carbohydrates 12 gm, cholesterol 0 mg, sodium 70 mg

MARBLED LEMON CHEESECAKE

SERVES 12

INGREDIENTS	AMOUNT/U.S.	METRIC
Lemon Curd:		
Cornstarch	2 tsp.	6 gm
Lemon juice	8 fl. oz.	240 ml
Lemon zest	2	2
Eggs	3	3
Crust:		
Sugar	5 oz.	140 gm
Graham cracker crumbs	12 oz.	336 gm
Vegetable spray	as needed	as needed
Batter:		
Sugar	8 oz.	224 gm
Cream cheese, fat-free	24 oz.	672 gm
Eggs	3	3
Lemon juice	2 Tbsp.	30 ml
Lemon zest	½ tsp.	1 gm

PREPARATION

LEMON CURD (CAN BE MADE A DAY AHEAD)

1. In stainless steel mixing bowl, combine cornstarch with ¼ of the lemon juice. Combine with eggs. Whisk mixture until frothy.
2. In a clean saucepan, combine remaining juice, sugar, and zest, heat to boil.
3. Temper egg mixture over hot water bath for 2–3 min while whisking and add to the boiled juice mixture. Bring combined mixture back to a boil to thicken.
4. Remove from saucepan and place in clean bowl. Cool curd thoroughly before continuing.

CRUST

1. Spray 9″ cake pan with vegetable spray, and coat with graham cracker crumbs.

BATTER

1. Preheat oven to 325°F (165°C).
2. In a clean stainless steel mixing bowl, cream together sugar and cream cheese until smooth.
3. Add eggs one at a time and fold in completely. Scrape sides of bowl after each addition.

4. Add lemon juice and zest.

5. Pour batter into pan, and spoon curd on top. Marble the two mixtures gently.

6. Bake in a water bath for approximately 1 hour, until a knife inserted comes out clean, or to an internal center temperature of 170°F (75°C).

7. Chill cake well before unmolding.

PRESENTATION

Serve cheesecake with fruit puree or fresh fruit compote.

NUTRITION PER SERVING

Calories 322, protein 13 gm, fat 5 gm, carbohydrates 59 gm, cholesterol 116 mg, sodium 490 mg

MERINGUE SHELL

YIELD: 8 INDIVIDUAL SHELLS

INGREDIENTS	AMOUNT/U.S.	METRIC	CHEF'S NOTES
Egg whites	4	4	*Use meringue shells as a base topped with berries or fresh fruits.*
Cream of tartar	⅛ tsp.	60 mg	
Sugar	6 oz.	168 gm	

PREPARATION

1. Preheat oven to 250°F (125°C).

2. Place egg whites in clean mixing bowl. While whipping egg whites, slowly add cream of tartar and sugar. Beat until stiff.

3. Line cookie sheet pan with parchment paper. Shape 8 meringue shells onto parchment paper. Bake 1½–2 hours until hardened.

NUTRITION PER SHELL

Calories 89, protein 2 gm, fat 0 gm, carbohydrates 21 gm, cholesterol 0 mg, sodium 26 mg

APPLE-RUM RISOTTO WITH CINNAMON GLACÉ OR CINNAMON GELATO

SERVES 12 (3 OZ. SERVING)

CHEF'S NOTES

The flavor will depend on the type of apples and cider used.

The risotto should not be too sweet; add only enough brown sugar to bring up the flavors. Additional sweetness is provided with the Cinnamon Glacé or Gelato.

The risotto is best when served at once. If left for longer periods, some additional liquid may be necessary to retain the creamy texture.

INGREDIENTS	AMOUNT/U.S.	METRIC
Granny Smith apples, peeled, ¼″-diced	2	2
Butter	1½ oz.	42 gm
Sugar	3 Tbsp.	45 gm
Rum	1 Tbsp.	15 ml
Vanilla	1 Tbsp.	15 ml
Arborio rice	12 oz.	336 gm
Apple cider or juice	40 fl. oz.	1200 ml
Brown sugar	3 oz.	84 gm
Cinnamon	to taste	to taste

PREPARATION

1. In a clean saucepan, sauté apples in ½ oz. butter and sugar until tender. Finish with rum and vanilla. Reserve.
2. In a clean saucepan, melt 1 oz. butter, add rice, and sauté for 2 minutes, stirring continuously.
3. Add enough apple cider/juice to fully cover rice, and bring to simmer, stirring frequently. As the liquid is absorbed, add more cider/juice, until rice is tender and creamy, but not mushy. Cooking time will be approximately 20–25 minutes.
4. Add sautéed apples, and adjust flavor with brown sugar and cinnamon (see Note).

PRESENTATION

Serve risotto on its own or with Cinnamon Glacé or Cinnamon Gelato (p. 345).

NUTRITION PER SERVING OF RISOTTO

Calories 236, protein 2 gm, fat 3 gm, carbohydrates 49 gm, cholesterol 8 mg, sodium 7 mg

CINNAMON GLACÉ

SERVES 30 (1 1/2 OZ./42 GM SERVING)

INGREDIENTS	AMOUNT/U.S.	METRIC
Yogurt, nonfat	24 oz.	672 gm
Ricotta, part skim	16 oz.	448 gm
Sugar	12 oz.	336 gm
Cinnamon, ground	1 tsp.	2 gm

PREPARATION

1. In food processor, combine all ingredients and puree gently for 3–5 minutes to incorporate mixture smoothly.
2. Remove from processor bowl, place in deep stainless steel insert, and freeze in ice cream freezer.

NUTRITION PER SERVING
Calories 77, protein 3 gm, fat 1 gm, carbohydrates 14 gm, cholesterol 5 gm, sodium 36 mg

NUTRITION NOTES

Serve on top of warm risotto, or use with fresh fruit compotes. Nonfat ricotta can also be used to make this recipe virtually fat-free.

CINNAMON GELATO

SERVES 25 (1 1/2 OZ./42 GM SERVING)

INGREDIENTS	AMOUNT/U.S.	METRIC
Cornstarch	2 oz.	56 gm
Milk, low-fat (1%)	32 fl. oz.	960 ml
Sugar	6 oz.	168 gm
Cinnamon, ground	1 tsp.	2 gm

PREPARATION

1. In small, clean stainless steel bowl, make slurry of cornstarch and a small amount of the milk.
2. Combine remaining milk, sugar, and cinnamon in saucepan. Bring to boil, and thicken with cornstarch slurry.
3. Remove from heat and place in a clean deep stainless steel insert pan. Cool thoroughly, and freeze in ice cream machine.

NUTRITION PER SERVING
Calories 51, protein 1 gm, fat 0 gm, carbohydrates 11 gm, cholesterol 2 mg, sodium 20 mg

CHEF'S NOTES

When making a variation of sorbets or sherbets, use only fresh seasonal fruits, but these too can be frozen until you need them. Their flavor can be enhanced with citric acid, which is readily available, or with lemon juice.

VANILLA SAUCE

SERVES 24

INGREDIENTS	AMOUNT/U.S.	METRIC
Nonfat, skim milk	32 fl. oz.	960 ml
Sugar	8 oz.	224 gm
Vanilla bean, seeds from	1	1
Cornstarch	3 tsp.	8 gm
Egg substitute	8 fl. oz.	240 ml

PREPARATION

1. Combine skim milk, sugar, vanilla bean, and cornstarch in saucepan. Bring to boil.
2. Place egg substitute in mixing bowl. Using a whisk, add skim milk mixture and blend well.
3. Return mixture to saucepan and heat over low heat, stirring constantly, until slightly thickened.
4. Remove from heat and allow to cool. Strain to remove lumps. Refrigerate.

NUTRITION PER 4 TBSP.

Calories 58, protein 2 gm, fat 0 gm, carbohydrates 12 gm, cholesterol 0 mg, sodium 36 mg

FRUIT STRUDEL
WITH RED WINE SAUCE

YIELD: 15 PORTIONS

INGREDIENTS	AMOUNT/U.S.	METRIC
Brown sugar	2½ oz.	70 gm
Amaretto	2 fl. oz.	60 ml
Red wine	2 fl. oz.	60 ml
Orange juice	8 fl. oz.	240 ml
Lemon juice	2½ fl. oz.	75 ml
Cinnamon stick	1	1
Cloves, whole	2	2
Apples, peeled, cored, coarsely diced	3	3
Pears, peeled, cored, coarsely diced	3	3
Plums, pitted, coarsely diced	12	12
Raisins	1 oz.	28 gm
Lemon peel, grated	½ tsp.	1 gm
Filo dough	12 sheets	12 sheets
Almonds, toasted	6 Tbsp.	60 gm
Powdered sugar, sifted	as needed	as needed
Vegetable spray	as needed	as needed

PREPARATION

1. Preheat oven to 450°F (230°C). In saucepan, combine brown sugar, amaretto, wine, orange and lemon juice, cinnamon stick, and cloves. Bring to boil.

2. Add apples, pears, plums, raisins, and lemon peel. Simmer gently over low heat for 10 minutes. Remove, drain, and cool the fruit. Reduce liquid over low heat slowly.

3. Place 1 filo sheet on clean surface, spray with vegetable oil. Layer on three additional sheets, spraying each except the top sheet. Sprinkle with one-third of the toasted almonds.

4. Spread one-third of the fruit compote on top and roll into cylindrical shape. Spray top with vegetable oil; fold edges over.

5. Repeat with remaining filo and fruit to make two additional strudels. Make four small cuts in top of dough, to reference portions as well as to release heat during baking.

6. Place in oven and bake for 8–10 minutes or until golden brown. Remove from oven and let rest prior to slicing. Cut on an angle and dust with powdered sugar. Serve strudel with the reduced compote liquid poured evenly onto plates.

NUTRITION PER SERVING

Calories 226, protein 3 gm, fat 6 gm, carbohydrates 40 gm, cholesterol 0 mg, sodium 78 mg

CRANBERRY-APPLE COBBLER
WITH YOGURT-RICOTTA ICE

SERVES 10

INGREDIENTS	AMOUNT/U.S.	METRIC
Filling:		
Red Delicious apples, peeled, cored, diced	1¼ lb.	567 gm
Dried cranberries, plumped in boiling water	12 oz.	336 gm
Cinnamon sticks	2	2
Honey	¼ cup	60 ml
Batter:		
All-purpose or pastry flour	4½ oz.	126 gm
Sugar	2 Tbsp.	30 gm
Baking powder	½ tsp.	2½ gm
Baking soda	½ tsp.	2½ gm
Kosher salt	1 tsp.	5 gm
Yogurt, nonfat	1 cup	224 gm
Nonfat, skim milk	1 Tbsp.	15 ml
Vanilla	1 tsp.	5 ml
Egg white	1	1
Sugar	1 Tbsp.	15 gm

PREPARATION

1. Preheat oven to 350°F (175°C).
2. Combine filling ingredients in stainless steel saucepan and cook gently until apples are soft, stirring frequently. Set aside.
3. For batter, sift together dry ingredients. Add yogurt, milk, vanilla, and egg white; stir to combine thoroughly.
4. Fill 10 cobbler dishes with apple filling and spread batter in thin layer over the top.
5. Sprinkle with about 1 Tbsp. sugar and bake for 25–30 minutes.

PRESENTATION

Top with a scoop of Yogurt-Ricotta Ice (p 349).

NUTRITION PER SERVING OF COBBLER

Calories 145, protein 3 gm, fat 0 gm, carbohydrates 33 gm, cholesterol 0 mg, sodium 346 mg

YOGURT-RICOTTA ICE

SERVES 48

INGREDIENTS	AMOUNT/U.S.	METRIC
Ricotta cheese, part skim	2¼ qt.	2016 gm
Yogurt, nonfat, plain	3¼ qt.	2912 gm
Maple syrup	1 qt.	960 ml
Honey	6 fl. oz.	180 ml
Vanilla beans, split, seeds removed	4	4
Orange, zest of, finely grated	2	2

PREPARATION

1. Puree ricotta cheese in food processor. Add yogurt, maple syrup, and honey, mix all thoroughly.

2. Add vanilla bean pulp and orange zest, mix thoroughly.

3. Remove mixture from food processor bowl, place in deep stainless steel insert, and freeze. Serve with Cranberry-Apple Cobbler (p. 348).

NUTRITION PER ½ CUP SERVING

Calories 181, protein 9 gm, fat 4 gm, carbohydrates 28 gm, cholesterol 16 mg, sodium 108 mg

LIME-GINGER CHEESECAKE
SERVES 14

INGREDIENTS	AMOUNT/U.S.	METRIC
Ricotta cheese, nonfat, drained	3 cups	672 gm
Yogurt, nonfat, plain, thoroughly drained	¾ cup	168 gm
Sour cream, nonfat	½ cup	112 gm
Eggs	2	2
Egg white	1	1
Maple syrup	2 Tbsp.	30 ml
Lime juice	2 fl. oz.	60 ml
Orange, zest of, grated	1	1
Lime, zest of, finely grated	1	1
Sugar	1 cup	224 gm
Ginger, fresh, grated	1½ tsp.	5 gm
Vanilla beans, fresh, seeds removed	2	2
Graham Cracker Granola Crust (p. 351)		

PREPARATION
1. Preheat oven to 350°F (175°C).
2. Line bottom of sprayed 9½" springform pan with crust.
3. Combine the ricotta, drained yogurt, sour cream, eggs, egg white, maple syrup, lime juice and zests, sugar, ginger and vanilla in a mixing bowl. Beat or whisk until smooth. Pour filling over crust.
4. Bake for approximately 1 hour until filling is just set. Transfer to cooling rack and cool to room temperature.
5. Refrigerate overnight. Remove from springform and serve.

PRESENTATION
Could be served with fruit puree or stewed fruits.

NUTRITION PER SERVING
Calories 205, protein 11 gm, fat 4 gm, carbohydrates 35 gm, cholesterol 36 mg, sodium 123 mg

GRAHAM CRACKER
GRANOLA CRUST

YIELD: ONE 9 1/2" SHELL

INGREDIENTS	AMOUNT/U.S.	METRIC
Graham cracker crumbs	4 oz.	112 gm
Granola cereal, low-fat, coarsely ground	4 oz.	112 gm
Canola oil	2 Tbsp.	30 ml
Apple juice	3 Tbsp.	45 ml

PREPARATION

1. Combine all ingredients and mix until crumbly.
2. Press mixture into bottom of sprayed 9½" springform pan.

NUTRITION PER ¼ OF SHELL

Calories 80, protein 1 gm, fat 3 gm, carbohydrates 13 gm, cholesterol 0 mg, sodium 62 mg

SPONGE CAKE

SERVES 12

CHEF'S NOTES

For a chocolate sponge-cake, reduce the cake flour to 4 ¾ oz. (132 gm) and add 1 ½ oz. (42 gm) cocoa powder and 1 tsp. baking powder.

INGREDIENTS	AMOUNT/U.S.	METRIC
Egg whites	14 fl. oz.	420 ml
Cream of tartar	1 tsp.	.5 gm
Powdered sugar	7 oz.	196 gm
Cake flour, sifted	6¼ oz.	175 gm
Lime zest	⅛ oz	3½ gm
Orange zest	⅛ oz.	3½ gm
Butter, browned	1 fl. oz.	30 ml
Vanilla bean, scraped, seeds removed	1	1
Vegetable spray	as needed	as needed

PREPARATION

1. Preheat oven to 350°F (175°C).
2. Coat 10″ cake pan with vegetable spray. Line bottom with parchment paper.
3. In large mixing bowl, combine egg whites, cream of tartar, and powdered sugar. Beat to a firm meringue.
4. Gently fold sifted flour and zests into meringue.
5. Combine cooled, browned butter with vanilla and fold into batter.
6. Pour batter into cake pan and bake 25–30 minutes, until cake pulls ¼″ away from sides of pan (or until toothpick inserted comes out clean).

NUTRITION PER SERVING
Calories 153, protein 5 gm, fat 2 gm, carbohydrates 28 gm, cholesterol 5 mg, sodium 58 mg

CINNAMON-ALMOND COOKIES

YIELD: 80

INGREDIENTS	AMOUNT/U.S.	METRIC
Flour	1¼ cups	160 gm
Powdered sugar	1¼ cups	160 gm
Almond paste	6 oz.	168 gm
Egg whites	6	6
Vanilla extract	1 Tbsp.	15 ml
Cinnamon	1 Tbsp.	15 gm
Nonfat, skim milk	4 fl. oz.	120 ml

CHEF'S NOTES

These cookies are also called hippenmasse, which are very fine almond paste cookies. They are made with, or without, a cookie template.

PREPARATION

1. Preheat oven to 325°F (165°C).
2. Put all dry ingredients and almond paste in food processor and mix for 5 minutes. Whip egg whites to soft peaks in large mixing bowl. Fold dry mix into egg whites, and add vanilla extract, cinnamon and milk.
3. Drop spoonfuls of batter onto greased and floured baking sheet, or use a cookie template for desired shape. Bake for approximately 5 minutes or until golden brown. While baking, check cookies frequently to prevent burning.

PRESENTATION

May be served with Yogurt-Ricotta Ice (p. 349) as garnish or shaped to desired form.

NUTRITION PER COOKIE

Calories 26, protein 1 gm, fat 1 gm, carbohydrates 4 gm, cholesterol 0 mg, sodium 5 gm

APRICOT-RICOTTA ICE

SERVES 8

INGREDIENTS	AMOUNT/U.S.	METRIC
Dried apricots	4 oz.	112 gm
White wine	8 fl. oz.	240 ml
Ricotta cheese, part skim	6 oz.	168 gm
Yogurt, nonfat	8 oz.	224 gm
Maple syrup or sugar	4 fl. oz.	120 ml
Vanilla extract	1½ tsp.	7 ml

PREPARATION

1. Combine apricots and wine in small saucepan and bring to simmer. Cook until nearly sec. Allow to cool.
2. Puree apricots and ricotta cheese in food processor until a silky smooth texture is developed. Stop processor several times and scrape the sides of the bowl to ensure that all of the cheese is processed.
3. Add all remaining ingredients and process until incorporated.
4. Refrigerate until needed, then freeze in an ice cream freezer.

NUTRITION PER SERVING

Calories 151, protein 5 gm, fat 2 gm, carbohydrates 25 gm, cholesterol 7 mg, sodium 62 mg

CHOCOLATE-PRUNE TORTE

SERVES 8

INGREDIENTS	AMOUNT/U.S.	METRIC
Chocolate, unsweetened	1 oz.	28 gm
Prune puree, canned	¼ cup	75 gm
Nonfat, skim milk	2 Tbsp.	30 ml
Egg whites	2	2
Vanilla	1 tsp.	5 ml
Sugar	1 cup	224 gm
Kosher salt	¼ tsp.	1.25 gm
All-purpose flour	¼ cup	35 gm
Unsweetened cocoa powder	2 Tbsp.	30 gm
Walnuts, chopped	2 Tbsp.	30 gm

PREPARATION

1. Preheat oven to 350°F (175°C). Melt chocolate over low heat or in microwave at low power setting for 2–3 minutes.
2. Combine prune puree, skim milk, egg whites, vanilla, sugar, and salt, mix thoroughly. Add chocolate and mix.
3. Combine flour, cocoa, and walnuts. Carefully fold into prune and chocolate mixture, being careful not to overmix.
4. Lightly spray 8 small soufflé cups or oven-safe coffee cups with vegetable spray. Divide mixture into cups.
5. Bake for approximately 20–25 minutes or until firm to the touch. Allow to cool slightly before serving.

PRESENTATION

Turn cakes out onto plates and garnish with Apricot-Ricotta Ice (p. 354).

NUTRITION PER SERVING

Calories 174, protein 3 gm, fat 3 gm, carbohydrates 36 gm, cholesterol 0 mg, sodium 92 mg

PEPPERED SPICED PEARS

SERVES 8

INGREDIENTS	AMOUNT/U.S.	METRIC
Pears (Asian, Bosc, or Anjou), ripe	8	8
Spring water	16 fl. oz.	480 ml
Lemons, juice of	5	5
Oranges, juice of	8	8
Red Rioja wine (from Spain)	24 fl. oz.	720 ml
Fresh, cracked black pepper	1 Tbsp.	15 gm
Brown sugar	3 Tbsp.	45 gm
Cinnamon stick, cracked	1	1

PREPARATION

1. Clean and peel pears, leave whole, and place in mixture of 1 cup spring water and juice of 2 lemons to keep blonde.
2. In stainless steel saucepan, place remainder of lemon juice and spring water, orange juice, wine, pepper, brown sugar, and cinnamon stick. Bring to boil.
3. Remove pears from lemon water and add to poaching liquid.
4. Slowly poach pears over low heat until tender. Test after 40 minutes with baking needle.
5. Cool in liquid, then chill.
6. Before serving, remove pears from liquid. Strain liquid and reduce over heat by one-third. Tighten with a little cornstarch slurry, if needed.

PRESENTATION

Serve with about 2 Tbsp. of hot syrup per pear.

NUTRITION PER SERVING

Calories 220, protein 2 gm, fat 1 gm, carbohydrates 40 gm, cholesterol 0 mg, sodium 12 mg

HERBED CORNBREAD

INGREDIENTS	AMOUNT/U.S.	METRIC
Cake flour, sifted	12 oz.	336 gm
Yellow cornmeal	5 oz.	140 gm
Brown sugar	6 Tbsp.	90 gm
Cilantro, snipped	4 Tbsp.	20 gm
Parsley, snipped	4 Tbsp.	20 gm
Serrano chili peppers, seeded, diced	3	3
Baking powder	2 Tbsp.	28 gm
Kosher salt	2 tsp.	10 gm
Eggs	5	5
Water	10 fl. oz.	300 ml
Canola oil	6 fl. oz.	180 ml
Vegetable spray	as needed	as needed

PREPARATION

1. Preheat oven to 350°F (175°C).
2. In food processor, place flour, cornmeal, brown sugar, cilantro, parsley, peppers, baking powder, and salt. Add eggs, water, and oil. Cover and process for 1 minute. Scrape down sides and process another minute. Place container in refrigerator.
3. Spray 20 small muffin molds with vegetable spray. Heat molds in oven for 5 minutes. Fill with cornbread mixture and bake for 15 minutes.

PRESENTATION

Serve warm with soup and salad.

NUTRITION PER SERVING
Calories 188, protein 4 gm, fat 10 gm, carbohydrates 22 gm, cholesterol 53 mg, sodium 253 mg

HERB CREPES

SERVES 6 (2 CREPES PER SERVING)

CHEF'S NOTES

*These crepes can be served
with a savory filling for
an entree or appetizer. Or
omit the parsley and salt
and use with a sweet filling for a dessert crepe.*

INGREDIENTS	AMOUNT/U.S.	METRIC
Egg substitute	6 fl. oz.	180 ml
Nonfat, skim milk	8 fl. oz.	240 ml
Water	4 fl. oz.	120 ml
Kosher salt	1 tsp.	5 gm
Flour	4½ oz.	126 gm
Olive oil	1 Tbsp.	15 ml
Parsley, snipped	½ oz.	14 gm

PREPARATION

1. Place all ingredients in blender. Blend slowly at medium speed until mixture is well incorporated. Stop and scrape down the sides, and blend for an additional 10 seconds. Allow to rest for 1 hour. Or whisk eggs lightly by hand, add milk, water, salt, and olive oil. Last, whisk in flour and parsley. Be sure mixture is free of lumps. Allow to rest for 1 hour.
2. Spray hot nonstick 6″ skillet or crepe pan with vegetable spray. Using a 1 oz. ladle, pour batter evenly into pan. Cook crepes over medium heat; do not overbrown.

NUTRITION PER SERVING
Calories 127, protein 7 gm, fat 3 gm, carbohydrates 19 gm, cholesterol 1 mg, sodium 459 mg

HONEY ROLLS

YIELD: 20 ROLLS

INGREDIENTS	AMOUNT/U.S.	METRIC
Yeast	2 pkg.	2 pkg.
Nonfat, skim milk, warm	8 fl. oz.	240 ml
Flour	18 oz.	504 gm
Egg whites	6	6
Honey	2 tsp.	14 gm
Kosher salt	½ tsp.	2.5 gm
Margarine, melted	5 Tbsp.	75 ml

PREPARATION

1. Preheat oven to 350°F (175°C).
2. In large bowl, combine yeast, warm skim milk, and half the flour. Set in a warm place for 15 minutes.
3. In separate bowl, combine remaining ingredients, and mix into yeast mixture. [Do not have the margarine over 100°F (38°C).] Knead for 10 minutes. Let dough rest in a warm place for 30 minutes.
4. Punch dough down and shape into rolls. Place on greased cookie sheet and allow to double in size in a warm place. Bake for 10–15 minutes.

NUTRITION PER ROLL

Calories 137, protein 5 gm, fat 3 gm, carbohydrates 22 gm, cholesterol 0 mg, sodium 117 mg

CORNMEAL HONEY BREAD

YIELD: 2 DOZEN ROLLS OR 2 LOAVES

INGREDIENTS	AMOUNT/U.S.	METRIC
Yeast	1 Tbsp.	50 gm
Warm water	6 fl. oz.	180 ml
Milk, nonfat, warm	12 fl. oz.	360 ml
Bread flour	22½ oz.	630 gm
Honey	2½ fl. oz.	75 ml
Kosher salt	1 tsp.	5 gm
Yellow cornmeal	8 oz.	224 gm

PREPARATION

1. Preheat oven to 350°F (175°C).
2. In large bowl, combine yeast, lukewarm water, milk, and half the flour. Set in a warm place for 15 minutes.
3. In separate bowl, combine all other ingredients. Add to yeast mixture and mix. Knead dough for 5–10 minutes. Let dough rest for 30 minutes in a warm place.
4. Punch dough down and shape into 36 rolls or 4 loaves. Place rolls in greased muffin molds or loaves in greased loaf pans. Let rest in a warm place until doubled in size.
5. Bake for 10–15 minutes or until golden brown.

NUTRITION PER 1 ROLL OR ½2 OF LOAF SLICE

Calories 154, protein 5 gm, fat 1 gm, carbohydrates 32 gm, cholesterol 0 mg, sodium 91 mg

SIMPLE SOFT BREAD ROLLS

YIELD: 3 DOZEN 1 OZ. ROLLS

INGREDIENTS	AMOUNT/U.S.	METRIC
Yeast	1½ oz.	42 gm
Warm water (105°–115°F or 40°–60°C)	4 fl. oz.	120 ml
Bread flour	8 cups (or 2 lb. 4 oz.)	1012 gm
Sugar	2½ oz.	70 gm
Kosher salt	2 tsp.	10 gm
Olive oil	2½ fl. oz.	75 ml
Water	6 fl. oz.	180 ml

PREPARATION

1. Preheat oven to 350°F (175°C).
2. In large bowl, combine yeast, water, and half the flour. Set in a warm place for 15 minutes in order to activate the yeast.
3. In separate bowl, mix all other ingredients and add to yeast mixture. Flour and knead dough for 5–10 minutes. Allow dough to rest for 30 minutes in a warm place.
4. Punch dough down and shape into 1 oz. rolls (about 36). Place rolls on greased cookie sheet and set in a warm place until doubled in size.
5. Bake on a greased cookie sheet for approximately 15 minutes or until golden brown.

NUTRITION PER ROLL

Calories 138, protein 4 gm, fat 3 gm, carbohydrates 25 gm, cholesterol 0 mg, sodium 131 mg

SUN-DRIED TOMATO BREAD OR ROLLS

YIELD: 3 DOZEN 1 1/2 OZ. ROLLS OR 4 LOAVES

CHEF'S NOTES

Optional: Sprinkle tops of rolls or loaves with grated parmesan cheese or fresh herbs before baking.

INGREDIENTS	AMOUNT/U.S.	METRIC
Sun-dried tomatoes	1½ oz.	42 gm
Water	16 fl. oz.	480 ml
Active dry yeast	½ oz.	14 gm
Tomato water	4 fl. oz.	120 ml
Bread flour	5 cups	633 gm
Egg white	1	1
Butter	2½ Tbsp.	37 gm
Sugar	2 Tbsp.	30 gm
Kosher salt	4 tsp.	20 gm
Basil, fresh, snipped	1 oz.	28 gm
Oregano, fresh, snipped	½ oz.	14 gm

PREPARATION

1. Cover sun-dried tomatoes with 1 cup water. Let sit overnight or simmer until soft.
2. Remove tomatoes; reserve ½ cup excess tomato water for the dough.
3. Preheat oven to 375°F (190°C) for rolls or 400°F (205°C) for loaves.
4. Combine 1 cup lukewarm water with yeast to dissolve. Let rest in a warm place for 15 minutes.
5. In large mixing bowl, combine dissolved yeast and tomato water with all remaining ingredients except the herbs and tomatoes. Mix with a dough hook on low speed (#2 speed) to form a smooth dough, or knead by hand until a smooth dough develops (about 5 minutes). Add basil, oregano, and tomatoes. Mix until incorporated.
6. Remove from bowl, and cover dough. Let rise in a warm place until doubled in size.
7. Punch dough down and divide into 1½ oz. rolls (about 36) or 4 loaves. Place rolls on greased cookie sheet or loaves in greased loaf pans. Let rest in a warm place until doubled in size.
8. Bake until golden brown (about 20 minutes).

NUTRITION PER 1 ROLL OR ⅛ OF LOAF SLICE
Calories 84, protein 3 gm, fat 1 gm, carbohydrates 16 gm, cholesterol 2 mg, sodium 242 mg

WHOLE-WHEAT BREADSTICKS

YIELD: 32 STICKS

INGREDIENTS	AMOUNT/U.S.	METRIC
Active dry yeast	2 pkg.	2 pkg.
Sugar	4 tsp.	20 gm
Warm water (105–115°F or 40–46°C)	16 fl. oz.	480 ml
Whole-wheat flour	13 oz.	364 gm
All-purpose flour	9 oz.	252 gm
Wheat germ	8 oz.	224 gm
Kosher salt	1 tsp.	5 gm
Canola oil	4 fl. oz.	120 ml
Egg whites whip loosely	3	3
Coarse kosher salt (optional)	as needed	as needed

CHEF'S NOTES

Breadsticks are good served with soup or salad and as a snack food.

NUTRITION NOTES

The addition of wheat germ to this bread product increases calories from fat, however it also improves the fiber content.

PREPARATION

1. Preheat oven to 350°F (175°C).
2. In stainless steel bowl, combine yeast, sugar, and water; rest for 5 minutes. Stir in flours, wheat germ, salt, and oil. Combine thoroughly.
3. Turn dough out onto clean, lightly oiled surface. Cut dough into eight sections, then into 32 sections.
4. Between the surface and the palm of your hands, roll each piece out into a rope-like strand of approximately 16″ in length.
5. Place sticks on sheet pan, 1½″ apart, brush with egg white, and sprinkle with salt (optional). Let sticks rise for approximately 30 minutes.
6. Bake for approximately 30 minutes, until golden brown and crisp.

NUTRITION PER STICK

Calories 128, protein 5 gm, fat 5 gm, carbohydrates 18 gm, cholesterol 0 mg, sodium 74 mg

OATMEAL MUFFINS

SERVES 12

INGREDIENTS	AMOUNT/U.S.	METRIC
Oatmeal flakes	4 oz.	112 gm
Buttermilk, low-fat	8 fl. oz.	240 ml
Margarine, melted	2 fl. oz.	60 ml
Egg whites	2	2
Brown sugar	3 oz.	84 gm
Flour	3 oz.	84 gm
Whole-wheat flour	1 oz.	28 gm
Baking soda	½ tsp.	2 gm
Kosher salt	1 tsp.	5 gm
Vegetable spray	as needed	as needed

PREPARATION

1. Preheat oven to 375°F (190°C).
2. Combine oatmeal and buttermilk. Soak for 1 hour in refrigerator.
3. In large bowl, mix margarine, egg whites, and brown sugar together thoroughly.
4. Sift together flours, baking soda, and salt. Stir into egg white mixture, alternating with oatmeal and buttermilk mixture.
5. Spray muffin tins with vegetable spray and fill two-thirds full. Bake for 20 minutes until golden brown.

NUTRITION PER SERVING

Calories 143, protein 4 gm, fat 5 gm, carbohydrates 21 gm, cholesterol 0 mg, sodium 308 mg

APPLE-BRAN MUFFINS

SERVES 12

INGREDIENTS	AMOUNT/U.S.	METRIC
Bran flakes, finely crushed	10 oz.	280 gm
Oatmeal flakes	4 oz.	112 gm
Brown sugar	3 oz.	84 gm
Cinnamon	¾ tsp.	1.5 gm
Baking soda	¾ tsp.	4 gm
Baking powder	1 tsp.	4 gm
Vegetable oil	2 Tbsp.	30 ml
Egg white	1	1
Applesauce, unsweetened	8 fl. oz.	240 ml
Nonfat, skim milk	4 fl. oz.	120 ml

PREPARATION

1. Preheat oven to 375°F (190°C).
2. In stainless steel bowl, combine all dry ingredients thoroughly.
3. In a clean stainless steel mixing bowl, combine all wet ingredients and mix thoroughly.
4. Fold wet ingredients into dry mixture.
5. Line muffins tins with paper muffin cups and spray with vegetable spray. Divide batter equally into 12 muffin cups. Bake for 20 minutes until golden brown, or until a wooden toothpick inserted in center comes out clean.

NUTRITION PER SERVING

Calories 173, protein 5 gm, fat 3 gm, carbohydrates 34 gm, cholesterol 0 mg, sodium 308 mg

OAT BRAN MUFFINS

SERVES 24

INGREDIENTS	AMOUNT/U.S.	METRIC
Oat bran, dry	5 oz.	140 gm
Whole-wheat flour	4 oz.	112 gm
Baking powder	1 Tbsp.	12 gm
Raisins	2 oz.	56 gm
Nonfat, skim milk	4 fl. oz.	120 ml
Honey	2 fl. oz.	60 ml
Vegetable oil	2 Tbsp.	30 ml
Egg whites	3	3
Orange juice	4 fl. oz.	120 ml
Vegetable spray	as needed	as needed

PREPARATION

1. Preheat oven to 400°F (205°C).
2. In stainless steel mixing bowl, mix together all dry ingredients, including raisins.
3. Add wet ingredients and mix thoroughly.
4. Line mini-muffin tins with paper muffin cups and spray with vegetable spray. Divide mixture into cups. Bake for 15 minutes until golden brown, or until a wooden toothpick inserted in center comes out clean.

NUTRITION PER SERVING

Calories 75, protein 3 gm, fat 2 gm, carbohydrates 13 gm, cholesterol 0 mg, sodium 50 mg

BLUEBERRY MUFFINS

INGREDIENTS	AMOUNT/U.S.	METRIC
Flour	8 oz.	224 gm
Baking powder	2 tsp.	8 gm
Baking soda	1 tsp.	4 gm
Kosher salt	½ tsp.	2.5 gm
Brown sugar	4 oz.	112 gm
Yogurt, nonfat, plain	8 oz.	224 gm
Egg whites	4	4
Margarine, melted	2 fl. oz.	60 ml
Blueberries, fresh	8 oz.	224 gm

PREPARATION

1. Preheat oven to 375°F (190°C).
2. In stainless steel mixing bowl, combine flour, baking powder, baking soda, salt, and brown sugar.
3. Add yogurt, egg whites, and margarine and combine well. Fold in the cleaned blueberries.
4. Line muffing tins with paper muffin cups and spray with vegetable spray. Divide mixture evenly into muffin cups. Bake for 20 minutes until golden brown or until a wooden toothpick inserted in center comes out clean.

NUTRITION PER SERVING

Calories 110, protein 3 gm, fat 3 gm, carbohydrates 19 gm, cholesterol 0 mg, sodium 201 mg

CHOCOLATE-FRUIT MUFFINS

SERVES 12

INGREDIENTS	AMOUNT/U.S.	METRIC
Flour	8 oz.	224 gm
Sugar	4 oz.	112 gm
Cocoa powder	4 Tbsp.	60 gm
Baking powder	1 Tbsp.	12 gm
Kosher salt	½ tsp.	2.5 gm
Nonfat, skim milk	8 fl. oz.	240 ml
Vegetable oil	2 fl. oz.	60 ml
Egg whites	3	3
Dried cherries or cranberries, high quality	8 oz.	224 gm

PREPARATION

1. Preheat oven to 375°F (190°C).
2. In stainless steel mixing bowl, combine the flour, sugar, cocoa powder, baking powder, and salt.
3. Add milk, oil, and egg whites and combine wet and dry mixtures. Fold in cherries or cranberries.
4. Line muffin tins with paper muffin cups and spray with vegetable spray. Divide mixture into muffin cups. Bake for 20 minutes until golden brown, or until a wooden toothpick inserted in center comes out clean.

NUTRITION PER SERVING

Calories 175, protein 4 gm, fat 5 gm, carbohydrates 29 gm, cholesterol 0 mg, sodium 202 mg

POPPY SEED MUFFINS

SERVES 12

INGREDIENTS	AMOUNT/U.S.	METRIC
Flour	8 oz.	224 gm
Poppy seeds	3 tsp.	9 gm
Kosher salt	½ tsp.	2.5 gm
Baking soda	½ tsp.	2 gm
Sugar	8 oz.	224 gm
Margarine, soft	3 Tbsp.	45 ml
Egg whites	4	4
Yogurt, nonfat, plain	8 fl. oz.	240 ml
Vanilla bean, scraped, seeds removed	1 tsp.	3 gm
Vegetable spray	as needed	as needed

CHEF'S NOTES

This recipe can also be used as a cake; add additional flavorings such as lemon or almond.

PREPARATION

1. Preheat oven to 375°F (190°C).
2. In small bowl, combine flour, poppy seeds, salt, and baking soda.
3. In stainless steel mixing bowl, cream together sugar and margarine, then whisk in egg whites. Add yogurt and vanilla bean and whisk mixture vigorously.
4. Fold in flour mixture and combine thoroughly.
5. Line muffin tins with paper muffin cups or spray with vegetable spray. Divide mixture into muffin cups. Bake for 15–20 minutes until golden brown, or until a wooden tooth pick inserted in center comes out clean.

NUTRITION PER SERVING
Calories 187, protein 4 gm, fat 3 gm, carbohydrates 35 gm, cholesterol 0 mg, sodium 199 mg

A GOOD MEAL SOOTHES THE SOUL AS IT REGENERATES THE BODY; FROM THE ABUNDANCE OF IT FLOWS A BENIGN BENEVOLENCE.

Frederick W. Hackwood

THE KITCHEN IS A COUNTRY WHERE THERE ARE ALWAYS DISCOVERIES TO BE MADE.

Grimod de la Reynière

COOK FOR THE CUSTOMER, BUT IMAGINE YOURSELF SITTING DOWN TO ENJOY THE FOOD YOU'RE COOKING.

Chef Ronald De Santis, CMC

INDUSTRY ISSUES

℮

℮

Genetically engineered food products: What are the pros and cons, and how does genetic engineering work?

All cells contain DNA, the long molecule shaped like a double helix. A gene is a swatch of DNA that controls a certain characteristic of the organism. In the 1970s scientists discovered that they could clip off a gene-length swatch from a DNA molecule, and later they learned to affix it to a different DNA molecule. This "cut and paste job" became known as gene splicing and results in what is now called recombinant DNA. Today many biotechnology experts are optimistic; they see consumers around the globe benefiting from a new genetically engineered green revolution.

In the future, the advent of genetic engineering will most likely be remembered as the brain-power technology revolution. It will alter plants, animals, and possibly human beings. Genetic engineering has the potential to cure genetic disease and alter genetic characteristics.

Part Five provides food service professionals with information concerning this nationally debated issue of biotechnically altering food products and the effects this will have on food service.

CHAPTER 13

A PERSPECTIVE ON GENETIC ENGINEERING

@

The culinary arts are primarily an artistic vocation; however chefs today must ready themselves and actively pursue the importance of the developments in genetic engineering. As these products enter the market, they will certainly demand more scientific knowledge and higher skill level from chefs in the future. Chefs are considered experts on food, but they must accept the challenge that technology has brought about. When properly informed and educated on the subject, chefs will be ready and able to handle the changes as they apply to the profession and the food service industry as a whole.

Due to the magnitude of this issue, it is imperative that ample and accurate information is available on the subject and is disseminated to food service industry employees. In addition, the same information should be available to consumers so they are able to make informed decisions regarding how to use, or not to use, a product that has undergone chemical alteration.

The general public and the end consumer do not find this sort of information as readily available as do members of the hospitality industry who can obtain such information through trade magazines, trade newspapers, and journals. It is therefore crucial for food service employees to be properly educated and informed on the subject, as consumers will depend on them for guidance on food and its byproducts.

The scope of the perspective of this chapter is limited, to the extent that we merely attempt to address how food service professionals should prepare themselves to deal with food products that have been chemically engineered or altered.

Through the interview questionnaire, the following areas of concern were addressed:

1. Has a change in lifestyles and demographics brought about a "dietary schizophrenia"? What should be done to help educate consumers to bring balance to their future eating and purchasing decisions?

2. Who actually supports and who does not support the decision on bioengineering?

3. What is the responsibility of government and industry?

4. What influence will bioengineered food have in the role of chefs of tomorrow?

5. Should chefs be required to take food technology courses in order to comprehend the science involved?

6. Should correct and adequate labeling be required to inform the chef and consumer on the products they are purchasing?

7. What are the effects of bioengineering from a cultural, ethical and religious standpoint?

8. What concerns are there for future health effects possibly caused by the consumption of bioengineered foods?

9. Will chefs of tomorrow find themselves in reversed roles from artistic to scientific? How will they proportionally link themselves in these roles?

10. In the food industry of tomorrow, the edge in the marketplace will be decided by a unique or uniquely improved product. Will under-nutrition take hold?

11. If protein is to be the commodity of the future, is seafood the answer?

12. Should the food service industry aggressively pursue training workshops on the changing foods of the future? If so, what exactly should be suggested as the focus of these workshops?

Fifty business leaders, industry executives, educators, executive chefs, food manufacturers, dietitians, and health-care food service directors were interviewed at random on this subject. Following is an evaluation and analysis of the responses received from the participants of this market research project.

1. Has a change in lifestyles and demographics brought about a "dietary schizophrenia"? What should be done to help educate consumers to bring balance to their future eating and purchasing decisions?

This question prompted the most consistent answer from all respondents. It was felt that the more knowledge we in the industry can bring to the public about the makeup of food items, particularly as they relate to protein, the more beneficial. The evolving variety of regional and native foods allows the public to become better educated and make informed decisions. Their understanding of the effects of these products will enhance their ability to understand that dieting is not really the answer. But balanced eating and purchasing habits will give them the lifestyle that they wish to achieve.

There is an explosive demand for low-calorie, low-sodium, low-fat, low-prep-time, "no cook" types of products in every category. The new labeling regulations now in place will assist the consumer in making better purchasing decisions based on nutritive value. The chef and the dietitian should also form a partnership, sharing the synergy of their talents for the benefit of the public health by identifying ways to make foods more healthful through cooking techniques, and by offering alternatives without sacrificing quality.

Increased consumer educational programs could continue to bring about greater awareness among consumers. Many consumers today, although more knowledgable about foods, still face the challenge of applying what they know.

One important point that was stressed primarily by the educational respondents was that we need to avoid having the consumer fear food as something bad. The lifestyle change has forced fast food service giants like McDonald's to fry french fries in polyunsaturated fats. The education of the dining public is evolutionary. It is a cultural change that will continue to evolve over time. Also, in the food manufacturers' responses, it was clear that the news media has helped bring about this "dietary schizophrenia."

Almost every day a new study is released making claims about the health benefits of a certain food, or that eating a particular item is hazardous to your health. The food manufacturers reported that honest media coverage, through magazine articles, credible television cooking shows including dietitians and chefs, and various government agencies, could focus on the topic of genetic engineering and distribute factual and consistent information to the consumer.

All respondents indicated that basic, sound, comprehensible information and education should be offered to help create a nation that will place greater importance on a balanced diet. Great strides have been made in this regard, as is evidenced by the U.S. Department of Agriculture's Food Guide Pyramid, but the nation as a whole must change its eating habits to comply with the food guide and dietary guidelines. Proper nutrition starts at home. The population should be reeducated through the media or perhaps government mailings. Parents must start their children early on a healthy diet. Schools should continue the process by educating children on proper dietary habits and demonstrate examples with a sound school lunch program.

2. Do you support genetic engineering and genetically engineered food products?

The overall consensus regarding support of genetic engineering and genetically engineered food products was positive, although with certain reservations. Particular concern was expressed regarding the safety of the food and water supply and the degree of improvement in product quality. Respondents also indicated that as the world's food supply decreases, and the demand for food becomes more difficult to balance with nature, genetic engineering of food will be an inevitable conclusion. Genetic engineering, in the form of conventional cross-breeding, has actually occurred throughout the history of civilization.

All respondents agreed that this technology has been widely used in medical research laboratories for the development of vaccines and drugs to prevent diseases. They also agreed that it would be natural to apply genetic engineering to food products, provided that quality and safety were maintained and the

@

basic nature or composition of the food was unchanged. Respondents also stressed the need for great caution as we proceed with genetic engineering, to assure protection from products which may prove to be harmful after extended research.

Deriving more efficient means of food production and more nutritional sources is in the best interest of the world population. Without continued work in bioengineered food products, the earth's population may outgrow the food supply.

Several respondents in the health-care sector expressed the idea that genetically engineered foods could potentially be more disease resistant, thereby reducing crop loss and pesticide use, but even more significantly, that engineered food products could contain more disease-fighting components. However, other respondents did not agree, nor philosophically accept the prospect of genetically improved food products that have been produced from dissimilar species (genes from one species transferred to another).

Respondents believe that bioengineering offers several benefits to the agricultural community; through the use of bioengineering, chemical pesticides could be reduced drastically. Farmers would be assisted economically by growing plants that are resistant to disease and toxic to pests. Through genetic engineering, great advances in food production technology are possible. Various crops could be adapted to harsher growing conditions and different climates, therefore yields might be greatly increased and costs reduced. As an example, Calgene Fresh, Inc. has taken the gene that signals the tomato to soften, and reversed it. The result is a tomato (Flavr Savr) that takes seven to eight days longer to soften on the vine, which, in turn, harvests a better tomato.

Another consideration was the benefit in the fight against world hunger, especially as it relates to storage potential for various food products and the increased ease with which goods could be transported. From a culinary standpoint, improvement in the product could be possible in the areas of flavor, texture, and appearance. We might even see some exotic new hybrids.

All of this will have an impact on the chef and in the kitchen of the future—in all areas of the food service cycle. Because we expect that genetically engineered food products may be vastly different in shelf-life, moisture content, nutritive value, and flavor, it will be important for chefs to understand these characteristic changes and what new methods of handling will be required of the chefs of tomorrow.

3. What is the responsibility of government and industry?

The overall concurrence was that there is a need for government and industry to regulate the genetic engineering process. Ideally, this regulation would ensure a safe and wholesome food supply and consistent disclosure of all treatment. Interestingly enough, though, the food manufacturers questioned felt that government involvement should be for compliance only, to ensure product safety and integrity. They also felt that the government should have quality inspection teams to ensure standardized manufacturing practices. However, they felt that labeling and regulating in other aspects of manufacturing should be the responsibility of industry. The biotechnology industry must set high standards of control, testing, and ethics, or it will face stronger government regulation like hundreds of other industries.

The industry executives stressed that government and industry need to work in tandem to ensure the safety of products being developed, particularly as it relates to nutrition and flavor.

As the United States is the world's largest producer of food, we have a responsibility to develop products that will be available to the developing world. The food service respondents felt that the government must regulate the genetic engineering industry to prevent the possibility of any potentially harmful products entering the marketplace. Once genetically altered products enter the market, they must be clearly labeled, enabling consumers to know exactly what they are purchasing and whether there are known potential risks involved with consumption of these products. The distinction that needs to be made in labeling is whether or not related genes are introduced, as in the case of creating a hybrid tomato by crossing two tomato varieties, as opposed to the introduction of a totally foreign substance, for example, an animal gene to a vegetable.

Overall, respondents reported that the responsibility for the safety of genetically engineered products entering the marketplace rests in government regulation, as it does today in the case of pharmaceuticals. However, from the food service industry's perspective, it may not be entirely practical to inform the consumer every time a genetically altered tomato has been incorporated into their pasta sauce.

Dietitians and health-care respondents concurred with the Environmental Defense Fund's (EDF) viewpoint that the Food and Drug Administration (FDA) should regulate ingredients under the 1958 Food Additive Amendment. In addition, it is believed that it is the industry's responsibility to conduct product testing, in compliance with preestablished standards, to ensure that products developed are safe for public consumption. Respondents generally were of the opinion that the government should be responsible for regulation and inspection, and industry for research, production, and delivery. Respondents in the health-care sector expressed that both government and industry should support appropriate research, such as the Designer Food Project, and offer chemo prevention, basic research, and chemical trials. They also stressed that the public should be educated on this information as it relates to nutrition-related chronic diseases, including heart disease, cancer, osteoporosis, and stroke.

The educational sector suggested that reasonably appropriate government procedures are already in place, and that the government will not test items that are derived from the same species (tomato to tomato or broccoli to cauliflower), unless an allergen is involved (such as peanuts). However, they test all products involving allergens or cross-species engineering (such as flounder genes in tomatoes). Some respondents in the educational sector felt that current FDA policy falls below the acceptable level of control needed in the biotechnology industry.

4. What influence will bioengineered food have in the role of chefs of tomorrow?

The overall consensus was that chefs must have a basic understanding of the science involved in chemistry and physics. In the future the chef's knowledge of the science must progress, and the chef of tomorrow will need to be knowledgable of the food crops that are candidates for redesign. Knowing the source of the many new genes and the purpose of engineering will help the chef to prepare for potential changes in food-handling practices. In addition, educating chefs on other new processes, such as irradiation, is essential for the present and the future.

The influence of these products will largely depend on their quality, price, and availability and the availability of non–genetically engineered foods. The exciting part of this process could be the availability of a greater variety of products with improved flavor, texture, and appearance.

Several respondents in the health-care sector felt that being a chef is primarily an artistic vocation. Conversely, they saw bioengineering as improving efficiencies in production, delivery, and nutritional sources. To them, the two seem quite different in pursuit.

The health-care sector thought that chefs should become involved in helping researchers understand the food properties required when certain techniques are used in cooking. This would help identify characteristics needed in the raw form.

A small number of respondents from the educational sector reported that bioengineering will improve the availability of high-quality, economically affordable products for preparation. These products, in addition to being disease and rot resistant, will be nutritious as well. They felt that the influence of bioengineered food on the chef of tomorrow will be that he or she will find it easier to prepare high-quality, nutritionally sound food at a lower cost. However, the question that remains is the eventual success level of bioengineering. Most respondents felt that integration of new products will be a gradual process, and that we will not see a flooded market. But as new genetically engineered products are introduced, the changes may require new methods of handling by the chefs of tomorrow.

5. Should chefs be required to take food technology courses in order to comprehend the science involved?

Sixty percent of the respondents in all categories supported the idea of chefs taking food technology courses in order to fully comprehend the science of food. The educational sector believed that food technology courses should be required as part of the chef certification process. In addition, they thought that chefs should take food technology courses to broaden their general knowledge of the field, not just to increase their knowledge of genetic engineering. Such education will benefit chefs as future developments occur in genetic engineering. The food manufacturers felt that in order to educate the consumer, chefs need a working knowledge of any controversial ingredient. The chef must know the reason for an ingredient being added to a particular product. They also felt that a fundamental course in food science should be part of the chef's certification process. Major corporations often assist chefs by conducting seminars, such as the L.J. Minor Corporation's educational seminar entitled "The Truth about Ingredients on Food Service Labels." These types of seminars provide chefs with the necessary information concerning the science of bioengineering.

The health-care respondents felt that initially more emphasis should be placed on the area of nutritional sciences. Then the focus should proceed on to food technology as it relates to genetic engineering. They expressed the belief that chefs must comprehend the science involved but also understand the ethical aspects and future potential opportunities for bioengineered food in the industry. However, they did not believe that this should be a requirement. In addition, they felt that food technology would become an integral part of balancing the art of preparation with the science of genetically altered ingredients.

6. Should correct and adequate labeling be required to inform the chef and consumer on the products they are purchasing?

All respondents felt that correct and "adequate" labeling should be required on genetically engineered foods, similar to what is now on all foods with the new FDA labeling regulations. Although food manufacturer respondents pointed out that ingredients should be listed in order of their predominance, by weight, they stress that too much information on the label is both costly to the manufacturer, adding to their delivery costs, and confusing to the consumer. They questioned, as did other respondents, what is "adequate" and for whom, and felt that it could harm the food service industry. However, they also agreed that the public should be notified of allergens or products that are the result of cross-species engineering. Operators felt that information in simple terms that can be placed on a label to inform the consumer is significant and gives the end user a choice in deciding what goes into their bodies. If foreign elements have been introduced to the product they purchase, they should be informed. The health-care respondents felt strongly that end users have a right to fair and accurate listing of ingredients. This should be in terms that the average consumer can comprehend, with particular emphasis on food additives in genetically altered products.

With regard to the issue of labeling foods, the consensus was that it is important for any purchaser to be able to make a choice. Choice is and will be an

important aspect of purchasing anything that the consumer feels to be of benefit. Therefore, bioengineered foods should be labeled so as to ensure proper
disclosure of changes made to the product and to provide correct and adequate
labeling to consumers.

A special note that must be mentioned is the need to inform the public of
the seal, code, or emblem that will be used to identify an altered product.

7. What are the effects of bioengineering from a cultural, ethical, and religious standpoint?

The overall consensus from respondents can be summarized as follows:
The key to the success of bioengineering of food products in the American culture is a continuing educational process of the underlying economic efficiencies
and health benefits that may be derived from these bioengineered products. As
we become more knowledgable about altering our environment, we must accept the responsibility to pursue and use these technologies. Religion and
ethics give guidance. Culture defines and is defined by the environment.

Food manufacturer respondents indicated that throughout history people
have developed thousands of new procedures for the good of humankind.
Therefore, the process of creating bioengineered food should not affect culture,
religion, or ethics. They see this technology primarily as an effort to feed the
world's population now and in the future.

Respondents in the health-care sector were of the view that manipulating
the structure and function of foodstuffs raises many anxieties about what the
future will hold for the human race. Respondents in the educational sector felt
that this comes down to a personal decision, and one should not reduce religious or cultural beliefs to a scientific level. Some respondents felt that religious convictions will remain unchanged, especially since the religious point of
view has survived centuries of wars, political activism, and other tribulations
without change.

Health-care respondents indicated that the cultural impact could be
greater since regions would be able to obtain a greater variety of products that
are normally not accessible and could enhance their cuisine. The same respondents felt that the expectancy of the ethical principle can be successful as long
as food retains its integrity.

Respondents in the operator sector expressed that most people, regardless
of their religious or cultural viewpoint, would understand that bioengineering
could be an answer to the millions of today's starving people. However, they
also stressed that the religious implications of creating food products from dissimilar species are noteworthy, especially in relation to the Hindu, Muslim,
and Jewish faiths where certain food products are controlled. For example, at
what point is pork present in a product, in its natural muscular form or as a mi-
croscopic gene used to make a carrot more orange?

Because of the vast differences in resources between the wealthy and the
poor in this country, and the resulting gap in education and flow of informa-

tion, it is quite possible that underprivileged members of the population would not even know they were consuming altered products.

We know that genes are the template of life. Mark Cohen, one of the interviewees, may have expressed the controversy best: "Will our entire food supply be genetically engineered to provide enough fresh nutritious food to feed the entire planet, or will it be filled with new food products that cause unpredictable reactions?" Will science fulfill our greatest hope, that the human race will be relieved of genetic imperfections? Or will it prove our greatest nightmare, that our personalities, individualities, even our souls are only the result of biochemistry?

8. What concerns are there for future health effects possibly caused by the consumption of bioengineered foods?

All respondents were in accord that our knowledge of health effects is limited based on the research that has currently been released. For example, there are concerns that exist in current literature in relation to toxins created when genes are altered and in relation to new allergies that could develop from gene splicing.

Some respondents in the health-care sector believe that the effects of genetic alterations will be significant but that we will not know the total impact for years. They expressed the belief that appropriate education and adequate research and development must be completed to understand long-term benefits and any harmful effects that may come to those who utilize bioengineered foods and food products.

This anxiety or concern may be appropriate, and we should continue to challenge anything that may appear to be healthy but may have long-term harmful effects. At the very least, people should be made aware of potential side effects that may result from utilization of bioengineered food products.

In principle, the more bioengineered foods mimic natural foods in "makeup and breakdown," the lower the risk. When the reward for their use outweighs the risks of unknowns, acceptance and use will increase.

Some of the respondents in the educational sector indicated that, except for the introduction of allergens, the "hype" of negative aspects of bioengineering would be speculative at best. They also felt that the health benefits should be identified and that, through education, individuals will form their own opinion. We will continue to get conflicting information about the possible benefits and harm of the foods we eat.

The operators all felt that the public, as a whole, is concerned about bioengineered foods. This concern comes from the fact that very few people understand the makeup of foods, as well as any health problems that could possibly be caused. They felt very strongly that education is the answer and that all of food service has a responsibility to help educated the public. They also stressed testing and regulation by the government as a solution to the concerns.

@

9. Will chefs of tomorrow find themselves in reversed roles from artistic to scientific? How will they proportionally link themselves in these roles?

All respondents indicated that chefs of tomorrow will be challenged to enhance their skills and refine their talents in a new marketplace. Chefs will continue first and foremost to play an artistic role, making use of available resources and products, bioengineered or otherwise. They responded that being a chef requires a balance between art and science, because today's healthy approach to cooking demands a more scientific understanding of food while still maintaining all artistic abilities.

However, respondents in the food manufacturing sector believed that chefs will need to become more scientifically aware to understand new processes in the food industry and to make educated decisions as they relate the processes to their particular situation.

It was interesting to see that respondents in the education sector view the culinary profession as one of true craftsmanship as well as artistry. If it were to become a profession simply of science rather than enjoyment, they question how many chefs would still want to be involved in the profession. They all indicated that the chef of tomorrow will still be an artist but with greater scientific understanding. Some chefs may find themselves in a reversed, more scientific role, for instance, in research. However, the educators believed that most chef roles will continue to be artistic and managerial.

Some respondents in the health-care sector felt that the food innovations of today will produce new opportunities for the chef to break away from the traditional viewpoint of their role as a "cook." It will place them on the consumer's wish list as the food expert who can offer solutions to the public's food dilemma. Again, they felt education would be the key to understanding.

In the future, chefs must allocate a significant percentage of their time to understanding the architecture of food from a composition standpoint. To prepare for the new role, further formal instruction in food technology and nutrition is needed.

10. In the food industry of tomorrow, the edge in the marketplace will be decided by a unique or uniquely improved product. Will undernutrition take hold?

The majority of respondents did not understand or agree with the premise of this question, and perhaps a clearer statement should have been made initially. Respondents stated that "improved" implies better, unless either the consumer is deceived, or the understanding of the change made in the product is not complete. Undernutrition would not be an issue. However, the health-care respondents stated that undernutrition without malnutrition is predicted to be evidenced as we approach the year 2000.

While the consumption of a nutrient-dense, low-calorie diet is promoted to maximize life span and minimize the aging process, health-care respondents believe that this model requires further study due to the limited amount of research in human subjects. Presently there is no concrete answer to this issue of genetically altering food, although it will present additional challenges to both nutritionists and dietitians.

Some respondents in the educational sector indicated that because of the development of engineered food products, there will be a capability to create higher yields of products with greater nutritional value and perhaps more widespread nourishment for the world population. They also felt that access to and distribution of desired products will be another key driver in the marketplace demand. One respondent felt that undernutrition will not be an issue, as humankind inherently wishes to live longer and undernutrition will not be more prevalent in tomorrow's food industry than it is today.

One food manufacturer's response was that undernutrition will not occur in the future because the modern consumer will be so well educated on all aspects of food production that taking a new process or product to the point of undernutrition is not a concern. It was also indicated that unique products will always be in demand by consumers, but they would not supplant quality and value.

Nutrition can be favorably contained in the food industry of tomorrow provided that adequate education takes place. All believed that the government, specifically the FDA, will have to play a more dominant leadership role to ensure that the change in food product makeup is understood and is convincingly presented to the general public. Some operators suggested that the idea of undernutrition would be revolutionary, and the thought of all food available to the consumer being nutrient-packed and low-calorie, unique.

11. If protein is to be the commodity of the future, is seafood the answer?

Respondents in the health-care sector felt that farming of seafood offers great potential for supplying the volume of high-quality protein needed to sustain our planet, provided that the safety and sanitation of the water supply remains intact. They also felt that natural sources of seafood products will shrink unless traditional fishing becomes more regulated and controlled. As it stands, certain fish species will become extinct due to overfishing; therefore, aquaculture will continue to grow over the next decade. Only one respondent in the health-care sector disagreed. This subject indicated that protein-rich substitutes or other cheaper sources made to resemble more expensive products would be the sensible choice.

In the educational sector, several respondents favored seafood as one of the answers but questioned the increased costs involved, and suggested that certain plants high in protein count could have a greater impact in filling the protein void. These are quinoa, bundle flower, kelp, and also leguminous vegetables such as soybeans. Furthermore, they suggested that the traits of these kinds of plants could be engineered into common vegetables that consumers would recognize and enjoy.

Food manufacturers reported that meat and poultry would also continue to be major sources of protein. Considering some of the new genetic engineering practices in place, red meat could be produced with a significantly lower fat and cholesterol level.

Respondents in the operator sector expressed the view that protein will certainly be a major commodity in the future and while they see seafood as a major source, it certainly will not be the only source. Like respondents in the educational sector, they felt that there may be a much greater potential in certain plants that are not yet fully understood. Aquaculture has great potential, but certainly grains and legumes are among the most viable possibilities.

12. Should the food service industry aggressively pursue training workshops on the changing foods of the future? If so, what exactly should be suggested as the focus of these workshops?

Respondents in the educational sector indicated that there should be workshops, and the exact focus of the seminars should be relevant to the issues at hand. The history of biotechnology, limitations of current research, government policy, and positioning should all be considered as focal points. They also stated that these workshops should identify the different genetically engineered foods and provide nutritional analysis and comparisons with similar products. Side-by-side taste tests could assist in dispelling false impressions and would allow for comparison of genetically engineered foods to regular food products. In addition, the results of such workshops should be made available to food manufacturers and the public. Furthermore, they indicated that by explaining the basic process of bioengineering, such workshops would provide an avenue for feedback from grassroots levels to end users. The emphasis should be on what our bodies truly need from a medical perspective and understanding those foods which provide a balanced diet.

Respondents in the health-care sector expressed that training is mandatory to keep the skills of the chef competitive in the high-tech food marketplace. They suggested a multidisciplinary approach including hands-on training, more formal instruction on all issues concerned, and exposure to consumer trends through industry experts.

Respondents in the food manufacturers and operators sector point to holding continuing education seminars and workshops for everyone involved in the food service industry today. The main focus of these workshops should be on the current research in a broader sense and how it impacts the food service industry. Initially it would not be important to learn the details of the biogenetic engineering process but rather to understand it in general terms and the impact it has on the food service industry. They also indicated that this educational process should start with young culinarians in school and continue throughout their culinary career. It should then be a part of recertification training in conjunction with all major national professional food service associations.

The issue of genetic engineering has strengths and weaknesses that must be presented to both the public and the culinary profession. We are obviously in the early stages of genetic engineering and do not know all of its consequences. We should most certainly proceed with genetic engineering as long as it is quality oriented, without changing the basic nature and composition of food, because we are on the threshold of exciting advances in foods and nutrition.

Today researchers are learning how diet can prevent heart disease, vascular diseases, and cancer. These chronic diseases are the major threat to our health today and will only get worse in the future unless effective preventative measures can be developed and widely disseminated. However, caution should be exercised as we proceed with genetically engineered food in order to avoid the creation of any products that might ultimately prove to be harmful.

Current research is being done to assess an individual's disease risk based on genetic analysis. With these areas of altering foods and nutrition converging, specific dietary recommendations can be produced for adding or subtracting nutrients to reduce this risk. With the specific disease-preventing guidelines in place, chefs of tomorrow will be able to plan menus accordingly. It is evident that postgraduate education and training workshops on changing foods will be valuable, especially as knowledge accumulates. The future holds a technology that makes almost anything possible. But it will clearly be determined by what people say they want.

The professional chef and the registered dietitian have a unique opportunity to bring a host of choices to the American public that are linked to a healthy future. Although there will be a greater scientific understanding, chefs of tomorrow will still be primarily artistic, because tasty, well-prepared, and well-presented food will remain essential to good healthful eating. The most healthful bioengineered food is worthless if it tastes bad.

To date, there is no known scientific evidence that product development using biotechnology exhibits harmful characteristics. Intensive evaluation during the product development stage, as well as regulatory scrutiny, should ensure the safety of these products.

In the future, chefs should allocate a percentage of their time to the study of the architecture of food from a composition standpoint. The balance will be in food choices (scientific) and food preparation (artistic). Both are extremely important, and with continued education and added food science courses, chefs will have the opportunity to remain current. Awareness and understanding of cooking and nutritional theories will be necessary to enhance the artistry of the chef.

In conclusion, from the answers to the survey, it was clear that education is the key to public understanding and proper evaluation of biotechnology. Survey results indicate the need to explain biotechnology in simple terms and put the process into a familiar context. Most likely, it should be described as a set of techniques that can be applied in a manner that offers ultimate benefits for both the consumer and the environment. It is clear that the role of the biotechnology industry must be clearly and carefully constructed, and educational endeavors should be viewed as impartial. Furthermore, financial resources are required for meetings and materials.

As well, industry grants to educational programs for unbiased, thought-provoking, and factual presentations would assist in overcoming the credibility questions. Industry most definitely could begin to facilitate the exchange of information by openly sharing all reference materials. Although the dissemination of the information might not always resolve doubt or eliminate the concern of the end user, it will allow for more informed decisionmaking based on likely benefits, risks, and personal and social values. Unless we address the public's concerns, the benefits that biotechnology has to offer will never be realized.

Biotechnology is an evolving field. Although numerous food applications have been envisioned, it is clear that many face technical obstacles that remain to be overcome before they are ready for commercialization.

CHAPTER 14

A POSITION ON MARKETING

@

As the food service industry changes and evolves, the marketing and sales end of our business, whether commercial or noncommercial, is increasingly confronted with new, corresponding needs. It is our job as food service professionals to manage those changes effectively and productively.

One of the most fundamental management responsibilities is often ignored—that of staying in touch with the customer and satisfying his and her every need and request. Ordinary service meets the customer's needs, whereas extraordinary service anticipates them. In the food service industry, customers are at the center of everything we do everyday, or they should be! Therefore, food service requires an unconditional commitment from all those involved, if an operation is to be truly successful.

MARKETING TOOLS

Marketing a food service operation takes careful planning from the beginning. Marketing is really everything we do to promote our business. It starts with the name, and runs through every aspect of a good business plan. Marketing should be kept in mind when defining the product, or service, that you offer. The packaging and color of your product, the location of your facility, the advertising and public relations, the sales training, the sales presentation of your service or product, and the procedures to accommodate inquiries about your business are all facets of your total marketing effort.

If a business is going to be successful, we as managers must look at every detail as a potential marketing tool. Business cards for everyone! That's right, everyone! Business cards will build a sense of employee ownership, and increase pride among the staff in their individual jobs. Be sure that business cards make the most of the opportunity to tell the person who receives it as much as possible about your business. Every member of the team can be a salesperson for your company when armed with their own business card. Chances are your staff is diverse and encompasses a multitude of special interests. Do not rule out the potential of newfound markets within your own workforce.

Stationery is another great opportunity for getting your message out. Take time to think of ways you can make your stationery deliver more than the words printed on it. Let stationery help create your image and give impact to your message.

Matchbooks, napkins and beverage napkins, logo wear, packaging, your phone number, a signature item—no detail of your business is too small to play a role in the total marketing game.

Great ideas are nothing without creative marketing. After all, who is going to buy your product or service if they have never heard of it?

The most obvious first step is to decide who is your current customer. Do this analysis in great detail. Then look at who *could* be your customer, and why they are not. Be brutally honest with this step. Think "out of the box" and come up with the customer who is not currently yours, but should be yours.

By now you should feel your mind beginning to stretch and the excitement building for your "about to be born" new marketing ideas. Especially during this process, be sure to keep a journal or notepad with you at all times to write down your own brilliant ideas as they come to you on the freeway or in an elevator. Also, write down the brilliant idea you see someone else using that you can revise, rework, refine, and reuse to work in your specific operation.

Remember, not all great ideas have to be original. Be very analytical of what other successful businesses are doing. A great idea for your business can be inspired by something another business, totally unrelated to food service, is using successfully.

Positioning is probably the most critical key to marketing success. If you do not appeal to the right person, the one who will buy your product, all your efforts will be wasted. You must fully understand your business, your goals, your strengths and weaknesses, your competitor's strengths and weaknesses, and the needs of your target market. Ask yourself, what value does your product or service deliver? Who will buy your product or service, and does it deliver a real benefit? When you are comfortable with the answers to all these questions you will have a clearer picture of your market position. How you position your marketing efforts will play a large part in your success.

Once you realize that marketing encompasses all areas of your business, and is not limited to advertising, you will realize the real power of creative marketing.

The forms creative marketing will take are very different from one segment of the food service industry to the next. Food service in the health-care industry must first overcome the stereotypical idea that one would not eat the food served there by choice. Some hospitals are combating this label by rethinking and refocusing their food service program. By hiring professional chefs to lead the culinary staff, and focusing their menus on delicious foods that are well prepared and artfully presented, a few hospitals are differentiating themselves from the status quo. The more "creative thinking" hospital food service teams see patients and hospital staff as potential customers, and have developed programs to sell to them directly.

One such program offers complete, delicious, and ready-to-eat meals for take-out. This same food service team opened an area in the hospital where the staff could buy high-quality convenience foods in individual-size servings for personal use. Another idea was to market the food service program by offering interesting, healthful, and consumer-friendly cooking classes that are promoted through the local media. The case study details the possibilities for such a program.

@

CASE STUDY
CULINARY ENHANCEMENT
PROGRAMS

Culinary Enhancement Programs can be a very effective marketing tool in the noncommercial food service arena where the environment is traditionally not associated with the glamor of commercial food service.

When searching for a specialization in the culinary arts, it is human nature to look beyond an obvious, and for some, very fulfilling choice. With a reported $11 billion slice of the national food service industry and some 6,000 kitchens, health-care institutions are in need of well-trained culinarians, and very few have such personnel.

Working in the health-care area today has many benefits. In addition to the opportunity to be creative, a culinarian will find good hours, good pay, efficient equipment, and the opportunity to train other culinarians, build relationships with customers, develop other revenue sources such as outside catering and gourmet take-out, and design new menu concepts and recipes.

Our experience in health-care cooking at Zale Lipshy University Hospital in Dallas has been surprising and unexpectedly inspiring. This hospital is a private, 152-bed referral hospital, and we are faced with the daunting task of not only overseeing the food service for internal customers, but also of servicing the cafeteria, which serves 800 meals a day to faculty members, staff, and visitors. We also offer a catering service, which provides special lunches, receptions, and formal dinners for development, physicians, and hospital board functions. Patients take on a whole new light when you view them as *customers* rather than a captive audience.

Zale Lipshy is a high-customer-service hospital. We call it "high-tech, high-touch." Trying to meet the individual needs of each customer is very challenging.

There were a lot of expectations for the food service when the hospital opened in 1989. In general, people are more educated about food, and many of the customers had very high expectations. Today people do not accept unappealing food, even in an institution setting. They want food to be familiar, tasteful, and well presented.

The food production staff was determined to take the "bland" out of hospital food. We believe that we have always had good food service for a hospital, but our quality and presentation were not always consistent. We wanted to bring first-class hotel concepts of fine dining to our hospital, so we initiated the Culinary Enhancement Program.

@

The initial goal in a Culinary Enhancement Program is to evaluate the production staff and determine how the kitchen is being run. Basically it is a back-to-basics approach.

The next step is to hire a well-rounded production manager or executive chef to head the culinary division. The chef is provided the same opportunities that come with working in any other sector of the food service industry.

Working with a dietitian can open a chef's mind to more possibilities. It invites one to experiment with other flavor enhancers rather than simply adding fats to make a recipe delicious. It also challenges one to make a healthy dish taste even better.

Culinarians can help change hospital food by influencing purchasing decisions and introducing breads, fresh produce, less convenience foods, and more fresh meats.

Having a strong culinarian as the executive chef helps to open the door in recruiting other qualified culinarians. When training staff, a very effective tool is to expose your culinarians to other dining establishments, places where some of their guests and customers might regularly dine. This process will simultaneously help to increase the self-esteem of staff members and make them more proud of their professional environment.

Having an executive chef oversee the hospital kitchen has numerous benefits. Previously, food service directors were more involved in the actual preparation of the food, as well as planning all in-house, cafeteria, and catering menus.

Today it is the chef who supervises the food preparation. He or she also does a great deal of menu planning, creating daily specials, and catering for special functions, all approached from a nutrition-conscious standpoint.

Traditionally, hospital kitchens prepared everything from "scratch"; most even had their own bakeries. But as recently as a decade ago, hospital cooking became more about reheating and serving food than about cooking it. Because of a lack of trained staff and the sheer volume of meals that need to be prepared, hospitals buy lots of prepared products, big pans of lasagna, instant mashed potatoes, preformed meat patties, and canned and frozen vegetables, and reheat them.

A Culinary Enhancement Program can show an operation how to improve cooking techniques and include more fresh products into the operation. Some things cannot be changed about hospital food, especially at a surgical hospital. Food must be therapeutic. Working with a chef can prove that food can be healthy *and* flavorful. For example, once an operation begins using fresh herbs and fresh juices as seasonings, a whole new approach to cooking develops.

Most operations today already use canola or olive oil instead of the traditional cooking oils. However, small and simple improvements can be made, such as preparing mashed potatoes from scratch and using fresh, seasonal vegetables, both of which will make a major difference in quality. We have learned that the chef and dietitian can complement each other by creating delicious recipes that are low in fat and low in salt. Also, by the addition of fresh herbs, a simple dish can be transformed into a more interesting flavor profile.

Not only is retraining necessary with the kitchen and service staff, but we must also introduce our customers to the concept of healthy eating. We must establish "buy in" from the customers and staff, so that they will be positive and accept a new approach to food preparation.

Many customers still like traditional menu items. For instance, an old-fashioned chicken potpie with top and bottom crusts and a white sauce has traditionally been a bestseller in the hospital cafeteria. To change that formula to chicken and fresh vegetable pie in a natural broth with an herb crust on top takes getting the word out first!

It is definitely an educational process, but the job of the nutrition services department in a hospital is taking care of customer meals. It is easier to accomplish this goal by providing delicious, appealing meals that customers want to eat. Food is an important part of treatment in a hospital, because it brings back a customer's appetite, nourishes them, and allows them to return home sooner. It can also educate the customer about correct food choices and food preparation.

Working with the concept that "all foods can fit" into a healthy diet allows the food service professional more creative freedom. This means including "comfort" foods on the menu, such as a regional Texas specialty like chicken-fried steak. The use of monounsaturated oil, leaner, smaller cuts of meat, and less breading are necessary adjustments in its preparation. The most important consideration is to provide added comfort while tastefully and healthfully serving your customers, visitors, and guests.

Many major causes of illness are diet-related. While a customer is hospitalized, a dietitian has a unique opportunity to assist the individual in modifying his or her eating behavior. For example, an individual who has experienced a heart attack may need to learn to eat differently at home. If the first experience with low-fat cooking is bland and boring, a person will be less likely to continue with the modified eating behavior.

Many hospitals believe they cannot afford a Culinary Enhancement Program. However, in our experience a hospital cannot afford not to have such a program.

For one thing, prepared food can be more expensive than fresh ingredients. You are paying for someone else to do the preparation work. With a culinarian guiding the kitchen, we do the preparation ourselves and, as a result, have a better product. Also, a professional culinarian knows how to eliminate waste.

For a food service operation to spend time on food preparation and service and end up with a mediocre food product is not a good marketing strategy. Rather, the focus should be on a long-term plan to enhance the food service program.

Relationships between chefs and dietitians have often been misunderstood. However, creating a positive partnership between dietitians and chefs will offer them the unique opportunity to have a positive impact and lasting effect on the eating behavior in America.

Health-care food service facilities should participate in being an active externship site for culinary students, as well as dietetic students from health science schools. Energetically seek to build early alliances between culinary students and dietetic students as they work side by side in your department.

At Zale Lipshy, we continuously collaborate on the technique that highlights the approach to healthy cooking, eliminating the need to calculate the fat and calorie content of every morsel of food. Our philosophy is based on good food, simply prepared, which has the added bonus that it is healthy for you.

Our approach is to use real foods, small amounts of rich ingredients, and creative cooking techniques that minimize calories yet maximize flavor. The result is a marriage of delicious food and good nutrition.

Another result of our collaboration at Zale Lipshy has been a series of Saturday cooking classes at the hospital, open to both in-house individuals and the public, featuring well-known local chefs. The chefs send their recipes to the nutrition services director and her staff, who evaluate them in terms of calories, fat, and sodium. They then make suggestions to the chef on how to modify the recipes to make them applicable to the department concept. It is a continuous learning process for chefs and dietitians alike. Working together they can maintain the taste of a recipe while making it more healthful.

These cooking classes are part of our mission to teach the public about healthful cooking. As a health-care institution, we should serve as an example of how to eat right without having to count every calorie and fat gram. Research has shown that "diets" don't work; people need to be eating healthful foods, and we believe that through cooking classes and a user-friendly cookbook we are making a meaningful step in that direction.

The process of changing food service in an institutional setting may take many years, to train the staff, to change the way food is purchased and from whom it is purchased, but in the end we believe it is well worth the effort.

Americans have a newfound appetite for good taste and good nutrition. Health-care institutions should be setting an example of how the art of cooking and the science of nutrition can merge into a new delicious and satisfying way to eat.

GETTING THE MESSAGE ACROSS

How one chooses to get the message across is just as important as the message itself. While low-fat, healthful food may have a negative connotation, we have chosen to put a positive spin on the high flavor, creative selection, and quality ingredients that make up our menus. With a commitment to using only select and freshest available products, we do not rely on nutritional labeling or symbols to convey the message that our food is "nutritious and delicious." Instead, we combine innovative recipes with our "Top 10 Things We Do to Make Our Food Nutritious and Delicious." This strategy enables us to educate our customers about the healthfulness of our meals.

1. We provide fresh salads daily and offer only fat-free or reduced-fat/calorie salad dressings and mayonnaise.

2. Seasonal fresh fruits are available at each meal, and we select only those with the freshest flavor.

3. We find the leanest cuts of meat on the market. Our kitchen utilizes contemporary cooking techniques such as roasting, dry sautéing, grilling, poaching, stewing, and stir-frying.

4. We enhance meat flavors naturally by pairing with and utilizing salsas, vegetable slaws, fruit purees, and vegetable and/or bean ragouts. By complementing the meat without significantly increasing the fat or calories, we are able to enhance both the flavor as well as the texture of our recipes.

5. We serve meats or proteins in 3 to 4-ounce portions. The illusion of a larger portion of protein is created when it is paired with vegetables and starches. For example, we are able to extend entrees by adding such items as risotto, paella, and white bean ragout.

6. Our kitchen utilizes monounsaturated fats such as olive and canola oil. Oils are chosen with flavor in mind. We select oils that will provide the most flavor in the smallest amount possible. Fats are used only as a condiment.

7. Our chefs enhance vegetable flavor by using fresh herbs, stocks, pungents, and aromatics. The color and flavor of fresh vegetables shouldn't be masked by heavy sauces and creams.

8. Our culinary team routinely utilizes low-fat or nonfat dairy products. In most instances a low-fat dairy product can easily be substituted for a high-fat product. For example, a low-fat buttermilk product is used for our in-house mashed potatoes. In addition, we add flavor enhancers such as roasted garlic, fresh herbs, and caramelized onions. Butter is only added if it is needed to help impact the flavor.

9. Our menu frequently includes plant-based entrees, such as pasta primavera, fresh tomato basil pizza, and cheese enchiladas with roasted vegetable chili. These items continue to impress our vegetarian and nonvegetarian customers alike.

10. We stress variety at every point, from our entrees to our cooking techniques. We offer appetizing, comforting, healthful foods that are seasonal and that add interest to the plate.

One thing is clear, in today's competitive market all areas of food service must begin to think more creatively and market themselves more effectively.

In some segments of food service, such as the hotel industry, catering is considered the nucleus and catalyst of the food and beverage operation, particularly with regard to revenue and profit producing capabilities. This makes the marketing of your catering services critical to the overall financial success of your business.

Catering is exposed to a market that is driven by a consumer who demands top quality, value, and convenience, and all for a reasonable price. Catering and providing high-quality special events that are executed to the last detail are a top priority of today's demanding customer. Accomplishing this consistently is in itself a 24-hour commitment and responsibility of the catering professional.

As in the hotel industry, the chef in hospital food service is an integral part of the overall catering and marketing plan. The property that knows how to market its product and its key players could gain the competitive edge over its competitors.

Today, catered events can take many forms, such as

- Conventions and business meetings
- Special holiday parties (Easter, Christmas, Passover)
- Special-occasion events (weddings, engagements, bar mitzvahs, bat mitzvahs, christenings, anniversaries, groundbreakings, grand openings, housewarming parties, etc.)
- Chef's table luncheons and dinners
- Off-site events (country picnics, barbecue events, yacht parties, etc.)
- Corporate breakfasts, lunches, and dinners
- Promotional events (social, corporate, community, etc.)
- Charity events (ballet, museum, zoo, medical causes, etc.)
- Birthday and tea parties
- Theme parties (Gatsby, Treasure Island, Halloween, Indonesian, Polynesian, Star Trek, Cuisines of the World, Bountiful Harvest, '50s Bebop, casino parties, etc.)

Whether preparing a meal for 10 or 2,000 guests, every catered event should be a celebration on its own, with pronounced quality ingredients, passionately prepared and served in style and elegance. The chef always plays a key role in the success of any special event, and in the case of large events the chef will be the pivotal point for the support departments. The other key players must know the "game plan" before the event and execute their part as if building a foundation for the work of the culinary department. This includes the important ingredients provided by the steward, house persons, banquet, beverage, and housekeeping departments. The catering coordinator must communicate the details and expectations of the guests to all other key members of the team, with 100 percent accuracy. For example, the set-up of the furniture and equipment is crucial to the success of the overall event and must happen in a timely manner, allowing the culinary department enough time to complete their part for the event and allow a safety net of time to correct any unexpected difficulties (e.g., a broken ice carving, faulty extension cords, stained linens that must be replaced, etc.).

Coordination and communication are the keys to a successful catered event. Much like a symphony, each department has its part to play and all the parts must work in harmony to ensure the success of the entire event.

Successful banquets and special events depend on advance planning and organization with the complete involvement of many professionals. Once the client decides on the specific occasion and date, a menu and theme are developed and finalized.

Give close consideration to the following when planning a menu:

1. Offer a good variety of choices that are interesting and diverse, yet sensible to the theme or occasion. Build the menu to fit the occasion.

2. Consider the costs; is there an established budget?

3. Take into account the time of year and seasonal temperatures. Focus on seasonality of the food.

4. Introduce dishes that add excitement from the food product as well as from the preparation standpoint.

5. Offer appropriate progression of the different courses.

6. Consider who will be attending the event. Will there be children, or guests with special dietary requirements?

7. Understand special requests of your client regarding specific tastes, likes, and dislikes.

8. Remember that the high point of the menu is always the main course.

9. Build a balanced menu, with enough diversity throughout to hold the guests' interest.

10. Decide on the format, i.e., buffet or seated service, table cookery or classical silver service, plated service or preset service.

11. Review the equipment needs prior to finalizing your menu: tables, chairs, china, silver, props, decor, flowers, printed menus, beverage needs, carving stations, electrical needs, ventilation restrictions, audio and visual requirements, etc.

Special theme events are always popular, particularly with convention and social event planners. Every property has a unique challenge when it comes to creating interesting theme parties. Usually one can create a theme party that is linked to the location, for example, Hawaii for luaus, Texas for barbecues, New England for clambakes and boiled dinners, and so on. But what if you are in a location where more imagination is required or you have a client that wants something truly unusual? All major cities of the United States are fortunate to have rental companies and theme party planning services that, for a fee, will provide the ideas and props necessary for a one-of-a-kind event. The chef can then complement the idea selected by the client with the props, entertainment, costumes, and overall menu theme. Also, equipment such as extra buffet set-up items, china, silver, and so on, can be rented and added to the price of the catered event.

However, the property with a creative and committed team can create its own array of unique party ideas complete with table props, backdrops or scenes for decoration, costumes for the servers, and options for entertainment. In a property that generates a great deal of banquet business this can be very profitable.

The catering team that wants to develop interest and excitement in their services can create a theme unique to their individual property. Through the development of a photo album that will be used to sell future clients on the idea, promoting the theme through the local media, and using the excitement of each event to attract new convention and social business, a catering department can develop a new identity and dramatically increase its revenues.

Keep in mind that there is more to be gained than producing a wonderful party, there is a reputation to be built as an enterprise that creates unique events for all occasions!

To implement this plan, the key players will first brainstorm to gather theme ideas. Assign one, two, or more people to develop each idea down to the last detail. Gather the start-up costs for the props and other equipment needed. Initially there will be start-up costs, but these will be quickly recovered provided the theme is correctly developed and marketed.

Select the best ideas, the ones that are most likely to sell and attract new business. Then decide on a "one-time" cost to create this party for a particular event, keeping in mind that this event, if executed with care and attention to detail, can be sold over and over. Once the initial theme costs are recovered, through renting this theme for catered events, a profit will be generated. Now is the time for the next great idea that came out of your brainstorming session to become an additional theme offering!

In time some of the props will need to be replaced or refreshed, but with repeated rentals the necessary capital will be available. One must also consider storage and security of the theme equipment since it will be a valuable commodity. An enterprise can become known for its wonderful theme events if they are well conceived, professionally executed to the last detail, and consistently promoted.

Some of the best theme parties are the ones that cross many lines of age, culture, and so on. A favorite is the '50s Bebop Party, complete with servers in poodle skirts or James Dean–style attire. Decorations can include a vintage car on the dance floor (or backdrop look-alike), which can also be used as a backdrop for the photographer. The photographer can create party favors by taking Polaroid photos of the guests with a Marilyn or Elvis look-alike. Of course the theme will require a great band or DJ for entertainment. Food offerings should include "period" items such as mini-cheeseburgers and fountain drinks. The area can be further decorated with backdrops reminiscent of the drive-in restaurants with servers on roller skates, or a drive-in movie theater setting complete with a movie playing and a popcorn stand!

These are just a few ideas, however it is most important to select a theme that the players support. A good theme must be fully developed with unique ideas and abundant details that will make it a truly successful, desirable, and profitable theme!

A successful catering operation will depend heavily on a positive relationship built between the community and the event coordinators. An effective public relations program will provide the groundwork for the catering service and enable the caterer to become, or be perceived as, a central part of the community social life and business activities. The public relations department should keep in mind all the targeted audiences of an operation, not only addressing the social functions but also taking a keen interest in the conventions, seminars, markets, and the corporate arena.

The catering operation should have a clearly defined operating philosophy. The food and beverage products and services offered should be in line with today's trends and be consistent in their promotion and execution. Once the products and services are clearly identified and everyone knows what needs to be accomplished, the marketing strategy on how to reach the markets can be developed. Only then can the team go forward to be a competitor in the marketplace of catered events!

Catered events for the repeat customer are always a challenge. Theme parties geared around seasonal food items make excellent points of difference, with quality and freshness showcased, and offer the customer an alternative menu choice which many guests today expect. Focus on a bountiful harvest with, perhaps, asparagus, wild mushrooms, tomatoes, beans, and fruits as the featured centerpiece items of a menu. A chef can create unexpected and interesting items with a fresh, contemporary approach that perhaps the guests have never experienced before, and still be culturally sensitive to the traditional fare.

Overall, catering is an area where a love for diversity and an expanded imagination come in very handy!

CHEF'S NOTES

☙ *When ordering a meal in a restaurant, look for calorie- and fat-reducing terminology such as roasted, baked, braised, grilled, steamed, or poached. Ask for au jus, sauces, butter, and salad dressings on the side. Most restaurants over-sauce and over-dress food items, particularly salads. Having the sauces and dressings on the side will give you real control over the fat and calories.*

◎ *Many soups, most breads, all fresh fruits and vegetables, and definitely water are low in calories and fat and will help make you feel satisfied. Enjoy and take time to appreciate everything you eat; savor the flavors rather than coveting the quantities. Identify and relish the textures, colors, aromas, and preparation of your meals.*

◎ *When selecting take-out foods, remember that many restaurants and home meal replacement markets offer simple grilled foods, such as chicken or fish, with accompaniments of salsas, chutneys, fresh citrus relishes, chilies and spice blends, baked potatoes, steamed vegetables, and fresh salads. Order an extra portion of your favorite pasta, poultry, or soup when choosing take-out, and freeze for later consumption.*

◎ *Have crunchies ready and waiting, such as fresh vegetable sticks or fruit; plain yogurt seasoned with cucumbers, onions, and dill; cold pasta; pretzels; or baked tortilla chips for an afternoon snack.*

◎ *When purchasing frozen meals, seek out high-quality, conventional oven as well as microwavable, healthful meal options, but be aware that these can contain excessive amounts of sodium, processed foods, and even fat.*

◎ *Incorporate a Mediterranean flair into your lifestyle. Eat like the French, walk like the Portuguese, drink like the Spanish, and moderate like the Moroccans!*

APPENDIX A

CONVERSIONS
AND EQUIVALENCIES

WEIGHT CONVERSION

Grams		Ounces	Kilos		Pounds
10g	=	⅓ oz	0.5 kg	=	1.2 lb
20g	=	⅔ oz	1.5 kg	=	3.3 lb
40g	=	1½ oz	2 kg	=	4.4 lb
100g	=	3½ oz	2.5 kg	=	5.5 lb
150g	=	5⅓ oz	3 kg	=	6.6 lb
200g	=	7 oz	3.5 kg	=	7.7 lb
250g	=	8¾ oz	5 kg	=	11 lb
300g	=	10½ oz	7.5 kg	=	16.5 lb
400g	=	14 oz	10 kg	=	22 lb
454g	=	16 oz (1lb)	12.5 kg	=	27.5 lb
500g	=	17½ oz	25 kg	=	55 lb
1000g	=	1 kilo	32 kg	=	70.5 lb

VOLUME CONVERSION

Millilitres		Fluid Ounces	Litres		Pounds		Gallons
15 ml	=	½ fl oz	1 l	=	1 pt 14½ fl oz	=	0.22 gal
150 ml	=	5 fl oz	1.5 l	=	2 pt 12 fl oz	=	0.33 gal
200 ml	=	7 fl oz	2 l	=	3 pt 9 fl oz	=	0.44 gal
250 ml	=	8½ fl oz	2.5 l	=	4 pt 6 fl oz	=	0.55 gal
330 ml	=	11½ fl oz	4 l	=	6 pt 18 fl oz	=	0.88 gal
500 ml	=	17 fl oz	5 l	=	8 pt 16 fl oz	=	1.1 gal
710 ml	=	24½ fl oz	10 l	=	16 pt 32 fl oz	=	2.2 gal
750 ml	=	26 fl oz	20 l	=	32 pt 64 fl oz	=	4.4 gal
1 l	=	34½ fl oz					
			2.6 kg			=	½ gal
1000 ml	=	100 cl	5 kg			=	1 gal

EQUIVALENCIES (ENGLISH)

pinch or dash	less than ⅛ tsp.	
3 tsp.	1 Tbsp.	½ fl. oz.
¼ cup	4 Tbsp.	2 fl. oz.
½ cup	8 Tbsp.	4 fl. oz.
1 cup	16 Tbsp.	8 fl. oz.

TIN SIZES APPROX.

Size		Ounces
A1	=	10 oz
A1T	=	16 oz
A2	=	20 oz
A2½	=	28 oz - KC1
A5	=	43 oz
A6	=	6 lb 12 oz - KC3
A10	=	6 lb to 7½ lb
KC5	=	10 lb

TEMPERATURE CONVERSION

°F to °C: (°F − 32) ÷ 9 × 5 = °C
°C to °F: (°C × 1.8) + 32 = °F
Examples: 212°F − 32 = 180 ÷ 9 = 20 × 5 = 100°C
100°C × 1.8 = 180 + 32 = 212°F

OVEN TEMPERATURES

Fahrenheit		Celsius
250°F	Moderately Warm	125°C
300°F	Warm	150°C
350°F	Medium Hot	175°C
400°F	Hot	205°C
450°F	Very Hot	230°C

OTHER USEFUL TEMPERATURES

°C	°F	
−18	0	storage of frozen goods
0	32	freezing point
1	33.8	storage of fresh fish
2	35.6	storage of fresh meat and poultry
5	41	normal refrigeration temperature
7	44.6	
8	46	storage of fresh vegetables
10	50	
37	98.4	proofing temperature for yeast goods; holding Hollandaise Sauce.
76	168.8	coagulation of eggs; making Sauce Anglaise
93	199.4	poaching temperature
100	212	boiling temperature
160	320	sugar for glazing
180	356	caramelization of sugar

FOODS OF THE SEASONS

@

January	Apples	Cauliflower	Potatoes
	Arugula	Celery	Spinach
	Avocados	Citrus Fruits	Sweet Potatoes
	Beets	Lettuce	Tangerines
	Cabbage	Peas	Winter Pears
February	Apples	Beets	Grapefruit
	Artichokes	Broccoli	Lemons
	Arugula	Broccoli Raab	Lettuce
	Asparagus	Cauliflower	Naval Oranges
	Avocados	Celery	Potatoes
March	Apples	Broccoli	Citrus Fruits
	Artichokes	Cabbage	Fennel
	Asparagus	Carrots	Leeks
	Avocados	Cauliflower	Potatoes
	Beets	Celery	Spinach
April	Apples	Broccoli	Fennel
	Artichokes	Carrots	Lettuce
	Asparagus	Cauliflower	Pears
	Avocados	Chard	Peas
	Beets	Citrus Fruits	Spinach
May	Asparagus	Cherries	Peas
	Avocados	Citrus Fruits	Potatoes
	Beets	Lettuce	Spinach
	Cabbage	Mâche (Corn Salad)	Strawberries
	Carrots	Mangoes	Sweet Corn
	Celery	Onions	Tomatoes
June	Apricots	Cucumbers	Peppers
	Asparagus	Figs	Plums
	Avocados	Honeydew Melon	Potatoes
	Bush Berries	Lemons	Snap Beans
	Cantaloupe	Lettuce	Snap Peas
	Carrots	Nectarines	Strawberries
	Celery	Onions	Summer Squash
	Cherries	Oranges	Tomatoes
	Corn	Peaches	Watermelon
July	Apricots	Cabbage	Celery
	Avocados	Cantaloupe	Cucumbers
	Bush Berries	Carrots	Eggplant

	Figs	Musk Melon	Potatoes
	Grapefruit	Nectarines	Strawberries
	Green Beans	Okra	Summer Squash
	Green Lima Beans	Onions	Sweet Corn
	Honeydew Melon	Peaches	Sweet Corn
	Kohlrabi	Pears	Tomatoes
	Lemons	Peppers	Valencia Oranges
	Lettuce	Plums	Watermelon
			Zucchini

August

Avocados	Figs	Pears
Boysenberries	Grapes	Peppers
Cabbage	Honeydew Melon	Persian Melon
Cantaloupe	Lettuce	Plums
Celery	Lima Beans	Potatoes
Chili Peppers	Mangoes	Snap Beans
Citrus Fruits	Okra	Summer Squash
Cucumbers	Onions	Sweet Corn
Eggplant	Oranges	Tomatoes
Escarole	Peaches	Watermelon

September

Apples	Grapes	Pears
Bokchoy	Green Beans	Peas
Cabbage	Green Lima Beans	Peppers
Cantaloupe	Honeydew Melon	Plums
Citrus Fruits	Lettuce	Prunes
Corn	Onions	Squash
Cucumbers	Oranges	Tomatoes
Eggplant	Parsnips	Turnips
Figs	Peaches	Wild Mushrooms

October

Apples	Figs	Persimmons
Broccoli	Golden Beets	Pomegranates
Brussels Sprouts	Grapes	Potatoes
Cabbage	Hard Squash	Snap Beans
Carrots	Lemons	Sweet Corn
Cranberries	Lima Beans	Sweet Potatoes
Cucumbers	Okra	Tomatoes
Dates	Pears	Valencia Oranges
Eggplant	Peas	Wild Mushrooms
Fennel	Peppers	Winter Squash

November

Almonds	Celery	Peas
Apples	Dates	Peppers
Avocados	Eggplant	Persimmons
Broccoli	Gourds	Potatoes
Brussels Sprouts	Grapes	Sweet Corn
Cabbage	Green Beans	Sweet Potatoes
Carrots	Lemons	Walnuts
Cauliflower	Lettuce	Winter Squash

December	Almonds	Celery	Lemons
	Apples	Chayote	Naval Oranges
	Arugula	Dates	Red Beets
	Avocados	Frissee (curly	Spinach
	Broccoli	French endive)	Sweet Potatoes
	Brussels Sprouts	Grapefruits	Walnuts
	Carrots	Kumquats	Winter Squash
	Cauliflower		

SPEED SCRATCH SAUCES AND STOCKS

@

Demi-Glacé Gold®
Classic French Demiglacé
Demi-Glace Gold® is reduced four times from the classic and allows you to make elegant finished French sauces quickly and easily.

Nutrition per 2 tsp serving (¼ cup/11 gm prepared): Calories 35, protein 3 gm, fat 1.5 gm, carbohydrates 2 gm, sodium 230 mg

Glacé de Viande Gold®
Classic French Brown Stock Reduced to Glacé
Glace de viande for use in all fine sauces or to enhance the flavor of a variety of stocks, sautés, roasted items, etc.

Nutrition per 2 tsp. serving (¼ cup/11 gm prepared): Calories 35, protein 3 gm, fat 1.5 gm, carbohydrates 2 gm, sodium 230 mg

Glacé de Poulet Gold®
Classic French Roasted Chicken Stock Reduced to Glacé
A reduction of French chicken stock with deep, rich, roasted color and syrupy consistency. Glacé de Poulet Gold® provides pure intense flavor to enhance finished sauces.

Nutrition per 2 tsp. serving (1 cup/11 gm prepared): Calories 15, protein 2 gm, fat 0 gm, carbohydrates 1 gm, sodium 330 mg

Jus de Poulet Lié Gold®
Classic French Chicken Stock Bound with Starch
Jus de Poulet Lié Gold® allows you to make all the classical lighter-colored chicken-based sauces.

Nutrition per 2 tsp. serving (1 cup/11 gm prepared): Calories 20, protein 2 gm, fat 0 gm, carbohydrates 3 gm, sodium 270 mg

Fond de Poulet Gold®
Classic French White Chicken Stock
Fond de Poulet Gold® is a pure chicken stock for use in all basic preparations within a commercial kitchen.

Nutrition per 1 tsp. serving (1 cup/6 gm prepared): Calories 10, protein 1 gm, fat 0 gm, carbohydrates 1 gm, sodium 170 mg

Veggie-Glacé Gold®
Vegetarian (Meatless) Demiglacé Substitute
Veggie-Glace Gold® is excellent for use in light cooking or vegetarian entrees. It is a "vegan" product.

Nutrition per 2 tsp. serving (¼ cup/11 gm prepared): Calories 15, protein 0 gm, fat 0 gm, carbohydrates 3 gm, sodium 75 mg

All the above natural classic French sauce bases are produced by More Than Gourmet™, and are made with consistency of quality from the finest and freshest ingredients. Nutrition Facts for More Than Gourmet™ products were provided by the manufacturer.

Demi-Glacé Gold

Nutrition Facts
Serving Size 2 tsp (11 g/¼ cup prepared)
Servings Per Container about 40

Amount Per Serving

Calories 35   Calories from Fat 15

	% Daily Value*
Total Fat 1.5 g	2%
Saturated Fat 0.5 g	3%
Sodium 230 mg	10%
Total Carbohydrate 2g	1%
Protein 3g	

Not a significant source of Cholesterol, Dietary Fiber, Sugars, Vitamin A, Vitamin C, Calcium and Iron.

*Percent Daily Values are based on a 2,000 calorie diet.

Fond de Poulet Gold

Nutrition Facts
Serving Size 1 tsp (6 g/1 cup prepared)
Servings Per Container about 112

Amount Per Serving

Calories 10

	% Daily Value*
Total Fat 0 g	0%
Sodium 170 mg	7%
Total Carbohydrate 1g	0%
Protein 1g	

Not a significant source of Calories from Fat, Saturated Fat, Cholesterol, Dietary Fiber, Sugars, Vitamin A, Vitamin C, Calcium and Iron.

*Percent Daily Values are based on a 2,000 calorie diet.

Jus de Poulet Lié Gold

Nutrition Facts

Serving Size 2 tsp (11 g/¼ cup prepared)
Servings Per Container about 40

Amount Per Serving

Calories 20

	% Daily Value*
Total Fat 0 g	0%
Sodium 270 mg	11%
Total Carbohydrate 3g	1%
Sugars 1g	
Protein 2g	

Not a significant source of Calories from Fat, Saturated Fat, Cholesterol, Dietary Fiber, Vitamin A, Vitamin C, Calcium and Iron.

*Percent Daily Values are based on a 2,000 calorie diet.

Glacé de Poulet Gold

Nutrition Facts

Serving Size 2 tsp (11 g/1 cup prepared)
Servings Per Container 42

Amount Per Serving

Calories 15

	% Daily Value*
Total Fat 0 g	0%
Sodium 330 mg	14%
Total Carbohydrate 1g	0%
Sugars 1g	
Protein 2g	

Not a significant source of Calories from Fat, Saturated Fat, Cholesterol, Dietary Fiber, Vitamin A, Vitamin C, Calcium and Iron.

*Percent Daily Values are based on a 2,000 calorie diet.

Veggie-Glacé Gold

Nutrition Facts

Serving Size 2 tsp (11 g/¼ cup prepared)
Servings Per Container about 40

Amount Per Serving

Calories 15

	% Daily Value*
Total Fat 0 g	0%
Sodium 75 mg	3%
Total Carbohydrate 3g	1%
Sugars 1g	
Protein 0g	

Not a significant source of Calories from Fat, Saturated Fat, Cholesterol, Dietary Fiber, Vitamin A, Vitamin C, Calcium and Iron.

*Percent Daily Values are based on a 2,000 calorie diet.

DIET MANAGEMENT TABLES

SOFT/TRANSITIONAL DIET

Food Group	Foods Allowed	Foods to Avoid
Beverages	All.	
Breads/Cereals/ Grains/Starchy Vegetables	Cooked or ready-to-eat cereal; potatoes; rice; pasta; white, refined wheat, light rye bread or rolls; graham crackers.	
Desserts/Sweets	Gelatin, sherbet, ice cream without nuts, custard, pudding, cake, cookies without nuts or coconut, fruit ice, popsicle; sugar, honey, jelly, candy without nuts or coconut; flavorings.	Nuts, coconut.
Fats	Butter, margarine, non-dairy creamers, cream, oil, gravy, crisp bacon, salad dressing	
Fruits	Cooked or canned fruit, soft fresh fruit, fruit juice.	Raw fruits except bananas.
Meat/Poultry/ Fish/Egg/ Cheese	Moist, tender meat, fish, or poultry; eggs; cottage cheese; mild flavored cheese; creamy peanut butter; soft casseroles.	
Milk/Yogurt	Milk, milk beverages, yogurt without seeds or nuts.	
Miscellaneous/ Condiments	Seasonings, mildly seasoned condiments, cocoa.	
Soups/ Combination Foods	Broth, bouillon, cream soup, mildly seasoned soup.	
Vegetables	Soft, cooked vegetables; lettuce and tomatoes; limit gas-forming vegetables and whole kernel corn.	Raw vegetables except those listed.

MECHANICAL SOFT DIET

Food Group	Foods Allowed	Foods to Avoid
Beverages	All.	
Breads/Cereals/ Grains/Starchy Vegetables	White, refined wheat or light rye bread or rolls; graham crackers as tolerated; cooked or refined ready-to-eat cereals; potatoes; rice; pasta.	
Desserts/Sweets	Gelatin, sherbet, ice cream without nuts or fruit;, custard, pudding, fruit ice popsicles; sugar, honey, jelly, candy; flavorings.	Nuts, coconut.
Fats	Butter, margarine, non-dairy creamers, cream, oil, gravy, salad dressing	
Fruits	Cooked or canned fruit without seeds or skins, banana, citrus without membrane, fruit juice.	Raw fruits except for those listed.
Meat/Poultry/ Fish/Egg/ Cheese	Ground or finely diced, moist meats or poultry; flaked fish; eggs; cottage cheese; cheese; creamy peanut butter; soft casseroles.	
Milk/Yogurt	Milk, milk beverages, yogurt without seeds or nuts.	
Miscellaneous/ Condiments	Seasonings, condiments, cocoa.	
Soups/ Combination Foods	Broth, bouillon, cream or broth-based soup.	
Vegetables	Soft, cooked vegetables without hulls or tough skin (e.g., peas, corn); juice	Raw vegetables.

SAMPLE MENU

Breakfast	Lunch	Dinner
Orange juice	Cream of vegetable soup	Cream of pea soup
Cream of wheat	Ground pork with gravy	Ground chicken with gravy
Scrambled egg	Mashed potatoes	Buttered rice
1 Slice toast*	Buttered green beans	Buttered carrots
Margarine	Applesauce	Sherbet
Jelly	Bread*	Crackers*
Whole milk	Margarine	Whole milk
Coffee	Whole milk	Iced tea
Creamer	Iced tea	Sugar
Sugar	Sugar	
*as tolerated		

APPROXIMATE NUTRIENT CONTENT OF SAMPLE MENU

Kcal–2302
Carbohydrate–258 g
Protein–95 g
Fat–100 g

Thiamin–1.7 mg
Riboflavin–2.8 mg
Niacin–18 mg
Vitamin B_6–2.3 mg
Folate–256 mcg
Vitamin B_{12}–5.4 mcg

Vitamin A–16990 IU
Vitamin C–81 mg
Calcium–1522 mg
Iron–11.1 mg
Zinc–10.1 mg

PUREED DIET

Food Group	Foods Allowed	Foods to Avoid
Beverages	All.	
Breads/Cereals/ Grains/Starchy Vegetables	Refined cooked cereal; mashed potatoes.	
Desserts/Sweets	Gelatin, sherbet, ice cream; custard; pudding; fruit ice popsicles; sugar; honey; jelly; candy; flavorings.	Those containing seeds, nuts or fruit pieces.
Fats	Butter, margarine, non-dairy creamer, cream, oil, gravy, white sauce, whipped topping.	
Fruits	Pureed fruit or fruit juices.	Fresh or canned whole fruits.
Meat/Poultry/ Fish/Egg/ Cheese	Pureed meat, poultry or scrambled eggs; cheese used in a sauce, soup or blended casserole; blended cottage cheese.	Whole meat, poultry, fish.
Milk/Yogurt	Milk, milk beverages, yogurt without seeds, nuts or fruit pieces.	
Miscellaneous/ Condiments	Seasonings, condiments, cocoa.	
Soups/ Combination Foods	Broth, bouillon, or blenderized cream soups.	
Vegetables	Pureed vegetables or vegetable juices.	Raw or canned whole vegetables.

SAMPLE MENU

Breakfast	Lunch	Dinner
Orange juice	Cream of vegetable soup	Cream of pea soup
Cream of wheat	Pureed pork with gravy	Pureed chicken with gravy
Scrambled egg	Mashed potatoes	Mashed potatoes
1 slice Toast*	Pureed buttered green beans	Pureed buttered carrots
Margarine	Applesauce	Sherbet
Jelly	Bread*	Crackers*
Whole milk	Margarine	Whole milk
Coffee	Whole milk	Iced tea
Creamer	Iced tea	Sugar
Sugar	Sugar	
*as tolerated		

APPROXIMATE NUTRIENT CONTENT OF SAMPLE MENU

Kcal–1935
Carbohydrate–228 g
Protein–75 g
Fat–81 g

Thiamin–0.9 mg
Riboflavin–2.4 mg
Niacin–10 mg
Vitamin B_6–1.9 mg
Folate–208 mcg
Vitamin B_{12}–4.9 mcg

Vitamin A–13915 IU
Vitamin C–103 mg
Calcium–1386 mg
Iron–10.9 mg
Zinc–8.9 mg

Food Group	Foods Allowed	Foods to Avoid
Beverages	Carbonated beverages, fruit drinks, juices. Coffee, tea.	Beverages made with cream, ice cream, egg, or 2% milk.
Breads/Cereals/ Grains/Starchy Vegetables	All enriched or whole grain bread or rolls. English muffins, bagels, plain corn or flour tortillas. Breadsticks, Melba toast, pretzels, matzos, rye wafers, saltines, rice cakes. Air-popped popcorn, baked corn tortilla chips. Low-fat/nonfat snack crackers. All without nuts, seeds, or coconut. Cooked cereal without fat. Plain potatoes, rice, pasta, sweet potatoes. All prepared without added fat, unless used in the amount prescribed.	Quick breads, biscuits, muffins, cornbread. Pancakes, French toast, waffles. Croissants, fritters, popovers. Donuts, sweet rolls. Popcorn and snack crackers prepared with fat. Regular granola cereals and cereals containing nuts, seeds, or coconut. Fried potatoes, fried rice. Potato chips, corn chips, chow mein noodles. Creamed, au gratin, fried, or buttered starches. Convenience casseroles and mixes.
Desserts/Sweets	Angel food cake, fat-free commercial baked products. Sherbet, fruit ice, nonfat frozen yogurt, fruit and juice bars, sorbet, popsicles. Gelatin, meringues, pudding made with skim milk, fruit whips made with skim milk, egg whites and sugar. Graham crackers, vanilla wafers, ginger snaps. Sugar, jam, jelly, marmalade, syrup, molasses, honey, hard candy, gum drops, marshmallows, jelly beans.	All other cakes, cookies, pies, pastries, ice cream, and most commercial desserts. Puddings made with whole milk or egg yolks. Desserts made with coconut, nuts, or chocolate. Candy made with with chocolate, nuts, coconut, or fat.
Fats (limit to four servings per day)	Five grams of fat per serving—one fat serving equals: 2 tsp peanut butter 1 tsp fortified margarine, butter, oil, shortening, or regular mayonnaise. 2 tsp regular gravy 1 T diet margarine, reduced-calorie mayonnaise, oil-based salad dressing, cream cheese, heavy cream, salad dressing. 2 T light cream, sour cream, low-fat salad dressing, reduced-fat cream cheese.	All others and any in excess of prescribed amount and/or more than four servings per day.

Food Group	Foods Allowed	Foods to Avoid
	6 small nuts 5 small olives 1 strip of bacon ⅛ of 4″ diameter avocado Fat-free: salad dressings, mayonnaise, gravy, cream cheese, and sour cream as desired.	
Fruits	All; avocado in limited amounts. (See fat list.)	None.
Meat/Poultry/ Fish/Egg/ Cheese (limit to 4 to 6 oz lean meat per day)	3 grams of fat/serving lean meat. Lean beef such as round, chuck, sirloin, and extra lean ground beef. Poultry breast without skin. Lean pork such as canned or cured boiled ham, tenderloin, chops. Canadian bacon. All cuts of veal. Lean lamb such as chops or leg. All fish, fresh, frozen, or canned in water. Luncheon meats, frankfurters that are at least 90% fat free. Skim milk cheeses. Cottage cheese (0–2% fat). Parmesan cheese limited to 3 t. One whole egg per day. Egg whites as desired. Cholesterol free egg substitutes.	Fried or heavily marbled and fatty meats, poultry, fish. Ground beef greater than 20% fat, corned beef. All types of organ meat. Duck, goose, poultry skin. Spareribs, salt pork, pig's feet, ham hocks. Oil-packed fish. Sausage, frankfurters, regular luncheon meats. Processed cheeses or cheeses made with whole milk. Cottage cheese (4% fat). Eggs prepared with fat or other ingredients not allowed.
Milk/Yogurt	Skim milk, nonfat buttermilk, nonfat dry milk, nonfat chocolate milk. Nonfat yogurt.	Whole milk, buttermilk and chocolate milk made with whole milk, whole milk yogurt.
Miscellaneous/ Condiments	Herbs, spices, flavorings, pepper. Lemon juice, vinegar, extracts. Condiments such as catsup, mustard, chili sauce, pickles, relish. Cocoa powder. Fat-free butter replacements.	All others.
Soups/ Combination Foods Vegetables	Fat-free broth, bouillon, fat-free vegetable soup, cream soups made with skim milk, dehydrated soups. All fresh, frozen, or canned. Vegetable juices. Fat may be used in preparation if used within prescribed amounts.	Soups made with cream, 2% milk, whole milk, or fat. Vegetables prepared with butter or cream sauces. Deep fried vegetables. Prepared tomato, spaghetti, or pizza sauces made with fat.

Tables pp. 411 to 417 reprinted with permission of the Dallas-Fort Worth Hospital Council.

Food Category	Recommended	Excluded
Beverages	Milk, buttermilk (limit to 1 cup daily); eggnog, all fruit juices; low-sodium salt-free vegetable juices; regular vegetable or tomato juices (limit to ½ cup daily); low-sodium carbonated beverages.	Regular vegetable or tomato juices used in excessive amounts; commercially softened water used for drinking or cooking.
Breads and cereals	Enriched white, wheat, rye, and pumpernickel bread; hard rolls and dinner rolls; muffins, cornbread, light biscuits, waffles, and pancakes; most dry and hot cereals; unsalted crackers and breadsticks.	Breads, rolls, and crackers with salted tops; instant hot cereals.
Desserts and sweets	All.	None.
Fats	Butter or margarine; vegetable oils; low-sodium salad dressing, other salad dressings in limited amounts; light, sour, and heavy cream.	Salad dressings containing bacon fat, bacon bits, and salt pork; snack dips made with instant soup mixes or processed cheese.
Fruits	All.	None.
Meats and meat substitutes	Any fresh or frozen beef, lamb, pork, poultry, fish, and most shellfish; canned tuna or salmon, rinsed; eggs and egg substitutes; regular cheese, ricotta, and cream cheese (2 oz daily); low-sodium cheese as desired; cottage cheese, drained; regular yogurt; regular peanut butter (3 times weekly); dried peas and beans; frozen dinners (< 600 mg sodium).	Any smoked, cured, salted, koshered, or canned meat, fish, or poultry including bacon, chipped beef, cold cuts, ham, hot dogs, sausage, sardines, anchovies, marinated herring, and pickled meats; frozen breaded meats; pickled eggs; processed cheese; cheese spreads and sauces; salted nuts.
Potatoes and potato substitutes	White or sweet potatoes; squash; enriched rice, barley, noodles, spaghetti, macaroni, and other pastas; homemade bread stuffing.	Commercially prepared potato, rice, or pasta mixes; commercial bread stuffing.
Soups	Commercially canned and dehydrated soups, broths, and boullions (once per week); homemade broth, soups without added salt, and made with allowed vegetables; reduced-sodium canned soups and broths.	Canned or dehydrated regular soups (more than once per week).

Food Category	Recommended	Excluded
Vegetables	All fresh and frozen vegetables; canned, drained vegetables.	Sauerkraut, pickled vegetables, and others prepared in brine; vegetables seasoned with ham, bacon, or salt pork.
Miscellaneous	Limit added salt to ¼ tsp/day used at the table or in cooking; salt substitute with physician's approval; pepper, herbs, spices; vinegar, ketchup (1 tbsp), mustard (1 tbsp), lemon, or lime juice; hot pepper sauce; low-sodium soy sauce (1 tbsp); unsalted tortilla chips, pretzels, potato chips, popcorn, salsa (¼ cup).	Any seasoning made with salt including garlic salt, celery salt, onion salt, and seasoned salt; sea salt, rock salt, kosher salt; meat tenderizers; monosodium glutamate; regular soy sauce, teriyaki sauce, most flavored vinegars; regular snack chips, olives.

MULTICULTURAL FOOD GUIDE PYRAMIDS

@

HARD-TO-PLACE-FOODS

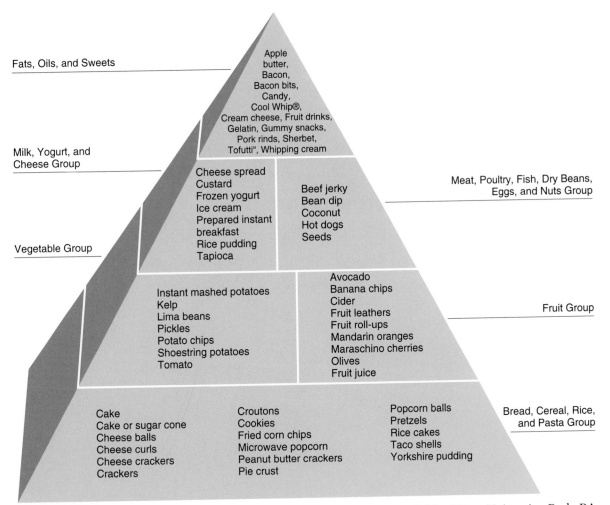

Fats, Oils, and Sweets

Apple butter, Bacon, Bacon bits, Candy, Cool Whip®, Cream cheese, Fruit drinks, Gelatin, Gummy snacks, Pork rinds, Sherbet, Tofutti", Whipping cream

Milk, Yogurt, and Cheese Group

Cheese spread
Custard
Frozen yogurt
Ice cream
Prepared instant breakfast
Rice pudding
Tapioca

Meat, Poultry, Fish, Dry Beans, Eggs, and Nuts Group

Beef jerky
Bean dip
Coconut
Hot dogs
Seeds

Vegetable Group

Instant mashed potatoes
Kelp
Lima beans
Pickles
Potato chips
Shoestring potatoes
Tomato

Fruit Group

Avocado
Banana chips
Cider
Fruit leathers
Fruit roll-ups
Mandarin oranges
Maraschino cherries
Olives
Fruit juice

Bread, Cereal, Rice, and Pasta Group

Cake
Cake or sugar cone
Cheese balls
Cheese curls
Cheese crackers
Crackers

Croutons
Cookies
Fried corn chips
Microwave popcorn
Peanut butter crackers
Pie crust

Popcorn balls
Pretzels
Rice cakes
Taco shells
Yorkshire pudding

Source: 1993 *Pyramid Packet,* Penn State Nutrition Center, 417 East Calder Way, University Park PA 16801–5633; (814) 865–6323.

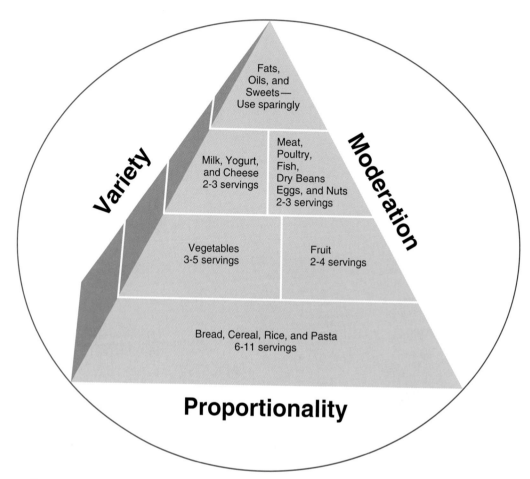

Fats,
Oils, and
Sweets—
Use sparingly

Milk, Yogurt,
and Cheese
2-3 servings

Meat,
Poultry,
Fish,
Dry Beans
Eggs, and Nuts
2-3 servings

Vegetables
3-5 servings

Fruit
2-4 servings

Bread, Cereal, Rice, and Pasta
6-11 servings

Variety

Moderation

Proportionality

Source: 1993 *Pyramid Packet,* Penn State Nutrition Center, 417 East Calder Way, University Park PA 16801–5663; (814) 865–6323.

FOOD GROUP NUTRIENTS

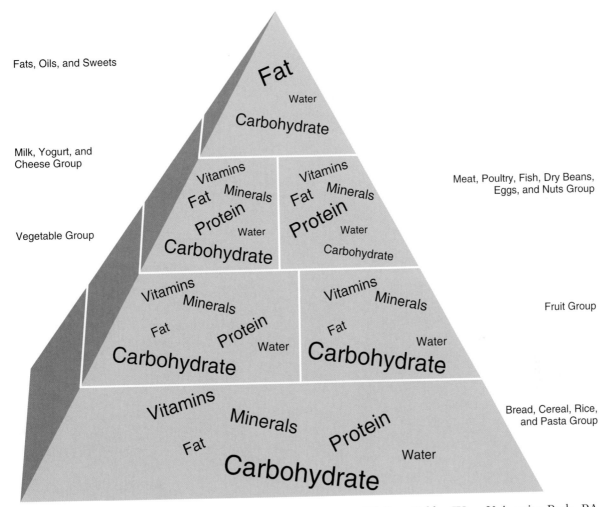

Fats, Oils, and Sweets

Milk, Yogurt, and
Cheese Group

Vegetable Group

Meat, Poultry, Fish, Dry Beans,
Eggs, and Nuts Group

Fruit Group

Bread, Cereal, Rice,
and Pasta Group

Source: 1993 *Pyramid Packet,* Penn State Nutrition Center, 417 East Calder Way, University Park, PA
16801–5663; (814) 865–6323.

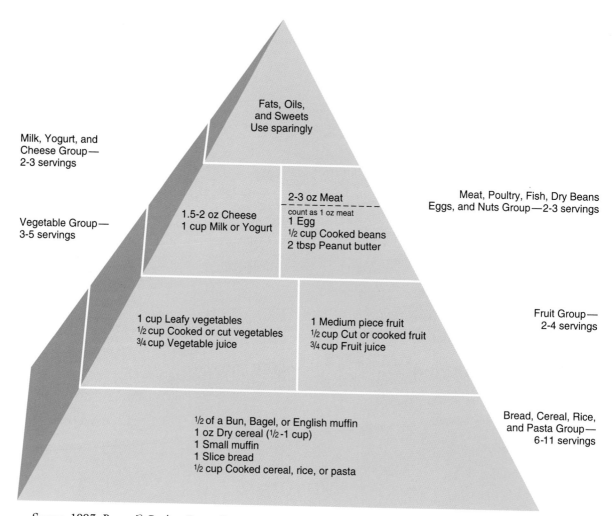

Fats, Oils, and Sweets
Use sparingly

Milk, Yogurt, and Cheese Group—
2-3 servings

1.5-2 oz Cheese
1 cup Milk or Yogurt

Meat, Poultry, Fish, Dry Beans Eggs, and Nuts Group—2-3 servings

2-3 oz Meat
count as 1 oz meat
1 Egg
½ cup Cooked beans
2 tbsp Peanut butter

Vegetable Group—
3-5 servings

1 cup Leafy vegetables
½ cup Cooked or cut vegetables
¾ cup Vegetable juice

1 Medium piece fruit
½ cup Cut or cooked fruit
¾ cup Fruit juice

Fruit Group—
2-4 servings

½ of a Bun, Bagel, or English muffin
1 oz Dry cereal (½-1 cup)
1 Small muffin
1 Slice bread
½ cup Cooked cereal, rice, or pasta

Bread, Cereal, Rice, and Pasta Group—
6-11 servings

Source: 1993 *Pyramid Packet,* Penn State Nutrition Center, 417 East Calder Way, University Park PA 16801–5663; (814) 865–6323.

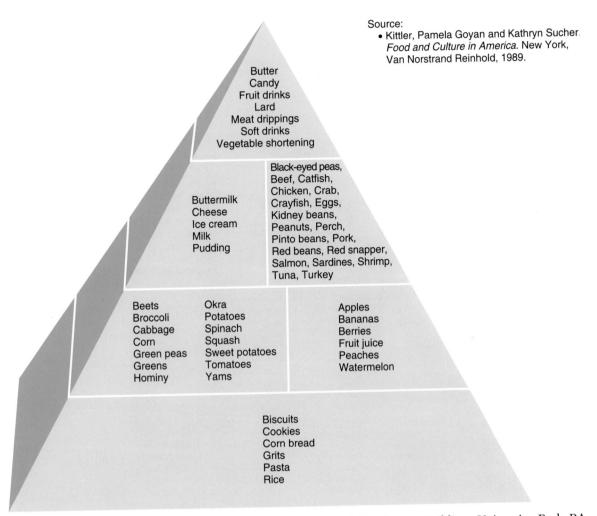

Source:
• Kittler, Pamela Goyan and Kathryn Sucher. *Food and Culture in America*. New York, Van Norstrand Reinhold, 1989.

Source: 1993 *Pyramid Packet,* Penn State Nutrition Center, 5 Henderson Building, University Park PA 16802; (814) 865–6323.

Sources:
- Barer-Stein, Thelma. *You Eat What You Are-A Study of Ethnic Food Traditions*. Toronto: McClelland and Stewart, Ltd., 1979.
- Dalal, Tarla. *Tarla Dalal's New Indian Vegetarian Cooking*. Bombay, India Book Distributors, 1986.
- Kittler, Pamela Goyan and Kathryn Sucher. *Food and Culture in America*. New York, Van Norstrand Reinhold, 1989.
- Madhur, Jaffrey. *A Taste of India*. London: Pan Books, Ltd., 1985.
- Sahni, Julie. *Classic Indian Cooking*. New York, William Morrow and Company, Inc., 1980.
- Santha, Rama Rau. *The Cooking of India*. Time-Life Books (Foods of the World). Time, Inc., 1969.

Prepared by: Uma Srinath

Butter, Chocolate, Coconut milk, Coconut oil, Ghee, Groundnut oil, Honey, Jam, Jaggery, Mustard oil, Sesame oil, Soft drinks, Sugar, Sunflower oil, Toffees, Vanaspati

Buffalo's milk, Buttermilk (lassi), Cow's milk, Curds, Chhena, Ice cream, Kheer, Khoya, Kulfi, Milk powder, Paneer, Peda, Raita, Rasmalai, Rossogolla, Sondesh, Srikhand, Sweet curds

Almonds, Cashew nuts, Chana, Chicken, Coconut chutney, Dal, Eggs, Groundnut, Kabob, Kheema, Mutton, Pappad, Pulses, Rajma, Rasam, Sambar, Soyabean nuggets, Sprouted beans

Aviyal
Bitter gourd
Brinjal (aubergine)
Cabbage
Capsicum
Carrots
Cauliflower
Cucumber
Drumsticks
Gourds
Green beans
Green papaya
Lotus stem

Lady's finger
Leafy greens
Onions
Pakora
Peas
Plantain
Potatoes
Pumpkin
Radishes
Salad
Sweet potatoes
Tomatoes
Vegetable curry

Apples
Bananas
Cheeku
Custard apple
Fruit chutney
Goose berries
Grapes
Guava
Indian pears
Jackfruit
Lychees

Mango
Melons
Oranges
Papaya
Pineapple
Plums
Pomegranates
Raisins
Sharbat
Sweet lime
Tamarind

Bhatura
Dhokla
Dosas
Idlis
Makai ki roti

Naan
Parboiled rice
Pressed rice
Puffed rice
Pullao

Puris
Roti (made from millet, rice flour)
Rice noodles
Sago

Steamed rice
Uppma
Vermicelli
White bread

Source: 1996 *Multicultural Pyramid Packet*, Penn State Nutrition Center, 5 Henderson Building, University Park, PA 16802; (814) 865–6323.

CHINESE AMERICAN FOODS AND THE FOOD GUIDE PYRAMID

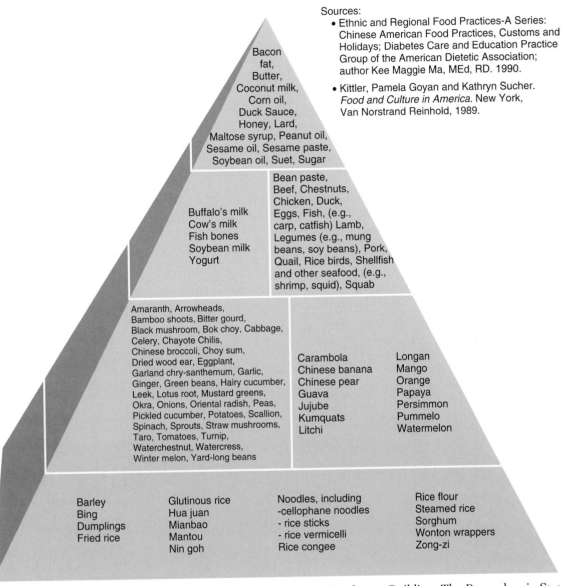

Sources:
- Ethnic and Regional Food Practices-A Series: Chinese American Food Practices, Customs and Holidays; Diabetes Care and Education Practice Group of the American Dietetic Association; author Kee Maggie Ma, MEd, RD. 1990.
- Kittler, Pamela Goyan and Kathryn Sucher. *Food and Culture in America*. New York, Van Norstrand Reinhold, 1989.

Bacon fat, Butter, Coconut milk, Corn oil, Duck Sauce, Honey, Lard, Maltose syrup, Peanut oil, Sesame oil, Sesame paste, Soybean oil, Suet, Sugar

Buffalo's milk, Cow's milk, Fish bones, Soybean milk, Yogurt

Bean paste, Beef, Chestnuts, Chicken, Duck, Eggs, Fish, (e.g., carp, catfish) Lamb, Legumes (e.g., mung beans, soy beans), Pork, Quail, Rice birds, Shellfish and other seafood, (e.g., shrimp, squid), Squab

Amaranth, Arrowheads, Bamboo shoots, Bitter gourd, Black mushroom, Bok choy, Cabbage, Celery, Chayote Chilis, Chinese broccoli, Choy sum, Dried wood ear, Eggplant, Garland chry-santhemum, Garlic, Ginger, Green beans, Hairy cucumber, Leek, Lotus root, Mustard greens, Okra, Onions, Oriental radish, Peas, Pickled cucumber, Potatoes, Scallion, Spinach, Sprouts, Straw mushrooms, Taro, Tomatoes, Turnip, Waterchestnut, Watercress, Winter melon, Yard-long beans

Carambola, Chinese banana, Chinese pear, Guava, Jujube, Kumquats, Litchi

Longan, Mango, Orange, Papaya, Persimmon, Pummelo, Watermelon

Barley, Bing, Dumplings, Fried rice

Glutinous rice, Hua juan, Mianbao, Mantou, Nin goh

Noodles, including -cellophane noodles - rice sticks - rice vermicelli, Rice congee

Rice flour, Steamed rice, Sorghum, Wonton wrappers, Zong-zi

Source: 1993 *Pyramid Packet,* Penn State Nutrition Center, 5 Henderson Building, The Pennsylvania State University, University Park, PA 16802; (814) 865–6323.

JEWISH FOODS AND THE FOOD GUIDE PYRAMID

Sources:
- Ethnic and Regional Food Practices-A Series: Jewish Food Practices, Customs and Holidays; Diabetes Care and Education Practice Group of The American Dietetic Association; contributors Catherine Higgins, MS, ED, CDE, and Hope S. Warshaw, MMSc, RD, CDE. 1989.

- Barer-Stein, Thelma. *You Are What You Eat-A Study of Ethnic Food Traditions.* Toronto: McClelland and Stewart, Ltd., 1979.

Cream cheese, Gribenes, Honey, Jelly, Margarine, Marmalade, Mayonnaise, Olive oil, Preserves, Schmaltz, Sesame seed oil, Sherbet, Sour cream, Sugar

Cottage cheese
Edam cheese
Farmer's cheese
Gouda cheese
Milk
Swiss cheese
Yogurt

Almonds, Beef, Beef tongue, Bob, Brisket, Chick peas, Chopped liver, Corned beef, Dry beans, Eggs, Flanken, Gefilte fish, Herring, Lentils, Lox, Pastrami, Poultry, Salmon, Sardines, Smelt, Smoked fish, Split peas, Tripe, Veal

Artichokes, Asparagus, Beets/borscht, Broccoli, Brussel sprouts, Cabbage, Carrot, Cauliflower, Corn, Garlic, Green beans, Greens, Latke, Leeks, Olives, Onions, Peas, Peppers, Pickles, Potatoes, Sorrel, Spinach, Squash, Sweet potatoes, Tomatoes, Turnips, Yams

Bananas
Citrus fruits
Dates
Dried apples
Dried apricots
Dried pears

Figs
Grapes
Melons
Prunes
Raisins
Sabra

Bagel	Bulke	Honey cake	Noodle pudding
Barley	Challah	Kasha	Pastry
Bialy	Crepe	Kichlach	Pita bread
Blintz	Dumplings	Knaidlach	Pumpernickel bread
Bubke	Farfel	Leckach	Rye bread
Bulgur	Hard rolls	Matzoh	Teiglach

Source: 1993 *Pyramid Packet,* Penn State Nutrition Center, 5 Henderson Building, University Park PA 16802; (814) 865–6323.

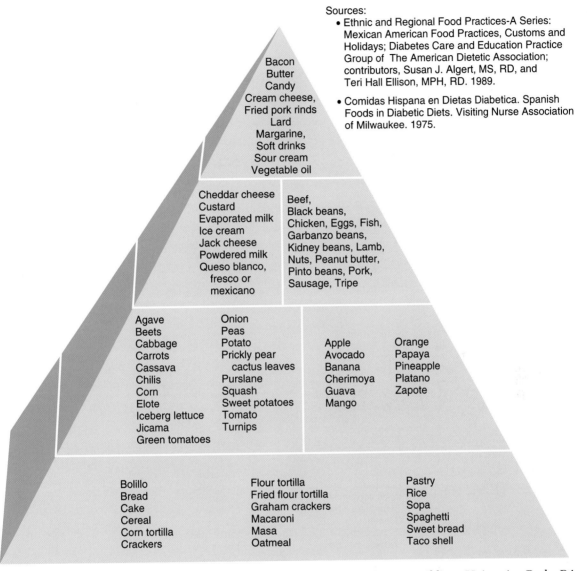

Sources:
- Ethnic and Regional Food Practices-A Series: Mexican American Food Practices, Customs and Holidays; Diabetes Care and Education Practice Group of The American Dietetic Association; contributors, Susan J. Algert, MS, RD, and Teri Hall Ellison, MPH, RD. 1989.

- Comidas Hispana en Dietas Diabetica. Spanish Foods in Diabetic Diets. Visiting Nurse Association of Milwaukee. 1975.

Bacon
Butter
Candy
Cream cheese,
Fried pork rinds
Lard
Margarine,
Soft drinks
Sour cream
Vegetable oil

Cheddar cheese
Custard
Evaporated milk
Ice cream
Jack cheese
Powdered milk
Queso blanco,
fresco or
mexicano

Beef,
Black beans,
Chicken, Eggs, Fish,
Garbanzo beans,
Kidney beans, Lamb,
Nuts, Peanut butter,
Pinto beans, Pork,
Sausage, Tripe

Agave
Beets
Cabbage
Carrots
Cassava
Chilis
Corn
Elote
Iceberg lettuce
Jicama
Green tomatoes

Onion
Peas
Potato
Prickly pear
	cactus leaves
Purslane
Squash
Sweet potatoes
Tomato
Turnips

Apple
Avocado
Banana
Cherimoya
Guava
Mango

Orange
Papaya
Pineapple
Platano
Zapote

Bolillo
Bread
Cake
Cereal
Corn tortilla
Crackers

Flour tortilla
Fried flour tortilla
Graham crackers
Macaroni
Masa
Oatmeal

Pastry
Rice
Sopa
Spaghetti
Sweet bread
Taco shell

Source: 1993 *Pyramid Packet,* Penn State Nutrition Center, 5 Henderson Building, University Park, PA 16802; (814) 865–6323.

CURRENT NAVAJO FOODS
AND THE FOOD GUIDE PYRAMID

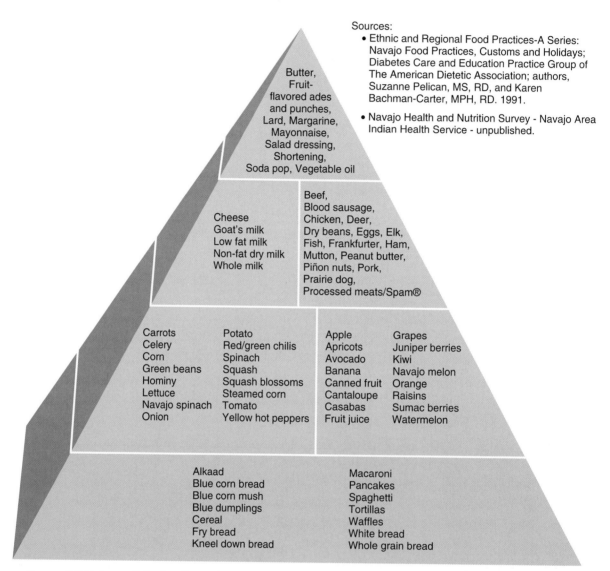

Butter,
Fruit-
flavored ades
and punches,
Lard, Margarine,
Mayonnaise,
Salad dressing,
Shortening,
Soda pop, Vegetable oil

Sources:
- Ethnic and Regional Food Practices-A Series: Navajo Food Practices, Customs and Holidays; Diabetes Care and Education Practice Group of The American Dietetic Association; authors, Suzanne Pelican, MS, RD, and Karen Bachman-Carter, MPH, RD. 1991.
- Navajo Health and Nutrition Survey - Navajo Area Indian Health Service - unpublished.

Cheese
Goat's milk
Low fat milk
Non-fat dry milk
Whole milk

Beef,
Blood sausage,
Chicken, Deer,
Dry beans, Eggs, Elk,
Fish, Frankfurter, Ham,
Mutton, Peanut butter,
Piñon nuts, Pork,
Prairie dog,
Processed meats/Spam®

Carrots
Celery
Corn
Green beans
Hominy
Lettuce
Navajo spinach
Onion

Potato
Red/green chilis
Spinach
Squash
Squash blossoms
Steamed corn
Tomato
Yellow hot peppers

Apple
Apricots
Avocado
Banana
Canned fruit
Cantaloupe
Casabas
Fruit juice

Grapes
Juniper berries
Kiwi
Navajo melon
Orange
Raisins
Sumac berries
Watermelon

Alkaad
Blue corn bread
Blue corn mush
Blue dumplings
Cereal
Fry bread
Kneel down bread

Macaroni
Pancakes
Spaghetti
Tortillas
Waffles
White bread
Whole grain bread

Source: 1993 *Pyramid Packet,* Penn State Nutrition Center, 5 Henderson Building, University Park PA 16802; (814) 865–6323.

PUERTO RICAN FOODS AND THE FOOD GUIDE PYRAMID *MAY BE USED WITH CUBAN AND DOMINICAN POPULATIONS.

Sources:
- Eliza B.K. Dooley, *Puerto Rican Cookbook* (Virginia: Dietz, 1948) 1-168.
- Internet: http://www.cu-online.com/~maggy/pr.html
- Internet: http://pubweb.acns.nwu.edu/%7Ecotto/pr.html
- Rivera, Jeanie. Personal Interview. 1 April 1996.
- Rufz, Leondro. Personal Interview. 26 May 1996.
- Unknown author, "Buen Provecho..." *Bienvenidos* 1994: 92-93
- Vasquez, Susana. Personal Interview. 10 April 1996.

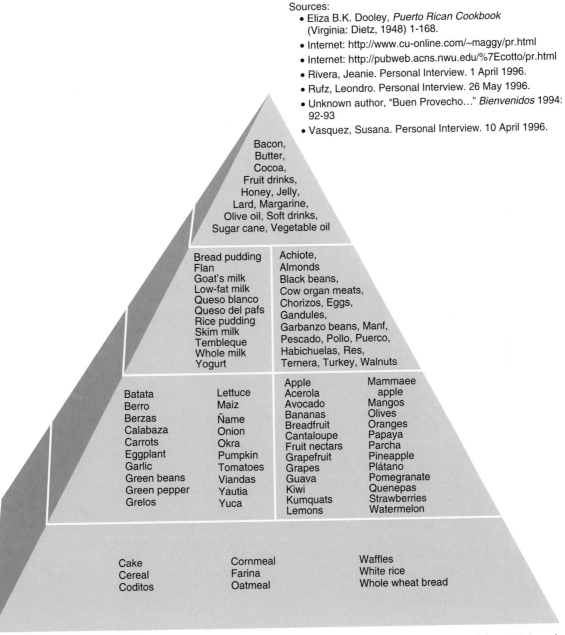

Bacon, Butter, Cocoa, Fruit drinks, Honey, Jelly, Lard, Margarine, Olive oil, Soft drinks, Sugar cane, Vegetable oil

Bread pudding
Flan
Goat's milk
Low-fat milk
Queso blanco
Queso del pafs
Rice pudding
Skim milk
Tembleque
Whole milk
Yogurt

Achiote,
Almonds
Black beans,
Cow organ meats,
Chorizos, Eggs,
Gandules,
Garbanzo beans, Manf,
Pescado, Pollo, Puerco,
Habichuelas, Res,
Ternera, Turkey, Walnuts

Batata
Berro
Berzas
Calabaza
Carrots
Eggplant
Garlic
Green beans
Green pepper
Grelos

Lettuce
Maiz
Ñame
Onion
Okra
Pumpkin
Tomatoes
Viandas
Yautia
Yuca

Apple
Acerola
Avocado
Bananas
Breadfruit
Cantaloupe
Fruit nectars
Grapefruit
Grapes
Guava
Kiwi
Kumquats
Lemons

Mammaee apple
Mangos
Olives
Oranges
Papaya
Parcha
Pineapple
Plátano
Pomegranate
Quenepas
Strawberries
Watermelon

Cake
Cereal
Coditos

Cornmeal
Farina
Oatmeal

Waffles
White rice
Whole wheat bread

Source: 1996 *Multicultural Pyramid Packet,* Penn State Nutrition Center, 5 Henderson Building, University Park PA 16802; (814) 865–6323.

VIETNAMESE AMERICAN FOODS AND THE FOOD GUIDE PYRAMID

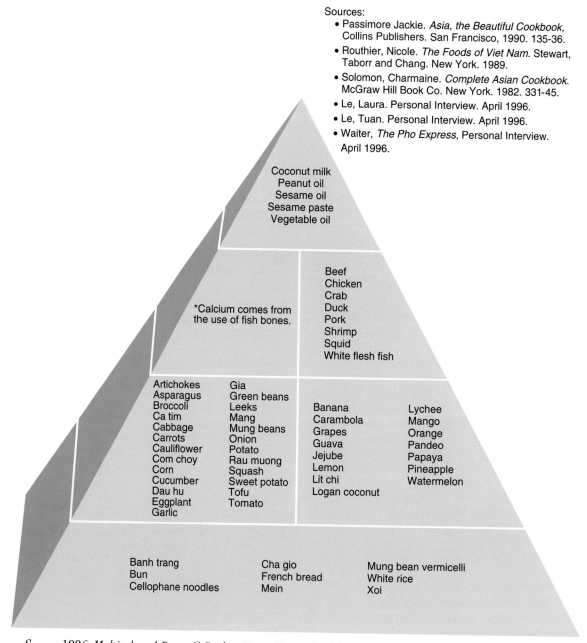

Sources:
- Passimore Jackie. *Asia, the Beautiful Cookbook,* Collins Publishers. San Francisco, 1990. 135-36.
- Routhier, Nicole. *The Foods of Viet Nam.* Stewart, Taborr and Chang. New York. 1989.
- Solomon, Charmaine. *Complete Asian Cookbook.* McGraw Hill Book Co. New York. 1982. 331-45.
- Le, Laura. Personal Interview. April 1996.
- Le, Tuan. Personal Interview. April 1996.
- Waiter, *The Pho Express*, Personal Interview. April 1996.

Coconut milk
Peanut oil
Sesame oil
Sesame paste
Vegetable oil

*Calcium comes from the use of fish bones.

Beef
Chicken
Crab
Duck
Pork
Shrimp
Squid
White flesh fish

Artichokes
Asparagus
Broccoli
Ca tim
Cabbage
Carrots
Cauliflower
Com choy
Corn
Cucumber
Dau hu
Eggplant
Garlic

Gia
Green beans
Leeks
Mang
Mung beans
Onion
Potato
Rau muong
Squash
Sweet potato
Tofu
Tomato

Banana
Carambola
Grapes
Guava
Jejube
Lemon
Lit chi
Logan coconut

Lychee
Mango
Orange
Pandeo
Papaya
Pineapple
Watermelon

Banh trang
Bun
Cellophane noodles

Cha gio
French bread
Mein

Mung bean vermicelli
White rice
Xoi

Source: 1996 *Multicultural Pyramid Packet,* Penn State Nutrition Center, 5 Henderson Building, University Park PA 16802; (814) 865–6323.

REFERENCES

@

American Dietetic Association. *Chef's Handbook: Low-fat Quantity Food Preparation/Project LEAN: "Low-fat Eating for America Now."* Chicago: American Dietetic Association, 1993.

American Dietetic Association. *Manual of Clinical Dietetics, 5th Ed.* Chicago Dietetic Association, South Suburban Dietetic Association, 1996.

American Dietetic Association. *New Survey Tracks American's Behaviors, Attitudes and Knowledge of Nutrition and Health Issues.* Chicago: American Dietetic Association, 1997.

American Heart Association. *Dietary Guidelines for Healthy American Adults: A Statement for Health Professionals from the Nutrition Committee.* Dallas: American Heart Association, 1996.

Bales, G. "A Guru's Gameplan." *Meat & Poultry Magazine* 35, (1989): 63.

"Basic Principles of Food Preparation." *Nutrition and the M.D.* 22 (August 1996).

Best, D. "Analogues Restructure Their Market." *Prep Foods New Product Annual* 158, (1989): 72.

Best, D. "Health Hooks Consumers." *Prep Foods New Products Annual* 157, (1988): 63.

Best, D. "Technology Widens Food Industry Horizons." *Prep Foods New Product Annual* 157, (1988):197.

Carney, M., and C. Shorney. *U.S. Food Industry Trends* (Stanford Research Institute International Report No. 760). 1988.

"Cholesterol-Reduced Fats: They're Here!" *Prep Foods New Product Annual* 158, (1989): 99.

"Cooking with Alcohol." *Good Housekeeping,* (November 1990).

Criqui, M. H., and Brenda L. Ringel. "Does Diet or Alcohol Explain the French Paradox?" *The Lancet,* Departments of Family and Preventive Medicine and Medicine, University of California, San Diego School of Medicine. 344 (Dec. 24 and 31, 1994).

Culinary Institute of America. American Dietetic Association 1996 Annual Conference, "Celebrate and Discover Techniques of Healthy Cooking" Workshop Presentation, San Antonio, TX, 1996.

Culinary Institute of America. *The Professional Chef's Techniques of Healthy Cooking.* New York: Van Nostrand Reinhold, 1993.

Dallas-Ft. Worth Hospital Council. *The Dietitian's Guide to Vegetarian Diets.* http://www.vrg.org.

Dallas-Ft. Worth Hospital Council. *Manual of Nutritional Therapy.* Fort Worth: Barr, 1996.

"Diet Foods Become Standard Fare." *Prep Foods New Product Annual* 156, (1987): 58.

Duyeff, Roberta L. *The American Dietetic Association's Complete Food and Nutrition Guide.* Minneapolis: Chronimed, 1996.

Elliot, P. "An International Study of Electrolyte Excretion and Blood Pressure." *British Medical Journal* 297, (1988): 319.

Food Marketing Institute. *Trends, Consumer Attitudes and the Supermarket.* Washington, D.C.: Food Marketing Institute, (1988).

Frost & Sullivan, Inc. *The Health, Diet Foods and Beverages Market.* New York: Frost & Sullivan, 1987.

Gelardi, R. C. "The Multiple Sweetener Approach and New Sweeteners on the Horizon." *Food Technology* 41, (1987): 123.

Hahn, Nancy I. "Variety Is STILL the Spice of a Healthful Diet: A Look at Proposed Revisions for the 1995 Dietary Guidelines for Americans." *Journal 95 of the American Dietetic Association* (October 1995).

"Hard Proof about Cooking with Alcohol." *Tufts University Diet & Nutrition Letter* 8, no. 4 (1990).

Hodges, Carol A. *Culinary Nutrition for Food Professionals,* 2nd Ed. New York: Van Nostrand Reinhold, 1994.

Heimbach, J. T. "Risk Avoidance in Consumer Approaches to Diet and Health." *Journal of Clinical Nutrition* 6, no. 4 (1987): 159.

Institute of Medicine. *Dietary Reference Intakes: A Report by the Institute of Medicine.* New York: National Academy Press, 1997.

Labensky, Sarah R., and Alan M. Hause. *On Cooking.* Upper Saddle River, NJ: Prentice Hall, 1995.

Lemaire, W. H. "Food in the Year 2000." *Food Engineering* 57, (1985):90.

The Lempert Company. *The Lempert Report: The Supermarket in the Year 2000.* The Lempert Co., 1987.

"Light Sweeteners Maneuver for Heavyweight Title." *Prep Foods New Product Annual* 158, (1989):91.

Mandel, T. F. *American Social and Consumer Trends in the 1990s* (Stanford Research Institute International Report No. 773). Stanford Research Institute, 1989.

Miller, G. A., and H. I. Frier. "Lifestyle-Driven Foods and the Ingredients Required for Their Development." *Food Technology* 43, (1989):136.

Murray, Joan. "The New Dietary Guidelines: How They Stack Up against the 1990 Version." *Food Service Director* (Feb. 15, 1996).

Nathan, J. "Food of the Future Is Ethnic and Fast." *New York Times* (Mar. 7, 1989).

National Research Council. *Diet and Health-Implications for Reducing Chronic Disease Risk.* Washington, D.C.: National Academy Press, 1989.

Netzer, Corinne T. *The Corinne Netzer Encyclopedia of Food Values.* New York: Dell, 1992.

"New Product Analysis." *Food Engineering* 60, (1988):89.

"News and Trends: But What about Frozens?" *Prep Foods New Product Annual.* 158, (1989):17.

O'Brien Nabors, L., and R. C. Gelardi. *Alternative Sweeteners.* New York: Marcel Dekker, 1986.

Pennington, Jean A. T. *Bowes & Church's Food Values of Portions Commonly Used.* Philadelphia: J. B. Lippincott, 1994.

Penn State Nutrition Center. *A Guide to the Pyramid Packet.* University Park, PA: College of Health and Human Development, 1996.

Pierson, T. R., and J. W. Allen. "Directions in Food Marketing: Responding to Consumers of Tomorrow." Paper presented at U.S. Department of Agriculture 1988 Annual Agriculture Outlook Conference, 1988.

Pilch, S. M. Physiological Effects and Health Consequences of Dietary Fiber. Contract No. FDA 223-84-2059. Washington, D.C.: Federation of American Societies for Experimental Biology, 1987.

"The Prevention Index: A Report Card on the Nation's Health." *Prevention.* 1989.

"The Prevention Index: A Special Look at the Baby Boomers, Age and Health Practices." *Prevention.* 1987.

Rubin, Karen Wilk. "Time for Another Look at Minerals in the Diet." *Food Service Director* (June 15, 1996).

Schutz, H., P. Judge, and J. Gentry. "The Importance of Nutrition, Brand, Cost, and Sensory Attributes to Food Purchases and Consumption." *Food Technology* 40, No. 82 (1986).

Sharkey, B. "The Chameleon Decade." *Adweek* (suppl.) (September 1989).

Sills-Levy, E. *U.S. Food Trends Leading to the Year 2000.* New York: Walker Group/Research, 1988.

Stevens, R. G. *Eating Out — The Growing American Obsession.* Chicago: Nader & Associates, 1985.

U.S. Census Bureau. *Current Population Survey.* Washington, D.C.: U.S. Census Bureau, 1986.

U.S. Department of Health and Human Services. *The Surgeon General's Report on Nutrition and Health.* Washington, D.C.: U.S. Government Printing Office, 1988.

"Under the Silver Dome: Top 20 Trends for 1998." *Restaurant Institutions.* 98, (1988): 126.

Vaclavik, Vickie A. *Essentials of Food Science.* New York: Chapman Hall, 1997.

Wiseberg, Karen. New Plastics, Shapes, Sizes, Roll In: Juice Packaging." *Food Service Director* (July 15, 1998): 92.

INDEX

@